Organizing
the
Unemployed

SUNY Series in American Labor History
Robert Asher and Amy Kesselman, Editors

Other books in this series include:

James J. Lorence

Organizing
the
Unemployed

Community and Union Activists in
the Industrial Heartland

STATE UNIVERSITY OF NEW YORK PRESS

HD 6515
.A82
I5754
1996

Cover Photo: Workers Prepare for Ford March, March 7, 1932 *(Archives of Labor and Urban Affairs, Wayne State University)*

Production by Ruth Fisher
Marketing by Nancy Farrell

Published by
State University of New York Press, Albany

© 1996 State University of New York

For information, address the State University of New York Press, State University Plaza, Albany, NY 12246

Library of Congress Cataloging-in-Publication Data

Lorence, James J.
    Organizing the unemployed : community and union activists in the industrial heartland / James J. Lorence.
        p. cm. — (SUNY series in American labor history)
    Includes bibliographical references and index.
    ISBN 0-7914-2987-3 (alk. paper). — ISBN 0-7914-2988-1 (pbk. : alk. paper)
    1. International Union, United Automobile, Aerospace, and Agricultural Implement Workers of America—History. 2. United States. Work Projects Administration—History. 3. Unemployed—Michigan—Political activity—History—20th century. 4. Automobile industry workers—Michigan—Political activity—History—20th century. 5. Industrial relations—United States—History—20th century. 6. New Deal, 1933–1939. I. Title. II. Series.
    HD6515.A82I5754 1996
    331.88'1292'097—dc20   95-33412
                                                                                        CIP

10 9 8 7 6 5 4 3 2 1

This book is for
Bill Williams

CONTENTS

LIST OF FIGURES

PREFACE

This book began in 1987 as a research project for William Sewell's NEH seminar at the University of Michigan, which explored the historical sociology of European and American labor since the Industrial Revolution. Determined to deepen my knowledge of the worker experience by examining the work lives of laborers themselves, I decided to explore the impact of the Great Depression's massive unemployment on workers and their families. In no state was the economic paralysis more complete than in Michigan. With ready access to the endless manuscript resources available in the Detroit–Ann Arbor area, I set out to determine how the state's workers and their organizations had responded to joblessness in the 1930s.

As the sources and questions multiplied, it became obvious that the topic comprised much more material than could be adequately dealt with in an article-length study. As a result, I embarked upon a more ambitious effort to develop an exhaustive analysis of the Michigan unemployed movement in all its phases and expressions. Early research revealed that organizational work among the state's jobless could not be understood apart from the dramatic story of the militant United Automobile Workers Union. It was inevitable that the story of unemployed workers in Michigan be told within the broader context of an evolving industrial union movement.

Before long, I also realized that the fate of the unemployed movement was inextricably linked to the ideological diversity of the

Michigan Left. At various times, Socialists, Communists, and liberals displayed sincere commitment to the casualties of the Great Depression. This study explores the hopes raised by the proponents of alternatives to production for profit, as well as the limits of liberalism and the failure of radicalism in the effort to devise solutions to the problem of cyclical unemployment. The tension between individualism and collectivism thus exposed and the measured response to radical appeals in 1930s Michigan reveal much about worker values and individual aspirations in a democratic society.

This book would not have been possible without the generous support of several institutions and foundations. The National Endowment for the Humanities provided funding for not only the seminar from which this study grew, but also a substantial travel grant administered by the American Association for State and Local History. The University of Wisconsin Centers provided a sabbatical leave which afforded me the opportunity to conduct sustained research in the early stages of the project's development. A research fellowship from the University of Wisconsin System and the University of Wisconsin–Madison Institute for Research in the Humanities enabled me to devote a full semester to research and writing as the study began to take shape. At various stages in my work, the University of Wisconsin Centers, the UWMC Foundation, the American Philosophical Society, and the Henry J. Kaiser Family Foundation at the Walter P. Reuther Library's Archives of Labor History and Urban Affairs supplied needed financial support to offset the expenses incurred as a result of travel to distant manuscript repositories.

The research task has been eased significantly by the untiring efforts of dedicated archivists and librarians at many institutions, including the State Historical Society of Wisconsin, Archives of Labor History and Urban Affairs, University of Wisconsin Center–Marathon County, Michigan Historical Collections at the Bentley Historical Library in Ann Arbor, Library of Congress Manuscript Division, Minnesota Historical Society, National Archives, George Meany Memorial Archives, Harlan Hatcher Library's Labadie Collection at the University of Michigan, Burton Historical Collection at Detroit Public Library, Michigan Archives, Michigan State University Special Collections, Grand Rapids Public Library, Grand Rapids City Archives, Michigan Technological University Library, Herbert Hoover Library, Franklin D. Roosevelt Library, Catholic

University of America, Martin P. Catherwood Library Labor-Management Documentation Center at Cornell University, Immigration History Research Center and Social Welfare History Archives at the University of Minnesota, Tamiment Institute and Robert Wagner Labor Archives at New York University, New York Public Library, Woodruff Library at Emory University, Ford Motor Company Archives, Milwaukee County Historical Society, Morris Fromkin Collection and Area Research Center at University of Wisconsin–Milwaukee, Area Research Center at University of Wisconsin–Stevens Point, Midwest Labor Institute for Social Studies, University of Oregon, University of Virginia, Schomburg Center for Research in Black Culture, Reference Center for Marxist Studies, Northern Michigan University Learning Resource Center, and the Hoover Institution on War Revolution and Peace. I especially thank Harry Miller, David Myers, Peter Gottlieb, Warner Pflug, Ray Boryczcka, Tom Featherstone, Curt LeMay, Judy Palmateer, Todd Roll, Jeanette Fiore, Dale Treleven, Debra Bernhardt, Anthony Zito, Diana Shenk, Kris McCusker, Saundra Taylor, Peter Hoefer, Stuart Kaufman, Mary Anne Hill, Ellen Nemhauser, Hilary Cummings, Maier Fox, Linda Kloss, Martha Hodges, Diane Lachatañerè, Dorothy Swanson, George Tselos, Timo Riipa, John Haynes, Dorian Paster, William Cunningham, LeRoy Barnett, Richard H. Harms, and David Crippens.

Equally valuable in advancing my research were interviews with many veterans of the labor struggles of the 1930s. I have learned from all of them and am especially grateful to these men and women who dedicated their lives to the search for the common good in a period of great stress. I have benefited especially from the thoughtful recollections of Frank Zeidler, Victor Reuther, George Edwards Jr., Sigmund G. Eisenscher, Ben Fischer, Ethel Polk, Christopher Columbus Alston, Carl Winter, Louis Weinstock, Genora Dollinger, Carl Raymond Anderson, Rachel Kangas, Dave Moore, Stanley and Margaret Novak, Paul A. Rasmussen, Franklin Folsom, Carl E. Ross, Helvi Savola, Edwin Spiegal, Wilbert Salmi, Frank Sykes, Alan and Stuart Strachan, Charles Symon, Frank Walli, Lester Washburn, Gilbert Jewell, Saul Wellman, and Leonard Woodcock. Arthur Zipser aided me in gaining access to the useful pamphlet collection at the Reference Center for Marxist Studies. I thank them all for allowing me into their lives. Without their social commitment and sense of history, which so aided me in my work, there would be no book.

My debts to friends, colleagues, and critics within the historical profession are many. More than any other person, Bill Sewell is responsible for this study, for it was he who first saw potential for further development in my tentative explorations. For his encouragement and steadfast support I am deeply grateful. His criticism and suggestions helped shape the general outlines of the manuscript. I have also profited from the insightful criticism and the encouragement offered by Robert H. Zieger of the University of Florida, John Cumbler of the University of Louisville, and Roger Biles of Oklahoma State University, all of whom read portions of the manuscript in its early stages. Warner Pflug and Ray Boryczka of the Archives of Labor History and Urban Affairs were always accommodating in easing access to research materials, including restricted collections, while Christopher Johnson of Wayne State University provided a useful introduction to the outlines of the Detroit Left in the 1930s. Jon Saari of Northern Michigan University helped me to understand the Finnish Community of the Upper Peninsula, and Debra Bernhardt of the Tamiment Collection at the Wagner Labor Archives was instrumental in helping me secure an excellent interview with the unreconstructed radical Rachel Kangas of Iron River, Michigan. Kenneth West assisted me in the use of the University of Michigan–Flint Labor History Project Archives. Daniel Leab of Seton Hall University, James Sargent of Northern Virginia Community College, Eric Davin of the University of Pittsburgh, and Dave Riddle of Wayne State University were generous in sharing their own research materials with me. Crucial to my research was the cooperation of Ernst Benjamin of AAUP, who not only was a gracious host, but also granted unrestricted access to his father's personal papers.

Discussions and correspondence with many historians have enriched my knowledge of the labor movement and the American Left. Among those who were most helpful were Stephen Meyer of the University of Wisconsin–Parkside; Harvey Klehr of Emory University; Kenneth Waltzer of Michigan State University; William Pratt of the University of Nebraska–Omaha; Susan Rosenfeld of New Orleans; Erling Sannes of Bismarck, N.D., Charles Hyde of Wayne State University; Daniel Nelson of Akron University; Udo Sautter of the University of Windsor; Richard Jensen of the Newberry Library; Nelson Lichtenstein of Catholic University of America; Larry Lankton of Michigan Technological University; and John Haynes of the Library of Congress Manuscripts Division. My colleague Jeffrey Kleiman of UWC–Marshfield/Wood County, who read an early draft of the manuscript, has been an insightful critic. A very special note of thanks is due to my long-time friend, colleague, and critic, the independent scholar Stanley Mallach of Milwaukee. His exhaustive critique has made this a stronger manuscript.

The task of revision has been eased by the editors at SUNY Press. Clay Morgan was especially helpful in keeping me focused. I am especially indebted to series editor Robert Asher of the University of Connecticut, whose enthusiasm for this book reinforced my confidence in my work. His advice was crucial in my efforts to sharpen the manuscript's most important themes.

Several institutions and organizations generously granted me permission to reprint materials which had appeared in previous publications. I especially thank the George Meany Memorial Archives for allowing me to reprint large portions of "Controlling the Reserve Army: The United Automobile Workers and Michigan's Unemployed, 1935–1941," *Labor's Heritage* 5 (Spring, 1994): 18–37. Editors Stuart B. Kaufman and Robert D. Reynolds Jr. were very helpful in clarifying the article's themes. In addition, the Tamiment Institute authorized the use of quoted material from Alex Baskin, "The Ford Hunger March—1932," *Labor History* 13 (Summer, 1972): 331–360. Columbia University Press permitted me to compile two tables based on material drawn from David Ziskind, *One Thousand Strikes in Government Employment* (New York: Columbia University Press, 1940).

Among the other institutions that have allowed the use of materials from their collections are the New York Public Library Rare Books and Manuscripts Division, Astor, Lenox and Tilden Foundations (Norman Thomas Papers); the Labadie Collection, Special Collections Library, University of Michigan–Ann Arbor; Special Collections Department, University of Colorado at Boulder Libraries (Folsom-Elting Collection); Special Collections, Robert W. Woodruff Library, Emory University, Atlanta, Georgia (Theodore Draper Papers); Labor History Project Archives, University of Michigan–Flint; Archives of Labor and Urban Affairs, Walter P. Reuther Library, Wayne State University; Bentley Historical Library, University of Michigan; Severson National Information Center, Family Service America; Social Welfare History Archives and Immigration History Research Center, both at the University of Minnesota; Special Collections, Michigan State University Libraries; Manuscripts Division, Special Collections Department, University of Virginia Library (William Jett Lauck Papers #4742); Labor-Management Documentation Center, Martin P. Catherwood Library, New York State School of Industrial and Labor Relations, Cornell University; Department of Special Collections, Syracuse University; Special Collections Library, Duke University; Local History Collections, Grand Rapids Public Library, Grand Rapids, Michigan; and the State Historical Society of Wisconsin.

The following individuals have willingly authorized my quotation and citation of materials in their possession: Ernst Benjamin, Dave Riddle, Ethel Polk, and Genora Dollinger. The Michigan District, Communist Party, U.S.A., granted me permission to use and cite materials from its Red Squad Files.

The mechanical details of manuscript preparation were managed with good humor and expertise by Lucy Ruder, Charlene Schmidt, and Kathy Schulz, all capable and efficient professionals whose typing skills made an important contribution to the final product. At several points, the administration of the University of Wisconsin Center–Marathon County was generous in assisting with the inevitable expenses encountered in the completion of the book. Without creative institutional support, the task would have been much more complicated.

Finally, I owe an enormous debt of gratitude to my wife, Donna, who has lived with this project for nine years and contributed her own skills as research assistant and critic. Without her, there would be no project; she knows why.

J. J. L.

LIST OF ABBREVIATIONS

AAWA	Associated Automobile Workers of America
ADC	Aid to Dependent Children
AFL	American Federation of Labor
AIWA	Automotive Industrial Workers Association
AWU	Auto Workers Union
CCE	Central Cooperative Exchange
CCW	Central Cooperative Wholesale
CIO	Congress of Industrial Organizations
CLA	Christian Labor Association
CP	Communist Party
CPLA	Conference for Progressive Labor Action
CWA	Civil Works Administration
DFL	Detroit Federation of Labor
FHA	Farm Holiday Association
GRFL	Grand Rapids Federation of Labor
HUAC	House Un-American Activities Committee
IWA	International Woodworkers of America
IWW	Industrial Workers of the World (Wobblies)
LNPL	Labor's Non-Partisan League
MESA	Mechanics Educational Society of America
MIUC	Michigan Industrial Union Council
NLRB	National labor Relations Board
NMU	National Miners Union
NNC	National Negro Congress

NRA	National Recovery Administration
NUL	National Unemployed League
POUR	Presidents' Organization for Unemployment Relief
PWA	Public Works Administration
PWU	Project Workers Union
RCL	Renters and Consumers League
RFC	Reconstruction Finance Corporation
RWPA	Relief Workers Protective Association
SP	Socialist Party
SWOC	Steel Workers Organizing Committee
TUCUIR	Trade Union Committee for Unemployment Insurance and Relief
TUUL	Trade Union Unity League
UAW	United Automobile Workers
UCWU	United Copper Workers Union
UFL	United Farmers League
UPWOC	United Project Workers Organizing Committee
UWPAUWA	United WPA and Unemployed Workers of America
WAA	Workers Alliance of America
WESL	Workers Ex-Servicemen's League
WFM	Western Federation of Miners
YCL	Young Communist League

The Residue of a Failed Economy

There is no problem more vexing in a postindustrial society than the persistence of chronic unemployment that idles significant portions of the labor force, sometimes in periods of relative prosperity. At present, the American economy is undergoing a significant adjustment, accompanied by downsizing and restructuring, as well as structural unemployment which has left many workers bereft of the technological skills necessary for survival in the modern workplace. Dramatic as these changes have been, they are best understood against the background of a long history of employment instability, never completely absent from the capitalist economy in the United States.

As this study will demonstrate, economic crises have sometimes resulted in innovative institutional changes designed to alleviate the most damaging effects of systemic failure. The Great Depression of the 1930s forced important advances in the scope of the American welfare state and encouraged the development of labor unions, some of which worked to meet the broad social needs of their most vulnerable members. While the 25 percent unemployment of the early

1930s encouraged the development of new solutions by community and union organizers, the nagging joblessness of the 1980s and 1990s has created a major problem for modern labor unions struggling to assist workers caught in the structural reorganization now under way.

As scholars reflect upon the human wreckage of the modern economic readjustment, it can be useful to recall the crisis of the 1930s and the response of industrial unionism to the scourge of unemployment in another time. This analysis reminds unionists, community organizers, and policymakers that the labor movement once functioned as a social movement dedicated to goals that transcended the limits of business unionism. The postwar shift to massive bureaucratization in American labor should not obscure the creativity demonstrated by the United Automobile Workers and the CIO in their moment of intense social consciousness. For community activists and industrial unionists in Michigan, the Great Depression was in one sense, a great opportunity.

• • •

The numbers were staggering and the social damage extensive. As the scourge of joblessness spread across the economic landscape after the Crash of 1929, Americans struggled to adjust their expectations to the realities of scarcity. Personal misery and human dislocation were especially devastating to a generation schooled in the myth of benevolent capitalism and unlimited abundance long nurtured by the leaders of corporate America. When the grand dream of a new era dissolved before them, stunned workers were forced to confront unemployment unprecedented in scope and demoralizing in effect. An already bleak picture darkened until, by the end of the Hoover administration, nearly one-third of the labor force had been idled by the collapse of the economic system.

The sharp decline in employment during the Great Depression has often obscured the fact that chronic joblessness had become a recognizable feature of the American economic scene before 1900. By the first decade of the twentieth century, unemployment was a national problem, one not confined to the outcomes of the few well-publicized panics of the late nineteenth century. In 1900, 22.3 percent of the national labor force was idle in a period of relative prosperity. Michigan's 19.9 percent approximated the national level. Long before the collapse of the 1930s, therefore, unemployment had emerged as an element in American working class life and as a potentially serious social problem.[1]

During the generally prosperous 1920s, at least two trouble spots appeared in the Michigan employment picture. First, the economy of the urban southeast was marred by the phenomenon of recurrent seasonal unemployment. Although auto production, the heart of the regional economy, grew by 170 percent between 1919 and 1929, the annual model changeover resulted in regular periods of joblessness for large numbers of workers. While the months of layoff varied from year to year, a pattern of summer-fall seasonal unemployment in the auto industry had emerged by 1926.[2]

In the key industrial city of Detroit, these fluctuations in employment created significant relief needs and forced civic and business leaders to explore the causes of unemployment. As early as 1915, the Detroit Board of Commerce commissioned a survey that documented a chronic instability in the city's labor market and revealed a normal unemployment rate of about 10 percent. Following World War I, another wave of unemployment accompanied the reconversion cutbacks of 1920 and increased pressure on the Detroit welfare system. The return of prosperity after 1922 failed to bring stable employment to the auto industry, in which model changeovers continued to produce hardship for workers. The Ford Model A changeover of 1926 was especially devastating to Detroit-area workers, who flooded relief offices to seek public assistance. By the end of the 1920s, then, irregularity of employment plagued the working class of southeastern Michigan.[3]

A second pocket of employment decline appeared in the cutover lumber areas and mining districts of Michigan's remote Upper Peninsula. Between 1915 and 1929, over half the jobs in the copper mines of Houghton, Keweenaw, Ontonagon, and Baraga counties were lost. Despite these losses, a steady stream of outmigration to Detroit in the 1920s helped minimize the potential poverty and unemployment that might otherwise have developed. Local mine managers regarded the 1920s as a period of labor shortage. Moreover, management now moved to consolidate the largest companies in the Lake Superior copper district, while more than a dozen smaller mines closed. By 1929, the surviving corporations had lowered production costs, reduced output, and cut the size of the work force, thus placing themselves in what seemed a strong competitive position, only to have their hopes for profit dashed by the economic collapse of the 1930s.[4] Once the Great Depression set in, a reverse migration combined with a further contraction in employment to create a massive new relief burden which the communities of the UP were unable to bear.

Because of declining employment in the UP and the chronic seasonal labor market instability of the urban southeast, the industrial crisis and economic collapse following the stock market crash of 1929 were especially severe in Michigan. With its faltering automobile industry in decline, Michigan experienced unemployment levels unmatched in any other state during the early depression years. As early as 1930, 18 percent of nonagricultural workers were jobless. The proportion of unemployed workers in Michigan was the nation's highest, while the Detroit unemployment rate topped that of America's twelve largest cities. Between 1930 and 1933, Michigan's 34 percent average unemployment was substantially higher than the national average figure of 26 percent. With 485,000 out of work and a jobless rate of 46 percent in 1933, Michigan was perilously close to economic disaster.[5]

Although the plague of unemployment affected the entire state, the urban centers suffered most, particularly those most influenced by the automobile, textile, and consumer goods industries. In no city was the descent more dramatic than in Detroit, where a struggling auto industry dominated an economy geared to an ever-expanding market for America's number one luxury good. By 1931, economic conditions in the motor city had deteriorated so badly that Secretary of Commerce Robert P. Lamont described it as the "hardest hit of the nineteen cities sampled" in the special census unemployment report of that year.[6]

Even the grossly understated estimates recorded in the 1931 census confirm the fact that urban Michigan experienced the heaviest unemployment recorded in the state. Detroit, Hamtramck, Flint, Pontiac, Saginaw, and Jackson bore the brunt of joblessness, with jobless rates ranging from 8 percent to 16.7 percent. Intensity of unemployment in 1930 was most severe in Detroit and incorporated places over 50,000 in population, where 11 percent and 10.2 percent of the population, respectively, were unable to find work. But while the burden was greatest in the industrial southeast, the *relative* need for assistance was more dramatic in the economically devastated mining and lumbering districts of the Upper Peninsula. Between 1929 and 1933, UP mining companies discharged 6,000 men, and by 1934 one-third of the population was on relief. In hard-hit Keweenaw County, 75 percent of residents were receiving public assistance. According to Federal Emergency Relief Administration administrator Harry Hopkins, there were more persons receiving relief in the Copper Country than in any comparable area of the United States. One year later, Michigan relief administrator William Haber concluded that no area of the state had experienced intensity of unemployment (as measured by the ratio of unemployed workers to the total number of gainful workers) comparable to that endured by Upper Peninsula residents.[7] In sum, Michigan's hard-core unemployment was concentrated in two distinct areas of acute distress, the industrial heartland of the southeast and the remote districts of the far north, where extractive industry constituted the economic base.

In January 1935, 45 percent of the urban jobless were to be found in the manufacturing and mechanical industries; of these, nearly half had been employed in the dominant automobile industry, with the remainder spread throughout other industrial groups such as building and construction, iron, steel, machinery, food and allied industries, lumber and furniture, paper and printing, and chemical and allied industries. An overwhelming 84.7 percent of the unemployed were male, though in trade, domestic, personal, and professional services, the female jobless predominated. Finally, the unemployed were disproportionately found among the less skilled segments of the labor force. One-half of all the jobless workers were drawn from semiskilled and unskilled occupations. In the bellweather automobile industry, nearly 60 percent had been engaged in semiskilled occupations.[8]

For reasons related to traditional employment practices, the depression dealt Michigan's black population an especially hard blow. A larger proportion of the black population depended upon unemployment relief than was true of other racial groups. While 29 percent of the black population received relief at the time of the 1930 census, only 12 percent of the white population were on the relief rolls. Last to be hired and first to be fired, black workers were eventually to assume a prominent role in the unemployed organizing that took place in response to economic privation. During the 1920s, Detroit blacks had lacked even the minimal security acquired by other immigrant groups and had often sought city welfare services. Always marginal workers, they now took their places in the army of the unemployed.[9]

Just as black workers suffered disproportionately, immigrants felt the impact of Depression unemployment more than the native-born. Since the decade before World War I, the auto industry's work force had been culturally diverse. While auto workers were drawn from a variety of ethnic groups, Polish immigrants were especially numerous in Hamtramck and Detroit. Similarly, the UP labor force was composed of workers from an array of ethnic backgrounds, including Finns, Italians, Poles, Swedes, Germans, and Canadians, though Finnish immigrants predominated. While statewide statistics were unavailable, data from Detroit indicated that 43 percent of families on relief were headed by foreign-born whites, although only 39 percent of the city's family heads were foreign-born. The Detroit study prompted Haber to assert that foreign-born whites had been "more seriously affected" than their native-born counterparts.[10] Haber's analysis suggested that ethnic as well as racial outsiders were especially prone to joblessness.

While outsider status characterized the hard-core unemployed, long-term joblessness was a particular problem for those whose productive work lives were nearing an end. The authors of the state unemployment census of 1935 found that the security of the industrial worker was at risk at an unusually early age due to the demands of high speed mass production. Many employers were convinced that only younger workers possessed the requisite stamina, speed, and adaptability to perform effectively on the job. Consequently, the demand for laborers from more advanced age groups was sharply curtailed due to Depression circumstances, especially among workers over 45. In Detroit, for example, less than 12 percent of the male workers in the 25–40 age group were unemployed in January 1935, but the jobless figure for those over 40 was twice as high. Beyond 55, the percentage ranged between 28 and 35 percent.[11] Chronic unemployables were not only disproportionately black or foreign-born, but they were also likely to be older, experienced workers. (See figure 1.)

Despite abundant evidence that Michigan confronted exceptionally severe unemployment problems, there was relatively little inclination to recognize their gravity. Plans for dramatic government action generated only modest support. Moreover, many critics held stubbornly to the traditional assertion that any motivated job-seeker would ultimately be successful. Presidential investigator Roland Haynes of the Hoover administration's President's Organi-

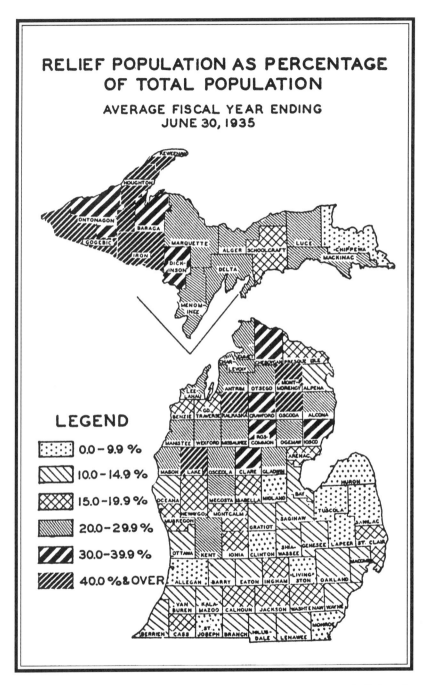

Figure 1 The Michigan Relief Crisis, 1935 (*"Unemployment, Relief, and Economic Security," Second Report of the State Emergency Welfare Relief Commission, Lansing, 1936*)

zation on Unemployment Relief reported in 1931 that Republican Governor Wilbur Brucker opposed a special legislative session that might revise the state's tax program and make "wasteful appropriations for relief." Similarly, POUR fieldworker Alice Stenholm asserted that despite pressure on Brucker, the governor's advisory committee on unemployment hoped to prevent legislative action. She noted that although government and community organizations in Michigan had been slow to organize, they were moving in a constructive direction by coordinating private and public resources. More remarkable was her accurate observation that the state's welfare authorities were confident that "Michigan will be able to handle its responsibility without outside aid."[12]

Contrary to this sunny forecast, the realities in Michigan were grim. Homes were lost, diets changed, and bills mounted as employment continued a precipitous decline. Detroit's agony was recorded in numerous popular articles. Social worker Helen Hall's analysis in *Survey* detailed the human impact of joblessness in several anecdotal accounts of courage, spirit, and resistance against the often unavoidable drift towards relief, regarded by many as evidence of failure and personal inadequacy. As unemployment mounted, Detroit job lines lengthened and superfluous people brooded darkly. The sullen men at the plant gates stood as stark evidence that the glowing optimism of the 1920s had turned to quiet desperation with the collapse of the capitalist edifice. Michigan's urban communities responded with penurious relief allowances, municipal lodging houses, food distribution programs, and resistance to further inmigration. Despite these palliatives, welfare rolls mounted steadily, and neither public assistance measures nor corporate relief programs seemed capable of stemming the tide of despair.[13]

Popular legend and modern historiography suggest that stunned workers drifted aimlessly, awash in a sea of self-blame and paralyzed by misfortune; and it is true that many responded with quiet resignation. Equally significant, however, was the spark of radicalism ignited by the widespread suffering. Resistance took many forms, including cooperative activity, family and neighborhood support groups, local supply networks, spontaneous political activity, occasional looting, and sometimes militant collective action. Radical organizers worked tirelessly to galvanize the unemployed into a social, economic, and political force and to promote in them a more advanced sense of class awareness than had previously been observed. Although the jobless often resisted radical ideology, they frequently responded to efforts to aid them in coping with their plight. These initiatives resulted in occasional successes for unemployed organizers, especially in the nation's largest urban centers. In no city was the potential for class militancy or the power of popular response more explosive than in Detroit, where the collapse of the automobile industry had created widespread hardship.[14]

This study traces the origins and development of organizational activity among the unemployed in Michigan from 1929 through 1941 and advances an explanation for the unique form taken by this workers' struggle. It identifies a clear link between the institutions created by and for the jobless and the conditions, circumstances, and organizations that prevailed in Depression-era Michigan. Given the state's social and economic environment, including the pervasiveness of the auto industry as an economic force, it was predictable that the United Automobile Workers Union would ultimately assume a significant role as an influence on the unemployed movement. The rise of industrial unionism shaped the struggle in lower Michigan and determined that unemployed activity in that region emerged in a form distinct from that which prevailed in most industrial states. Moreover, the Michigan organizational model created in 1937 by UAW welfare committees was doubly important because of its impact on the CIO's national commitment to the unemployed during the recession of 1937–1938 and in subsequent years.

While the CIO initiative and UAW activism dominated unemployed organizing in southern Michigan from 1937 on, the Upper Peninsula, with its unique economy, presented organizers with a special challenge. The weakness of an extractive economy combined with the political culture of Finnish radicalism to produce an alternative variety of unemployed activity. Beyond the reach of successful unionism for most of the 1930s, leftist Finns assumed leadership of the organized unemployed and created organizations that often expressed Communist Party ideology as they worked to aid the jobless. The Workers Alliance, which in the southeast offered spirited competition to the UAW, became the dominant unemployed organization in the UP. Here ethnicity and the absence of a viable union movement determined the course of the organized unemployed.

Ethnic tradition, religious institutions, and economic history were also significant in influencing unemployed activity in one additional geographic area of the state, the northern and western portion of lower Michigan. The relative weakness of unemployed organizations in this district is best understood in terms of its mixed urban-rural economy and the predominance of small and medium-sized cities. Without the concentrations of heavy industry or mass population that characterized the urban southeast, western Michigan appeared to be suffering economic contraction and joblessness less severe than that sustained in the Detroit, Flint, Lansing, and Jackson areas. Even if this flawed perception had been accurate, the local economic base and demographics would not have provided a full explanation for the region's relatively feeble unemployed organizations. An essential element in the story involves the penetrating influence in many western Michigan communities of the Dutch Reformed Church, the teachings of which embodied a Christian ethic of social harmony, cross-class cooperation, and deference to authority. This area, long hostile to labor unionism, was not fertile ground for the growth of militant unemployed organizations.

While geographic, economic, and cultural distinctions are important factors in any interpretation of unemployed organizing in 1930s Michigan, it is also necessary to consider separate phases of organizational activity. It is possible to identify several clearly defined stages of activism, during which various organizations worked to unite the unemployed in their own interest as well as that of their sponsors. At different times, Communists, Socialists, Trotskyites, Lovestoneites, and mainstream labor unionists were influential in attempts to mold the jobless into an effective economic, social, and political force.

These organizational efforts took place in two distinct phases, roughly separated by the advent in 1935 of the Roosevelt administration's Works Progress Administration program, the Social Security system, unemployment insurance, and the Wagner Act. The first, militant stage spanned the years between 1929 and 1935. In this period, unemployed organizers emphasized social action, community organizing, and the exertion of pressure through mass action. They employed various direct action tactics, including public demonstrations, welfare office sit-ins, eviction actions, and occasionally legislative pressure, to secure assistance for relief recipients and voice the broader demands of the jobless. At this point in their development, unemployed groups were often governed through a process of direct democracy in which the rank-and-file had substantial influence on policy and strategy. Often led by left-wing spokesmen, of whom the Detroit Communists were most active and influential, unemployed groups attempted to force public officials to accept responsibility for the casualties of the collapsed economy.[15]

The first period of unemployed organizing was itself divided into two substages of activism. Prior to the inauguration of Franklin D. Roosevelt, militants relied heavily on direct action to accomplish their objectives. In Michigan, Communists gave aggressive leadership to the unemployed, though their rank-and-file supporters often became involved in organizational work for essentially nonideological reasons. There is substantial evidence to indicate that jobless workers turned to the CP-dominated Unemployed Councils because of personal need and frustration, but that their participation in Council activities did not necessarily translate into endorsement of the Party. Rather, they saw the Communists as the only organization that offered them meaningful assistance. After 1933, however, other unemployed activists competed for the allegiances of the jobless. Socialists engaged the Communists within the Workers Alliance, which by late 1935 had made a promising start in Michigan. Between 1933 and 1935, the Unemployed Councils and their competitors responded to such New Deal programs as the Civil Works Administration, Federal Emergency Relief Administration, and Public Works Administration by assuming an advocacy and bargaining role for the jobless that began to resemble a labor union model.

Following Roosevelt's stunning legislative victories in 1935, unemployed organizing in Michigan entered a second major phase, during which attention focused on the development of a response to the newly created Works Progress Administration and the implementation of the Wagner Act in the auto industry and elsewhere. The central innovation in this period was WPA, a program rooted in the concept of the right to gainful employment. Because of this assumption, jobless organizers moved to apply the collective bargaining model to workers employed on WPA projects. In 1936 and 1937, the militant Workers Alliance assumed center stage, eventually gaining prestige, political acceptance, presidential patronage, and UAW cooperation. Since government employees seemed fair game for organizers and public employment legitimized collective action for them, the Alliance succeeded in establishing a position as the recognized union of the unemployed.[16]

However, once the UAW became firmly established in 1937, the ground rules for unemployed organizing in Michigan changed dramatically. The third and final phase of unemployed activity bore the indelible stamp of industrial unionism. This period is critical to an understanding of the political culture of unemployed workers and the limits of radicalism in the American social, economic, and political context. The direction taken by organizational activity after 1937 confirmed both the power of the CIO as a magnet for workers and, in the last analysis, the compelling attraction of mainstream liberalism for recently enfranchised unionists.

Joblessness was an inescapable dimension of the Michigan worker experience of the 1930s. And the definitive response to the challenge of unemployment from the recession of 1937–1938 onward emanated from the state's most powerful union, which embraced the jobless as both a service to the victims of a broken economy and as a matter of self-preservation. The rise of the UAW and CIO, whose social commitment reached far beyond the goals of traditional business unionism, holds the key to an explanation of organized unemployed activity in Michigan and accounts for its distinctiveness. The success of UAW in capturing the loyalties of jobless workers and harnessing their energies strongly reinforces an interpretation of the early CIO as not simply a powerful economic force, but also as a social movement of transcendent importance.

But was the drive to organize the unemployed itself a social movement in the accepted sense of the term? It was clearly perceived as such by those most active in its leadership ranks. Movement rhetoric was prominently featured in the public pronouncements of Unemployed Council and Workers Alliance organizers. Moreover, unemployed activism was geographically comprehensive, in that the work of Michigan's predominant organizations was matched by similar efforts throughout the United States, including not only the Councils and the Alliance but also the militant Unemployed Leagues of Pennsylvania, Ohio, and West Virginia and the West Coast Unemployed Citizens Leagues.

Some scholars have argued explicitly that Depression-era unemployed organizing constituted a classic social movement, including the requisite transformation of consciousness and behavior. Once the unemployed had denied the legitimacy of a system that had failed them and demanded that their right to survive be respected, they turned to defiant collective action to achieve their objectives. The result was spontaneous social protest that rose from the grass roots and ultimately expressed itself through a variety of organizational vehicles.[17]

In many respects, the development of unemployed organizations in 1930s Michigan displayed the definitive features of a social movement. In the first phase of activity, there is substantial evidence of spontaneity and grass-roots pressure, as well as a clear strain of democratic control from below. However, it is equally true that various organizations became active among the jobless in order to promote an ideology or advance a political agenda. The history of the Michigan unemployed reveals that idealism, social concern, and political/ideological self-interest combined to produce activities clearly seen by their adherents as a movement.

By the end of the 1930s, the personnel trained in the early years of unemployed activism had entered the larger labor movement. Indeed, it is plausible to argue that the work of organizers among the jobless constituted an early, preliminary stage in a larger national movement that climaxed after the enactment of the Wagner Act in 1935. The Michigan case supports the assertion that the protest which had flourished in the streets during the Hoover administration helped set the stage for the workplace insurgency that followed and provided many of the organizers who served the labor movement of the Roosevelt years.[18]

The direction taken by unemployed organizing in Michigan provides evidence that after the early expressions of mass protest and direct action, a combination of New Deal reforms and a bureaucratizing labor movement coopted the militants and drew many of them into a developing liberal consensus. As the New Deal welfare state extended benefits, including direct work relief, to the Depression's victims, some radicals were integrated into the relief administration's structure, while others played the role of willing collaborators who exerted controlled legislative pressure on Congress, as well as local relief bureaucracies. In Michigan, the final step in this integrative process was taken when the UAW launched its own drive to aid the unemployed and at the same time to preserve its hard-won gains.

The UAW's initiative, which brought the union into a closer relationship with New Deal work-relief agencies, undoubtedly played a role in the gradual domestication of the labor movement that accompanied state rationalization of the economy in the 1930s. It was, nonetheless, an innovative step for Michigan labor. While the casual ascription of blanket conservatism to the Detroit Federation of Labor and other state craft unions would be an oversimplification, the available evidence does suggest that in most cases affecting the interests of the unemployed, the building trades and other craft organizations were indifferent. Although AFL affiliates occasionally came to the aid of the jobless, as in the isolated efforts of the Kalamazoo and Grand Rapids Federations during the early 1930s, the predominant attitude of Michigan craft unions was closer to the suspicion of unemployed organizations regularly expressed by Frank Martel of the DFL. Partly for practical reasons and partly because of its social vision, UAW found it possible to think beyond the immediate concerns of employed dues-paying members. In contrast to Martel's skepticism, the UAW's acknowledgement of unionism's community dimension during the auto workers struggle for recognition at Flint and in subsequent years marked an important extension of union social consciousness. The union's grasp of the interrelatedness of unemployment, union community services, and the fate of its own organizational efforts became even more evident during the deep recession of 1937–1938.[19]

The nature and significance of that relationship are central issues in the analysis that follows. Equally important is an examination of the New Deal's impact on both the mass insurgency of the early 1930s and the evolution of the labor movement throughout the Depression years. For all participants in the struggle, whether radical organizers who advanced the immediate interests of the poor, ideologues who looked to the unemployed as the shock troops of revolution, union bureaucrats engaged in the institutionalization of their organization, or workers intent on gaining control of their lives and fortunes, one thing is certain: the union made a difference.

2

Radical Politics and Worker Response
Solidarity and Revolution, 1929–1933

For American workers the critical domestic issue of the 1930s was the search for economic security. In Michigan, unemployment had become a severe problem as early as April 1930, exacerbated as it was by the state's heavy reliance on manufacturing and its resultant sensitivity to cyclical economic fluctuations. The precipitous decline of 1929–1930 has sometimes obscured the fact that even in the relatively prosperous 1920s, the national army of the unemployed had grown substantially. Because of permanent job losses in the Upper Peninsula and the chronic instability of the labor markets of the southeast with its seasonal uncertainties, Michigan workers were already contributing to its ranks. By 1928 warnings against long-term high unemployment levels nationwide had emanated from such varied sources as the Bureau of Labor Statistics, the American Association for Labor Legislation, the League of Women Voters, the National Conference of Social Workers, and the American Federation of Labor. Particularly prescient was United States Commissioner of Labor Statistics Ethelbert Stewart, who in early 1928 warned that existing high levels of unemployment were but the "beginning of a more or less permanent unemployment" due to potential overproduction and underconsumption. Despite the forecasts, however, the sharp decline in employment that followed the stock market crash of October 1929 came as a brutal shock to the national economy and struck the auto industry with devastating force.[1] The reverberations were felt throughout the state as the Michigan economy slipped into the depths of depression.

Confronted with unprecedented economic and social distress, representatives of the labor establishment were slow to act on their awareness of a potentially explosive situation in Michigan's industrial heartland. Refusing to accept the prospect of long-term unemployment, the American Federation of Labor maintained a measured distance from the feverish unemployed organizing that occurred in the wake of the crash. Bound by an outdated commitment to voluntarism, the AFL not only avoided the organization of the jobless, but also fought against unemployment insurance until late 1932. Although as early as 1930, the AFL acknowledged "increasing support for unemployment insurance among working people," its executive committee stubbornly insisted that President William Green's rejection of any compulsory plan "accurately reflected" opinion within the Federation. Craft union avoidance of unemployed activity was wholly consistent with the elitist tradition of a skilled workers' federation suspicious of government intervention and historically committed to emphasis on the interests of the labor aristocracy.[2]

The Michigan trade union movement was equally unimaginative. Responding to pressure for tax cuts and government retrenchment from Detroit's financial elite, the Detroit Federation of Labor blamed unemployment and swollen relief rolls on the "insane manner" in which the "captains of industry" had kept the city "flooded with a surplus of labor" and urged restrictions on city hiring of nonresident labor. Meanwhile, the state Federation of Labor in Lansing looked to management for a solution. In January 1930, the Michigan Federation weakly endorsed Michigan Senator James Couzens' speech calling on corporate leaders to stabilize employment or face government-mandated unemployment insurance. More than a year after the crash, the state Federation's solution to the crisis revolved around the cautious scheme of work-sharing, whereby the work week would be limited without

Figure 2 Homeless Men Outside their Dugout Shelter in Detroit, 1930
(Archives of Labor and Urban Affairs, Wayne State University)

loss of pay. Beyond work-sharing and work relief, the Michigan Federation was unwilling to go. Its conservatism mirrored the dominance of the corporate elite in an oppressive open shop environment and a workplace peopled by a labor force divided by ethnic and racial differences.[3]

More committed to the search for a solution but no more effective were Michigan Socialists, who decried the system's failure to provide useful employment to motivated workers. By 1930, the state's small Socialist Party was only a shadow of a once vibrant institution that prior to World War I had offered a vigorous critique of capitalism. Although their efforts to aid the unemployed were poorly organized, Michigan Socialists were aware of the need for organization. Once Walter and Victor Reuther joined the party in Detroit, they soon became engaged in spirited debate with other Socialists over potential solutions to the economic crisis. A concern for the dispossessed was evident in their pamphlet attacking the system and contrasting the affluence of Detroit's wealthy with the plight of the city's unemployed. Yet their choice of a medium reflected the underlying weakness of Michigan socialism at the outset of the depression: its socioeconomic composition. Not only was the Michigan Socialist Party small by comparison with the parties in most surrounding states, but also the state organization was dominated by sincere yet ineffective middle-class intellectuals. As working-class Socialists, the activist Reuthers were atypical of a membership that had relatively little contact with workers or the unemployed.[4]

Despite the narrowness of its membership base, the Michigan Socialist Party tried to address issues of importance to workers. In 1930, for example, the Socialist state platform focused on unemployment as a contradiction to the individual's right to "occupation and plenty," which was to be ensured through state relief, public employment, unemployment insurance, and collective ownership. It was especially the concept of unemployment insurance that caught the imagination of the Michigan Socialists. Ever since the Couzens speech, discussion within the state party had centered on the state government's role in the stabilization of employment. In early 1931, Michigan Socialists embraced the idea of compulsory insurance, and by February, party members were immersed in an effort to force a referendum on the issue. Rejecting state representative Frank Darin's contributory plan, which required workers' payments, the SP insisted on a model bill advanced in the Socialist *Leader*. In an effort to establish worker solidarity in support of unemployment compensation, the party's Unemployment Compensation Committee appealed to the Detroit Federation of Labor for cooperation. The Socialist proposal, which reached DFL president Frank Martel in February 1932, drew no response. Long a conservative trade unionist, Martel was typically cool to leftist social schemes. Nonetheless, he had occasionally lent support to AFL organizing efforts among auto workers. The failure of Martel and the Federation to join in the SP campaign was no surprise, since Green and the AFL had not yet endorsed unemployment insurance. Moreover, as Victor Reuther later acknowledged, SP unemployed activists in Michigan were "not a highly-organized group." Their efforts were unsuccessful, though the failure of the insurance measure in Michigan was not simply the result of Socialist ineptitude. A more important factor was an increase in worker pressure for improved relief programs and a national unemployment insurance bill.[5]

Far more successful were Communist organizers, who assumed effective leadership of the struggle against unemployment. Not only was the Communist Party's initial analysis of the crisis more accurate than that of the nation's economic establishment, but Communists were ready to act on their convictions. Throughout the United States the Party assumed leadership in establishing Unemployed Councils under the auspices of its Trade Union Unity League. TUUL was the successor organization to the Trade Union Educational League, which until 1929 had been the CP's vehicle for working within existing AFL unions. After September 1, 1929, TUUL devoted its efforts to the establishment of industrial unions independent of AFL. Since Red union leaders were proud of their Party ties, there was no attempt to conceal them. And once the economy collapsed, TUUL openly sponsored the formation of Unemployed Councils that would include representatives of revolutionary unions, shop committees, mainstream unions, unorganized workers, and unemployed citizens. The Councils were affiliated with TUUL, which regarded the unemployed as the vanguard of the revolutionary movement. As a result, unemployed organizing became one of the Party's highest priorities and Communists came to view the fight against joblessness as the "tactical key" to the class struggle in America.[6]

Theodore Draper was essentially correct in identifying the period from 1930 to 1933 as the "purely Communist phase of the unemployed movement." Beginning with the massive demonstrations of early 1930, unprecedented public protests took place in the nation's major urban centers. Left-wing memoirs of the era are filled with testaments to the CP's catalytic role in mobilizing the jobless, and there is much truth in Wyndham Mortimer's assertion that "the only effective struggles against unemployment and evictions were those organized by the Communist Party." An important clue to the militance of these activists is the sometimes-overlooked fact of their own unemployed status, as well as the spontaneity of their actions. Many Communists were themselves unemployed, and the hard core did "manage to bring out ever increasing numbers of people for the various protest demonstrations."[7]

In Detroit the Party was stronger than in most industrial cities at the outset of the depression. Radical organizer Steve Nelson recalled

that Detroit was a one-industry town, and it was simpler to understand. Everybody had a common problem; you saw giant corporations, and you saw the mass of workers. . . . What you did, if you were male was hard industrial work. It was all very clear.[8]

On the shop floor and in the ethnic communities, the CP was an influence to be reckoned with. The party's ethnic composition made it by far the most effective radical group in working with Detroit's foreign-born population, particularly Poles, Finns, Ukranians, Lithuanians, and Russians. From the ranks of the workers came such party leaders as Phil Raymond, Bud Reynolds, and Al Goetz, all destined to assume leading roles in the early unemployed movement. They were familiar with conditions in the plants and avoided abstract intellectualism in their efforts to build an organization. To CP activists, the development of militant unionism was an essential prerequisite to any effective radical movement. Their work in the Auto Workers Union before 1930 ensured that the CP would be the predominant influence in the only union to challenge corporate hegemony and welfare capitalism in the pre–New Deal automobile industry.[9]

For Communists, the unemployed were a vital link in the chain that bound all workers in a class alliance. Consequently, Party energies shifted in 1929 towards organizational work among the jobless. The CP's crucial insight was to recognize that without "a high measure of united action between employed and unemployed, many of the organizing drives and strikes could not have succeeded." Driven by an advanced vision of solidarity, Michigan Party activists threw themselves into the drive to establish Unemployed Councils. In Detroit, Pontiac, Flint, and Hamtramck, Communists engaged workers wherever they congregated—at factories, shelters, welfare organization meetings, union halls, and relief offices. Committed to the promotion of "participation in the class struggle on a mass action basis," organizers urged recruits to create local committees which could "function as revolutionary centers" on the St. Petersburg model of 1905. Detroit Party leaders moved quickly in December 1930 to organize demonstrations that would call attention to the plight of the jobless and thereby capture their loyalty. Their Unemployed Council was the first organized in the United States. CP activist Herbert Benjamin later recalled that unlike previous unemployed movements, the Councils went out "to reach the unemployed in the community" and forced government "to provide relief to the unemployed." With some justification, Benjamin noted that they were the only workers' organization to make demands rather than requests in the pre–New Deal period before such actions became "rather safe."[10]

Dedicated as it was to organizing the unorganized, TUUL assumed a leading role in forging worker unity. It worked through its key affiliate in Michigan—the Auto Workers Union—which had consistently devoted heavy attention to the jobless. Originally a Knights of Labor affiliate, the United Automobile, Aircraft, and Vehicle Workers of America entered the AFL in 1891, where it remained until 1918 when it was forced out of the Federation after a clash with craft unions over jurisdiction in the auto industry. In its early years as an independent union after World War I, AWU grew rapidly in Michigan and elsewhere in the Midwest. However, the Palmer Raids and the economic recession of 1920–1921 combined to weaken the organization, which had been led by Socialists. After 1922, Communist influence in the union increased, and by 1927 CP members had assumed leadership positions, including Phil Raymond as head of Detroit Local 127 and Al Goetz as president of the national AWU. Before the Great Depression began, AWU was a small but prominent Red union.[11]

Analyzing the auto industry crisis in late 1929, AWU spokesman Phil Raymond identified rising unemployment in auto centers as an important stimulus to the union's early development. Raymond was in a position to know. Employed in Detroit's auto plants since 1924, he had emerged as the leading Communist organizer in the automobile industry. Because it was the only organization in the field, Raymond argued, workers had looked to AWU "for leadership in every major struggle that has broken out in our industry." Yet by 1930, growth in membership began to stagnate due to the deteriorating economic situation. With its expansion at a plateau, AWU now increased its emphasis on unemployed work with open meetings aimed at creating a mass organization that would solidify ties between employed workers and the jobless.[12]

Accelerated union activity coincided with increased worker militancy and CP activism. On 2 December 1929 large demonstrations occurred at the Murray Body and Briggs Highland Park plants, spontaneous outbreaks that revealed resentment among younger laborers, who were typically the first laid off in economic slumps. Convinced that the intensity and violence of these protests underscored the need for effective organization, AWU redoubled its efforts to recruit young workers who might "use their militancy on behalf of their class."[13]

Within two weeks AWU, TUUL, and the fledgling Detroit Unemployed Council Provisional Committee had announced a comprehensive program for unemployed relief, a rent holiday, and industrial unionism. For good measure, the Committee pressed these demands in a demonstration at the office of Detroit mayor John Lodge. It also urged workers to unite on the basis of class interest in full solidarity, encompassing both employed and unemployed. Only through "the organization of the unemployed into a powerful organization united in common struggle with those employed" would it be possible to "force the capitalists to consider the needs of the workers." Signed by CP operatives George E. Powers of TUUL, Committee Secretary Al Goetz, and Phil Raymond, the appeal was heavy-laden with Marxist rhetoric and bitter vitriol aimed at the AFL labor establishment, which drew a denunciation as the "agent of the bosses."[14]

By March 1930, the provisional committee was evolving into a more permanent Detroit Unemployed Council. These loosely organized bodies, though typically led by Communist organizers such as Raymond, Goetz, and Reynolds, were block and neighborhood organizations that operated on the basis of democratic control from below. Though group decision-making was sometimes manipulated by experienced activists, it is equally true that militancy often rose from the rank-and-file, which sometimes forced leaders to assume positions more extreme than they thought prudent. From the CP perspective, the Unemployed Councils could serve two purposes: to unite diverse ethnic and racial groups in struggle against economic hardship and to persuade the jobless that government and management bore primary responsibility for providing short-term relief and solving the long-term problem through a federal unemployment insurance program.[15] The achievement of these goals rested on a third important development, the establishment of a meaningful solidarity that linked employed and unemployed workers.

In the early months of 1930, the Councils began to escalate the battle for unemployment relief with a series of small demonstrations in Detroit, Hamtramck, and Pontiac. These skirmishes may have served to raise worker consciousness of their common plight, but the results were meager. In Pontiac, Raymond was jailed for "spreading discontent" after trying to see the mayor and later attempting to speak to a gathering of unemployed workers at city hall. Social worker Helen Hall found the allegation ironic, since she understood the simple truth that after six months of unemployment, "it doesn't take a Communist to make one feel discontented." Meanwhile in Hamtramck, Communist mayoral candidate George Kristalsky led an unemployed demonstration that coincided with a larger rally held in Detroit's Cadillac Square. These events matched several sporadic protest actions that took place elsewhere in the United States[16] as unemployed workers struggled to find a voice and left-wing activists worked to forge a policy that would provide structure for a national movement.

Business and political leaders were uneasy about the potentially explosive social environment, which was closely monitored in the Detroit *Industrial Intelligence Bulletin.* From this source Michigan employers learned that "the Red slogan is 'fight' " and that "whatever happens is their own responsibility." This remark was a direct reference to the Party's plans for the 6 March demonstration marking the eleventh anniversary of the Third International. (See figure 3.) Called by the Comintern as an international protest against unemployment, these demonstrations brought the CP national publicity for its role in organizing the jobless. Exhorting its readers to back the police, the *Bulletin* hoped that the Communists would be given "all the fighting they want."[17]

Despite DFL attempts to discourage participation, even some craft unionists displayed enthusiasm for the March protest. The Detroit Unemployed Council encouraged widespread involvement, arguing that "unemployment is the problem of *all workers,* employed, unemployed, organized, unorganized, negro, white, native, foreign-born, men, women, youth, and adult workers." In early March, Communists blanketed Detroit's working-class neighborhoods with leaflets and appealed for a large turnout. Convinced that they were on the verge of a major breakthrough, Council leaders exhorted members to attend a last-minute preparation meeting for an event that was certain to "draw . . . the unemployed into active work."[18]

Despite cautious optimism, however, even the demonstration's CP sponsors were stunned by the huge crowd on "Red Thursday," variously estimated at 50,000 to 100,000. The *Daily Worker* account of the national demonstrations ranked the Detroit turnout as second only to that of New York. Similar protests also occurred in Grand Rapids, Hamtramck, Kalamazoo, Lincoln Park, Lansing, Flint, and Pontiac, where sizable crowds turned out to demonstrate

Demonstrate *Detroit* *March 6* *1930*

Demonstrate on March 6th, 1 p. m.

— AT —

CAMPUS MARTIUS

OPPOSITE CITY HALL

DEMAND: WORK OR WAGES! FULL WAGES FOR PART TIME WORKERS! AGAINST WAGE CUTS AND SPEED UP! FOR SOLIDARITY OF EMPLOYED AND UNEMPLOYED!

WORKING MEN AND WOMEN OF DETROIT!

Each one of us feels the curse of unemployment. Not a worker's family is exempt from the monster of Unemployment. In every family there is at least one unemployed, one working part time. Those still at work, face daily an increasing speed-up and continual slashing of their wages. Fathers and mothers must watch daily the suffering of their little ones, compelled to go without food; leave for school with torn shoes, only to return home to a cold, unheated house.

About seven million unemployed in the United States, with over 150,000 in Detroit alone, sentenced by capitalism to death by starvation, while the bosses squander the wealth produced by our toil in magnificent luxury in their resorts in Florida an elsewhere.

CAPITALISM CANNOT SOLVE UNEMPLOYMENT

On the contrary in every capitalist country, unemployment is on the increase. Before Christmas, we were promised work after New Year; then within two weeks, and now they hold the prospect for Spring. Hoover boasts of "public works", while the City Council postpones its building program for the fall "when there will be more unemployment". Workers and their families can buy no bread with these promises. Only when capitalism is abolished as in the Soviet Union, can we eliminate unemployment in the U. S.

NEW ATTACKS AGAINST THE WORKERS! NEW ATTACKS AGAINST THE SOVIET UNION!

The bosses, in their greed for profits, try to shift the whole burden of the present crisis upon our shoulders. In the feverish competition on the already narrow market, they try to undersell each other at our expense by further wage cuts and speed up. This only increases the army of unemployed. The bosses are also preparing another imperialist war in order to secure new markets. Above all, we witness a capitalist united front against the Soviet Union, because they fear that the workers in all countries will follow the example of their brothers in the Soviet Union in overthrowing their oppressors and organize the rule of the workers.

WORKERS FIGHT BACK

The workers, unable to bear these conditions, are fighting back. The bosses use their agents—the American Federation of Labor officialdom, socialists and other misleaders, against us. They build up their Jerry Buckleys to try to lull us to sleep with their sweet words. Against their strategy of division, we must organize the united forces of labor; employed and unemployed, negro and white, native and foreign born, youth and adult workers.

The City Council and Mayor Bowles will do nothing for us. Instead, they increase the street car fare from 5 to 8 cents. They raise the salaries of their judges, who will send militant workers to long terms in jail. They are going to spend more millions for police and equipment to attack the workers. They are going to repeat the action of the Hoover government which returned hundreds of millions in taxes to the rich, by lowering the taxes of the rich in Detroit. Millions for the rich, but not a cent for the starving unemployed. This is the program of the City Council and Mayor Bowles.

TERROR, PROVOCATION—BOSSES' WEAPONS

In fear of the rising militancy of the working class, the capitalists are increasing their terror. Already "bomb plots" are being concocted by provocateurs in the police department. It is no accident that the police, as has been shown in the Gastonia investigation are closely connected with the underworld, receive this "tip" from gangsterdom; no doubt they receive more than mere "tips". As the workers prepare for March 6th, there will most likely be "revealed" more "Red Plots" and "Bomb Plots". They may even try to use the old frame-up as in California, where Mooney and Billings must rot in jail for life for a bomb planted by government provocateurs. The bosses and their government will stop at nothing in their efforts to destroy the Communist Party and the other workers' organizations.

Every worker knows that the Communist Party does not believe in individual terror and assassination. The Communist Party believes in the organization of the masses and in the mass struggle against the capitalist system.

FIGHT—REFUSE TO STARVE!

Long enough have we stood in submission. Alone we can do nothing; United, our power can make the bosses tremble. We must put forward our demands to the bosses, and their government. Let us build the Detroit Unemployed Council which is a section of the Trade Union Unity League into a mighty weapon of the working class.

Fellow Workers: MARCH 6th IS A BIG DAY FOR THE WORKING CLASS. March 6th is the day when the workers of the entire world, employed and unemployed, will demonstrate against unemployment, against speed-up, against wage cuts, and against imperialist war.

It is your duty to yourself—to your class, to join in the big demonstration called by the Communist Party, the Trade Union Unity League, and the Detroit Unemployed Council on March 6 at 1 p. m. at Campus Martius, opposite City Hall. Don't pay attention to any last minute announcements in the bosses' press, or the Jerry Buckleys that the demonstration was called off. IT WILL BE HELD ON MARCH 6th!

You must come with your wives and children. Bring your shopmates, your neighbors. All workers of Detroit must come to the streets and demonstrate for:

Work or Wages!

Unemployment Insurance to be paid out of the big profits of the bosses!

Full wages for those working part time.

Against Dismissals—go back to your shop and demand your job—don't accept dismissal as final!

Against wage cuts and against speed up! For 7-hour day!

For the 7-hour day!

For immediate emergency relief from the City Government!

Against Imperialist war!

For the defense of the Soviet Union!

Workers of Detroit! Organize and Fight! Refuse to Starve!

Join the Detroit Unemployed Council!

Join Trade Union Unity League and Auto Workers Union!

READ THE DAILY WORKER!

JOIN THE COMMUNIST PARTY!

COME WITH YOUR WIFE AND CHILDREN!

Figure 3 Handbill for Unemployed Demonstration in Detroit, March 6, 1930 *(Archives of Labor and Urban Affairs, Wayne State University)*

concern over the developing employment crisis. Auto workers were prominent in these actions, which provided many with their first organized working-class activity.[19] This training in grass-roots organizational work was an important service performed for auto workers by the Unemployed Councils.

After Detroit mayor Charles Bowles met briefly with Raymond and Powers, police moved to disperse the gathering, at which time two thousand officers waded into the crowd, attacking demonstrators and bystanders alike. For two hours confusion prevailed in the heart of the motor city. Before long, the violence escalated into what the *Detroit Times* labeled "indiscriminate clubbing," after which forty participants were arrested. Mayor Bowles reportedly concluded that the use of clubs was a "natural" measure designed to compel respect for police authority. The Detroit confrontation, like those in other major cities, shattered official optimism by revealing that many citizens were convinced that the CP and the Unemployed Councils "could help people face the deteriorating economic situation."[20] If the Detroit authorities had been in doubt about popular concern over unemployment, the day's events certainly dispelled those notions.

Less violence attended the demonstrations held in other Michigan communities. In the important auto center of Flint, where the Communist Party enrolled an anemic twenty-two members, 15,000 demonstrators participated in a peaceful protest. Here Phil Raymond and other AWU activists led a march to city hall, but no violence occurred. The day passed without major incident, in part because police officials had taken the precaution of locking up the city's leading Communists and holding them without filing charges. Similarly, Pontiac Communists were incarcerated to prevent any disturbance, thus leaving thousands of marchers leaderless. Repressive security procedures had helped keep the lid on. While the police worked to neutralize discontent, the Flint press dismissed demonstrators as "curious sightseers" and "gullible folk of limited mentality." Meanwhile, the Detroit Federation of Labor insisted that the 6 March protest was actually the creation of "the fertile brains of headline writers of the daily newspapers."[21]

The truth was far more complex. It is clear that city officials and the local labor establishment got more than they bargained for. The 6 March movement was, in fact, the first coordinated national reaction to the human misery created by the Great Depression. In retrospect, it is also clear that it marked the peak of CP political influence among the unemployed in the 1930s. (See figure 4.) Detroit Socialist Frank Marquardt later observed that "never before nor since in this country were the Communists so successful `when calling the masses into the streets.'" Even more significant, however, was the intensification of the national focus on joblessness.

Figure 4　Unemployed Demonstration in Detroit, March, 1930 *(Archives of Labor and Urban Affairs, Wayne State University)*

And among Communists, the immediate result was a renewed commitment to the organization of the unemployed.[22]

The *Auto Workers News* forecast an incipient mass movement by workers "not cowed by police clubs and official arrogance." Two days after the demonstration, the union pledged "to take up the struggle against wage cuts and for immediate relief." Reviewing strike activity since August 1929, AWU Secretary Phil Raymond insisted that despite widespread unemployment, the jobless had generally cooperated with other workers on the picket line. To Raymond, the March protest constituted the foundation for a mass organization to challenge the "reactionary strikebreaking Detroit Federation of Labor" by connecting the unemployed with shop locals in their former places of employment.[23]

On the national scene, the Communist Party now recognized that the plight of the unemployed provided an opening for substantial inroads among disenchanted workers. Consequently, the Party moved to create a national organization to pursue that goal. In

July 1930, a National Unemployment Convention in Chicago created the National Unemployed Councils of the United States. Although the meeting was dominated by Communists and endorsed TUUL's program for the unemployed, the new organization attempted to broaden its base by refusing to affiliate directly with TUUL, thus preserving at least a semblance of independence. However, there is no doubt that it was an extension of CP policy and the Party's conviction that unemployed organizing was among its highest priorities.

In Michigan, the practical outcome of the 6 March demonstration was intensification of CP unemployed activity. Raymond, Goetz, and other Communist activists soon succeeded in establishing Unemployed Councils in Detroit, Hamtramck, Pontiac, Lincoln Park, and Grand Rapids, all automotive centers. By April 1930, additional Councils were operating in Benton Harbor, Muskegon, Flint, and Jackson. Moreover, Michigan's TUUL planned a door-to-door canvas to "spread propaganda everywhere." In Detroit, where organizational activity was intense, fifteen Councils united 1500 community activists in 1931, more than Chicago's twelve and Philadelphia's seven.[24]

Asked by Congressional investigators to account for the growth of Communism in Michigan, Royal Oak's Father Charles Coughlin unhesitatingly cited massive unemployment and asserted that unless the problem was addressed, "you will see a revolution in this country." In the context of both the national crisis and the state's social and economic environment, his prediction seemed plausible. A sharp increase in Michigan unemployment levels had coincided with the growth of the Unemployed Councils. And when the TUUL Conference on Unemployment convened in New York, Detroit autoworker John Schmies, who also functioned as CP District Organizer, chaired the meeting that resulted in the adoption of a formal program for the nation's Unemployed Councils.[25]

Like Coughlin, other Detroit religious leaders perceived a "widespread growth of discontent" in the area, which they fought with the slogan "Every Church a Job Agency." Burgeoning Unemployed Councils implied radicalization, but most accounts suggest that membership was not synonymous with Party membership. Critics and participants alike acknowledged that the CP provided *leadership*, as well as assistance in securing relief and reversing evictions. Josephine Gomon of the Mayor's Committee on Unemployment, for example, remembered Communist organizational skills as welcome among the jobless. Unemployed workers responded positively to leaders who showed them how to protect themselves and "did not care whether they were Communists or who they were." Black activist (and Council member) Shelton Tappes was conscious of Communist Party initiative, but only in "a very abstract way." Recalling his own involvement, Tappes

> recognized that the leadership was coming from party people, but . . . never considered [himself] as actually participating in a Communist scheme. It was the people; that's the way they felt. It was necessary; the times called for it, and so the people responded to whatever leadership came along, and in this case the vocal leadership were communists, and I know nobody objected to it. People were glad to have somebody who would give them leadership.[26]

While CP leadership emerged, then, it was firmly based on pressure and initiative from the jobless community itself. Detroit Unemployed Council leader Frank Sykes stressed the "democratic process" employed in the neighborhood councils, in which the unemployed were frequently more militant than the leadership. When Council leaders assisted in the formulation of demands and programs, they would "try to hold them back, but the workers often took the initiative." In some cases, collective protests grew out of immediate crises. Young Dave Moore, a black teenager, was drawn into group action in response to the attempted eviction of a neighborhood family. Invited to help replace the ousted family's possessions by his friend, Chris Alston, Moore joined the ad hoc group to "chase hell out of the bailiff . . . and put the furniture back in."[27] From this simple act of defiance, a neighborhood gang developed. From spontaneous resistance it was a short step to the more systematic and organized activities of the Unemployed Councils, in which the leaders sometimes had to catch up with their followers. The Councils' appeal was the product of worker frustration, respect for activism, a need for mutual reinforcement, and the reality of results. Demonstrations, organizational activity, and eviction actions were important in creating a new sense of camaraderie and empowerment among the dispossessed. Out of shared adversity came a sense of community and hope for the future. Although the issues at stake were grave, fraternization bred excitement and optimism.[28]

Perhaps most remarkable was the racial accord evident in the ranks of the unemployed movement, especially among the young. Since blacks were disproportionately affected by the Depression, their active involvement in the Detroit unemployed movement was no surprise. Less predictable, but equally significant, was the Unemployed Councils' practice of full integration. Although the black establishment generally maintained its distance, some church leaders, such as Reverend Solomon D. Ross of Shiloh Baptist Church and Reverend Charles Hill on the west side, broke ranks to support the Councils. Black workers collaborated with Italians, Jews, and East Europeans on an unprecedented scale, particularly on Detroit's east side where they lived in close proximity with each other. For example, Mary Gosman, a Ukrainian Jew, taught Chris Alston and other blacks in his neighborhood "how to fight on their immediate issues." Alston later recalled that Gosman instructed them on eviction actions, the processing of relief requests, and the establishment of their own Unemployed Council. Such evidence of solidarity later led Dave Moore to assert that never before or since has there been "such unity exhibited between the blacks and whites in this town as [he] saw during depression days through the Unemployment Councils." The clearest expression of cooperation was the assumption of leadership roles by several black activists, including Frank Sykes, Joseph Billups, Shelton Tappes, and Walter Hardin. Most prominent as an unemployed organizer was Sykes, who eventually became chairman of the Detroit Unemployed Council.[29]

In many ways, the Councils made a difference for people. On one level, rallies, protests, and demonstrations enabled the unemployed to maintain political visibility. An important ally in these public activities was labor lawyer Maurice Sugar, himself immersed in the Detroit unemployed movement. Born in the Upper Peninsula to Lithuanian-Jewish parents, Sugar had witnessed the class struggle in the timber–paper mill country. By the 1920s he had become a conscious independent Marxist committed to the creation of mass movements, which led him to assist in the drive to establish industrial unions. As a speaker, organizer, and legal representative, he involved himself in the Councils' work. On one occasion, for example, it was Sugar who drew up a welfare program presented by the Detroit Council to Mayor Frank Murphy, portions of which were eventually implemented. Equally significant were the services provided by the Councils to relief recipients at the welfare offices, especially after Detroit welfare superintendent John Ballenger decided to permit Council representation of clients. Council tables were typically set up at the welfare stations so that assistance would be immediately available to persons stricken from the welfare rolls. Significant as the ombudsman role was, it was street militancy, particularly eviction actions, that drew the greatest popular support. Coordinated by a sophisticated network of block captains, the Councils were able to mobilize crowds at a moment's notice. Replacement of furniture sometimes resulted in a permanent solution for tenants because landlords refused to pay the constables for return visits. Council activist Joseph Billups recalled a deputy who simply said, "Just let us set them out and you can set them back." Such informal toleration of Council actions was widespread, since bailiffs were not concerned about what happened after their job had been done. As a consequence, according to journalist Edmund Wilson, the Detroit Councils "practically stopped evictions." One unemployed autoworker told Wilson that landlords were "so buffaloed that the other day a woman called up the Unemployed Council and asked whether she could put her tenants out yet." Small wonder that Earl Browder commended the CP Detroit district as the only one in the Party to have "systematically approached evictions."[30]

It was undoubtedly the pressing issues of food, clothing, and shelter that generated support for the radicals. Council veteran Chris Alston noted that the CP understood its primary commitment to be in the community, helping with urgent problems such as evictions and relief. Dave Moore agreed that the Communists "had it over other groups on the ability to organize" and "deal with hard human problems." He recalled that the Party also made its appeal on the grounds of equality. Polish organizer Stanley Novak emphasized CP commitment to meeting the needs of the poor, including the foreign-born. However, he also believed that Communists succeeded because only they had organization and leadership. Moreover, as New York unemployed leader Carl Winter noted, the Party possessed an additional advantage because of its trade union base, which enabled its organizers to "crystallize . . . and lead actions through a structured organization." By keeping the unemployed active, the CP succeeded in training local people to "organize in the neighborhoods" and "act on their own behalf."[31]

Once jobless workers were energized for community organizing, it was a short step to expanding the definition of community to incorporate a larger brotherhood and sisterhood. To black unemployed leader Frank Sykes, the genius of the CP was its ability to link the unemployed movement with other peoples' issues. He argued that the Party was the only organization that "made the connection between unemployment, poverty, capitalism, social discrimination, Scottsboro, Angelo Herndon, unionism, and solidarity." With this remark, Sykes identified a key theme in the story of the Michigan unemployed movement: the wider impact of the Councils on labor union history. There is universal agreement among veterans of the movement that the Councils were, in Alston's words, "a training experience for union organizers," many of whom eventually surfaced as the shock troops of the CIO. Not only did the Councils serve as a "recruiting agency" for the AWU in the early 1930s, but they also produced a significant by-product in the "leadership which was developed both in numbers and skill."[32] The importance of these organizational skills would not be fully appreciated until Council veterans took their places as CIO organizers after 1936.

Sharpened organizational skills and impressive local victories failed to produce significant gains in terms of Party membership or the development of long-term ideological commitments. At no time in the 1930s did any unemployed organization capture more than 5 percent of the jobless as dues-paying members. The ideological failure of the CP was illustrated by the frustration felt in the Unemployed Councils, which experienced substantial success in the period between 1930 and 1933. In Detroit, as elsewhere, the Unemployed Council became the predominant radical mass organization, but never succeeded in attracting a significant number of recruits for the Communist Party.[33]

Communist impatience first surfaced in September 1930, when the editor of *The Daily Worker,* Clarence Hathaway, published a scathing critique of the party's failure to organize the unemployed. Dwelling on the "central point" in the Party plan, Hathaway attacked a "fake unemployment insurance bill," which had been endorsed by Michigan liberals in the fall elections, as a betrayal of the worker. The Michigan proposal fell short of CP standards because it did not force employers to fund the program and failed to ensure worker control of its administration. As an alternative, he urged Communists to fight for the CP Workers Social Insurance Bill.[34]

Simultaneously, the Michigan Communist Party renewed its pressure for a state unemployment insurance program based on the TUUL model and pledged to utilize the 1930 campaign "to rouse the masses in the struggle." Coupling the legislative emphasis with mass action, TUUL and the Detroit Councils kicked off the drive with a Labor Day demonstration at Cass Park, where they denounced "fake relief proposals" such as mayoral candidate Frank Murphy's "unemployment insurance fund." In contrast to Murphy's plan for an employer-backed reserve fund, TUUL and the Councils insisted upon social insurance paid by employers and managed by insured workers, without state or management control.

Meanwhile, in the neighborhoods and at the community level, the party's new focus translated into demands for work relief, public assistance, medical care, tax exemption, abolition of vagrancy laws, and prohibition of evictions. Although their demands were impossible to meet, given the financial context in Detroit and other cities, it remains significant that only the Councils were so bold as to argue that relief should be a right rooted in justice rather than a privilege based on charity. Coupled with this assertion was a sharp attack on the speed-up as exploitation that exacerbated the problem of joblessness. Finally, the Councils' critique of existing remedies for unemployment, supported by the large crowds that endorsed their demands, was influential in altering the views of liberals like Frank Murphy. Left-wing exposure of the shortcomings of Murphy's policies, as well as the outdated voluntarism expressed by the mayor's Unemployment Committee, hastened the development of alternative programs.[35]

Once victorious in the special election of September 1930, Murphy handled Council protests with considerable skill. When Phil Raymond demanded $219 million in emergency relief and hinted that workers who preferred the "present system" might be "forced to solve their problems in some other way," the mayor listened intently and agreed to consider the obviously unmanageable request. Charged by the Councils with complicity in a "starvation conspiracy" as a "servant of the enemies of the workers," Murphy remained cool. Confronted later by a request for a demonstration permit to protest the "Murphy-Ford starvation conspiracy," he calmly overrode a subordinate's decision and authorized the meeting, which proceeded without incident. When a sharp street confrontation finally occurred in November 1931, Communists bore substantial responsibility because they insisted on congregating in a proscribed area of Grand Circus Park. Although the Unemployed Councils clashed with police and subsequently branded Murphy as the "agent of the bosses," his general liberality in dealing with protests placed the Councils at a disadvantage when they argued that free speech had been curtailed in Detroit.[36]

Radical rhetoric aside, Murphy was a labor mayor who believed that Americans would have to "substitute a socialistic sense for [the] individualistic sense." Convinced that "no one is secure until all are secure," he liberalized Detroit's existing relief policies. Despite its limitations, his Unemployment Committee established emergency residence lodges, set up municipal feeding stations, and coordinated job placement, where possible. Moreover, once apprised of the dimensions of the relief burden, the mayor became an early convert to the idea of federal responsibility for relief expenditures. In March 1931 Murphy addressed a conference of liberals in Washington on the relief needs of the cities. Murphy chastised the federal government for its neglect of the cities and demanded not only cash from Washington but also national unemployment insurance.[37]

As the mayoral election of 1931 drew near, the CP's rhetorical assault on Murphy intensified. In July, Bud Reynolds of the Detroit Unemployed Council chastised the mayor for his intimation that the Party planned violence on behalf of the jobless. Reynolds asserted that Communists opposed violence and preferred to base their appeal on "mass movements of workers" to "solve the problems growing out of capitalist exploitation." One month later hundreds of Unemployed Council supporters gathered at City Hall to demand better food and treatment at Detroit's lodging houses. Communist election literature denounced Murphy for tolerating police attacks on eviction fighters, a policy to be expected from a candidate of the "boss class." For his part, Murphy welcomed the relief issue as an opportunity to emphasize his administration's commitment to the unemployed and needy. Once the primary was over, he hoped to make the election a referendum on relief standards in Detroit, which he believed to be too low. A measure of his appeal was Murphy's resounding reelection by a two-to-one margin.[38]

By 1931, the Unemployed Councils were concentrating on efforts to raise their visibility in both Michigan and Washington. This acceleration in street action was part of TUUL's national plan to dramatize the issues of relief and unemployment insurance. In May, Michigan Communists coordinated a statewide Hunger March to Lansing designed to force Republican governor Wilbur Brucker and the State Legislature to provide a supplemental relief appropriation. Endorsed by eighty organizations, the mass demonstration drew support from all areas of the state, including Kalamazoo, Battle Creek, Pontiac, Wayland, and the UP, though as usual Detroit was the nerve center of activism.

As the unemployed army moved towards the state capital, large crowds of workers gathered to offer encouragement. When the delegation reached Lansing, 15,000 onlookers were present to greet them. Lodged in a ball park and surrounded by state troopers, the 250 marchers were virtually imprisoned. Denouncing the state's action as further evidence of repression, *Labor Unity* insisted that the Michigan march had "greatly advanced the movement" by radicalizing non-Communist workers and farmers "aroused by the brutal treatment of the marchers."[39] Hence, radicals insisted that even this dark cloud had a silver lining. The Lansing March, like those conducted in forty other cities throughout the United States, was only a preliminary exercise in preparation for the year's main event—a national hunger march to Washington, D.C.

By October 1931, elaborate preparations for a major national demonstration were under way, including the development of a detailed list of demands that centered on unemployment insurance, health insurance, a shortened work week, a moratorium on evictions, immediate payment of the World War I veterans bonus, and increased relief payments. To publicize the hunger march, CP planners launched a national program to step up eviction actions, local hunger marches, pressure on politicians, public hearings, veterans' organizing, and other forms of mass action. Finally, the march was to be representative, the delegates to be chosen by local Unemployed Councils, revolutionary unions, AFL unions, veterans' organizations, and fraternal organizations. The Michigan delegate allotment included forty representatives from Detroit and five from the UP.[40]

In Michigan, as elsewhere, support for the march extended beyond the narrow confines of the Communist Party. Because of the Unemployed Councils' pivotal role in the planning and execution of the event, endorsement from non-Communist sources has sometimes been overlooked. From the earliest planning stages an important Unemployed Council objective had been the development of a "Support the Hunger March" campaign inside sympathetic AFL unions, and some inroads were made. In December, for example, when the marchers passed through Michigan, organizers succeeded in arranging for food and lodging in Kalamazoo, where the Unemployed Councils had no local unit. In defiance of city officials and with the unanticipated support of the local AFL, march organizers arranged food and lodging for participants in Carpenter's Hall, home of the Carpenters' Union. Detroit Party activist Bud Reynolds regarded the Kalamazoo experience as evidence that many rank-and-file unionists opposed the policies of William Green and the national Federation. A carpenter by trade with a history of Party work within the AFL, Reynolds had long been convinced that the key to the revolution lay in militant labor organizing and alliance-building. To Reynolds the "practical tasks" of the hunger march had "borne political fruits of the highest order."[41]

The defection of the Kalamazoo AFL suggests that despite the national Federation's hard line against unemployment insurance, rank-and-file pressure was creating fissures within the craft unions on the question of proper government policy to combat the Depression. To be sure, the AFL maintained its opposition to unemployment insurance, but in 1930 and 1931, more and more orthodox union leaders embraced the idea. Meanwhile, Green and the Executive Committee pressed for "employment assurance" through shorter hours, public works, stable wage levels, and other nostrums from the past. Despite the mounting pressure from their increasingly restive followers in the field, they rejected the German and British models as "not suitable to American conditions." In February 1931, Green warned the Minneapolis City and County Employees that American workers would never "submit to the domination and control of the state" as did Europeans. His fears reflected the findings of an in-house study that revealed a drop in British union membership following the enactment of the British Unemployment Insurance Act in 1911.[42]

The end result of the rising pressure inside the AFL was the emergence in January 1932 of the AFL Trade Union Committee for Unemployment Insurance and Relief, headed by Communist Louis Weinstock of the New York Painters Union. This combination of twenty-one New York trade unions endorsed the Workers Unemployment Insurance Bill, later introduced by Minnesota Farmer-Labor congressman Ernest Lundeen, and worked to create a national pressure group to support the legislation. The Committee's proposed bill established an unemployment insurance program, funded by management and administered by workers, that would pay "full wages" to all unemployed laborers. This legislation, which closely resembled the Unemployed Councils' plan, became a rallying point for not only the AFL committee, but also for many unions and unemployed organizations throughout the United States that eventually embraced the bill.[43] For the old-guard resistance within the AFL, the appearance of dissent within the Federation marked the beginning of the end.

To hasten the Federation's acceptance of unemployment insurance, the New York Painters Union established contacts with union brothers in other states, who began to agitate for the insurance plan in their locals and central labor unions. The TUCUIR (usually referred to as the Rank and File Committee) established branches in most major cities, including Detroit. Its major objective was to build enough pressure within AFL to force the Federation to endorse the insurance concept, a goal that constituted a direct challenge to the AFL hierarchy. Before long, a Detroit AFL Committee for Unemployment Insurance appeared, under the leadership of the Painters Union's Richard Kroon. The Detroit Committee encountered spirited resistance from DFL president Frank Martel and the city's Central Labor Union, but despite the CLU's refusal to budge, the state Federation of Labor began to tilt towards a new pragmatism. In February 1932, President Frank Wade surprised the delegates to the Federation's Annual Convention in Kalamazoo by rejecting criticisms of the dole and urging the state organization to "give attention and study" to the protection afforded workers by unemployment insurance. While full employment was preferable, Wade argued that in its absence, labor would have to "continue a demand for this protection."[44]

While the AFL dissenters made progress within Michigan trade unions, radicals and their followers maintained direct pressure for business and government aid to the unemployed. As early as November 1931, the Detroit Young Communist League had mounted a demonstration at the Briggs Manufacturing Company Highland Park plant. This protest march was intended to call attention to the needs of recently laid off Briggs workers and to publicize the upcoming National Hunger March. Youth activist Nydia Barker later reported that YCL members, inspired by the work of the Unemployed Councils, decided to focus their attention on the Highland Park plant of Briggs Manufacturing Company, supplier of bodies for the Ford V-8. Focusing on the ravages of unemployment, the YCL consciously placed emphasis on collaboration between the employed and unemployed. Determined to expose the inadequacies of the Briggs welfare system, organizers worked with the Unemployed Council and other local organizations to mobilize unemployed Briggs workers around a program of unemployment insurance, food and shelter assistance, and the removal of racial and sexual discrimination.

In order to gain publicity for the Briggs march, demonstration planners issued promotional leaflets in the plant vicinity and staged a preliminary children's protest featuring signs which proclaimed: "Walter P. Briggs' children have their ponies. Briggs workers' starve. All out to the Briggs Hunger March." The following day, 23 November 1931, demonstrators succeeded in closing the plant, allowing workers inside to listen to speakers pledge that in the event of a strike, the jobless would refuse to provide scab labor. Stressing the importance of solidarity, Unemployed Council leaders asserted that all workers "must work together for unemployment insurance from the company." Workers locked inside leaned out the windows to observe a crowd of 5,000 witnessing the proceedings. After making their appeal for worker unity, the demonstrators marched on the Ford company store, where a pitched battle with police ensued. Out of this display of militance came tentative plans for a hunger march on the Ford River Rouge plant.[45] Unemployed organizers were elated by the results, and CP officials regarded the demonstration as a model for future efforts to dramatize the plight of the jobless and to link employed and unemployed workers. Now all eyes turned toward Dearborn.

Exhilarated by the Briggs demonstration, Council organizers and AWU activists began preparations for a more ambitious foray into the kingdom of Ford. Because of Henry Ford's stress on technological innovation, social experimentalism, paternalism, and self-reliance, he became a symbolic target of great significance to unemployed organizers determined to expose and exploit the harsh side of the Ford system. An extraordinarily complex thinker, Ford had pioneered a technological revolution that had radically altered the workplace after the introduction of the moving assembly line at his Highland Park plant in 1914. Moreover, he had broken new ground with the five-dollar day, which reflected his grasp of the relationship between consumer spending and long-term prosperity. Ford's embrace of the new technology had also had a deleterious effect, in that the investigations of the company's Sociological Department and its heavy-handed paternalism had produced resentment and sullen resistance in workers subject to external control. As the source of both economic opportunity and unwanted regimentation, Henry Ford therefore came to be perceived by workers in both a positive and negative light.[46]

So long as prosperity prevailed, the latent tension in worker attitudes towards Ford and the Ford Motor Company remained under control. However, the Great Depression unleashed forces that finally severed the bonds that had locked Ford and his employees in an uneasy embrace. An important factor in this estrangement lay in Ford's public posture during the early years of the Depression. Useful to critics of the Ford empire was his ill-considered announcement in 1931 that a depression was "a wholesome thing in general." Ford was a firm believer in self-reliance who demanded from his employees maximum effort at the point of production and high moral standards and frugality at home. Ford's philosophy of work assumed that motivated workers would gain employment and, at least from the worker's point of view, seemed to equate economic dependency with personal inadequacy. Always independent and sometimes arrogant, he stalled local relief efforts with his own brand of repayable relief to employees. Because of "Ford Relief," many workers were ineligible for public assistance but inadequately supported by company relief. Moreover, there was a glaring disparity between Ford's promises of employment and the economic reality for too many workers. Frank Sykes later recalled clearly the company's promise of jobs in March 1932 and the determination of the unemployed to claim them.[47] It is clear that by this time Ford's social and economic ideas had made him an important symbol for a failed economy and the badly eroded social assumptions that had once supported it.

Planning for a major demonstration in Dearborn had been under way for two months. In the wake of the National Hunger March, the CP Detroit District weekly letter urged the city's section committees and unit buros to intensify the class struggle at the neighborhood level and to prepare for factory hunger marches in the near future. In Detroit the Ford Motor Company became the primary target for the Party's mobilization of workers and unemployed citizens. The Detroit Red Squad, a Police Department division

Figure 5 Workers Prepare for the Ford Hunger March, March 7, 1932
(Archives of Labor and Urban Affairs, Wayne State University)

which closely monitored allegedly subversive activities in the city, clearly saw external (TUUL) initiative in the preparations for the escalation of unemployed pressure against local employers. By early 1932 there was substantial evidence of rising tension, such as the tear-gassing of job-seekers at the Ford employment office in February. Despite these skirmishes, however, few were prepared for the violence unleashed on the demonstrators on 7 March 1932. (See figure 5.) The AWU and the Unemployed Councils had organized a multiethnic and multiracial group of 3,000 demonstrators who planned to present a set of demands at the Ford employment office. At that point a committee was to present a statement seeking relief, limited hours, rehiring, guarantees against racial discrimination, a moratorium on foreclosures against Ford workers, and the right to organize. Herbert Benjamin later maintained that the Ford march was intended as a "major execution of classic unity" that would express the common interests of both unemployed and employed workers against the "common enemy." According to most accounts, the police initiated hostilities in a massive overreaction to an essentially orderly demonstration. What began as an "open organized protest" over what one observer described as the "terrible suffering, unemployment, and starvation of the Detroit working class" ended in the tragic deaths of five young men at the hands of the Dearborn-Detroit police and the Ford Service Department. Although led by Communists, such as Bud Reynolds and Al Goetz of the Unemployed Councils, the participants represented no single political viewpoint. On the contrary, *Forum* correspondent Charles R. Walker reported that most of the Ford marchers were not radicals, but rather "ordinary Americans" attempting to "demand redress of grievances." What united them was deep skepticism about the economic system and a conviction that employers bore responsibility for the job security and social well-being of displaced workers.[48] The bloody incident in Dearborn revealed the extent to which the social fabric had worn thin by 1932, as well as the sharpness of the conflict precipitated by the breakdown of capitalism.

What labor lawyer Maurice Sugar condemned as "brutal murder" produced a different analysis in the local press. First reaction in Detroit denounced the "communist outrage" and found CP leaders "morally guilty of the assaults and killings." Within two days, however, Detroit area moderates and liberals became more cautious. The *Nation* reported that a frightened business community "passed the word" to the Detroit newspapers, which began to reverse position. The normally prudent DFL found no evidence that the demonstrators had been armed, and a timid American Civil Liberties Union concluded that the marchers "were peaceful until their rights were interfered with" by police who "provoked such violence as the paraders resorted to." Similarly, the Michigan Socialist Party lodged a legalistic protest emphasizing the complicity of public officials in both the incident and the coverup that followed. Mayor Frank Murphy also moved quickly to distance himself from the events of "Bloody Monday," asserting that the marchers had not been interfered with in Detroit. His concern reflected both a troubled liberal conscience and a thick file of protests that reached his office after the events of 7 March. Equally disturbing was a *New Republic* article that found merit in Communist charges of the "frequently obscure interworking of the Detroit police with the Dearborn police."[49]

While liberals worried, the Detroit Employers Association and American Legion worked to foster anti-Communist hysteria. With a dragnet out to snare hundreds of suspected agitators, Red-baiting served to divert attention from the savagery of public and corporate violence for a time. Meanwhile, Ford management treated the event as the result of premeditated disruption. Ford executive E. G. Liebold saw the march as a "forcible invasion" by men who fully "intended to do destruction." Similarly, senior executive Charles Sorenson claimed that the "massacre" stemmed from a clash between the Communists and the police, and that "we [the company] were not in the picture at all." Before long, however, the enormity of the tragedy and the reality of an official error became clearer. A confidential investigation by the Presidents' Organization for Unemployment Relief was brutally frank in its assessment: the chief difficulty was the

> stupidity of the Dearborn police.... The Dearborn police, in number only about forty, apparently wanted to show that their small town was quite up-to-date.... All those hit by bullets were among the paraders or bystanders.
>
> In order to save their face and get a scapegoat, the police are blaming the Communists and are calling for a grand jury investigation. The Communists do not number more than 3,000 in the whole city of Detroit. William Z. Foster is accused of having excited the riot by an appearance on Sunday, the day before the trouble. It appears that all he said was something like this: "I hear you are going to have a march on the Ford factory tomorrow. All loyal Communists should join in."[50]

To this point, the POUR analysis was accurate. However, its author, Roland Haynes, went on to arrive at an astounding conclusion: that the incident was unrelated to discontent over the Detroit relief situation and had "nothing directly to do with unemployment."[51]

This remark reflected both uneasiness over mounting evidence of social unrest and a remarkable capacity for self-delusion concerning sources of radical activity in 1932, the peak year of Communist influence in the Detroit area. The volatility of the situation was implicit in one survey that found that 25 percent of unemployed workers thought that "a revolution might be a good thing." Many outside commentators reported a significant radicalization of unemployed auto workers in Detroit, where Mauritz Hallgren of the *Nation* observed "deep inroads" among workers impressed by Communist "vigor and promptness" in organizing against wage cuts, relief cutbacks, and the "dictatorship of the bankers." Following the Ford Hunger March, the YCL experienced considerable growth, reflected in a reported forty new applicants from Ford, Briggs, and Dodge within one week of the event. The radicalizing potential of violence was clear in Dave Moore's recollection of his personal recognition that there was "something terribly wrong with the system." At the Ford demonstration, he reached the point of consciousness: "when I saw the blood flowing there on Miller Road, that was the point I became a radical." Another young comrade, R. Rondot, wrote that after the impressive funeral for the victims, things looked clearer: "when our demands are just, logical, humane, and right, we do not hesitate to advance . . . even in the face of the violence offered us." Characteristic of a new resolve was a small act of personal courage by Ford worker B. Belenky who agreed to testify, fully aware that his job was in jeopardy. Belenky reasoned that if the Ford martyrs were "willing to give up their lives for the working class," he was ready to "give up a chance of losing [his] job."[52]

Common to these worker responses was a new sense of class awareness that crossed racial, ethnic, and gender lines. Symbolic of this solidarity was the role assumed by women, such as the Ukrainian Jewish immigrant Mary Gosman and the African-American Mattie Woodson, both of whom risked their lives by ministering to the needs of the wounded and dying. Dave Moore later speculated that "this unity was one thing the big wheels got scared as hell about" because they could no longer "pit one against the other."[53]

The Dearborn incident also provided Michigan Communists with a new rallying point, quickly exploited in the Party press. The *Daily Worker's* obituary for victim Joe York set the tone, declaring that the YCL organizer had been "murdered in the class war." Similarly, CP activist Mary Gosman wrote of bloodshed that "will never be forgotten by the working class." From another vantage point, *Workers' Age* reveled in the destruction of the "Ford myth" but warned of danger to the entire working class. Its answer was for all workers and workers' organizations to close ranks in "unbreakable class solidarity." Benjamin later argued that the clash advanced the program and demands of the jobless throughout the United States in part because it was the "first major battle" in the struggle that ended in the unionization of the auto industry.[54]

The Communists' short-term response was a program of militant worker demonstrations, coupled with an impressive full-dress Red funeral march for the victims. Crowd estimates varied from 8,000 to 70,000. Perhaps most reliable was Mayor Murphy's report of 30,000. It is clear that most mourners were non-Communist workers. Black participant George Owens later recalled: "when we got back downtown from the cemetery, the parade was still going on out there on Michigan. That was a funeral!" (See figure 6.) Murphy's decision to permit the march without police surveillance reflected his keen sensitivity to the negative publicity already generated by the tragedy. Almost universal revulsion had been expressed in the protests that flooded the mayor's office.[55]

Perhaps the most significant offshoot of the Ford incident was a heightened worker solidarity that foreshadowed an active union movement in Michigan. Historian Alex Baskin concludes that despite the emotional intensity of the Dearborn clash and its immediate aftermath, the major legacy of the Ford hunger marchers was the United Automobile Workers Union. In a similar vein, Martin Sullivan argues that the violence combined with the exoneration of the police to shock apathetic workers into a new receptiveness to

Figure 6   The Ford March Victims Lie in State, March 8, 1932 *(Archives of Labor and Urban Affairs, Wayne State University)*

unionization. The new consciousness was evident in the words of a funeral observer, obviously moved by workers who spoke of "fallen comrades" and the "necessity for organization and revolutionary vengeance." Reporting a questionable 2,000 applications for AWU membership at the funeral, the unidentified observer scrawled a half-finished memoir asserting that "out of their hate and anger, the workers were welding strength." To participant Mary Gosman, the creation of the UAW was the logical extension of the Ford march: she later asserted that "in this hour the union was born."[56] Although her oversimplified analysis was flawed, there can be no doubt that the sharpened class awareness created by the Ford massacre contributed to the advancement of industrial unionism in Detroit.

Industrial unionism was the wave of the future, but for the moment, the Unemployed Councils remained the most significant organizational force on the Michigan social and economic scene. Because Councils continued to stage demonstrations and press the demands of the jobless, clashes inevitably occurred, as in a disruptive and futile hunger march to the Briggs plant in June 1932. Moreover, the Councils renewed their emphasis on evictions and justice at welfare offices, which led them to step up their criticism of the Murphy administration. Citing Detroit as a model for unemployed organizing, the *Communist* endorsed the Councils' direct action tactics: through neighborhood organizing and mass action, the Michigan Party had attracted supporters who "would have remained outside our organization if we had confined ourselves, as we often do, to simply telling the workers about the good things unemployment insurance will bring for them."[57]

Although direct action at the local level dominated Council activity, Michigan organizers also became engaged in the national unemployed movement. During the veterans march on Washington in July 1932, five of the fifteen members of the Rank and File Committee of the Workers Ex-Servicemen's League represented Michigan, most of them from Grand Rapids. More significant was the leadership provided by John T. Pace of Detroit, veteran of the Ford march and Michigan organizer for WESL. An active Communist, Pace was at the forefront of the movement to occupy federal property in Washington.[58]

No sooner had the militant Pace returned to Detroit than he launched plans for the last national demonstration of the year, a veterans' march to Washington in December. As chairman of the WESL National Rank and File Committee, Pace established headquarters in Detroit, where he also planned to run for Congress in November 1932 on the Communist ticket. Almost immediately, the veterans' demonstration was subordinated to the CP's more ambitious plan for a second National Hunger March to Washington. The CP's selection of Michigan's Bud Reynolds as Hunger March chairman was fortuitous, since by November, Pace found himself in jail for leading a disruptive demonstration during the congressional campaign. Given the active involvement of both Reynolds and Pace, it is not surprising that the Michigan delegation was among the largest to reach Washington. Its 200 members was surpassed only by New York, Pennsylvania, and Ohio. The departure of the Michigan contingent was accompanied by major demonstrations in Detroit, Kalamazoo, and Muskegon, all intended to focus attention on the national march by coordinating state protests with the larger movement. Despite the flurry of activity, however, the CP–Unemployed Council influence in Michigan had reached a peak by mid-1932. Nonetheless, the estimated 7,000 marchers were sufficient to alarm the Employers' Association of Detroit, which feared that the CP had "most favorable conditions for the spread of their doctrine of sedition."[59]

The Communists' failure to build a stronger unemployed organization, both in Michigan and on the national scene, reflected near-insurmountable problems inherent in the task. It was extremely difficult to maintain a long-term organization because of a shifting, transient membership base of jobless workers whose work status was in a constant state of flux. Because of their mobility, the jobless did not develop the close bond with one another that might have facilitated the establishment of a more stable institution. Moreover, the coming of the New Deal and its sympathetic attitude towards labor reinforced the CP's (and workers') natural propensity towards shop floor organization rather than unemployed organizing as the first line of class struggle. Finally, Communists often imposed ideology on the unemployed organizations they sponsored, which sometimes separated organizers from the rank-and-file. In December 1931, for example, Detroit CP Section Committee No. 4 acknowledged that it was still working as the "Party *for* the working masses instead of the Party *of* the working masses." In a moment of candor the committee admitted that many needy unemployed workers had not turned to the Party. Convinced that they did not yet "know the life of the unemployed workers in [their] neighborhood," the frustrated organizers pledged to "overcome the isolation from the masses" by redoubling factory and neighborhood efforts and "applying Bolshevik discipline" to their educational work so that the workers of north Detroit would "fight against the capitalistic class."[60] The pedantic tone of the committee's self-critical analysis underscored the limitations imposed on Party progress by the Communist penchant for revolutionary posturing.

As Fraser Ottanelli has recently shown, however, important positive consequences flowed from the Party's work among the unemployed. In Detroit and elsewhere in Michigan, the CP was the most effective group speaking and acting on behalf of the jobless. In many instances, it was the only group. In some cases, the result was an improvement of relief benefits or living conditions for Depression victims. The experience gained in community organizing and protest activity was also invaluable in the union drives that began in 1933. And perhaps most important was the Communists' relentless pressure for unemployment insurance, which played a critical role in eroding the widespread social commitment to voluntarism that had long delayed the advent of the American welfare state.[61]

In Detroit and southeastern Michigan, one of the Unemployed Councils' most significant innovations lay in their insistence on racial equality and nondiscrimination in relief administration. As previously noted, the Councils had always professed and practiced racial equality in their work. For Dave Moore, the Ford Massacre left an indelible print on the future: the events at Miller Road forged a "bond of brotherhood" between the races that later resurfaced in Ford Local 600. Most black veterans of the unemployed movement stress the Councils' willingness to act on their commitment to racial equality. In 1933, for example, the CP assigned Detroit section organizer Frank Sykes to coordinate the mobilization of the jobless in the city's black community. One of the city's leading black activists, Sykes represented the North Side Unemployed Council. His growing visibility symbolized not only the Councils' policy of full integration in their work, but also the high priority the national Party placed on the organization of the black unemployed.[62] While some evidence of discrimination may be found in the unemployed movement, no institution in 1930s Detroit was more egalitarian in its practices than the Unemployed Councils.

By 1933, unemployed organizers had also moved to close ranks with employed workers. Recognizing that by their very nature, the Unemployed Councils were less viable as long-term organizations than labor unions, the CP shifted its primary emphasis to unionization and opportunistically used the Councils as a bridge to full solidarity. This strategy was evident in the landmark Briggs Strike of 1933, which revealed substantial unionist sentiment in Detroit well before New Deal labor legislation was in place. The stoppage also documented the influence of a small but very active Communist element among Michigan automobile workers.

In response to widespread safety violations, escalating layoffs, and significant wage cuts, preparatory organizing of the Briggs-Waterloo shop group began in November 1932. Detroit Red Squad observers later reported that in November and December, CP members and unemployed organizers had quietly drifted into the city and become engaged in undercover work in the Briggs plant and elsewhere. Part of this activity involved increased unemployed organizing in order to place a heavy burden on relief officials and public resources. According to CP union organizer Jack Stachel, AWU also found that the unemployed "could be used to secure contacts with the workers inside the shop." And from the first walkout at the Briggs-Waterloo plant following a 20 percent wage cut, an Unemployed Council representative sat on the strike committee, a development that reflected not only CP strength in the union but also the reality that a large block of AWU members were unemployed workers. More important, it indicated that the Council would play an important role in the strike by working to prevent the use of jobless workers as scab labor. It is also significant that many Briggs activists had prior experience as organizers for the Unemployed Councils. As was often to be the case in future years, labor drew upon the unemployed movement for effective organizers whose skills had been sharpened by previous confrontations with authority.[63]

As the strike developed, a united front seemed to promise that solidarity would prevail. Stressing the identity of interest among all workers, the CP cited the unity already shown by unemployed workers who had backed the strikers. In turn, the Party maintained that "support of the struggles of the unemployed for relief and unemployment insurance" was the best way of "cementing the unity necessary for victory in our common struggles." Not to be outdone, Socialists also threw their support to the Briggs workers by making a "concerted effort to reach the unemployed" and convince them that it was "in their best interest to present solidarity." The clearest indication of Socialist endorsement came when Norman Thomas addressed the strikers and joined them on the picket line. Another leader in the united front effort was Emil Mazey, who worked through the non-Communist Unemployed Citizens Council to mobilize the jobless in support of the strike. Mazey's Proletarian Party added its voice to the chorus on the left urging that employed and unemployed workers unite behind the strike committee in a display of class unity. Finally, an endorsement came from the YCL, which claimed that young workers had been the most militant activists in the strike. Denouncing Murphy, the Welfare Department, and the politicians for their alleged efforts to recruit scab labor, the YCL asserted that black and white youth were "sticking side by side," united against wage cuts and in favor of relief.[64]

For a time the reality of solidarity matched the radical rhetoric. The unemployed distributed handbills and staged a mass demonstration in support of the strikers. Frank Sykes later recalled that the Unemployed Councils "mobilized the unemployed for the picket lines and picketed in solidarity with the employed," which made it "impossible to scab." In a dramatic demonstration on 30 January 1933, Council members displayed banners proclaiming that "the unemployed won't scab" and "will help to win this strike." These developments prompted the seasoned labor journalist Joe Brown to observe that the strikers were "holding firm" and that there was "no evidence that the unemployed will scab." As late as February 1933, *Detroit Hunger Fighter,* organ of the local Unemployed Councils, could assert that the front remained intact: "the bosses' fond hopes that in the unemployed they had a great reserve of strikebreakers" had been "exploded" by an "outburst of mass anger."[65] Brave words—but premature.

Before long, optimism on the left began to fade. Although substantial community support for the strikers did develop, including somewhat equivocal cooperation from both Murphy and the DFL, the obstacles confronting the workers were virtually insurmountable. Despite tireless efforts of the Unemployed Councils, a labor pool estimated at 175,000 jobless dimmed long-term projects for complete solidarity. After the strike leadership's refusal of Walter Briggs's compromise offer, public officials and management took a harder line. At the same time, Phil Raymond and the strikers overextended their position with widespread mass picketing that brought on extensive police harassment and resulted in Raymond's arrest and detention in Highland Park. By the second week of February, over 3,000 strikebreakers had been employed at one Briggs plant, thus permitting the resumption of production and deliveries. Within another week the strike was broken.

As the workers' position deteriorated, a combination of internal division in the strike committee and Red-baiting of the AWU leadership disrupted the unity forged at the outset. Following Raymond's arrest on a criminal syndicalism charge, non-Communist strike leaders purged the remaining Communists from the strike committee and banned the Unemployed Councils from the picket line. With these actions, the strikers gave up experienced organizers and inexpensive legal assistance. Equally damaging was the dilution of outside support from the Councils, which had temporarily succeeded in counteracting pressure from a swollen reserve army of unemployed. The strike's collapse reflected the divisive force of anti-Communist sentiment, the labor surplus, and recalcitrant and calculating management, as well as the hubris of the Left.[66] The immediate result was the dissolution of the momentary solidarity achieved in the early stages of the dispute. More significant was the appearance of a problem that undercut the unemployed movement for the remainder of the 1930s: its vulnerability to charges of radical manipulation.

Despite the short-term setback, the Briggs strike marked a significant turning point in the history of auto workers unionism. The initial settlement at Briggs-Waterloo, which reversed the original wage cut, had demonstrated that even during a depression, strikes could be successful in the face of a labor surplus. Moreover, the massive turnout for the second Briggs Strike in late January exploded the myth that auto manufacturers presided over an army of contented and loyal workers. By August 1933, the CP estimated that 15,000–20,000 automobile workers had struck. For many observers, noted Josephine Gomon, the strike's "real significance" was "lost at the time." The Briggs strike was, in her words, the beginning of "organized mass labor" in Michigan, an event that inspired workers with a "real militant spirit" that carried over into the determination of the sitdowns. Although the Communists and the

AWU suffered a serious local setback due to their isolation in the late stages of the strike, they understood that a profound change had occurred. Jack Stachel's analysis caught the significance of the Briggs struggle as an important advance in the long-term evolution of worker protest and the development of worker solidarity. He also argued that by exposing the limits of "social-reformist policies and leaders," the battle revealed the necessity of "sharp struggle" in the ever-unfolding tension between classes. And by May 1933, Detroit Communist John Schmies had identified one aspect of the Briggs crisis as important for the future. He attacked the assumption that the union was exclusively for employed auto workers and the Council for the unemployed. Rather, as a "higher form of organization," the AWU was responsible for "giving guidance" to "auto workers generally, whether employed or unemployed."[67]

Schmies's treatment of the Unemployed Councils as a "more elementary movement" to deal with the "immediate needs" of unemployed workers suggested that they had reached a plateau in their development. As early as March 1933, the Councils and AWU were meeting jointly, which revealed that the Council was functioning as a leadership cadre more than a mass organization. By June 1933, unemployed activity in Detroit had begun to level off. Council assistance to the destitute continued and a running battle with the Murphy administration persisted, but the militance of the Briggs struggle declined. Although the Unemployed Councils remained active, their appeals assumed a highly sectarian form.

On March 4, 1933, Communists marked the occasion of Franklin D. Roosevelt's inauguration with a series of demonstrations that united all Detroit-area Party branches, including the Dearborn, West Side, East Side, North Side, Oakwood, Oakland, and Hamtramck units, in a demand for increased relief, the Bonus Bill, unemployment insurance, and union recognition. The protests were engineered and orchestrated by CP operatives such as Phil Raymond, Frank Sykes, Al Goetz, Bud Reynolds, Max Salzman, and George Kristalsky, whose remarks reflected the perspectives of the Councils, YCL, AWU, and WESL. On March 6, 1933, after Walter Eicker of WESL urged Roosevelt to remember the "forgotten man," Raymond blasted the new president as the "watchdog of Wall Street and the capitalists." Mayor Murphy, Senator Couzens, Governor Comstock, and Dearborn mayor Clyde Ford also drew criticism for alleged restrictions on civil liberties, insistence on forced labor for welfare recipients, inadequate relief benefits, and insensitivity to popular suffering. The scattergun attacks were peppered with Marxist rhetoric designed to appeal to the dispossessed, but the modest crowds at these events (estimated to be 2,000–8,000 at various locations)[68] suggest that the Party activists were preaching to the converted.

Perhaps the most notable outcome of the March demonstrations was a plan to commemorate the Ford march and honor the Dearborn martyrs. On March 7, an estimated 4,000 workers heard Bud Reynolds and Dearborn Unemployed Council organizer Max Salzman attack public officials from Washington to Detroit, as well as Henry and Clyde Ford. Reynolds told the Fords that the demonstration was a warning to the Ford Motor Company that the five deaths of 1932 had not been forgotten. He also threatened a new march on Ford headquarters that would bring workers "anything they want." Reynolds closed his remarks with an appeal to both the employed and unemployed to join the CP-dominated AWU so that they might "stick together and fight."[69] Like the inauguration day demonstrations, the Dearborn meeting was symptomatic of the Party's growing sectarianism as unemployed organizing became less intense.

The presence of a narrowing Party appeal did not alter the fact that the unemployed still suffered and the CP played a central role in publicizing their needs. Eager to exploit the Ford symbol, unemployed activists intensified their focus on Dearborn, the capital of the Ford empire. Determined to ease their plight, four hundred Ford Workers met in April to "organize and continue the fight for relief." Rebuffed by state officials in Lansing, the committee proceeded with the plan to undertake a second Ford Hunger March to dramatize the violation of civil rights in Dearborn and the urgent need for unemployment relief. At a meeting chaired by Frank Sykes, a unity committee of AWU, the Unemployed Council, and the Dearborn workers committee decided to request a permit for a march, which was promptly denied by Dearborn authorities. Eternally hopeful, the CP regarded the coalition as evidence of a new "united front in Ford-controlled Dearborn." The Party also saw the denial as evidence that Ford Motor Company was "prepared to repeat the murderous attack of March 7, 1932."[70]

Hoping to capitalize on residual popular sentiment against Ford, the Party mobilized its supporters among the unemployed, AWU members, black Ford workers, and the YCL. In preparation for a mass march in June 1933, the YCL and Unemployed Councils took the lead in appealing to Polish and Rumanian workers by screening motion picture footage of the last Ford Hunger March. Then in late May, the Councils, AWU, and the Ford Hunger March Committee seized on the police killing of Nicholas Jeftazek, son of an unemployed Ford worker, to establish a link with the Ford Massacre and stimulate interest in the 5 June march on the Ford plant. The main theme in the plans for the upcoming Ford March was an insistence that the Ford Motor Company assume full financial responsibility for meeting the relief needs of the workers it had brought to the Detroit area and left to fend for themselves. Unemployed organizers attacked both Ford's plans to decentralize production outside of Detroit and the Dearborn officials' denial of relief to an alleged 90 percent of the unemployed as evasions of the company's moral obligation to the workforce.[71]

On 5 June the march proceeded as a protest against evictions, inadequate relief, and the Ford repayable relief system. Appealing to employed workers, the protesters also attacked the "inhuman speed-up" in the Ford plant, and organizers reminded participants that they fought not only for themselves, but for all Ford workers. Denied permission to enter Dearborn, the marchers prudently stopped at the boundary, where, by one account,

> A line, invisible, stood between the City of Detroit and Dearborn. A line, invisible, stood between the Communists and the workers. So matters stood. To cross the invisible line and stand on Dearborn ground, the estate of Ford, meant violence . . . so in the warm sunshine of the day, the march broke up. No one crossed the invisible line in the tall green grass.[72]

The observer's imagery of separation, impotence, and alienation mirrored the social chasm opened by the Great Depression. It also recorded the growing distance between a more and more sectarian unemployed movement and the larger jobless constituency it hoped to serve. By 1934, even the CP acknowledged that the Detroit Unemployed Councils were "completely out of existence." Some workers lapsed into despair as the depression deepened, while others saw hope in Franklin D. Roosevelt's pledge of a "New Deal." Communists, once the undisputed leaders of the jobless movement, redirected their energies toward the imminent battle over union-ization.[73] The period of Communist predominance in the unemployed struggle was at an end.

Beyond the Core
Outstate Reactions to Economic Crisis, 1929–1933

B ecause the Communist Party and Unemployed Councils were extremely active in the Detroit area, it is tempting to focus exclusively on the dramatic events that transpired there in the darkest days of the early Depression. To do so, however, would distort the history of an unemployed movement that took other forms in less urbanized portions of a diverse state. In both the Lower Peninsula outside the urban core and the hard-hit Upper Peninsula, jobless workers lived in quiet desperation. Their responses to the crisis reveal alternative organizational patterns appropriate to the unique features of their respective ethnocultural, social, and economic backgrounds. An examination of the state's variegated unemployed movement demonstrates that while they could not match the vigor of the Councils, other groups did emerge to advance alternative solutions to the economic problems of the early thirties.

Along the most active new groups on the national scene in 1932 were labor educator A. J. Muste's Unemployed Leagues, which were very strong in Ohio, Pennsylvania, and West Virginia. Organized mainly in areas less influenced by the Unemployed Councils, particularly medium-sized communities, the Leagues carried out comparable programs and expressed demands that drew on the CP-Council model. Organized by Socialists and Trade Unionists from the Conference for Progressive Labor Action (CPLA), the Unemployed Leagues sought a non-Communist solution to the problems of the unemployed. Whereas CPLA had been primarily a propaganda and education organization, the Leagues were more concerned with meeting the immediate needs of the jobless. Employing patriotic symbols and slogans, they became identified with a variety of self-help organizations that drew censure from many radicals. The first stage of Unemployed League development climaxed in July 1933 when 800 delegates from thirteen states met in Columbus, Ohio, to form the National Unemployment Leagues.[1]

In part because they never developed a close connection with any political or economic group, Michigan's Unemployed Citizen's Leagues remained small organizations. In October 1932 their activities were confined to the Detroit area, but by March 1933 branches could be found in Lansing, Grand Rapids, Battle Creek, Owosso, and Bay City. However, only two Michigan delegates were present at the NUL founding meeting in July 1933. One year later a national organizer reported to NUL convention delegates that these organizations still needed to be "pulled together into a state League." Although the NUL managed to gain a modest foothold in Michigan, a shortage of experienced organizers, the lack of financial resources, and competition from the Unemployed Councils killed the state organization. This weakness was evident in NUL's classification of Michigan as a territory yet to be organized as of August 1934.[2]

Patterned after the Seattle organization by the same name, the Michigan UCL endorsed the principle of self-help as an antidote to joblessness and deprivation. Stressing "mutual self-help for self-aid," the League launched plans in 1932 to organize the state's unemployed into cooperative units to "provide for their own necessities" through the use of idle land, machinery, and buildings. Additional activities included the gathering of surplus farm produce and reconnection of gas and electricity lines after service had been cut off. League activist Emil Mazey of the Proletarian Party disingenuously noted that "we didn't think we were breaking the law." Nonpolitical and careful, UCL claimed the endorsement of many prominent state citizens and charitable organizations. The organization pointedly asserted that it embraced no political or economic philosophy and left the "solution to depressions" to other groups and agencies. Statewide in its aspirations, the League operated its own farm in St. Clair County and served 6,000 people in 1933. Yet by 1934, UCL found itself in financial straits, having failed to meet its financial obligations.[3]

Although the League professed political neutrality, it drew the endorsement of Michigan Socialists, who were sympathetic with the idea of cooperative self-help. Unlike their militant comrades in Chicago, who in 1931 had followed the lead of social worker Karl Borders to pioneer the Socialist Workers Committee on Unemployment, Michigan Socialist Party members were unable to unite on any program to organize the jobless. Borders and the Chicago Socialists, intent on offering the unemployed an alternative to the Unemployed Councils, had engaged in mass action, public protest, and legislative pressure activity. Similar Socialist organizations also developed in New York and Maryland, and the Workers Committee began to expand in some midwestern states. Michigan was not one of them. Torn by factionalism and dominated by the Old Guard reformists, the Michigan SP experienced near-paralysis between 1930 and 1932, which meant that Socialists were unable to offer activist leadership on the unemployed front.[4] The internal weakness of the Michigan Socialist party was to hamper its efforts to organize jobless workers throughout the pre-New Deal phase of unemployed organizing.

The one objective shared by the Socialists and the proponents of the Unemployed Leagues was the desire to counter the strong initiative gained by the Communists as a result of their militant and effective unemployed work. And the Unemployed Councils were sensitive to the challenge. Symptomatic of the Communist attitude was the *Detroit Hunger Fighter*'s sharp attack on the UCL program. In March 1933, the Council organ censured the League for its willingness to accept survival on surplus food and clothing. Arguing that 55 percent of the population could not live on the refuse left by 45 percent, the *Hunger Fighter* charged that "gleaning garbage is the program of those who flinch from the struggle for unemployment insurance, against evictions, and for the means of life from the owning class."[5] The CP's criticism clearly defined the distinction between the Communist and UCL perspectives on aid to the unemployed.

Alternative Responses to Economic Crisis:
Another Michigan

The bitterness of the Unemployed Councils' attack on self-help schemes reflected CP concern over the alternative models of unemployed organizing and service to the jobless explored by workers and communities throughout the state. The plight of the unemployed in the culturally distinct Grand Rapids area offers an instructive comparison, since the organizational results differed markedly from the pattern set by the Detroit movement. The behavior of workers and public officials in Kent County and other central-western Michigan locales is best understood as a reflection of the area's ethnic and religious background. Heavily populated by Dutch Protestant immigrants and their descendants, Grand Rapids and Kent County workers were influenced by the teachings of the predominant Christian Reformed Church, which had historically been suspicious of neutral (secular) organizations. Church members had been forbidden membership in the Knights of Labor and, by the 1930s, union membership was permitted only if workers were not required to commit "un-Christian acts."[6] Given the value system that grew from the Kent County ethnocultural heritage, the prospects for widespread organizational militancy on behalf of the unemployed were limited.

Politically and religiously more conservative than Wayne County, Grand Rapids responded to the plague of joblessness with heavy emphasis on work relief based on compensation in scrip. While the scrip system became a lightning rod for both left and right criticism, concentration on its shortcomings did not mean that the city escaped the popular pressures evident in Detroit. In some respects, then, the Grand Rapids unemployed movement mirrored patterns set in Wayne County, but the reflection proved to be a faint image by comparison.

A case in point was the 6 March 1930 "Red Thursday" demonstration staged by TUUL and the Unemployed Council, described in the *Grand Rapids Press* as "unusually quiet." A modest crowd of 3,000, mostly spectators, listened as Republican city manager George Welsh mingled with unemployed organizers, who expressed appreciation for his cooperation in preparing for the event. Local Unemployed Council spokesman Stanley DeGraff, in turn, confined his remarks to the organization's aim to create better working and living conditions, while others exhorted the audience to join TUUL. After the public demonstration, a parade was held, ending at International Workers Hall with more oratory and an "orderly mass meeting."[7] In short, the initial response to joblessness in Grand Rapids was cautious, wholly consistent with community values.

The official reaction to entreaties from the dispossessed gave little encouragement to unemployed organizers. In late 1930 the local Unemployed Council urged the Grand Rapids City Commission to create a relief fund, paid for by salary reductions and progressive taxes. The Council also urged a moratorium on evictions, utility cutoffs, and foreclosures, as well as food and shelter for the jobless. Finally, the organization proposed a city employment office administered by a workers' committee. Claiming to be "without jurisdiction," the commission simply filed the petition. Likewise, the Unemployed Council was denied permission to conduct a fundraising event to support the 1931 Hunger March to Lansing. Acting on the advice of the local Community Chest, the city commission rejected the proposal without explanation. Grand Rapids unemployed organizers did participate in state and national demonstrations in 1931 and 1932, and CP publications circulated in both the streets and shops; but by comparison with Detroit activism, left-wing activity was low-key and the worker response subdued. When the Unemployed Council did sponsor a protest of relief reductions and evictions in May 1932, repression followed quickly. The *Daily Worker* reported that increasingly militant workers had gotten into a "scrap" with police that landed five comrades in jail. Despite the altercation, military intelligence reports in August concluded that a local CP convention was a "tame affair" and that party activities were "very quiet."[8]

The most alarmist reaction to unemployed organizing came, ironically, from the Grand Rapids Federation of Labor, which warned of complacency in October 1930. Like Green and the AFL hierarchy, Grand Rapids trade unionists tended to overemphasize the influence of Communists in the unemployed activity that had only recently begun to develop in the city. Concerned that little official notice had been taken of "the Red band that is gradually increasing its numbers" and "worming its way into the city's factory and common labor ranks," the *Grand Rapids Labor News* urged city authorities to "adopt war measures." Taking aim at widespread unemployment, the Federation asserted that the times were right for Red propaganda to flourish:

> The man without a job, a starving family, and an empty belly, will listen to anything and see reason in it, if there is a tone of pitying persuasion behind it. Local authorities, don't be blind. Red propagandists are aggressive and they are getting results right here in Grand Rapids.[9]

The remedy adopted three months later was not what the Federation had in mind. The solution embraced by Grand Rapids city manager George Welsh and the city commission was work relief—with a twist. Under the Grand Rapids program, relief clients performed public service work and were compensated with scrip exchangeable for food and supplies at a city commissary. Before long the scrip system drew criticism. At the forefront were local grocers, whose businesses were adversely affected as former customers were forced to purchase at the commissary. In January 1930 the local Federation and the Carpenters and Joiners of America joined the opposition. To craft union leaders the forced use of the city store had established a principle "smacking of slavery." By 1932, the Michigan Federation of Labor had added its voice to the opposition and pressured the governor to help end the program, which it regarded as unconstitutional.[10]

The Left was equally outraged. Scrip payment drew censure from the Grand Rapids Unemployed Council, which presented Welsh with a full set of demands in February 1930. Characteristic of the response to unemployed organizers in Grand Rapids, the demands emerged from the Welsh conference as recommendations. The list emphasized not only an end to the scrip system, but also the restoration of free speech and assembly in Grand Rapids, a reflection of heavy-handed restrictions placed on local dissidents and demonstrators. In 1931, a lonely Socialist organizer, Walter Morris, also recorded opposition to scrip in a letter to national party secretary Clarence Senior. His words revealed much about the values of Grand Rapids workers, as well as the political culture of labor in the city:

> I do not know what to think of the working class here in Grand Rapids. There are very many unemployed here. Several thousand are working for scrips, which are only redeemable at the city store. And other thousands are working very

few hours per week in shops, yet they won't go to a meeting from which they would eventually derive a benefit. It is almost impossible to talk organization to them. It really is too bad that we must suffer along with these ignorant masses, who would have all the power in the world, if they would just use their heads.[11]

Not only did Morris's musings underscore the conservative proclivities of the city's proletariat, but his condescension clarifies the limitations inherent in the paternalism and intellectualism of Michigan's old guard Socialists in the early 1930s. His remarks also suggest that many of the Grand Rapids unemployed turned inward in the face of economic disaster. It is also likely that the 20 percent of the city's population who depended on the scrip system were reluctant to challenge it lest their support evaporate.[12]

The local Unemployed Council maintained the CP criticism of the city's relief system, emphasizing the superiority of the Party-sponsored Workers Unemployment Insurance Bill as a remedy for the ravages of joblessness. In its request for a parade permit in November 1931, the Council alleged "great dissatisfaction" with the scrip system among employed and part-time workers, who were assumed to prefer cash relief and workers insurance. When William Z. Foster took his presidential campaign to the city in July 1932, the local CP attacked Welsh as a "bourgeois demagogue" who served the city's bankers and furniture manufacturers by imposing the "scrip system of force labor" on jobless workers.[13]

Unfortunately for Welsh, the attack on the scrip program emanated from the Right as well as the Left. The result was the creation in 1932 of a citizens' committee to investigate the Grand Rapids welfare system. The Committee of 100 acknowledged what the unemployed already knew—that the scrip system was "destructive of morale" and produced "discontent on the part of those receiving it." For these reasons and because the system appeared wasteful, the Committee recommended that the city commissary be closed and that relief recipients be compensated in cash. By early 1933 the scrip system had been abolished and a cash reimbursement system was in place.[14]

While progressives and social workers applauded the outcome, not all approved. As early as October 1932, scrip workers had organized themselves into a Scrip Workers Committee, which accepted the system but demanded improved compensation. And in

January 1933 a new Grand Rapids Workingmen's Association, which had the support of a broad coalition of Communist, Socialist, labor, and ethnic organizations, insisted that the abolition of scrip not result in loss of employment and that cash payments for work relief be sufficient to maintain a stable standard of living. One month later, a mysterious community paper, *Our Gang,* warned that the "dole" would have destructive results:

> Groups of men are murmuring Revolution is in the air, whether those in power believe it or not—it is true. Nothing will ever be gained by fooling the people. Don't say "cash relief will replace scrip relief." It has never worked out in any city that tried it and invariably the end has been "dole" as is now in force here in Grand Rapids. DOLE MEANS IDLENESS. Idleness means revolution. Revolution means the end of our liberty. Is it worth the price? God grant politics be forgotten before it is too late.[15]

Thus, in a process that transcended the work of citizens' committees, an idea struggled to be born. With scrip, the commissary, and the dole unacceptable, the only alternative was work relief for cash compensation. But at this stage of development, no organization seemed strong enough to force a change.

Arguably more influential than the Unemployed Council, Workingmen's Association, Communist Party, or even the GRFL was another workers organization that expressed the unique political culture of the region—the Christian Labor Association. The CLA was organized in 1931 in Grand Rapids by several members of the Christian Reformed Church under the leadership of Dutch immigrant Berend Roeters, an unemployed construction worker. This body reflected the Dutch Reformed Church's preference for a separate Christian labor union over either AFL or CIO unions. CLA's original goals included the "improvement of general conditions in the field of labor and industry" and the establishment of "mutual ventures" of benefit to members only. Its proposal for "mutual welfare measures" incorporated not only an interest in wages, hours, and working conditions, but also a commitment to assist workers in times of unemployment. In 1931 and 1932, CLA attempted to operate primarily as an employment service for jobless members, but confronted by massive unemployment, it experienced little success. Only later, after the enactment of the Wagner Act in 1935, would the CLA concentrate on the organization of workers into Christian unions. As of December 1932, the organization operated in Grand Rapids, Holland, and Zeeland and had established representatives in Kalamazoo, Muskegon, Kelloggsville, and Lamont.[16]

The CLA's early interest in the problems of the unemployed led it to approach the Grand Rapids City Commission with a protest against a 10 cents per hour wage cut imposed on relief workers in late 1932. Its appeal revealed the fatal weakness in the CLA philosophy of labor relations, the unwarranted assumption that Christian charity would guide the relationship. On 20 December 1932, CLA asked that a wage rate of 40 cents per hour be restored for all relief workers, who needed to earn a "living wage." A sympathetic but unyielding Welfare Advisory Council told the Grand Rapids City Commission that they were paying the prevailing rate for skilled labor, a rate that was "just and fair." The advisory council concluded that the city should pay no more for any service than it could command on the open market.[17] In short, the marketplace rather than Christian charity guided public policy, even in Grand Rapids.

While the CLA searched for morality in the Kent County economy, elsewhere in central and western Michigan the Unemployed Councils struggled to cope in more traditional ways with the relief cutbacks of 1932. The *Daily Worker* claimed that while reductions were imposed in poorly organized communities, such as Kalamazoo, Lansing, and Battle Creek, an effective resistance developed in Muskegon, where the Council mobilized unemployed militants to halt the latest round of cuts. Only in those cities where the Communist Party and the Councils played a "decisive role" was the resistance successful. In Jackson, for example, the Unemployed Council had begun to wrest concessions from a Welfare Bureau that had formerly required "forced labor" as a prerequisite for the receipt of donated food, clothing, and supplies. Local Council leaders claimed to have secured weekly provisions and brought an end to the "forced labor" system. Less successful were Socialists Dean Selby and A. D. Gordon, who by October 1931 had established an unemployed organization in rural Three Rivers. Calling for a mortgage and rent moratorium, as well as free medical care, clothing, and public services, the new organization submitted resolutions rather than demands.[18]

Although the Socialist organizers reported great enthusiasm for their ideas, "local comrades and sympathizers" were "unable to support the movement." Three Rivers authorities were definitely unenthusiastic. After presenting his resolutions at city hall, Selby was jailed on charges of dubious validity. Despite wretched local conditions, something was sadly missing in Three Rivers: repressive authority was too strong and popular pressure too weak to force public action on the issues raised by a Socialist organization "so broke that they cannot afford to buy literature."[19] As of December 1932, the Michigan SP was even less prepared to lead a peoples' movement in the hinterlands than in the urban centers.

Radicalism in the Far North: Unemployed Activism on Michigan's Last Frontier

While the social and cultural values of central and western lower Michigan had not encouraged the development of a powerful unemployed movement, the economic, ethnic, and cultural peculiarities of the remote Upper Peninsula fostered an entirely different worker response to the scourge of unemployment than had developed elsewhere in the state. In the isolated and economically devastated UP, left-wing militants were on the move at an early date. As previously noted, the UP was the most depressed area in the entire state, in terms of both percentages of workers unemployed and percentages of families on relief. Because of the region's extractive economy, the economic distress was even more pronounced in the UP than that evident in other parts of Michigan. As mining and logging had declined, farming the cutover area had been overemphasized. The end result was a chronic economic problem for an area stripped of its primary resources and excessively dependent on mineral production that found no market. Since the mid–nineteenth century, the UP had provided natural resources to an expanding capitalist economy. The economic exchange had been unequal, and the result economic disorganization.[20] By the 1930s all ingredients were present for social and political upheaval.

The response to economic crisis in the UP cannot be understood without reference to one additional element in the recipe for radicalism—the ethnocultural composition of the population. In no other area of Michigan, Kent County included, was unemployed activism so firmly rooted in the ethnic character of the population. While the UP was culturally diverse, with a population base composed of Finns, Italians, Poles, Czechs, Slovenes, Swedes, and native-born Americans, it was undoubtedly Finnish political culture that accounted for the militancy of the jobless when an organized movement came into being. Not only were Finns the largest ethnic group in the UP, but in 1930, more foreign-born Finns resided in Michigan than in any other state. In Gogebic County, for example, Finns outnumbered Italians (the next largest ethnic group) by three to one in 1930, when 3,129 foreign-born Finns resided in that single county. Inheritors of a rich radical tradition, UP Finns immersed themselves in the hunger marches, Unemployed Councils, and other worker protest movements of the Depression years; they were the shock troops of the area unemployed movement.[21]

For leftist Finns, the central issue of the early Depression years was the deep split in the Finnish Cooperative movement that had occurred in 1929–1930. When in 1929 Communists in the Workers Party had demanded a $5,000 loan from the Central Cooperative Exchange in Superior, Wisconsin, Socialists, non-aligned leftists, and non-Communist Finns took control of the cooperative and refused to grant the loan. Despite their defeat in 1930, CP cooperators remained active in the movement and continued to attack the Central Cooperative Exchange. The main Communist tool in this offensive was the fledgling Farmers and Workers Cooperative Unity Alliance, which competed with the dominant CCW (CCE became Central Cooperative Wholesale in 1932) until the Unity Alliance's collapse in 1939. Like many CP mass organizations of the 1930s, the Unity Alliance maintained a united front with the unemployed and embraced the Unemployed Councils wherever they existed. At a unity conference at Superior in April 1933, for example, the Unity Alliance scored the CCW for its failure to support a "working class program" of "united action for workers and farmers." Calling for massive May Day demonstrations, the Unity Alliance pledged "full support to the struggle of the masses for unemployment insurance and immediate relief" and resistance "against foreclosures on farmers and small homeowners."[22]

Unity Alliance supporters deplored CCW's political neutrality, which led it away from a "working class attitude" towards a "business attitude." Unity organizer and cooperative manager Ernest Koski later accused CCW of class betrayal, in that its proponents deluded themselves into thinking they could build a socialist society simply by buying from cooperative stores while ignoring the fact that it was "a capitalist class that still held the reins." Koski defiantly accepted the Communist label, but like the black unemployed activists in Detroit, he later recalled that "you didn't have to be a Communist" to be politically and socially active: "if you were unemployed and hungry, and became militant, what the hell?" His perspective was widely shared within the leftist element in the UP's Finnish community, whose members saw the split and the development of right-wing coops as a repudiation of their ethnic heritage and "commitment to the workingman's struggle."[23]

Following the 1930 split in the cooperative movement, Communists worked to build the Party throughout the UP. The heart of Communist activity was to be found in Gogebic, Iron, Delta, Alger, Houghton, Keweenaw, and Marquette counties, particularly in the cities of Ironwood, Bessemer, Iron River, Crystal Falls, Escanaba, Rock, Gladstone, Negaunee, Calumet, Houghton, and Hancock. The Communist Party was "predominantly based among the Finnish population," according to party district secretary John Wiita. Party membership was almost identical with the local Finnish Workers Federation lists. While the CP was the dominant political organization, there were several pockets of IWW strength, such as those in Iron River and the Rock-Eben Junction area. Both Communists and Wobblies were progressive politically and able to work together through the Workers Federation. Predictably, both displayed great interest in the problem of unemployment, the touchstone of radical activism.[24]

Unemployed organizing in Michigan's Upper Peninsula must be understood within the context of a predominant iron and copper mining industry and its long history of troubled labor relations. Labor unrest and union organizational efforts were not new to the area. As early as 1872, the Copper Country had experienced its first strike, and during the 1880s and 1890s the Knights of Labor had engaged in substantial, though largely unsuccessful, efforts to build a union. A new era opened in 1903 when Jay Pallard of the Western Federation of Miners launched an organizational drive in the Copper Country. The WFM brought with it a reputation for radicalism earned during the bloody battles in the Rocky Mountain fields during the 1890s. UP management used a devastating blend of labor spies, detective agencies, paternalism, and ethnic discrimination in hiring to divide and intimidate the labor force. Nonetheless, the WFM slowly grew until it enrolled the majority of Copper Country miners, and in 1913 the union called a strike that closed the mines and eventually eroded support for unionism. The copper strike of 1913–1914 was a long and bitter clash that failed to win union recognition, split the worker community, destroyed the WFM in the Copper Country, and retarded the development of unionism in the UP for twenty-five years.[25] The strike's legacy to the Depression generation was a combination of paternalism and an insidious blacklist that produced an atmosphere of fear among workers even more dependent because of the retrenchment of the 1920s and the economic collapse of the mining industry in the 1930s.

Nowhere in America was the blacklist more feared than in the mining districts of the UP, where paternalism and corporate arrogance held sway. Because of the copper strike's bitter legacy, UP unionism seemed paralyzed at the outset of the Great Depression. But the radical heritage was firmly planted in the hearts of Finnish leftists, and in 1930–1931, many began to respond to the overtures of the National Miner's Union. Before long, unionism and unemployed activism were to mesh as inseparable parts of the same organizational process.

At first, NMU activity was low key, beginning with informal private discussions among Finnish miners, some of them CP members. For "reasons of safety," small groups met secretly in private homes. It was, in the words of Ironwood miner and Party organizer Frank Walli, "an underground movement" that led to the organization of the first NMU locals among iron miners in Gogebic and Iron counties. Comparable efforts were under way among workers in Negaunee and Ishpeming, while Hancock, Calumet, and Painesdale copper miners attempted to organize for the Mine, Mill, and Smelter Workers Union "despite the copper barons' elaborate spy–stool pigeon system." Moreover, by December 1931 a Communist-led farmer-labor coalition was developing in Houghton and Ontanagon counties. In Iron River, where mass layoffs accelerated the union drive, an anonymous miner reported in April 1932 that a NMU demonstration against a mine shutdown had stimulated union growth "until we have the strongest local in the whole metal mining district."[26] Among the most active organizers in these efforts were Finnish CP activists Frank Walli, John and Martin Maki, William Heikkila, and later Gene Saari.

The rising militancy of the mineworkers was an essential precedent to the development of the unemployed movement in the UP. Frank Walli recalled that CP union activists soon became involved in the next step, namely the organization of unemployed groups. Eventually, NMU urged its organizers and workers to enter Mine-Mill, advice Walli complied with in 1932. Now blacklisted, he learned that the Mine-Mill constitution made unemployed workers ineligible for full union membership. Thus, "unemployed militants were out," leaving men like Walli "free to work full time in the unemployed movement."[27]

Because large numbers of NMU members were unemployed and others worked no more than two days per week by 1932, there was a firm base in Iron and Gogebic counties for organizing the jobless. Iron River union member John Kova reported that NMU had finally discovered "correct united front tactics," which began to pay dividends. Because most members were jobless, the union now began organizing new unemployed branches, which in 1932 cooperated with employed workers in several militant demonstrations. Walli noted that after reading of the Detroit area Unemployed Councils, UP activists began organizing similar groups.[28] The outcome was a new measure of solidarity that constituted an unprecedented threat to local management and their community allies.

The acceleration of efforts to organize the UP unemployed reflected the Communist Party's conscious decision to broaden its base with an appeal to the region's jobless workers. In late summer 1930, a regional Party conference at Ironwood resolved to intensify organizing activity in upper Michigan, where miners' groups were still pitifully weak. As a result, CP organizer William Heikkila transferred from Minnesota to Hancock in the UP, from which he launched an organizing drive among the jobless that took him to Mass, Iron River, and other communities throughout the peninsula. Heikkila was a member of a Finnish Socialist family who had absorbed Socialist doctrine at home. Heikkila later remembered that his primary activities involved leadership in the "economic struggle" rather than participation in everyday Party work. From autumn 1930 to late 1933, he criss-crossed the UP as an itinerant unemployed organizer and worked to weld the jobless into a social force to be reckoned with.[29]

For people like Heikkila, progress was measured in small increments, though the little victories were viewed as part of a constantly unfolding advance towards the hoped-for radical triumph. In July 1931, a Communist delegation disrupted an Iron County board meeting, taking over a school building to hold its own session and demand adequate relief. Later, under Heikkila's leadership, the Iron River–Caspian Unemployed Council joined with the NMU to fight for and win a raise in compensation for relief workers that doubled their pay rate. And in February 1933 the unemployed workers of Crystal Falls pressured the Iron County Poor Commission to rescind a relief workers pay cut, increase relief payments, and halt discrimination in relief payments. Although the commission failed to grant these demands, the jobless workers received a courteous hearing, which tended to increase their stature in the worker community.[30]

Mass action had increased the pressure felt by representatives of the ruling elites in UP communities, but the power structure was fully prepared to respond to popular agitation. In Iron, Houghton, and Keweenaw counties, the corporations either dispensed relief themselves or controlled the public welfare systems indirectly. Although the Copper Country mines closed one by one between 1931 and 1933, traditional corporate paternalism held sway. Both Calumet & Hecla and the Copper Range Mining Company adopted a policy of spreading the work, with preference to those with heavy family responsibilities. Most companies allowed gardening and woodcutting on company land and permitted laid-off workers to reside in company housing, often rent-free. Both Copper Range and Calumet & Hecla also provided direct relief to employees, at least through 1932. But by January 1933 the companies could no longer absorb the burden. Looking to the government for a solution to the relief crisis, Copper Range executive Ward Paine asserted that the company's "sole objective" must be to remain viable as a "permanent source of employment," though on a restricted scale. The federal government would have to be the employer of last resort, as corporate welfare proved inadequate in the face of the unprecedented economic crisis faced by the one-industry communities of the UP. In 1933 Washington did in fact assume most of the Copper Country relief load.[31]

Confronted by relief demonstrations and a united front between the Councils and union miners, management responded with diverse strategies to contain a radical initiative that demonstrated public appeal and potential for growth. In Gogebic and Iron counties, the blacklist was the preferred vehicle for social control. By 1933, an alternative scheme emerged in the Copper Country, where Calumet & Hecla launched an Employee Representation Plan which, contrary to management protestations, was a company union without the dues. Most dramatic were events in Iron County, where in late 1931 joint meetings between mining officials and local government authorities began in an effort to blunt the edge of radicalism. In Iron River, a new citizens committee searched for a means to meet the workers' needs through charity and finally settled on two-day work weeks as an antidote to the "discontent of the miners as a result of Communist agitators." By 1933, local NMU activists had concluded that with extensive unemployed organizing complete and the mines operating again, if only on a part-time basis, "it won't be long before we are on fighting edge again."[32]

Bold rhetoric masked continued fear of company repression. Closer to the truth was an anonymous iron miner's assertion that "the steel trust terror" was pervasive and that "the iron bosses kept the two thousand miners under a grip of terror." In fact, the reality of community pressure was harsh. Not only were workers intimidated by corporate dominance, but the local business elite worked with management and local government to break unions and disrupt unemployed activities. Recalling her own efforts to assist the jobless and their families, CP community organizer Rachel Kangas agreed that "the fear was great." The combination of business-government collusion and workers' awareness of their own vulnerability helps to explain why Unemployed Councils on the Detroit model developed slowly in the UP.[33]

It remains to determine the reasons for the Communist Party's organizational success in the face of community pressure and corporate paternalism. An explanation must begin with the Finnish tradition of activism and group consciousness. Finns were cooperators and organization builders. Most observers also acknowledge that the CP was effective because it had direction, motion, and organization. Through these instruments, the Party was able to provide leadership, a scarce commodity. TUUL, NMU, the Finnish Workers Federation, Unity Alliance, and YCL were all active in the UP during the early Depression years, and each was willing to "raise issues with which workers and the unemployed could identify." The CP used intelligent tactics, emphasizing problems of intense popular concern. And Communists were willing to invest effort in tedious, but indispensable, "nitty gritty organizational work."[34]

Although Unemployed Councils appeared later in the UP than in the industrial southeast, they had become a feature of the local scene by 1932. Moreover, the independent community organizing initiated by UP social activists resembled the work done by urban organizers. Reacting to mass layoffs, Rachel Kangas of Iron River established a personal reputation as a militant ready to assist neighbors and friends in dealing with welfare authorities in Iron County. She quickly learned that the only way to get county officials to understand the plight of the jobless was to "go to the relief office and make demands right there." Using leaflets, pamphlets, mimeos, and personal contacts, Kangas and other CP workers helped educate the needy on their rights under the law. After receiving six hundred votes for Register of Deeds on the Communist ticket in 1932, Kangas found middle-class citizens more willing to help provide relief. On some occasions, the only effective way to elicit a response from management or government was to exert pressure through public protest. When the Davidson Mine in Iron River closed in 1932, for example, social workers "simply ignored people." After mining officials used a public meeting to urge the jobless to have patience, Kangas assumed leadership in a spontaneous act of personal courage. Never intending to "get up on a soap box," the fiery young woman challenged management:

> I got up and asked the woman "how many of you can feed your babies on patience? When you eat patience, how much does it fill your stomach."[35]

Unable to respond, the mining officials slipped away, but not long thereafter, the social workers' attitude became more cooperative.

The first documented mass demonstration in the UP had occurred in Negaunee more than a year earlier, when in February 1931 an impromptu unemployment insurance committee led seventy men in a march on city hall. The *Marquette Mining Journal* dismissed the demonstrators as transients "who never sought employment in prosperous times and would not work." The marchers presented a set of extreme demands for emergency relief and protection against evictions, including a worker-administered relief fund of $500,000. The local press correctly saw the protest as Communist in origin, "evidence that the Communist movement, even if slenderly supported, has outposts scattered about the country." Unable to conceive of worker alienation, the *Journal* argued that "it speaks well for the labor of the Upper Peninsula that more of them were not spoon fed with the dose sent out from Communist headquarters."[36]

Whatever the dosage, UP patients continued to respond to the medication. During the next few years, similar outdoor demonstrations took place in Ontonagon, Mass, Iron River, Newberry, Ishpeming, Painesdale, Munising, Ironwood, and elsewhere. And when the Michigan Hunger March reached Lansing in May 1931, a large Copper Country delegation was present.[37] As always, Finnish Communists were prominent as leaders of these public events.

On May Day 1931, Ernest Koski of the Cooperative Unity Alliance and CP activist Gene Saari of Hancock led a demonstration at Ontonagon in defiance of a local ban on the celebration. Apprehended while addressing the crowd, both Koski and Saari landed in jail, charged with conducting a street meeting without permission and resisting arrest. While the criminals languished in custody, the Ontonagon American Legion paraded into the night, asserting that "the Communists are where they ought to be." Bailed out by a Finnish farmer, Koski was later acquitted of the charges, though he was forced out of his position as cooperative manager a year later because the board of directors sought to remove the store's Red image.[38]

The significance of the May Day incident lies in the evidence it provides of growing farmer-labor collaboration in the UP. The drama of the worker struggles in the copper and iron industries should not obscure the fact that a smaller but substantial group of Finns and other settlers had pioneered an attempt to farm the cutover areas of Upper Michigan, and that they too, confronted the ravages of the Depression. Inheritors of the same cultural tradition of social activism that inspired organizational efforts among workers in the mining districts, many rural Finns supported the leftist Unity Alliance following the split in the cooperative movement. It was logical, therefore, for them to look to the Left as they attempted to cope with the Depression's impact on the farm economy. Their organized response constituted the rural analogue to the urban unemployed movement.[39]

One of the most common responses to joblessness in the UP was a back-to-the-land movement, which resulted in a significant inmigration of urban dwellers who returned to the soil as unemployment worsened. Hunting, fishing, and subsistence farming became a way of life for many UP citizens who were unable to find work in the mines or the urban centers. Because of contracting employment elsewhere in the state of Michigan, moreover, a reverse migration from the Lower Peninsula also occurred. This population movement placed Depression migrants in the very areas experience had proven least capable of supporting a farm population and providing a reasonable living standard. As a result, in deeply depressed Houghton County the population actually increased by 4,000 persons. In sum, the land held a powerful attraction in times of economic despair.[40]

For the permanent farm population, the Depression too often meant loss of home, land, and living. Angered and confused, many responded with mass action to protect the holdings they regarded as their birthright. For leadership in their hour of peril, cutover farmers turned to persons and institutions they had long trusted: the cooperatives, their leftist managers, and often the CP organizers well known to the Finnish community. The organizational expression of this militance was the Communist-sponsored United Farmers League, which rallied American farmers around a program of direct action to prevent mortgage foreclosures, promote tax forgiveness, and provide relief to farmers and rural workers in need. Like all CP mass organizations, UFL also called for a united front with urban workers and the unemployed in the battle against capitalism. By November 1931, a farm crisis in the UP was imminent. Confronted with the prospect of sixty foreclosure sales in Ontonagon County and a similar situation in Houghton and Baraga counties, eight hundred farmers attended organizational meetings in many communities to prepare for a confrontation with authority. The UFL organ, *Producers News,* reported that rebellious farmers were electing "committees of action" designed to forcibly resist public officials who attempted to execute foreclosure actions. These committees operated extensively throughout upper Michigan, Minnesota, and Wisconsin in a manner parallel to the Farm Holiday Association of the plains states; indeed, in some states FHA and UFL cooperated closely at the local level to prevent legal action against farm debtors.[41]

Typical of the "committees of action" demands were the resolutions of the Snake River–Chassel rebels, who called for postponement of tax payments, cancellation of delinquent loans, a moratorium on foreclosures, an end to evictions, delayed mortgage payments, free medical aid, county public works projects, and salary cuts for public officials. More dramatic was the action of two-hundred Ontonagon County farmers, who blocked a foreclosure on 24 November 1931. After an attempt to dissuade the sheriff from carrying out a foreclosure order, the large crowd disrupted the sale by preventing serious bids on the property in question. The boldness of the Ontonagon protestors reflected the rapid growth of UFL in Michigan's Upper Peninsula.[42]

Equally aggressive were the UFL delegates who in December 1931 assailed the Houghton County Board of Supervisors for their subservience to the "Copper Trust" that controlled county politics. *Producers News* described a courtroom packed to the walls with "husky farmers" who were present to "back up" their committee's demands. The Houghton rebels endorsed heavy taxation of industry, tax relief for farmers and unemployed workers, a moratorium on evictions, protection of public employees' jobs, and the assignment of public works jobs only to needy workers. The Houghton declaration clearly aimed to foster a farmer-labor alliance to advance the interests of the jobless, both urban and rural. After the supervisors adjourned in self-defense, the angry farmers took over the courtroom to hold their own meeting and threaten their reluctant hosts with a larger protest if action was not taken, not to mention vengeance at the polls.[43]

The dam had clearly burst. In county after county UFL committees of action sprouted up to express popular outrage over the effect of the economic collapse on rural workers. In Alger County, the committee demanded that the county unemployed commission provide "relief or work." When Munising mayor C. G. Kemp told the unruly husbandmen to make requests rather than demands, he found himself castigated as an "agent of the capitalist class." Moreover, the farmers insisted on relief work that was not to be regarded as charity, but rather "something to which every unemployed worker is entitled."[44] In short, UP workers, like the unemployed elsewhere in Michigan, were redefining the state's responsibility to the citizenry and claiming a right to gainful employment as a part of a social safety net.

Through the UFL, UP farmers had found their voice. What the UFL actions taught participants was that in dire economic and social circumstances, there was a place for extralegal mass action, and that sometimes, the result might be redress of grievances. A case in point was the UFL's success in preventing a foreclosure on the Fred Seubert farm in Ontonagon County. In December 1931, after an angry mob had forced the sheriff to halt the sale, the county board declared postponements of foreclosure illegal. For the UFL militants, however, the law resided in their ability to "scare those politicians out of their wits." *Producers News* noted that "when enough pressure is brought to bear" by an aroused public, somehow "the postponement becomes legal."[45]

By January 1932, UFL leaders had laid the basis for an effective organization. Finnish leftists had been able to broaden their base of support in the UP. In the process, the cultural tradition of collective action for the common good had asserted itself in those areas where left-wingers and the Unity Alliance were strongest. These convictions were evident in the demands of Iron County farmers, who in December 1931 insisted that work relief jobs be assigned on a nondiscriminatory basis. The group found it necessary for their own self-preservation to "act collectively in organized fashion" on the "life and death questions" involved in securing relief.[46] It was this perspective that had animated the great relief rebellion of late 1931.

Between April 1932 and early 1933, the UFL moved towards a more collaborative approach to the problems of insecurity on the farm and widespread unemployment. During this period, UFL intensified its effort to establish links with jobless workers. In April 1933, when a major county board protest occurred in Houghton, a strong workers contingent joined the farmers in an open threat to withhold tax payments. This warning induced the county supervisors to promise that they would prevent foreclosures, if facts warranted such action. Even more militant were the 3,000 farmers and workers present on 3-4 July for the Finnish Workers Club festival in Negaunee and Ishpeming. When Ishpeming's mayor called on spectators to interfere with a mass parade, his suggestion was flatly ignored.[47] (See figure 7.)

By early 1933 the UP farmer-labor coalition seemed to be taking shape. On 14 January 1933 a Baraga County UFL relief conference at L'Anse devoted most of its attention to urban-rural collaboration. UFL regional organizer Frank Arvola stressed "organized united action" as the only way to halt both foreclosures and evictions. The conference embraced the Workers Unemployment Insurance Bill and attacked Henry Ford's UP enterprises. Finally, the

Figure 7. Finnish Demonstrators Demand Food in Negaunee, 1932 *("Finnish Workers Federation of the United States Records," Box 2, Immigration History Research Center, University of Minnesota)*

delegates demanded worker-controlled relief committees at the county level. On 25 February, five-hundred Baraga County workers and farmers marched to the court house to demand cash relief, the eight-hour day for relief workers, and increased relief payments for the unemployed. In Houghton County, UFL protestors challenged evictions and forced rent payments by the mining companies in Paavola. Meanwhile, workers and farmers in Painesdale and Ontonagon were engaged in private meetings aimed at the development of a united front unemployed movement. Determined to organize a more sweeping struggle for relief, members of YCL, NMU, and UFL joined to create the United Front Action Committee.[48]

Just as the UFL unity drive crested in the UP, rural protest spilled over into the northern reaches of Michigan's Lower Peninsula, an area previously unaffected by the radical virus. In isolated Newaygo County, one thousand protestors massed in Manistee to halt a foreclosure action in February 1933. On 10 March, an equally large band of "irate farmers," armed with axe handles, took charge of an auction in Ithaca, where they jostled a bank agent, forced a sale, and bid low to save another rural homestead. And three hundred farmers at Ludington organized a united front farmers committee that included not only UFL members, but also Farm Bureau and unaffiliated representatives. The radicalizing potential of the Depression was evident in the words of the participants. One Farm Bureau member declared that although he was not Red, "we'd all be Reds" unless farm relief was forthcoming. Similarly, an unaffiliated farmer angrily asserted that "if we have to be Reds to stick up for our rights, then we'll be Reds." By March 1933 the mood in northwest Michigan had begun to turn ugly.

The tension escalated into open confrontation at White Cloud, where on 15 March, five Michigan farmers were arrested and held, two of them on criminal syndicalism charges, after they had participated in a foreclosure protest. Among those charged were Michigan farm organizers Clyde Smith, John Rose, John Babcock, and John Casper. Casper was a militant UFL activist who had recently been the Communist congressional candidate, while the others had worked to unite farmers in resistance to foreclosures. The CP's leading national farm activist, Lem Harris, later argued that the aggressive and outspoken Rose had been targeted because of his effectiveness. *Producers News* condemned the arrests as a "threat to farmers everywhere" and to the homes they were trying to save. Less diplomatic were the resolutions of the Muskegon County farmers' committee of action, which blistered the authorities for their actions but expressed gratification at the evidence that at White Cloud, farmers and workers had finally realized that by "uniting all of their own forces," they could "smash the capitalist frameups" and destroy the "whole rotten capitalist system."[50] It is clear that the radicalism that had drawn substantial popular endorsement in the UP now threatened to spread southward. The events of early 1933 demonstrated that while Communist ideology was almost incidental, the idea of militant protest found a receptive rural audience in places where desperate conditions bred desperate people.

Although militant insistence upon the government's responsibility to the dispossessed gained vocal expression, the impoverished farmers of the UP explored other alternatives in response to the collapsed economy. No study of the area's unemployed in the 1930s would be complete without examination of the "Karelian fever" of the early Depression years. Convinced that American capitalism was beset by contradictions that damaged the human spirit and limited social progress, thousands of Finnish-Americans decided to reemigrate to Soviet Karelia, where they might participate in the construction of a workers' society. It is important to recognize, however, that some of the return emigrants were not Communist. Many were simply Finns disillusioned with the failure of the American dream. Yet enough were Party members to create concern within the CP over the loss of some of its most active American supporters.[51]

The venture originated in 1931 shortly after Otto Kuusinen gained influence as secretary of the Comintern. The plan gained momentum when the Soviet Karelia Technical Committee, headed by Matti Tenkunen, was established in New York. One important recruiter was Unity Alliance cooperative manager Ernest Koski of Ontonagon. Koski, who remembered the venture as a success, noted that the prime motivation for reemigration was economic: returnees "could see that the United States was in a general depression." Modern scholars place greater emphasis on the Karelian and Soviet government initiatives of the early 1930s, rooted in their need for technical assistance and skilled labor. It is also clear that many returnees were farmers of at least moderate means. Yet the lure of ready employment was undoubtedly one factor in the Finnish American response to the recruitment campaign. The emigration, which drained ten thousand Finns from Canada and the United States, was heavy between 1931 and 1934, reaching a peak in 1932, the nadir of the American Depression.[52]

Since most reemigrants paid their own passage to Karelia, it is obvious that the poorest element in Michigan's Finnish population was not prominent in the exodus. It is more likely that the explanation for the extensive reverse immigration lies in the extraordinary idealism that possessed so many Finns in American capitalism's darkest hour. An elderly Eben Junction resident recalled the emotion of a search for a "promised land." Great admiration was evident among the four hundred local cooperative members who in 1931 packed Finn Hall in a farewell tribute to comrades who chose a social gamble. Another returnee later recalled that he "had to find out for [himself] about the great 'social experiment' in the Soviet Union." Typical were the reemigrants who left *Tyomies* a greeting filled with penetrating social vision as they departed for

> the country where a heroic giant of labor is standing, in one hand a dreadful sword with which he has beaten numerous enemies and will beat enemies in the future; and in the other hand a trowel with which he is creating, unknown before in

the history of mankind, heroism and energy, a new and happier society, a society in which each and everyone feels that he is a human being among people. Side by side with them we all promise that we will give our best to this glorious cause.[53]

Imbued with optimism, the pioneers were unprepared for the hardship encountered in the Karelian woods. Before long, the initial idealism wore thin, as shortages, harsh living conditions, and restrictions on personal liberties became clearer. The result was a substantial new return migration to Finland, the United States, and Canada. Perhaps the most important long-term outcome was the weakening of the Finnish-American Communist movement in the UP and elsewhere. Combined with the disastrous split in the cooperative movement, the Karelian experiment sapped the party of some of its most able leaders.[54]

For the purpose of this analysis, "Karelian fever" provides evidence of the rich diversity with which frustrated Americans reacted to the economic dislocations of the early Depression. Just as urban ethnics, black inmigrants, and transplanted Southern whites had shaped responses to deprivation consistent with their social needs and relevant to the economic situation in southeastern Michigan, so it was that many Finns in the UP adopted an approach to social crisis that expressed their unique political culture. They shared a collective social ethic that brought Finns of many political persuasions into a common protest against the loss of personal and family security that resulted from the collapse of the economy. Whether unemployed miners, jobless lumberjacks, or harried farmers, the victims of the crisis united in the demand for immediate relief and in protest against unacceptable losses. Their non-Finnish neighbors endorsed these objectives and often supported their efforts. That the CP embraced the cause did not make it less just, and for all but the true believers, ideology was a relevant but secondary concern.

In the outstate areas of lower Michigan, a conservative political culture produced a weaker response to the ravages of unemployment. Here, too, ethnic heritage was a factor, especially in the west central region, where the Dutch Reformed tradition and a somewhat diversified economy combined to reinforce social values more resistant to radical ideology and militant mass action. Yet by 1933, even the state's conservative heartland had been affected by the economic debacle of the early Depression years, and the Unemployed Councils, Scrip Workers Committee, Christian Labor Association, Workingmen's Association, and United Farmers League had made their appearances.

As a new administration took office in Washington, the dispossessed of both the UP and lower Michigan had found common ground on several important points. First, many workers had concluded that since there was no escape from economic reality, traditional voluntaristic assumptions needed modification. As a corollary, the majority of citizens were prepared to expect a more comprehensive solution to the nation's economic problems from a more activist government. For most workers in both regions, public employment for cash compensation loomed large as a potential response to an unprecedented crisis. A consensus in favor of work relief had emerged in the UP, the rural–small town lower Michigan area, and the urban southeast. Moreover, militants in all areas had concluded that an urban-rural worker coalition would be an effective tool in advancing the agenda of Michigan's unemployed. Though the coalition existed more in theory than in practice, the events of late 1932 and early 1933, especially in the UP and the north, seemed to hold the promise of future success.

In spring 1933, workers representing a broad spectrum of Michigan's population looked to Washington for the domestic solution that had evaded them. Unemployed activists, their numerous organizations, frustrated labor and farm groups, and the larger community of the jobless watched anxiously as a new president, Franklin D. Roosevelt, embarked on his search for that elusive remedy. The rest of this study concentrates on those unemployed who organized to help find it.

4

New Leadership and New Opportunity
Organizing for Action, 1933–1935

With the establishment of the New Deal, the context within which the unemployed movement operated changed dramatically. In both Michigan and the United States, organizers now dealt with programs and agencies created by an activist government and with workers who increasingly viewed government employment as work not significantly different from that in the private sector, except for the important assumption that public employment was a temporary phenomenon. As a result of this shift, new unemployed organizations entered the field and older, established groups found it necessary to alter their approaches to the mobilization of jobless workers. Perhaps the most striking change was that the new public employees perceived themselves as jobholders, which made the labor union model relevant for organizational activity.

Scholars have long pondered the question of the New Deal's impact on labor. Until recently, the liberal interpretation of the New Deal as a boon to unorganized and unprotected workers predominated. Since the 1960s, however, historians have emphasized the co-optation of worker movements, including the unemployed insurgency of the early 1930s, by a New Deal that essentially domesticated worker organizations and drew their leaders into an evolving labor relations system that originated with the National Recovery Administration and matured under the Wagner Act of 1935. Close examination of Michigan's unemployed organizations suggests that theirs was a movement that welcomed this co-optation. As a result of this process, mass organizations were integrated into a new corporatist order under the watchful eye of a paternalistic state. Simultaneously, worker organizations themselves became increasingly bureaucratized as they took their place in the new pattern of labor-management relations.

The remainder of this study explores the impact of the New Deal on the unemployed movement in Michigan as it matured after 1933. In this period, the number and variety of participating organizations increased and the ideological basis of unemployed activity became more diverse than had been true during the Communist phase of the Michigan movement. Eventually, the unique character of unemployed organizing in Michigan became evident, especially after the labor movement emerged as an economic force to be reckoned with. For the jobless, the results were momentous.

Among the themes that surfaced in the Roosevelt period, none was more significant than the development of the idea that the unemployed were workers subject to organization on a labor union model. Starting with the Civil Works Administration in 1933 and 1934, both public works employees and the unemployed organizations viewed relief work as gainful employment and relief workers as legitimate subjects of quasi-union organizational activity. As a result, the movement towards collective bargaining and union recognition quickened between 1933 and 1936. During these years, the AFL rallied behind skilled labor and the union scale and, at least temporarily, explored the organization of project workers. However, other competitors came to dominate the field and the craft unions reverted to their traditionally cautious approach to jobless workers and their problems. The unionization of the unemployed worker was a concept introduced in this period and eventually embraced by the Workers Alliance, which promised to become an influential advocate for the jobless. Yet for Michigan, the union organization of the unemployed remained a visionary idea whose time had not yet come.

•   •   •

By the time Franklin D. Roosevelt took office in March 1933 the troubled Michigan economy had reached a new low. Unemployment continued to rise relentlessly, and was soon to peak at 722,000. By the end of the year, 800,000 men, women, and children were on the relief rolls—17 percent of the state's population. Although relief agencies expanded their services, the need for public assistance remained great. In the view of the State Emergency Welfare Relief Commission, Michigan's economic life suffered from "mass stagnation." Symbolic of this paralysis was Democratic governor William Comstock's closure of the state's banks in mid-February 1933. So severe were Detroit's financial problems that the city's banks remained closed for many months following Roosevelt's national bank holiday, accounting for 40 percent of the combined assets of all closed banks in the United States as late as October 1933. The Detroit jobless were also in deep trouble in early 1933. When Mayor Frank Murphy resigned to become governor-general of the Philippines, five out of six unemployed Detroit workers received no assistance from public or private sources.[1] The future looked bleak.

Despite the Hoover administration's tentative exploration of a new financial relationship with the states in late 1932, a crisis atmosphere prevailed in Michigan when Roosevelt assumed control. This sense of desperation reflected a great disparity between state needs and federal resources, as well as the long shadow of voluntarism. By the time of the interregnum, a loose urban coalition had developed around the issue of stronger federal involvement in relief funding. This alliance, of which Frank Murphy had been a part, had succeeded in dramatizing the unmet needs of the urban unemployed and the financial limits under which municipal governments worked. Without a doubt, there was a large gap between the resource bases and social obligations of the nation's city governments.

Equally significant, at least in Michigan's case, were the outdated assumptions held by conservative politicians, who endorsed self-reliance and remained suspicious of federal intervention. In

Michigan, Republican governor Wilber Brucker was very slow to accept federal funding for relief expenditures. Although the cities of Flint and Muskegon Heights had received federal loans and the Reconstruction Finance Corporation had essentially assumed full financial responsibility for relief programs in the Upper Peninsula, Brucker remained uninterested in a major loan for statewide unemployed assistance. Even after RFC prodded Brucker in late 1932 to support a request for an appropriation, the state failed to act. Michigan continued to resist RFC pressures until the New Deal's Federal Emergency Relief Administration threatened to deny Michigan access to direct relief grants, after which the state complied with federal requirements. As a result of this decision, Michigan was one of the first seven states to receive a FERA grant in May 1933.[2]

To deal with the nationwide crisis, the Roosevelt administration created not only FERA, but also the Public Works Administration and later the Civil Works Administration. Both PWA and CWA were steps towards the work relief approach advocated by the unemployed organizations that had become so strident in their demands by 1933. By embracing the idea of public work for cash remuneration, these agencies implicitly acknowledged the principle that in times of economic crisis, government should become the employer of last resort. The administration thus legitimized a concept widely endorsed within the organized unemployed movement. Its implementation soon stimulated the further growth of unemployed organizations. It also raised thorny questions for the American labor movement, which was still dominated by craft unions and burdened by notions of voluntarism that had outlived their usefulness.

To its credit, in late 1932 the AFL had reversed its long-standing position of hostility to the idea of unemployment insurance. Under great pressure from the Weinstock Rank and File Committee and dissenting unions within the Federation, the Executive Council finally acted in July 1932. Bowing to the wishes of the dissidents, the Council instructed Green to draft a bill that would protect the rights and jobs of organized workers. Green acted promptly to implement their decision, but still faced last-ditch resistance from Federation conservatives at the 1932 convention. On the left, moreover, he confronted a challenge from the Rank and File Committee, which demanded a hearing for the Workers Unemployment Insurance Bill. Predictably, the convention embraced the Green proposal, a moderate plan that preserved the "freedom and liberty" of the worker and "continuity of employment." With this action the Federation essentially caught up with the workers it represented. The combination of deep depression and popular pressure had moved craft unionism along the road to the corporate liberal state and induced union leaders to insist on one of the foundation benefits of the modern social welfare system.[3]

The shift in the Federation's position suggested that the AFL might be prepared to offer more concrete support to jobless workers. In March 1933 the *American Federationist* proposed that Central Labor Unions "serve as the advocate of the unemployed." With this suggestion, the *Federationist* seemed momentarily to tilt towards a more comprehensive definition of craft unionism, arguing that "the outlook of the trades union movement must be larger than just our union group."[4]

To DFL president Frank Martel, this position implied that federal relief workers might be recruited into unions. A product of the International Typographical Union with a background in Socialist politics, Martel had been a consistent supporter of autoworkers unionism. Given his early record as a builder of bridges among competing groups, his initial interest in unemployed organizing was not surprising. Before long, however, the AFL hierarchy dismissed Martel's argument. AFL secretary Frank Morrison soon reminded the Detroit Federation that national policy forbade the issuance of charters to relief workers. Such organizational efforts would work "in opposition to the philosophy of the labor movement" if unions demanded relief when their primary goal was to "organize workers to readjust conditions of labor in industry" in order that all workers have an opportunity to earn a living "without having to appeal for relief from public agencies."[5]

The message from Washington served to reinforce long-held assumptions in the DFL. Since the onset of the Great Depression, the local Federation had viewed the unemployment problem through the lens of craft unionism and member interests. Consequently, DFL sought to gain influence in the administration of federal relief programs, ensure access to jobs for its members, and uphold union wage and workplace standards. These themes were to reappear throughout the 1930s as the guiding principles of DFL policy with regard to CWA, PWA, and WPA employment programs.

Frank Martel's strength had always been in the building trades. Of greater significance in Michigan, however, was the emergence of the Mechanic's Educational Society of America (MESA), which under the leadership of transplanted Englishman Matthew Smith had grown significantly by Summer 1933. A left-wing democratic union led by a militant Socialist, MESA united highly skilled auto tool-and-die makers. When MESA struck against General Motors in September 1933, the leaders of the declining AWU threw their support to the new union. Closing ranks, AWU's John Schmies called for a united front in the Flint struggle, a move reinforced by MESA's endorsement of collaboration with the Unemployed Councils. Recognizing the need for solidarity, MESA organizer Jack Levy stationed himself outside the Chevrolet employment office, where he enjoyed some success in recruiting the unemployed into the new union. The rise of MESA coincided with AWU's loss of members and influence, as well as the Communist Party's decision to work within other mass unions, including those inside the AFL.[6]

Elsewhere in Michigan, conditions among the unemployed produced a new interest in organizational activity. Since mid-1932, RFC had extended loans to UP counties, which expended these funds on both direct relief and public works programs, especially road-building projects. After Roosevelt took office, the federal government assumed primary financial responsibility for direct and work relief in the region. By Spring 1933, pressure for unemployed organization had begun to build, and the initiative for collective action came increasingly from below. In March 1933, the miners of the Copper Country responded to new layoffs with group action. House meetings were held in Atlantic Mine, South Range, Painesdale, Mass, and Bruce Crossing in preparation for a Houghton County relief conference and hunger march. When the conference convened in April 1933, eighty-nine militant farmer-labor delegates hammered out a sweeping set of demands for cash relief, work relief at increased wages, nondiscriminatory hiring, free medical care, and recognition of farmers' and workers' organizations. The proceedings at Houghton, coordinated by the United Farmers League, revealed deep worker resentment against welfare bureaucrats whom they perceived to be hostile towards the clients they served. One month after the Copper Country conference, the Gogebic County Unemployed Council staged a major demonstration to protest wage cuts, unacceptable hours, and poor working conditions on relief jobs. In April 1933, the dissidents marched on the county seat at Bessemer to demand an eight-hour day at 40 cents per hour and present their grievances to the county board. Concerned about the economic future, the Council demanded economic justice for the young who were "lacking much that young men look forward to."[7]

Judicious though the demonstrators were, they were too aggressive for Gogebic County's emergency relief authorities, who focused on the Council's Communist leadership. Isolating Frank Walli, relief director William McNamara curtly notified the CP organizer that since he was dissatisfied with the relief committee's regulations, his name had been removed from the county payroll. Militants paid a price for activism, but despite such intimidation, the movement continued to grow. In May and June, mass demonstrations and marches occured in Ahmeek, Allouez, Fulton, and Hancock. In Houghton County, relief strikers demanded cash payments, provisions, and adequate medical care. Denouncing management's domination of the relief system, the newly organized Relief Strike Committee also urged Governor Comstock to launch an investigation of the area's "copper trust controlled relief officials." Meanwhile, strikers on the Keewenaw County road project staged a demonstration in protest of "intolerable conditions" in the county's "forced labor" program. While the changes were not disclosed, the *Daily Worker* claimed that worker militancy had resulted in improved conditions.[8]

After a moment of hesitation during the summer of 1933, UFL intensified its drive to organize the unemployed farmers and workers of northern Michigan and the UP. This renewal in organizational activity coincided with the ascendancy among CP rural activists of Party agricultural secretary Henry Puro (John Wiita), the Finnish left, and the most militant elements within the councils of the national UFL, which had taken on an even clearer Communist tone. In the UP, this activism centered around a renewal of the struggle against foreclosures and evictions and for adequate relief. In September, the UFL's UP organizer, Frank Arvola, described an intense pressure campaign carried out by angry farmers and workers, who descended upon the county courthouses of Upper Michigan to demand redress of grievances and ultimately to win increases in work programs and direct relief. Arvola maintained that non-Communist farmers and "workers on the sidelines" supported the UFL's direct action program as "the only way to protect [themselves]."[9]

In order to cast a wider net, UFL sponsored a major conference at Painesdale in October 1933, attended by ninety-nine delegates from nine UP counties. Coordinated by Arvola, this meeting was designed to "unite farmers organizations and unorganized farmers around a program against those forces which threaten the farmers with ruin." The conference featured a plan for tighter grass-roots organization. The program had been drafted by UFL national secretary Alfred Tiala, a Puro protegé, who urged a program of mass action to promote the interests of dirt farmers. Delegates responded with a protest resolution attacking the persecution of the Michigan Farmers League's White Cloud leaders, who had been imprisoned for their defiance of government authority. To complement this protest, the conference adopted a set of demands that reiterated the right to adequate relief, security in homes and property, relief from debts and taxes, and freedom of assembly and protest.[10] The Painesdale proceedings revealed that with the support of a sympathetic Finnish population, the UFL had established itself as an important, if numerically small, element in the social and political life of the UP.

The strength of the Michigan contingent in the Communist Party's rural ranks became evident in November 1933, when the Party-based Farmers National Committee for Action convened a national farm protest conference in Chicago. Among the conference vice-chairs were Clyde Smith and Margaret Hacht of the Michigan Farmers League. They were also elected to the Farmers National Committee for Action, along with Arvola and three other Michigan delegates. And the toast of the convention was John Rose, the hero of the White Cloud eviction fight, only recently released from Jackson prison after the Michigan Farmers League's successful appeal to the state supreme court. Rose's appearance was consistent with the conference theme of reliance on direct action as the only way to protect rural workers against the bankers, trusts, and middlemen. As the delegates endorsed mass action and a militant program, including the farm strike as their ultimate weapon, external forces were operating to dull the edge of rural radicalism. Few anticipated the power of federal largesse to undermine the left-wing appeal to hard-pressed rural workers. In Michigan, as on the national scene, the period of highly publicized eviction fights was at an end rather than a beginning.[11]

After the inauguration of the Civil Works Administration in November 1933, the concept of a relief workers union surfaced in

Iron County, where under Communist leadership, four hundred CWA workers organized the Iron County Labor Union. A reflection of Iron County's traditionally strong Communist movement, the organization formulated and presented a set of demands focusing on wages, hours, and working conditions on the projects. The protest grew out of the Iron County CWA officals' failure to pay the CWA rate of 50 cents per hour for common labor. The union persuaded the County Board of Supervisors to endorse their request for an increase, but their action failed to allay criticism from various quarters. Alarmed that Iron County workers had launched the state's first CWA union, the conservative *Marquette Mining Journal* asserted that unless challenged, the budding unionists would be "emulated by some of the men in other counties." In a similar vein, the Ironwood *Daily Globe* warned that CWA projects might be cancelled "if Communists are allowed to run the show."[12] In short, the contagion had to be contained before the Red virus spread. Despite all efforts to squelch the principle, however, the idea of unionism on government projects could not be destroyed. Within four years, the UAW-CIO was to express the idea in a much more sophisticated and effective form.

While the UP jobless edged towards unionism for relief workers, the AFL elsewhere in the state fought to protect prevailing wages for skilled workers. On 15 December 1933 the Muskegon Trades and Labor Council attacked the CWA's failure to pay union scale for skilled labor and promised a protest to Labor Secretary Frances Perkins. Two weeks later a similar complaint emanated from the Ann Arbor Trades and Labor Council, which resented having to "fight tooth and nail" for rates skilled workers were entitled to. Perhaps most outspoken was Frank Martel, who publicly criticized the Macomb County CWA Committee for "deliberately withholding" from skilled workers money the federal government had intended them to receive.[13] By the time he was escorted from the room, Martel's commitment to the union scale for trade unionists could not be doubted.

It was therefore no surprise that, in early 1934, the DFL circled the wagons in defense of craft unionism. Exalting the virtues of skilled workers, DFL president Frank Martel and Ed Thal of the Detroit Building Trades Council insisted that Wayne County CWA officials erred in their readiness to employ the nonunion unemployed. Dismissing the needs of the economic underclass, the DFL baldly demanded that trade unions be given preference in employment. In response, John Carmody of CWA reminded his Michigan administrator, Fred Johnson, that "when organized labor is called for, organized labor should be supplied as long as it is available." Washington's reaction to DFL pressure was wholly consistent with national CWA policy, which embodied skill classification, the prevailing rate, and often, cooperation with local unions. As was true in most states,[14] CWA maintained generally warm relations with Michigan labor, despite occasional differences over preferential treatment for the AFL.

Even after CWA went out of existence, Ed Thal maintained a running critique of CWA policies on remaining projects, where "terrible unsatisfactory conditions prevailed." What the Building Trades meant was that allegedly unqualified workers had deluged the projects, where skilled unionists saw their work being done by "a lot of people who are either misfits or do not give a damn how or where the money is spent." Thal's words revealed much about the labor aristocracy's contempt for their unskilled brethren. He was brutally frank in arguing that "Building Trades activities" on the projects should be "entirely divorced from this damnable welfare" so skilled tradesmen could be "given a decent break."[15] No clearer statement of the chasm separating Detroit Federation leaders from the unorganized masses could have been made.

Waiting in the wings was an opportunistic Communist Party that was quick to capitalize on the fears created by the termination of CWA. As early as March 1934, the party staged mass demonstrations in Detroit to protest the end of CWA. By summer, the struggle was under way on several fronts. Leading the drive was the weakened AWU, which in June kicked off a campaign to rally autoworker support for laid-off relief workers with a set of demands that stressed immediate assistance to victims of the cutoff. Simultaneously, the remnants of the Unemployed Councils joined the AWU for a series of demonstrations to maintain pressure for adequate relief payments, unemployment insurance, and, significantly, the right of relief clients to join unions of their own choice. In June, YCL president Gil Green reported to the League's national convention that in several cities, including Detroit, the struggles for immediate relief and unemployment insurance remained high priorities. Acknowledging that the Roosevelt program had reduced the appeal of radicalism, Green urged redoubled efforts to bring youth into the Unemployed Councils.[16]

The broader, renewed drive to organize the unemployed had originated in the Communist-sponsored Washington Conference on Unemployment in February 1934. Michigan delegates represented Unemployed Councils, the AWU, the Small House Owners League, the Workmen's Association, and four AFL locals; they were drawn from organizations in Detroit, Grand Rapids, Kalamazoo, Ann Arbor, Jackson, Saginaw, Pontiac, Berkley, Dearborn, Lincoln Park, and Muskegon. Out of this meeting came a keen interest in the CWA and relief workers as the fulcrum of organizational work. In addition, the conference endorsed the League of Struggle for Negro Rights and rededicated Party workers to a policy of racial solidarity, with special emphasis on the fight against discrimination in relief distribution, relief work, and CWA employment. The energy generated by the Washington conference resulted in a flurry of organizing among CWA workers, especially in Detroit. The Communist-backed Relief Workers Protective Association endorsed a sweeping program that included jobs for all workers, guaranteed 30-hour weeks, union wages, nondiscriminatory hiring, workers' control of registration, and the right to organize on the projects. As a result, when relief cutbacks led to fewer hours on the projects, several strikes hit the city's construction programs, including work under way at Wayne University and River Rouge. Once again the AWU embraced the cause, urging relief workers to build their union, the RWPA, and strengthen the united front with the Unemployed Councils in a "fight of all the workers, employed and unemployed."[17]

Detroit relief workers were Michigan's most militant, but federal cutbacks produced resistance throughout the state in 1934. Reacting to a July pay cut, 2,500 Washtenaw County FERA employees went on strike in Ann Arbor, encouraged by Communist John Pace's impassioned plea for the "formation of a permanent united front." The Bonus Expeditionary Force veteran took particular pride in the cooperation received from skilled AFL workers on the projects, all of whom walked off the job in an unusual show of solidarity. To Pace, the strike committee, which included Unemployed Council representatives, CP organizers, Labor Council delegates, and AFL members, was the embodiment of the "united action" that would bring gains to employed and unemployed alike. The key to success lay with the AFL rank-and-file, whose jobless members ignored warnings from their leaders in forging worker unity.[18]

In Grand Rapids, there was little evidence of such solidarity. Since 1933, the local AFL had confined itself to the prevailing wage issue. Intent on protecting skilled workers, the Federation urged the city commission to fight for a 50-cent-per-hour minimum wage for unskilled workers and the prevailing wage for skilled labor. However, when CWA workers organized to demand adequate wages, they found themselves without support. Meanwhile, the conservative Christian Labor Association proposed a 33-cent-per-hour minimum wage for project workers, with flexibility to pay higher prevailing wages where local conditions justified them. More aggressive but clearly isolated were members of the Kent County Workingmen's Association, which in February 1934 sponsored an abortive relief protest at city hall. Led by Communists, the strikers demanded the "right to live" and "security for the workers," including unemployment insurance. Never known for its tolerance of dissent, the Grand Rapids Police Department brutally suppressed the protest, which a military informer called "a small riot." The observer dispassionately noted that "the police handled the situation very well, arresting a number and breaking the skulls of a number of others." Hapless though the small CP contingent was, local authorities were intent on silencing critics of the welfare and relief system. Official motives were obvious in the watchdog's assertion that "it is hoped that it will be possible to take them out of circulation for a few months."[19] The right of peaceable assembly was not a high priority in Grand Rapids, always barren ground for radical activity.

Sporadic resistance to the relief cutbacks resulting from the termination of CWA persisted throughout 1934 and into 1935, reaching even isolated areas of the state. For example, on two separate occasions, Owosso relief workers struck for better compensation; in August 1934, 572 persons walked off the job, while 600 participated in a strike two months later. A federal labor conciliator reported that a "professional labor organizer" kept these "unfortunate people" in a "continuous inflamed state of mind." After the August dispute, most workers returned, but in October, the strikers "compelled the local welfare commission to resign." Other disturbances occurred in Detroit, Pontiac, Hamtramck, Dearborn, Ludington, and Flint, in many cases instigated by the CP-dominated Revolutionary Workers Protective Association.[20]

Of particular interest is the Party's work in Flint, where the shadow of General Motors loomed large over a depressed community. Here, as in Detroit, the Socialist Party was present, though in modest numbers, while the CP showed signs of significant growth. The Socialists did maintain a large chapter of the League for Industrial Democracy in 1934, but were somewhat handicapped by the intellectualism of the Norman Thomas wing of the Party, which in the words of SP activist Genora Dollinger, "had little understanding of the actual working man." More organized than the Socialists or the left-wing splinter parties, the CP assumed leadership of the city's unemployed movement in 1934. Communist leader William Weinstone claimed a Party membership of three hundred in Flint at this time, a somewhat inflated number. Among them was Charles Killinger, who would eventually emerge as the most active CP unemployed organizer in the community. While the AFL set up a "complaint committee" for the jobless, its limited services were available primarily to those who "belong to the family of the AFL." The Flint Federation's major interest lay in setting prevailing wage levels, upon which even skilled unionists disagreed. In the words of FERA fieldworker Louisa Wilson, "the divergence of opinion among the small fry of the AFL" was "enough to make one's head ache."[21] Only the Flint Unemployed Council seemed to have the relief workers' broad concerns in mind.

Wilson's November report to Harry Hopkins revealed a clear understanding of the political forces at work among the unemployed in this open shop company town, where workers were "hard babies" in their attitude towards relief as a right. Not only were they willing to demand relief, but their use of organization to advance the interests of the jobless was sophisticated. Unemployed Council leader Robert Young told the FERA investigator that his group, "looking realistically on relief as a program to stay, was fighting for more and better relief." The oldest and strongest of the two major jobless organizations (the other was the Socialist Workers Alliance), the Council represented relief clients considered by industry "not acceptable" as recipients. Despite CP influence, Wilson believed Council members were "motivated little by Communism" beyond their insistence on "mass treatment" to avoid being "reduced to a peon class."[22]

Flint welfare workers also reported that the Unemployed Council was becoming powerful, its strength "clinched" in November 1934, when it protested successfully against a proposed cut in relief payments. Impressed by the result, demoralized relief workers became convinced that "the biggest hollerer gets it," which led them to use community pressure through the Council. Complementing the 300-member Unemployed Council, a second jobless group pursued self-help activities and practiced the politics of the "unity front against possible cuts." Although their leadership was "feeble," Wilson concluded that they too, were "creating sentiment." No longer apologetic about relief, the Flint "unemployables" were "beginning to show a little strength."[23]

So assertive had the Flint unemployed become by November 1934 that they began to fight within the AFL for the rights of the jobless. Working through Federal Labor Union 18512, Communist organizer Charles Killinger now attacked AFL policy as "negligent" in efforts to "safeguard the welfare" of unemployed union members. Convinced that aiding the jobless would increase AFL membership, Killinger warned the Flint Federation not to "shirk [its] duty" to unemployed union members or "forget those who are struggling against odds for a mere existence."[24] Killinger's Buick local called for a relief conference to address the problems of laid-off workers. Their demand was one more indication of rising pressure against the labor establishment from a restive rank-and-file.

Comparable militance surfaced in Hamtramck in response to the relief cuts of 1934. In April, a relief strike organized by the local Painters Club yielded increased work hours, though wages remained stable. Hamtramck was reportedly a "hotbed of Communism," according to Louisa Wilson. Perhaps more to the point was her observation that a politically conscious Polish population was "extremely demanding" and willing to "use the local Unemployed Council more vehemently than is true in most other districts of Detroit." With nearly half the population on relief, many Hamtramck Poles had undergone a radicalization process in the early Depression years, which strengthened the local unemployed movement considerably. Hence, in December 1934, when CP section organizer George Kristalsky appeared in Hamtramck to discuss the concept of unemployment insurance, he was met by an enthusiastic throng of seven hundred, which promptly endorsed the Workers Unemployment Insurance Bill.[25]

Out of economic despair came a new wave of worker militancy and community organizing in Hamtramck. These efforts produced an aggressive Unemployed Council and the militantly leftish Peoples League. The League demanded increased relief, union wages on the public projects, prohibition of labor spies, and an end to racial, ethnic, and religious discrimination in the administration of relief programs. Moreover, the jobless demonstrations gave rise to the Housewives League to Fight the High Cost of Living, which was led by Mary Zuk, the wife of an unemployed auto worker. In July 1935, a series of demonstrations protested excessive food prices and set the stage for a larger movement that matured into an organized meat boycott. With strong support in Hamtramck's Polish neighborhoods, the demonstrations and boycott became more and more confrontational when housewives and butchers clashed over price-gouging. Although the boycott failed to permanently alter meat prices, it launched an important political career with Zuk's election to the city council in 1936. The important supporting role of the Unemployed Council also provides an excellent example of the interplay between the many peoples' issues that sustained the Left. Moreover, a sharpened political consciousness in the Polish community revealed the importance of radicalized European ethnic groups to the unemployed movement and the Communist party base in the Detroit area.[26] And finally, the meat strike, including the leadership provided by the militant women of Hamtramck, demonstrated the extent to which unemployment and its consequences were family issues that galvanized workers across gender lines.

The heightened militancy of 1934–1935 was especially intense in the Copper Country of the UP, where resentment smoldered over management control of the public relief apparatus. In Hancock, for example, relief recipients reported to the Quincy Mine to collect their checks, a symbolic ritual which reinforced the fears that had forestalled the development of unionism for so long. Yet not all workers bowed to the pressure. In 1934, angry relief workers confronted relief administrator Herman Rahn in his Calumet office, where a verbal confrontation occurred before the protesters were forcibly removed. More significant was the two-week relief strike of June 1934, when 220 workers closed down the Laurium airport project. Led by CP organizer Richard Hirvonen of Houghton County, the militants demanded better commodity distribution, higher relief payments, and an end to discrimination among FERA clients by the authorities. After halting work on the project, the dissidents clashed with police, who arrested eight demonstrators, including four strike leaders, on dubious charges of "intimidating the workers."[27]

In July 1934, five of the demonstrators were found guilty as charged. However, in September, Timber Workers Union legal counsel Henry Paull succeeded in having the convictions overturned on appeal. While the cases would not stand, the legal vendetta carried out by public officials was characteristic of the repressive practices commonplace in the Copper Country. In a moment of candor, a Michigan State Police investigator who later reported on these events admitted that the case was dismissed "it seems for lack of evidence."[28] By this time, of course, the incident was long-forgotten and the strike had been broken.

Elsewhere in the UP, radicals remained vigilant in their critique of the New Deal relief program. From the May Day conference and celebration in Ironwood to the Iron County Welfare Relief Workers Union protest of October 1934, unemployed workers worked collectively to improve wages and working conditions for relief workers.[29] The common thread that united the unemployed of the north with their comrades throughout the state was an insistence upon prevailing wages and a commitment to organization as the key to the realization of their goals.

As the new year approached, unemployed organizing had undergone important changes. Both Communists and Socialists perceived a new vitality and diversity in the movement. Looking to the future, S. L. Devin of the Socialist *Unemployed News Service* predicted that before long, the competing unemployed organizations would unite to create one national federation. Concerned over a possible fragmentation in unemployed activity, the Communist Party also edged towards cooperation. Confronted by CWA unions, Relief Workers Unions, State Workers Alliances, the Chicago and New York Workers Committees, the National Unemployed Leagues, and more-activist trade unions, the CP concluded that there existed a stable national membership base of 200,000 jobless workers who should not become the object of divisive competition. To Communist analysts, the Unemployment Councils (the renamed Unemployed Councils) remained strong. In truth, however, diversity had meant competition, and several organizations had presented a strong challenge to the Councils' early leadership of the organized unemployed. Accelerated organizational activity had resulted in a marked increase in militant relief struggles and project strikes from thirty in 1933 to seventy-six in 1934. Not only had new groups entered the field, but pressure from below had forced the major organizations to react. The result was tentative movement, beginning in 1934, towards unity or at least affiliation among existing bodies.[30]

The first stage in this unity movement culminated in the establishment of the Workers Alliance at a major national convention in March 1935. Formed in Washington, D.C., under Socialist auspices, the Alliance united 400,000 unemployed workers from eighteen states in a "permanent non-partisan federation" that included most of the large unemployed organizations in the United States. Its original program advocated immediate improvements for project workers and government action on long-range solutions to the problem of unemployment. Asserting in a rhetorical flourish that the "master class" was "attempting to use the depression to permanently reduce the standards of living of the unemployed," the new organization pledged a "fight for the abundance possible in this, the richest country in the world."[31]

While leaders of the established non-Communist unemployed organizations had cemented their ties in order to prevent excessive competition, they had also been drawn together by their common interests. Of these, none was more significant than their endorsement of unemployment insurance, which Alliance activists shared with not only the CP Unemployment Councils but also the AFL. The cresting wave of support for the insurance concept so evident by 1935 virtually ensured that one of the foundation stones of the welfare state would soon be laid.

A critical impediment to the enactment of unemployment insurance legislation had been removed in late 1932 when the AFL national convention had moved to endorse compulsory unemployment insurance. Bowing to irresistable rank-and-file pressure, Green worked to draft a plan for state implementation that would protect unionists and the "American standard of living," as an alternative to an "impossible Communist plan." In Detroit, the Federation acknowledged this reversal of position as necessary to "prevent the rajahs of industry from casting their employees out in the cold at the whim and caprice of indifferent and duty-dodging employers."[32]

With the dragon of voluntarism slain, the basic issue became the nature of the insurance plan to be implemented. By 1934, the focal point for discussion was the legislation proposed by New York senator Robert F. Wagner and Maryland representative David J. Lewis, a bill that incorporated a federal payroll tax that might be offset by a tax credit for employers in states in which state taxes funded suitable unemployment insurance programs. The Wagner-Lewis Bill thus preserved state prerogatives in accordance with the tradition of American federalism, while alleviating Green's fears of centralized control. It was the Wagner-Lewis tax offset plan that in June 1934 drew the endorsement of the United Automobile Workers Federal Labor Unions at their first national conference in Detroit. In part because Roosevelt preferred a comprehensive approach to the entire problem of old age dependency and unemployment, the Wagner-Lewis Bill failed to pass during the Seventy-third Congress. After the legislation died in the House Ways and Means Committee, unemployment insurance fell within the purview of a new presidentially appointed Committee on Economic Security, which drafted the legislation that eventually emerged as the Social Security Act of 1935.[33]

In the meantime, however, pressure also built for the more radical Workers Unemployment Insurance Bill (H.R. 7598), endorsed by the CP and sponsored in Congress by Minnesota Farmer-Labor representative Ernest Lundeen. Although the Lundeen Bill drew only lukewarm congressional backing, its strong rank-and-file support helped shape the debate that ended in the creation of the American unemployment insurance system. The substantial popular interest in the CP alternative ensured that a lively controversy would develop over a plan labeled "impossible" by the AFL hierarchy. Heading the leftist forces was the AFL Rank and File Committee for Unemployment Insurance, the guerilla organization that since 1932 had spoken for dissidents inside the house of labor.

In Detroit, Martel did all within his power to squelch union support for the radical measure. Despite his attempt to scuttle an organizational meeting in November 1933, maverick locals such as the Plasterers persisted in bucking the Federation leaders. The outcome was a statewide conference, headed by Earl Reno of the struggling Unemployed Councils, that united forces drawn from AWU, AFL, IWW, MESA, the Michigan Rank and File Committee, and the Councils. Their deliberations resulted in the delegation of sixty representatives to lobby the state legislature for relief measures. And in February 1934, Michigan was well represented at the Washington conference on unemployment insurance.[34]

The focus of the escalating drive for legislation was H.R. 7598, introduced by Lundeen in February 1934 at the urging of CP unemployed leader Herbert Benjamin. Its authorship has been variously attributed to Benjamin, Mary Van Kleeck of the Russell Sage Foundation, and the Communist Party. Whatever its origins, it is clear that the CP was the driving force behind the bill. Despite the Michigan AFL's reservations, in April eight AFL locals broke ranks to back the measure, including the Painters, Railroad Carmen, Bakers, Flint Patternmakers, Plumbers, Bellmen, and Retail Drug Clerks. Combined with the support of MESA, the Unemployment Councils, the International Workers Order, and the remnants of AWU, these DFL defections reflected growing impatience even among craft unionists over the insurance issue. The expanding consensus on the left became evident when the national Musteite and Socialist unemployed groups embraced the Lundeen Bill. All of which failed to move Martel, who dismissed the growing AFL Unemployment Insurance lobby as nothing more than a "Communist group," whose missionary work for the Lundeen Bill was part of its plans for "causing disturbances in the labor movement."[35] Communist-dominated it was, but supporters of the Lundeen Bill pursued goals that transcended the promotion of sectarianism, and their increasing success was socially significant.

Bucking the AFL's "reactionary leadership," the Michigan Rank and File Committee, led by R. M. Kroon of the Painters Union, challenged Detroit unionists to support the Lundeen Bill's basic principles in September 1934. Easily able to move the Painters (organizational home of national Rank and File Committee leader Louis Weinstock), Kroon faced formidable opposition in the DFL. The grass-roots pressure escalated in September, when a national meeting of the Rank and File Committee convened in Detroit to prepare for the AFL convention. Broadly representative, with fifty-two delegates from steel, auto, rubber, building trades, and other industries, the body adopted a sweeping program grounded on an endorsement of the Lundeen Bill. As chairman of the Detroit Committee, Kroon was an open target for the DFL leadership. The result was his expulsion from the AFL as a Communist. An alternative view prevailed within the Rank and File Committee, which hailed its martyr as a "progressive fighter against the machine in the central body."[36]

Undaunted, Kroon moved in November 1934 to stage a city wide conference on relief and unemployment insurance, which claimed to represent 20,000 workers in 38 unions, 10 unemployed leagues, and 46 fraternal and social organizations. The meeting resulted in the adoption of a set of demands for increased welfare benefits to the jobless, subsequently presented to the Wayne County Relief Commission. Rebuffed by Relief Commissioner John Ballenger, the body laid plans for a mass demonstration on behalf of the unemployed, as well as a planning meeting to prepare for the upcoming Washington Conference for Unemployment and Social Insurance. As part of a concentrated effort to promote H.R. 7598, the unions in attendance also voted to bring their program before the DFL for its endorsement, though such a result was unlikely to occur. Finally, in a move that anticipated future trends in union concern for the jobless, delegates urged all locals represented to form unemployed committees to advance the interests and meet the needs of their own unemployed members.[37]

Alarmed by the growth of grass-roots worker support for more aggressive policies on relief and unemployment, Martel responded with Red-baiting attacks on Kroon and the entire conference, clothed in expressions of dissatisfaction over their alleged misrepresentation of union sponsorship. By December 1934, however, there were signs that Martel's "slanderous campaigns" had begun to lose effect. When the DFL leader confronted conference planners in the Central Labor Union, he met stiff resistance to his effort to kill an endorsement of the conference results. Guided by Green's attack on the upcoming Washington Congress for Unemployment and Social Insurance, Martel limited discussion and squelched the endorsement resolution. The *Daily Worker* reported disagreement with Martel's position, including the dissent of one thirty-year DFL veteran, who asserted that "although I am not a Communist, I am wholeheartedly in favor of the work of the Conference and National Congress."[38]

The veteran unionist identified the DFL's central problem: the velocity of events and changing opinions had left them behind, awash in a sea of outdated assumptions. So it was that when the rebel conferees reassembled for a follow-up meeting at Danish Brotherhood Hall on December 10, thirteen AFL locals sent delegates, a clear signal to the CLU that the Federation's obstructionism on the unemployment issue had run its course. The militants launched plans for a major demonstration to protest the latest round of relief cuts imposed by the Wayne County Relief Commission, and in defiance of Martel, took steps to recruit a Michigan delegation of two hundred to the Washington Conference scheduled for January 1935. By 1935, then, the united front seemed to be taking shape in Michigan.

And although the center of activity was clearly Wayne County, echoes of the unity movement could be heard in areas as distant as the UP. At the same approximate moment as the dramatic events occurred in Detroit, the Unity Alliance cooperatives approached the Central Cooperative Wholesale with an offer of a united front on unemployment insurance. Despite a rebuff from non-Communist leaders, the leftists reported some success at the grass roots. Ignoring resistance from cooperative officials, some rank-and-file cooperators organized united fronts and claimed success over the heads of the CCW leadership.[39]

The popular pressure crested in January 1935 with a major national demonstration to support the Lundeen Bill. Among the groups endorsing the legislation were MESA; AWU; Railway Carmen; Machinists; Mine, Mill and Smelter Workers; the rebel AFL unions; and a large number of ethnic and fraternal organizations. Predictably, the urban southeast and chronically depressed UP were well represented. Moreover, some Michigan leaders played prominent roles in the Washington deliberations, including John Pace, J. F. Chapman, and Richard Kroon, all of Detroit. Each assumed important subcommittee responsibilities, and Pace spoke for the Unemployment Councils in attacking several unemployment compensation schemes then under discussion, especially Green's proposal for federally subsidized state programs. The repercussions from the increasingly divisive national debate reverberated within the Michigan labor movement. In February 1935, the recalcitrant Kalamazoo Federation of Labor broke ranks to urge the Michigan Federation to endorse the legislation (now H.R. 2827) at the MFL state convention in Lansing. Although the state Federation followed AFL national policy to kill the resolution, the necessity for internal debate revealed a division of opinion among Michigan craft unions on the controversial issue of unemployment insurance. Rank-and-file enthusiasm for Lundeen was strong, but Benjamin later acknowledged that the bill was essentially a bargaining chip containing "higher demands than what the administration or the Congress would be willing to grant."[40]

It had long been clear that Roosevelt would insist on a comprehensive social insurance program. Since June 1934 the Committee on Economic Security had labored to draft recommendations for a wide-ranging social welfare system, which was to include unemployment insurance. The result of these deliberations was a conservative plan for a federal-state system that omitted mandatory national benefit standards. By January 1935 these principles had been incorporated into a weakened Wagner-Lewis Bill that became the basis for the Social Security Act. There can be no doubt that the work of the Committee on Economic Security was the key to the legislative enactment of an unemployment insurance program, in that the conservative approach was best-designed to survive in Congress in 1935.

While the Wagner-Lewis Bill and a conservative legislative strategy made sense given the political context in 1935, the National Congress for Social and Unemployment Insurance and the Lundeen Bill were important in creating the pressure that ensured the enactment of at least the modest unemployment provisions of the Social Security Act of 1935. Much to the surprise of administration managers, the House Labor Committee reported the Lundeen Bill favorably on May 15, which indicated that a radical unemployment insurance plan was not without Congressional support. However, Roosevelt had read the mood of Congress accurately, and the Wagner-Lewis Bill became law in Summer 1935.[41] Congressional approval of moderate legislation was due in part to mass pressure that spanned the political spectrum within organized labor, yet it is plausible to argue that the Lundeen Bill was a fairly accurate barometer of rank-and-file sentiment on an unemployment insurance program in 1935.

By the time the Social Security law was enacted, the unemployed movement had undergone significant change. In Detroit and southeastern Michigan, the militancy of the early Depression years decreased after the early successes of the Unemployed Councils as advocates for the dispossessed. Gone was the radical potential that had surfaced in the dark days of 1932 when the clash between capital and labor had brought bloodshed in the streets of Dearborn. In September 1934, the Councils were struggling to regain the initiative by focusing on demands for direct relief to unemployed workers. Yet by late 1934, Louisa Wilson could report to Hopkins that the Detroit Unemployed Council was "a very quiet affair" under the leadership of a "very genteel New Yorker." Although most relief families were not actively involved in the Council, Wilson concluded that "it influences relief policy." The gradual integration of the Council's activities into the structure of the nascent welfare state was evident in its chairman's remark to a local relief administrator: "Don't tell me your back is against the wall because you have no funds. Your back is turned the wrong way. Why don't you help me get more money from Mr. Hopkins?"[42] Even the Councils looked to Washington.

Their perspective was understandable in view of political, social, and economic trends, for in 1935 the state closed ranks with the corporate community to establish a social welfare system that sustained marginal men and women and dulled the edge of radicalism. While it had fought for more comprehensive federal legislation, the unemployed movement was essentially a partner in this process. While the Social Security Act had set the welfare state's foundation, moreover, another important dimension of New Deal policy was expressed through the Works Progress Administration, which was to provide employment of last resort for one-third of the nation's jobless between 1935 and 1942.

Understanding the impact of WPA is essential to an analysis of the Michigan unemployed movement's second phase, since the new agency had significant ramifications for both worker self-image and the future of the unemployed organizations. Crucial to a renewed organizational drive was the extension of FERA/CWA assumptions concerning workers' rights. WPA employees regarded themselves not as relief clients, but rather as government workers. A corollary assumption held that, as employees, they enjoyed the same privileges as workers in the private sector, including collective bargaining guarantees. In turn, unemployed organizations and eventually industrial unions came to perceive them in a similar light.[43] Any interpretation of unemployed activity in Michigan after 1935 must begin with an awareness of these attitudes.

Since 1934, there had been a splintering of unemployed organizations, as a myriad of new groups entered the field. Once the Unemployment Councils had lost ground, they were forced to compete with the Unemployed Leagues, Workers Committees, CWA unions, Workers Alliance, and even the formerly distant AFL. Of these, the most important was the Workers Alliance, which grew rapidly as a national organization after the formal federation of state unemployed groups took place. By late 1935, the National Unemployed Leagues were engaged in unity negotiations with the growing Workers Alliance. Like the Alliance Socialists, the Musteites saw the need to close ranks with organized labor.[44]

As early as 1934, new organizations had challenged the CP for control of the Michigan movement, even in the Party stronghold of

Detroit. Among the local activists were members of the Unemployed Leagues, Workers Alliance, and the Proletarian Party. Only the Alliance held potential for significant growth, in part due to an increasingly serious commitment from the Socialists. In some respects, little had changed within the Michigan Socialist Party since the failures of the early 1930s. Weak organizationally, rent by factionalism, and effectively checkmated by more disciplined Communist organizations, the SP had languished. Even party members acknowledged weakness in a state that in the words of Clarence Senior "had been closed to us for a good many years." With a party membership of 537 in 1933, the Michigan SP ranked ninth in size among parties in eleven major industrial states. As late as June 1935, activist Alan Strachan, struggling to organize SP auto workers, admitted that he had "never seen the party here at such a low level."[45]

Although Strachan thought the Michigan party "hopelessly confused," it had been sufficiently organized to assign him to unemployed organizing in 1934. In an effort to build the fledgling Detroit Workers Alliance, the party notified each branch to contact local non-Communist unemployed organizations to acquaint them with the Alliance and recruit members. In this way, Strachan was able to attract the support of Emil Mazey, who had organized for the Unemployed Citizens League. Detroit-area Socialists made a modest start towards the creation of an effective organization, and the Michigan party enthusiastically endorsed the creation of a nationwide unemployed organization in 1935. However, at this stage of its development, the Michigan Alliance suffered because its organizers were always more interested in the larger problem of building an industrial union in the auto industry.[46]

Nonetheless, the SP began to make headway. At Ford Federal Local 19374, workers unveiled plans in March 1935 to create an independent unemployment committee to aid jobless union members. Using a dues exemption authorized by the UAW, they also intended to recruit unemployed Ford workers into the union. Similar plans were under way in Bay City, where SP members were dissatisfied with the existing organization. Meanwhile, Grand Rapids Socialists made common cause with a changing AFL to create an Unemployed Workers Union, dedicated to the enactment of the Frazier-Lundeen Bill (now H.R. 2827) and the improvement of relief benefits.[47]

The linkage of skilled with unskilled labor reflected a rising interest in cooperation within the national AFL. This collaboration was an early response to the organizational opportunity created by WPA, as well as the appearance of the Workers Alliance as a non-Communist alternative for unemployed organizing. An early indication of the AFL's new departure came when Green informed the Alliance's national chairman, David Lasser, that the Federation would urge locals to work closely with Alliance leaders to "maintain and preserve wage standards, hours, and conditions on public works and public relief projects." One month later the MFL pledged itself to cooperate with the Alliance. Driven by a keen desire to maintain union wage standards on the projects, Green now committed the Federation to the protection of the "interests of both the employed and unemployed."[48]

The AFL's sudden interest in the jobless did produce action on WPA projects. By midsummer, the wage issue resulted in widespread protests, as workers balked at the "security wage" assumption that low pay would encourage the acceptance of private employment. In August, the first convention of the UAW-AFL in Detroit endorsed the prevailing wage concept, expressed solidarity with WPA strikers, and urged that AFL formulate a plan to organize WPA workers into the Federation. Demands for the prevailing wage on government projects poured into Washington from Lansing, Flint, Jackson, Grand Rapids, and Bay City, as unionists and unemployed organizers rallied around hard-won wage levels and traditional work standards. Perhaps most significant was the action of the Michigan Federation. Secretary John Reid bitterly attacked WPA wage policy as a "destructive" guideline likely to end in the "demoralization of the living standards of workers now employed." Reacting to labor pressure throughout the country, Hopkins resolved the issue in September by adjusting hours downward to ensure that monthly earnings on the projects conformed with prevailing wage standards. It was a small victory for the new coalition, but one that was illusory from the project workers' viewpoint, since total employee income remained stable and fiscal problems soon surfaced.[49]

Socialist, AFL, and Alliance activism increasingly overshadowed the state Communist Party, which had lost the initiative in unemployed work. More and more Party attention was devoted to agit-prop, as in an abortive attempt to exploit memories of the Ford

Massacre with mass demonstrations. In Dearborn, CP organizers continued to work on laid-off Ford workers, but were not notably successful. An occasional breakthrough occurred, such as the creation of a project workers union on one of Detroit's large WPA sites. And in Grand Rapids, Socialist unemployed organizer D. B. Hovey, impatient with the AFL connection, temporarily moved towards the CP to support a labor party. A military informant in Grand Rapids simply reported that "open action on the part of the Communists, as Communists, in strikes or any subversive effort is not being resorted to anymore." Meanwhile, the Grand Rapids Federation of Labor was now subsidizing the city unemployed organization as a recruitment measure.[50]

Despite the social vision and enlightened self-interest evident in the Grand Rapids approach, the national AFL held firm to its standing policy, denying charters to project workers unions while opposing the security wage in self-defense. Similarly, the Michigan labor establishment maintained its focus on the wage problem, to the exclusion of organizational activity among the jobless. In retrospect, the Federation's decision to eschew unionization of project workers seems incredibly short-sighted in view of the swirl of grass-roots organizational activity evident in late 1935,[51] a movement that harnessed energies with great potential for union-building and worker solidarity. However, despite the MFL's disinterest in organizing the unemployed, its drive to increase WPA wages found a sympathetic audience within the Workers Alliance and opened the door to cooperation with the Alliance, at least in its formative period.

While the Michigan labor establishment temporized, pressure for the organization of the unemployed built from below. In September and October 1935 the Workers Alliance joined with AFL unions to promote wage increases on the projects. Their collaboration indicated that the needs of the jobless coincided with the interests of skilled workers, in that both supported union wages on the projects. Simultaneously, unemployed workers coalesced in Niles, Menominee County, Bay County, Detroit, and Flint to lay the foundations for what national Alliance leaders hoped would be a powerful new state organization. Stretching Green's April statement of cooperation to its limits, Lasser and the Alliance launched a vigorous campaign to woo AFL support for the jobless groups that were appearing throughout the United States in late 1935. The Alliance pledged support for AFL proposals for the thirty-hour week, union scale, and the abolition of company unions, and called for solidarity in strike situations both on the picket line and at the relief office. Once Lasser had taken the initiative, the Alliance's national secretary Paul A. Rasmussen brought the organizational effort to Detroit in October 1935. In an attempt to capitalize on the Michigan Federation's recent protest against WPA wage policy, Rasmussen worked to arrange a meeting with union and SP officials, including Martel and Strachan. One month later, Rasmussen told John Brophy of the United Mineworkers that he had secured "pledges and indications of real cooperation" from several prominent state unionists, including Martel. Aware of UMW's previous record of interest in the unemployed, the Alliance appealed to Brophy and John L. Lewis for badly needed help. In a reference to the Lewis agenda, Rasmussen assured Brophy that when labor "decides the time is ripe" for the organization of the mass industries, including automobiles, it would "find a powerful and militant mass movement of the unemployed ready and willing to support their employed brothers." In short, Alliance members were *pledged never to scab*."[52]

Despite Rasmussen's exertions, the Workers Alliance grew slowly in Michigan. Part of the reason for this lag in development lay in the absence of a firm Socialist base like that which had sustained the Alliance in other areas, such as Wisconsin, Illinois, and Ohio. In 1935, the Michigan party had not yet developed the labor orientation that was later to be evident in Wayne County Branch 2. Rasmussen later recalled Wayne County Socialism in the pre-UAW era as heavily intellectual, separated by class barriers from workers, welfare recipients, and the unemployed on the projects. He remembered "not one outstanding natural leader among all those white collar neo-liberals, Christian Socialists, and Populists." Although the SP had a "goodly number of trade union functionaries" in MESA, the Machinists, and the Farmers Union, there were "no rank and file leaders" until the early auto unions emerged. All of which made the political and social base for a Socialist-driven unemployed movement in Michigan and Detroit very weak in 1935.[53]

This weakness did not mean that there was an absence of agitation, certainly not in the Detroit area. Other forces were as busy as Rasmussen in October and November 1935, and some were more successful in Wayne County. Anticipating an end to direct federal relief and the shift to WPA employment, Michigan Communists prepared for another battle for the loyalty of the unemployed. Internal party publications exhorted supporters to "get a move on," and several comrades were assigned to full-time unemployed work. Their goal was to perfect the organization of the Project Workers Union while accelerating neighborhood work among those not placed on the projects. Detroit Communists created a "committee for Organization of WPA Workers," which launched an aggressive grass-roots campaign in the city's working-class districts. Meanwhile, the Party worked to revitalize the Unemployed Councils as a vehicle to represent those relief recipients unaffected by the WPA program. While the PWU program rallied project workers in support of the thirty-hour week at 60 cents per hour, community organizers stressed the continuation of direct relief and an ongoing struggle against racial discrimination. Both interest groups worked to improve the unemployment insurance system through enactment of H.R. 2827. When a union organizing committee met to draft demands for WPA workers, charges of Communist initiative were deflected by chairman Richard Harrington, who asserted that politics were irrelevant and that the key issue was "a living wage for all of us irrespective of political or religious affiliation." Harrington, a CP organizer with prior experience in the Unemployed Councils, eventually became the business agent for the PWU. One anonymous informer alleged that both Harrington and the militant Frank Sykes had CP instructions to foment a WPA general strike, and that Sykes had boasted that "if he can't pull these jobs on strike, he will no longer consider himself a good organizer."[54] More to the point, however, was the evolution of unionism as an approach to the ongoing economic and workplace problems of jobless WPA workers. A corollary development entailed an increased emphasis on the relief worker rather than "unemployables," which meant that the Unemployed Councils took a back seat to the new WPA union.

In its formative period, the WPA Project Workers Union extended a hand to Martel and the Detroit Federation by creating its own "committee on friendly relations with the AFL" and suggesting an early meeting with a comparable DFL delegation. For a time, collaboration seemed possible, since the WPA union became Local 830 of the AFL Laborers Union, thereby gaining the support of Detroit AFL organizations. Cooperation peaked in December 1935 when Ed Thal threw the support of the Detroit Building Trades Council behind the demand for union standards, including a WPA wage increase. Endorsing the PWU position before the Detroit Common Council, Thal insisted that the city find a way to supplement the wages permitted by WPA allocations. He later joined Harrington to blast the WPA "policy of transferring and firing men for union activities on WPA projects."[55]

Before long, however, an onslaught of Red-baiting weakened the temporary alliance. Attempting to undercut the workers' position, Commissioner Laurance Lenhardt and Secretary William Walker of the Detroit Department of Public Works charged that Local 830 was "a Communist group of 200 members who are trying to control 20,000 WPA workers in the city." More damaging to the solidarity already achieved was Martel's assertion that union president Frank Sykes was engaged in Communist activities, a claim that, to him, justified withdrawal of the Local 830 charter. Although PWU leaders ridiculed the attack, Sykes saw clearly that Martel's charge threatened to disrupt the fledgling organization. As a result, the black activist withdrew as union president, while promising to "stick by his political convictions and remain active in the union."[56] Despite Sykes' decision, the seeds of discord had been sown, and the PWU was destined to be hampered by identification with CP activism during future struggles.

Red-baiting in Detroit and elsewhere failed to impede the growth of WPA unions throughout Michigan. In Muskegon, for example, nine hundred workers struck in November for prevailing wages and paid transportation to the projects. With the tacit support of the local Building Trades Council, flying squadrons roamed the projects, pulling workers as soon as they arrived. WPA administrators in Michigan discounted the "trouble started by the Unemployed Workers Union" as the work of the IWW, which had also been active in Escanaba and Newberry. After meeting with the Muskegon rebels, State WPA Labor Management Director James G. Bryant counseled officials in Washington against any further publicity for the dissident group since its demands "cannot be satisfied" and compromise would only mean "they would have more demands later on." Similar criticisms of wage policy reached WPA officials from Washtenaw County, Hazel Park, and Jackson. Characteristic of local agency attitudes towards the myriad of organizations that appeared in late 1935 was the reaction of Jackson WPA Director A. W. D. Hall, who complained about "having more or less trouble with the workers in this county due to the activities of agitators who claim to represent the Workers' Protective Union."[57]

There was an element of accuracy in Hall's analysis of the rising discontent in Jackson. A Red Squad observer's report of the CP District 7 Plenum in mid-December confirmed an increase in Party organizational work in outstate areas, including Jackson, Muskegon, Grand Rapids, and Flint. There were three themes in CP reports of progress in the field: first, CP organizers throughout the state had found WPA workers eager for union organization. In addition, an important second dimension of Communist activity entailed collaboration with the AFL. Finally, the Popular Front made a difference. Since Communists were no longer obligated to build their own mass organizations, they felt free to collaborate with Socialists to organize WPA workers on a "united front basis." In every instance, the CP unemployed unions saw obtaining AFL charters as the next step in their development. One leading Detroit Communist predicted that this detente would promote the growth of a new solidarity within the framework of industrial unionism. He asserted that when veterans of the WPA unions reentered the factories they would be prepared to "spread the industrial unionism idea."[58] Here, in an embryonic form, was an idea that was eventually to be translated into action when the UAW became the dominant force on the labor scene in urban Michigan. (See Table 1.)

Table 1   Location of Strikes on Public Employment Projects in Michigan (August 1935–August 1937)

	1935	1936	1937	Total
Delta County	1	0	0	1
Detroit	0	3	5	8
Niles	0	6	0	6
Dowagiac	0	1	0	1
Berrien County	0	2	0	2
Cass County	0	2	0	2
Gogebic County	0	0	2	2
Muskegon County	1	0	0	1
Ottawa County	0	4	1	5
Iron River	0	0	0	0
Bay County	0	1	0	1
Menominee	0	1	0	1
Ludington	0	1	0	1
Flint	0	1	0	1
Mason County	0	1	0	1
Grand Rapids	0	1	0	1
Total:	2	24	8	34

Source: David Ziskind, *One Thousand Strikes of Government Employees* (New York: Columbia University Press, 1940), 138–76.

In the short run, WPA administrators were unresponsive. Moreover, their emphasis on radical agitation revealed little awareness of the social and economic forces that propelled unemployed workers towards collective action. Absent from the administrative reaction to the new WPA unions was any recognition that the substantial support they generated could have reflected legitimate worker grievances and economic needs. In fact, project jobs were often physically demanding and worker grievances justified. Moreover, while some WPA jobs involved socially useful work, makeshift projects were often devised by lackluster administrators. Under these circumstances it was difficult to maintain the employee's creativity and sense of purpose. Given such conditions, labor unrest on the projects is easily understood.[59]

Equally significant as a stimulus to worker militancy was the early success of the WPA unions, particularly Detroit Local 830. As a result of union pressure, WPA state director Harry Lynn Pierson announced wage increases in Detroit and throughout the state. In January 1936 WPA workers received salary hikes ranging from $1

Figure 8   Detroit Women in WPA Training Program, ca 1936 *(Archives of Labor and Urban Affairs, Wayne State University)*

to $9 per month, depending on local prevailing wage levels. Local 830 argued that the percentage of increase from community to community bore a direct relationship to the extent of labor organization in affected localities. While nonunion workers typically received small increases, Detroit WPA employees got 9 percent raises and their brothers and sisters in Jackson and Muskegon saw a 19 percent jump in monthly income. To Local 830 unemployed organizers the message was clear: "It pays to organize."[60]

WPA News, the voice of Local 830, maintained that these victories were just the beginning of the improvements that would result from intensified organizational activity. When workers saw these results, they reportedly "flocked by hundreds" to the union, which by January 15 had grown to 1,200 members. So appealing was the union's message that Detroit police worked to intimidate organizers by confiscating large quantities of the *WPA News* when they attempted to distribute the union paper on the projects. This police action was part of a pattern of petty harassment that included the confiscation of union literature, extinguishing warming fires on the projects, and temporary detention of union leaders. It is clear that local officials disliked the union presence among WPA workers and attributed unrest on the projects to "Communist activities."[61]

Given the escalation of local Red-baiting, the endorsement of the AFL was especially useful to WPA union leaders in Local 830's formative period. This cooperation was perceived by one Detroit Public Schools' observer as "an attempt on the part of the AFL" to "organize the WPA as a member of the AFL." Reporting to his supervisors on a WPA meeting at Cass Technical High School, the informant described a "strong plea" from Frank Martel that WPA workers join the AFL. By February 1936, then, it seemed that progress had been made. With Local 830 recognized as the bargaining agent for project workers, the new union stood poised for a sweeping organizational drive in Wayne County.[62]

The WPA union's apparent success actually produced ambivalence within the DFL, a somewhat uneasy ally since the strikes of 1935. On one front, Martel maintained pressure for prevailing wages on the projects and even urged that WPA workers organize to achieve this goal. Having persuaded Pierson to cut hours but maintain full wages for skilled workers, however, the DFL president downplayed the problems of unskilled workers, reportedly telling the WPA administrator that there were too many men on the projects, where the unskilled were "falling all over each other." Martel's suggestion that "fewer men work fewer hours"[63] placed a strain on the already tense marriage between Local 830 and the Federation.

Further complicating the relationship was the recurrent charge that the Detroit WPA union had fallen under the influence of the Communists, a clear reference to the organizational role played earlier by Frank Sykes, Richard Harrington, and Richard McMahon. Noting that one alleged Communist (Sykes) had been "removed from the scene by the responsible officers of the American Federation of Labor," *Detroit Labor News* insisted that the unemployed union was not part of a CP movement. As late as March 1936, Martel was supporting the AFL endorsement of the Workers Alliance (and by implication its affiliate, Local 830) as a legitimate unemployed organization. At this point, however, the pot began to boil when Local 830 demanded that the deposed Frank Sykes be reinstated, maintaining that the radical activist had lost his WPA job due to union activity. Martel's perspective on the escalating controversy became clear when the DFL representative on the WPA arbitration board called for a new business agent to represent the union, thus attacking Harrington as well. At a special board meeting, the Detroit Building Trades Council, DFL, and Hod Carriers Union presented their own intelligence report on Local 830, which detailed the Communist activities of several members, including Sykes, Harrington, McMahon, James Anderson, Walter Crocker, John Wanot, and Nat Wald. The Hod Carriers spokesman told the board that "the thing has got down to a point where it [Local 830] is so full of Reds we are going to cancel their charter." The AFL delegation also pledged to withdraw sponsorship of the local immediately. Almost overlooked in the bombast over Communist subversion was a revealing acknowledgement of the AFL's limited concern for the unemployed. The Federation's motives were clearly stated in the Hod Carriers' assertion that it "took an interest in this WPA Local" for "only one reason," which was its determination "to keep the rate of wages we had worked years to establish."[64] This remark illustrated the gap that separated labor's insiders from the unskilled and unorganized, as well as the development of an increasingly cordial relationship between the DFL and the administrators of the New Deal labor system.

In contrast, it was unquestionably those on the bottom rail who provided the shock troops of the Workers Alliance and its affiliates in most communities. In Flint, for example, many Alliance members were almost "declassed." In the words of one observer, "they were low. . . . They came through the Depression and they were still in it." In the Alliance's formative period, the Flint AFL still cooperated by providing union halls for unemployed meetings. Under the leadership of Communist Charles Killinger, jobless auto workers "went into the field" to organize the unemployed and "get them moving, get them doing something for themselves." By late January 1936, the Flint Project Workers Union claimed 1,000 members, which, according to the *Daily Worker*, made it the largest labor organization in a nonunion city.[65] A start had been made, but the greatest achievements were yet to come. Not until the 1937 sitdown did the organized unemployed in Flint assert themselves as a social force, when they assumed a supporting role in the establishment of automobile unionism.

Table 2   Strikes on Public Employment Projects in Michigan, (August 1935–August 1937)

Issue	1935	1936	1937	Total
Prevailing Wage Through Reduction in Hours	1	5	2	8
County Reclassification to Higher Rates	1	5	0	6
Wage Increase Beyond Security Wage	0	1	2	3
Hours (Lost time)	0	4	0	4
Weather Protection	0	3	0	3
Free Transportation	0	1	0	1
Pay Roll Delay	0	1	0	1
Change Supervision	0	1	0	1
Union Recognition	0	1	0	1
Miscellaneous	0	2	4	6
Total:	2	24	8	34

Source: David Ziskind, *One Thousand Strikes of Government Employees* (New York: Columbia University Press, 1940) 138–76.

While jobless workers in the General Motors empire moved cautiously, agitation grew rapidly in several western Michigan communities during the winter of 1935–1936. In this period, no outstate unemployed organization was more active than the militant Workers Alliance of America, which was becoming a force to be reckoned with in the Michigan unemployed movement. An early center of activity was the former railroad hub at Niles in the southwestern corner of the state. Paul A. Rasmussen, the Alliance's national organizer, recalled that although the organization was relatively weak at the time, some Kalamazoo Socialists with connections to unemployed activist Mary Fox and the University of Chicago SP group made a start. These jobless groups in southwestern Michigan were responsible for a rise in Alliance work in Niles, Dowagiac, Benton Harbor, and Buchanan. In Niles, Lon Statle assumed responsiblity for spreading the movement throughout the region. Before long, the Niles militants graduated to direct action when two hundred WPA workers stormed the local relief offices and held hostages until assured that their tardy checks would arrive the next day. The national Alliance saw great promise in an affiliate that expanded when its members "took matters into their own hands and won their point."[66]

While Alliance loyalists were "learning that in union there is strength," not all jobless workers rallied to the cause. One recalcitrant project worker endorsed "real labor unions" but rejected the "radical outfit" operating in Niles. His words underscored a formidable obstacle faced by unemployed organizers everywhere: "Do they think that real American men want to strike against the government when our government is trying to make conditions better for us as fast as possible?"[67] In short, the need was great and workers preferred earned income to the dole. The Roosevelt program was undoubtedly a powerful deterrent to the growth of radicalism.

For most project workers, the issue was never ideology. The majority of collective actions centered on bread and butter issues. While modest protests emanated from the western Michigan communities of Jackson and Jonesville, other project workers in Niles, Ludington, and Holland were more aggressive in demanding higher wages. In Ludington, a bitter dispute erupted over the wage scale, ending in a two-week walkout by an estimated 500–900 workers. Although all Mason County projects closed down, a conference with WPA administrators resulted in a return to work. However, hard feelings outlived the strike. Similar dissatisfaction was evident in an Ottawa County demand for a pay classification comparable to neighboring Kent and Muskegon counties. The always active Niles Workers Alliance echoed these demands and pointedly reminded Hopkins that the Democrats would need worker support in the coming election, which made Berrien County's 20,000 Alliance votes important. Although two hundred Niles workers walked out, halting work on four projects, WPA authorities in Lansing did not anticipate "any particular trouble from this group" beyond continued pressure for shorter hours and more money.[68]

Contrary to this cheery forecast, a Michigan WPA internal analysis for March 1936 acknowledged "tension in the labor situation" that was only gradually easing due to prompt payroll management and warmer weather. The agency concluded that the only trouble experienced by the Michigan WPA had been with the Workers Alliance. Despite the Alliance's growing strength, Pierson was confident that his administration could manage the situation. The state administrator's strategy was clear: "through the cooperation of the American Federation of Labor we can control this organization."[69] In short, the Michigan WPA was prepared to make common cause with the labor establishment to curb radical unionism among the unemployed.

The agency's concern mirrored the emergence of the Michigan Workers Alliance as a formidable pressure group. Symptomatic of this trend was an Alliance-sponsored meeting in Lansing, where delegates from statewide unemployed organizations told WPA administrators that more should be done to publicize the right to organization and bargaining on the projects. Agreement was reached on this issue, but no progress was made on wages and hours. Most significant was the dramatic development of a statewide Alliance organization in Michigan, acknowledged within the WPA administration. The new labor situation was noted by WPA administrative aide Frederick Schouman, who wrote:

> While Michigan so far has not experienced any serious or prolonged strikes, WPA unions have been organized in every section of the state, with a definite effort on the part of radical and Communist leaders to gain control of such unions. In Detroit . . . Communist leadership of this organization [Local 830] has been largely eliminated. . . .

In the other industrial cities, however, radical leaders are heading the WPA Unions.[70]

The Lansing meeting revealed a burgeoning popular movement, led by the Left but encompassing a broad reserve army of the dispossessed. Recognizing an opening, the Workers Alliance now assigned the dedicated Ford Thompson of Niles to be state organizer in the erroneous belief that he had been responsible for the recent acceleration of unemployed organizing.[71] While the Niles group had been early on the scene, the expansion of 1935–1936 was more the product of spontaneous action, worker resentment, new opportunity, and radical activity than of missionary work centered in outstate Michigan.

In no region beyond Detroit was the radical initiative more influential than in the far reaches of the Upper Peninsula, where the Left had long dominated unemployed organizing due to the strength of Finnish political culture. Because of the UP's traditional receptivity to collective action, Thompson made it a primary target area for the Workers Alliance's organizational drive of early 1936. The UP unemployed welcomed the Alliance's interest.

A leader in this drive was Carl Raymond Anderson, the central figure in the militant Delta County unemployed movement, which originated during the statewide organizing struggle of late 1935. A CP member since 1934, Anderson took a leading role in the effort to "develop a consciousness of the plight of the unemployed" in the Escanaba-Gladstone area. Noting the AFL's disinterest in the jobless, Anderson helped organize a local Party group and establish the United Workers of Delta County (a Workers Alliance affiliate). For Carl Anderson, the Alliance was the first step in a long career as a labor activist in the Escanaba area. The WPA program was but one week old when his organization lodged its first protest, an attack on favoritism and discrimination in job assignments based on political affiliation. Two weeks later a spontaneous march by the Gladstone Alliance's Women's Auxiliary liberated canned milk and beef from the local relief station, while police stood by without making arrests. The adoption of the direct action approach probably reflected the influence of militant anarcho-syndicalists in the Gladstone group. Their aggressiveness paid off: after nervous relief officials had been held hostage for several hours, food orders were reluctantly issued to the protestors' families. In addition, local WPA authorities agreed to send the demonstration chairman to Lansing for a personal protest to state administrator Pierson.[72]

The waves from Gladstone had barely receded when the new Delta County Workers Alliance launched a protest strike on the Escanaba projects, aimed at the $44 monthly wage. The CP was firm in its support of a strike deemed "absolutely necessary to the welfare of labor in Delta County." Arguing that the walkout would determine the future of labor in the area, the Party's Escanaba Section urged all UP workers to stand with the strikers to "stop the government's wage-slashing program." Alliance leaders were aware of a 10 percent discretionary wage margin available to WPA administrators, but the regional authorities insisted that they lacked authority to further adjust wage levels. Undaunted, the strikers persuaded state senator John Luecke and Congressman Frank Hook, both UP Democrats, to intercede on their behalf. Eventually, some adjustments in hours occurred, and workers won the right to remain off the job when harsh weather conditions made outdoor work a physical challenge. Confronted by the reality of worker militance, the *Marquette Mining Journal* nervously maintained that the revision in work rules was unrelated to the strike. What most alarmed the conservative press was abundant evidence that the Delta County militants were spreading the virus of resistance in Ishpeming, Menominee, and Manistique. The *Mining Journal* warned the WPA administration that such concessions "would be used in other parts of the state to get something of what the WPA workers desired," and that the trend thus set would end in "country-wide chaos."[73]

Although the mass walkout, which idled eight hundred project workers, shook the establishment, the Delta County strike was broken. However, modest gains had been made, and a broader lesson was learned by UP unemployed activists: a single county protest held limited prospects of success. In the wake of the Escanaba struggle, WPA administrators openly conceded that in the event of a concerted union effort in several counties, strikers' demands would have to be considered. Mindful of the advantages in united action, the Gladstone militants offered a defiant parting shot with a vow to "organize every county in Northern Michigan into the Alliance."[74]

Even more active were Gogebic County unemployed organizers, long among the most aggressive in the UP. A key figure in the growth of this group was CP organizer John Wiita, who arrived in Ironwood in November, 1935. Recognizing the limitations of the

Party's near-exclusive Finnish base in the region, Wiita launched an effort to broaden the organization by extending a hand to native-born elements in the population. Central to this effort was the Americanization of the unemployed movement, as well as local Communist Party groups. By organizing an Ironwood discussion group that included Democratic liberals like County Supervisor Raymond Garvey, the Party initiated a highly visible public debate on the economy and the unemployment issue. The Democrat Garvey, regarded by CP activists as an "opportunist," served as an important bridge between radicals and the wider unemployed community. Recalling that the unemployed movement "didn't question your background" but stressed an individual's view of the cause, CP activist Frank Walli asserted that the movement was perfectly willing to use the liberals to build consensus. Hence, once a solid working relationship had been established, Wiita unhesitatingly deployed Garvey as an emissary to the loosely organized jobless groups outside Ironwood. For his part, Garvey used the unemployment question to his personal advantage as the ticket to political success as a local and state legislator. Other local backers of the jobless included Ironwood politicians Ed Marander, Rudolph Anderson, and Lauri Lahti. Although the Finnish Workers Federation continued to dominate Party activities among the unemployed in Iron County, the sophisticated integration of the Gogebic County movement resulted in an extension of radical activity well beyond Finn Hall. To Wiita, this was a great success because it meant the "Americanization of the Party" and "widening its influence among the general public."[75]

In contrast, Finnish influence dominated unemployed activity in Iron, Houghton, and Keweenaw counties. While the Finnish Federation worked to secure relief and transient lodging for unemployed timber workers in the Iron River vicinity, the Workers Alliance soon became the main voice of the Copper Country jobless. Leftist Finns like Richard Hirvonen were among the most active organizers, but only "those Communists that were more diplomatic" served as Alliance leaders. CP organizers often remained in the background and, to avoid publicity, allowed others to function as official contacts with the state Workers Alliance. And not to be overlooked was the role of non-Communist Finns such as Walter Salmi, a key figure in the Toivola Alliance. Salmi's rise to prominence reflected a conscious effort to downplay ideology and stress the common needs of all workers in an area plagued by chronic unemployment. Given this emphasis, it was perfectly reasonable for politically moderate Finns to gravitate towards the organization best equipped to deal with their needs. Another factor in the Copper Country Alliance's growth was the lack of a real union movement in Houghton and Keewenaw counties. In the absence of a miner's union, the Alliance assumed significance as a transitional vehicle on the road to unionism. As such, one of its important contributions was the development of leaders, who often rose from the rank-and-file. In Calumet, for example, CP worker Ed Spiegal later became Alliance President when he simply "went on stage and learned to become a leader."[76]

The entire UP movement gained new life when the CP-liberal coalition in Gogebic County joined forces with Delta County militants to sponsor an area-wide organizational conference at Ironwood. Conscious of the Delta County strike's limited effect, Clyde Berry of the Escanaba Alliance issued a call to "consider WPA problems" and unite all UP WPA employees behind a "uniform program." Setting a tone for the meeting, Garvey and the ad hoc Michigan Workers Committee on Unemployment released a protest of recent increases in hours of employment on WPA projects (without compensatory wage hikes) and demanded that Gogebic County WPA manager S. P. Fitzpatrick rescind the work order. *Workers Alliance* viewed the impending conference and the rapid growth of its UP affiliates as evidence that the Alliance led the "march of the workers." Even more optimistic, Jim Allen of the *Daily Worker* saw both the conference and the recent Delta County strike as harbingers of "discontent and radicalization."[77]

When the conference convened on 11 January 1936, the Democrat Garvey opened the attack with a blast at the "capitalistic gang" that had controlled Ironwood for forty years. Only the "united workers of the Upper Peninsula" could solve problems so long "neglected by the corporation gang in the lower part of the state." Elected conference secretary, Frank Walli argued for higher wages, shorter hours, and a "decent standard of living" on WPA, asserting that if workers "don't put a stop to the treatment we are receiving," then "nobody will." Fired by the rhetorical blast, delegates adopted sweeping demands for an eighty-eight–hour month, increased compensation, supplementary relief, free transportation, and limited work in inclement weather. Despite the sound and fury, federal, state, and local officials refused to grant the workers' demands.

Hopkins' office politely referred Walli to state officials, one of whom had already asserted that there was "no labor trouble in the 6th district."[78]

The deeper meaning of the conference lay not in its public pronouncements but rather in the momentary unity forged from political diversity. Present were 111 delegates from the Communist, Socialist, Democratic, and Farmer-Labor Parties, as well as the IWW, Workers Alliance, Iron County Labor Union, Michigan Workers Committee, and the Mine, Mill and Smelter Workers Union. Claiming to represent 10,000 unemployed workers from eight UP counties, the assemblage was the living embodiment of the recently proclaimed Popular Front that united antifascists of all political stripes. And for a time, the united front seemed close to reality. An apparent consensus marked Walli's final report, which committed delegates to work out a joint program, create a joint committee, and act on conference demands.[79]

Despite the momentary harmony, however, hidden tensions existed from the beginning. Democrats loudly protested the Michigan Farmer-Labor Party's advocacy of a third party, while Socialists brooded over the substantial CP influence at the meeting. Their concerns were well-founded in view of the prominent role played by Walli, John Maki, Matt Savola, and other party operatives. For their part Communists maintained that the interest of unemployed workers mandated cooperation across ideological lines. Socialist Paul Rasmussen, by 1936 the Workers Alliance's national secretary, recalled that the CP was "in full control" of the organizational apparatus at the Ironwood conference. The delegates had fought snowstorms and cold weather to attend the meeting and, according to Rasmussen, the "atmosphere was cold politically." While the CP account stressed cooperation, some Party hard-liners tried to prevent Rasmussen from delivering his own message of unity. Finally gaining the rostrum, he presented the Alliance argument for "united struggles of all WPA workers, independent working class political action, and the possibilities of life in America if all workers were united politically in an effort to gain peace and security for all."[80] Behind the conciliatory words was an awareness that regardless of the Popular Front ideal, a power struggle for the heart of the Alliance was taking shape.

While the leaders of the UP unemployed movement jockeyed for position, the workers' battle went on at the local level. In Iron County, members of the Finnish Federation launched an effort to organize WPA employees, but experienced little success. Still present was a pervasive fear that militance might result in the loss of WPA employment, and only with great difficulty were workers persuaded that they had a right to speak. Yet in many communities, radicals worked with confused and angry citizens to encourage small acts of defiance against a system gone awry. In the Iron River vicinity, leftists were aware of the resistance to evictions that had developed in the urban centers. Hence, when one local widow faced the loss of her home, a determined crowd gathered to aid in resistance to authority. Seizing the moment, CP activist Rachel Kangas told the authorities that if the proceeding went forward, "the people here won't like it." She then threatened to replace items removed and warned that the officials "better leave the furniture in" lest they "have trouble." They never returned, and eventually the property reverted to the family after the state acquired the land for taxes. Sporadic strikes, eviction struggles, and protests also occurred in Marquette, Menominee, and Sault St. Marie,[81] but no action better revealed the radicalizing impact of adversity than the spontaneous resistance of the Iron River rebels.

The clearest organizational expression of the new militance was found in the Workers Alliance of America, which had experienced such rapid growth in Michigan during the winter of 1935–1936. Whether lobbying for the Lundeen Bill, agitating for increased WPA benefits, sponsoring strikes, or promoting demonstrations, the organization spoke forcefully for the jobless. By 1936, WAA had become a pressure group of national stature. While it was the largest unemployed group on the labor scene, in March 1936 it had reached a plateau in its development. Like the Unemployed Councils and Unemployed Leagues, the Alliance had begun to lose some of its most aggressive local leaders, many of whom left the unemployed movement to become organizers for John L. Lewis and the Congress of Industrial Organizations. The CIO, which had recently launched the drive for industrial unionism, sapped the unemployed organizations by depriving them of their most effective grass-roots activists.[82]

Their foothold as the nation's leading unemployed organization secure, President David Lasser and the Alliance leadership now worked to enlarge the organization's power and expand its membership base by absorbing the Unemployment Councils and the National Unemployment League. The Alliance initiative coincided with Benjamin's effort to implement the Councils' desire to perfect a Popular Front with all labor unions and unemployed organizations. Intent on "unifying all the unemployed organizations of the country into one mighty national organization," Benjamin saw an opportunity to revive the sagging Councils in a merger with the expanding Alliance. He noted that for some time the Councils had "followed a policy of merging their local organizations with the Alliances, Leagues, or AWU"[83] in hopes of attracting mass support. As in the case of Detroit Local 830, the process of integration was well under way throughout the state of Michigan.

In plain fact, CP willingness to amalgamate reflected both Popular Front ideology and the declining fortunes of the Unemployment Councils. It is equally true that the rapidly expanding Workers Alliance, under Socialist leadership, had "so outdistanced other unemployed organizations" that by April 1936, when the Alliance, Council, and League met in Washington to create an enlarged Alliance, "absorption of practically every important unemployed group was possible." Under these circumstances, CP labor spokesman Jack Stachel came to the unity meeting to propose the "liquidation of the Councils and their integration into the Workers Alliance." Once the marriage had been consummated, Lasser argued that political ideology should take a back seat to the interests of the unemployed. With a majority on the executive board, non-Communist Alliance leaders were optimistic. Although some Socialists resigned from WAA when the merger took place, most followed Lasser and Rasmussen into the enlarged organization.[84] With Lasser as president and Benjamin as secretary, the new Alliance embodied the Popular Front mentality, which prevailed in the 1930s Left following the Comintern's endorsement of a Communist-Socialist alliance in the fight against fascism.

Alliance growth at the national level accelerated more rapidly than its activity within the state of Michigan, though the advances of 1935–1936 were promising. Detroit Communist Nat Ganley recalled that the unity convention reflected concerted action by Left forces with a "social view" and that both Communists and Left-Socialists "played an important part in cementing this employed-unemployed activity." Michigan delegates to the unity conference, representing both urban and outstate organizations, enthusiastically supported the merger. Compared with other industrial states, however, Michigan was unplowed ground, a "vast new area for the

WAA," where an effective state office remained to be established as a base from which to organize. This analysis was confirmed by Chris Alston, who later asserted that the Alliance was not a predominant force in Detroit, partly because its actions were too often the result of decisions made in New York or Washington by leaders unfamiliar with the community's unique problems and needs. Rasmussen agreed, though his explanation stressed the relative weakness of the SP base and the absence of "natural" working-class leadership as reasons for the original Alliance's stunted growth in Michigan before 1936.[85]

With unity achieved at the national level, the state unemployed movement faced an uncertain future. A promising start had been made, and the pace of organization had quickened in the months before merger created a powerful national pressure group. Yet the progress of the Michigan Workers Alliance was uneven and plagued by uncertainty. Handicapped by a narrow Socialist Party base and weakened by allegations of radicalism, proponents of an effective united front among the jobless confronted still another challenge, as yet only dimly perceived. With the rise of militant unionism, the organized unemployed increasingly competed with another mass movement of greater proportions and immense popularity. Any further successes in Michigan depended upon a strong link with an expanding labor movement. Perfecting that relationship proved a formidable task for all concerned.

5

Finding a Place
The New Unemployed Movement and the Rise of UAW, 1936–1937

B
y spring 1936, the social and economic context for unemployed organizing in Michigan had changed dramatically as
a result of the rapprochement between Socialists, Communists, and even a cautious AFL. Groups which had formerly competed for the loyalties of the jobless were now united as members
or affiliates of an expanded Workers Alliance, which prepared for
a new drive to organize the state's unemployed legions. While the
Alliance remained mindful of the needs of the wider unemployed
community, it focused its attention on the thousands of project
workers who swelled the WPA rolls in 1936.

Not long after the Workers Alliance had swung into action, however, another organizational development began to occupy the attention of Michigan labor activists when the CIO moved to organize the
state's automobile industry. Liberated and empowered by the Wagner
Act's provisions for a government-monitored labor relations system,
CIO operatives soon inaugurated an organizing drive that culminated in the recognition of the United Automobile Workers Union at
General Motors and Chrysler in 1937. The organizational process

that had begun with the AFL's creation of federal unions in 1934 soon evolved into a competitive labor struggle characterized by independent organizing through several unions, including MESA, the Associated Automobile Workers of America (AAWA), Automotive Industrial Workers Association (AIWA), as well as the federal unions. Finally, in 1935 the contending forces merged and created the United Auto Workers (UAW), still under the auspices of an autocratic AFL, whose president, William Green, named Francis Dillon to be the auto workers' first president. At its South Bend convention one year later, a rebellious UAW, in which Communists, Socialists, liberals, and other progressives now cooperated, forced the election of their own chief executive, vice president Homer Martin, former president of the Kansas City local. With this united-front action, the delegates literally took their own union from the AFL hierarchy. Armed with a new international charter, the newborn UAW stood ready to challenge automobile management in the landmark General Motors confrontation of 1936–1937. With CIO support, industrial unionism came to the auto industry.

These events transpired against the background of the emerging Popular Front. After the CP had abandoned dual unionism and embraced Popular Front politics in 1935, it worked to create a united front in both the labor and unemployed movements. During the UAW's formative period, the well-organized Communist faction practiced the politics of self-restraint, most obviously in 1936 when it chose to support Martin for president rather than CP activist Wyndham Mortimer. As a result of CP pragmatism in both UAW and CIO circles, it was possible for progressives within the labor movement to collaborate in the creation and early development of the auto workers union in 1936.[1]

This same element of cooperation was to surface again during the General Motors struggle of 1936–1937. During the pivotal battle at Flint, the unemployed were to emerge as one component of the broad coalition that contributed to the UAW's success. And as the union movement gained impetus throughout the state of Michigan in 1937, the unemployed were consistently found in the camp of organized labor. Thus began a collaboration between employed unionists and jobless workers which was destined to grow into a symbiotic relationship with the ultimate triumph of unionism. For a moment, at least, the CIO took on the characteristics of a social movement and assumed broad community and political functions.

To social activists, the promise of industrial unionism seemed unlimited.

• • •

By late spring 1936, a Michigan WPA analyst confidently reported that while there had been some unrest on the projects, "no labor trouble of any consequence" was then evident. This pause in militant activity masked the quiet organizational work that followed the Workers Alliance national unity meeting. Although AFL national secretary Frank Morrison had pledged cooperation, the Federation had offered little but words of encouragement. The Michigan Alliance harbored continuing suspicion of the AFL, which was expressed in March by Ford Thompson of Niles, who wondered why the Federation would make common cause with unemployed workers when two years earlier they had refused them recognition.[2] As summer approached, there was precious little evidence of organizational progress.

In Detroit, the Alliance scored a modest victory in June, when a project workers' strike ended in increased benefits for single men on relief. An oversimplified report by an FBI informant identified the group as a CP organization composed of the "remnants of the old Communist Unemployed Councils." The observer noted that the Alliance was "in the process of organization in Detroit," and that it already included a "strong branch" in Hamtramck headquartered at the Russian Communist Club and headed by Unemployed Council veteran George Kristalsky. Because it represented non-WPA unemployed workers and welfare recipients, the Detroit Alliance placed special emphasis on increases in direct relief, while its affiliate, Local 830, maintained pressure for improved wages and hours for project workers.[3] (See figure 9.)

For the WPA union, the summer's hottest issue was the prevailing wage. After Hopkins announced in June that all projects would respect the local standard, Local 830 became engaged in a running battle with government administrators over wage levels. In this struggle, the union demanded that prevailing wages be paid on all projects. Local 830 argued that WPA workers were entitled to a thirty-hour week and a monthly income of $72. By August, strike threats filled the air, as business agent Richard McMahon blasted "certain industrialists" and "reactionary elements in the WPA" for

Figure 9 Michigan Workers on the Job Again, June, 1936 *(Harry Lynn Pierson Collection, Bentley Historical Library, University of Michigan)*

resisting federal policy in order to hold down the wage level. Although Hopkins's office agreed to reinvestigate Detroit rates, the local press launched a broad attack on the union position, which the *Detroit News* dismissed as "dangerous nonsense." McMahon retaliated with a public letter defending a 60-cent-per-hour minimum and the right to union organization. Next the defiant workers sent a delegation to Washington to make their case before WPA authorities, simultaneously staging a sitdown strike on the Wayne County projects.[4]

Despite McMahon's audacious gesture, the strike was doomed. Not only was the decision left in the hands of Michigan WPA administrator Harry L. Pierson, but the confrontation also exacerbated simmering tensions between Local 830 and Hod Carriers officials, who repudiated their uncontrollable affiliate. Denouncing McMahon and other "communists and agitators," the Hod Carriers' national president, John W. Garvey, announced that he didn't want his union "dirtied by such people." Unsuccessful in its wage demands and rejected by its AFL parent organization, Local 830 endured a rocky summer. In fact, the abortive walkout was characteristic of a national trend towards WPA strikes in 1936. Detroit alone experienced at least seven such stoppages in a fourteen-month period in 1936–1937.[5]

Despite the failed protest, the Workers Alliance (in Detroit, an umbrella organization that encompassed Local 830) found reason for optimism in the summer's events. After a Washington conference between a national Alliance delegation and WPA assistant administrator Aubrey Williams, the Alliance gained formal recognition as bargaining agent for WPA workers in Detroit and a few other cities. Herbert Benjamin considered this decision an important breakthrough for the unemployed movement, which no longer consisted of "loose groups that come together like a fire brigade when some emergency arises." In late 1936 he reported to the CP national convention that in Detroit the administration had been "compelled to recognize" the Workers Alliance's job stewards as representatives of project workers. Benjamin saw in this advance an important step in the movement, as the Alliances emerged "like trade union instruments for collective bargaining."[6] In short, workers perceived unemployed organizations as unions, and now government recognition reinforced their perception.

Outside Detroit, organizational activity in southern Michigan lagged in the spring and summer months. Several strikes occurred, some of them centering on charges of WPA discrimination against Alliance members for union activities in such places as Niles and Jackson, but none was of major consequence. Not surprisingly, therefore, Lasser's report to the WAA national executive board in

September spoke of Michigan in terms of unrealized potential rather than the reality of growth. Even in Detroit, the FBI's watchdog concluded that "nothing important has been accomplished yet." Finally, in October 1936, no less an authority than Herbert Benjamin candidly admitted to CP officials that the Party's unemployed work in Michigan was "weak."[7]

With the exception of Detroit, the main hot spot for unemployed agitation was the UP, where dismal economic conditions fueled the fires of discontent. For the jobless, the first priority was the wage level on WPA projects. When the MFL journeyed north to Escanaba for its July convention, it brought with it an endorsement of prevailing wages, to be achieved, if need be, by a reduction in working hours on the projects. This message was small comfort to the militant UP unemployed organizations, which by August 1936 were again focusing on the problem of substandard wages. The renewed agitation originated in Houghton and Keweenaw counties, where unemployment was severe and the CP was strong. In September 1936, the Copper Country Workers Alliance, headed by James Myers of Calumet, tested the limits with a sweeping demand for increased wages, reduced hours, and union recognition. While concessions were not made, WPA officials did agree to discuss the wage rate in the context of the UP prevailing wage. The endorsement of the Houghton County Board of Supervisors notwithstanding, state and local administrators were powerless to increase wage levels set by federal regulations.[8]

The Copper Country demands paralleled the position taken by an eight-county UP workers' delegation that met in Iron Mountain with district WPA officials on August 31. After consultation with state administrators, the existing $44 per month wage was reaffirmed, the rate established by a cutback in hours. Misreading federal policy, diehard Alliance supporters in Iron River rejected the new policy, and requested a federal investigation of the Sixth District administration, which it insisted was "in gross violation of the rules and regulations." They were no more successful than their Copper Country counterparts. The response from Washington was courteous but clear: prevailing wages would remain in effect though monthly income could not be raised.[9] In effect, the MFL's position had been reaffirmed.

The controversy over compensation for WPA workers made it inevitable that New Deal public works programs and labor policies would become issues in the 1936 campaign. Since 1935, Roosevelt had presided over the first stage of a revolutionary change in both the labor relations system and federal welfare and relief policy. The administration's success in securing a $5 billion appropriation for emergency relief, including the establishment of WPA as employer of last resort, had already had a profound impact on workers, who had begun to accept the idea that public employment constituted legitimate work. This in turn led many relief workers to the principle of union organization. Even more profound in their impact were the Wagner Act's bold guarantee of collective bargaining rights and the National Labor Relations Board's emergence as the administrative mechanism that policed the collectively bargaining state. As a result of these momentous changes, American workers had streamed into the unions in record numbers. But as the labor movement extended its reach, tension between craft union leaders and the proponents of the new industrial unionism had brought an end to internal harmony within the house of labor. By November 1936, the dynamic CIO stood ready to engage corporate leadership in the major mass industries, including auto. Just as conservatives decried the banishment of voluntarism and the onset of government paternalism, traditional craft unionists looked askance at the onrush of industrial unionism.

The widening rift in the labor movement spilled over into the politics of the unemployed movement in September 1936, when Lasser asked Green and Lewis to state their positions with regard to organizing the unemployed and protecting their interests. Green's reply emphasized efforts to raise WPA wages to prevailing levels, a matter of deep interest to the AFL. He also pledged to support the Alliance's efforts to achieve that goal. Lewis made a similar commitment, but went further to promise an effort to guarantee jobs to the unemployed as "a matter of elementary justice." More to the point, the CIO leader endorsed organization and collective bargaining for WPA workers under the protection of the law. Lewis praised the Workers Alliance for presenting solidarity in its refusal to scab and pledged UMW support in the fight for more WPA jobs at a living wage.[10] It is clear from this response that Lewis and the CIO regarded unemployed organizing as one important dimension of the accelerating drive to organize the unorganized that was the product of the Wagner Act. It is also evident that Lewis and Green were maneuvering for position as they established their working relationships with the Workers Alliance.

Given the imminent disruption of the labor movement and the brutal shocks that had shattered traditional conceptions of the individual's relationship to the activist state, it was a foregone conclusion that the Roosevelt policies would become the subject of acrimonious political debate during the election campaign. In Michigan, the WPA program and Republican charges of favoritism and cronyism in relief administration were staple items of political discourse in 1936. In Detroit, for example, Democratic gubernatorial candidate Frank Murphy made an open campaign pitch to an audience of 2,500, more than half of them WPA workers. Attacking the "reactionary" press, Murphy warned his enthusiastic audience against anti–New Deal propaganda spawned by wealthy citizens who objected to taxation that supported "those less well off." Meanwhile, in the UP, Democratic congressman Frank Hook came under attack for alleged coercion of WPA workers. Bordering on demagoguery, he blasted lumber interests for subsidizing his GOP opponent, attorney John B. Bennett, then making the first of several congressional runs that featured heavy criticism of the New Deal and its job programs. Supporting the challenger's charges, the Houghton *Daily Mining Gazette* insisted that politics "does enter into the administration of relief." Apparently oblivious to the views of an electorate dependent on WPA and sympathetic to Hook, the *Gazette* attacked the Roosevelt administration's relief program as a "national scandal" that had created a "shameless political machine."[11] Hook was reelected handily, with the strong support of the public charges so despised by the Republican establishment.

In the wake of the Roosevelt landslide, the Michigan Workers Alliance rededicated itself to an intensive organizational campaign. Meeting in Jackson, the state executive board elected Glenn McCoy of Ludington to the position of state organizer and vowed to extend the Alliance throughout the state. In December, organizer "Hoot" Rasmussen of the Indiana Alliance warned his Michigan friends of threatened WPA cutbacks. He insisted that only strong organization could counteract the persistent attacks on WPA from business groups. Agree as they might, the hard fact was that despite much fanfare, the Michigan Alliance was no stronger than it had been the previous summer, and its organizational campaign had not advanced beyond the planning stage since the Washington unity meeting. Other factors, primarily an expanding labor movement, had absorbed the attention of militants on the left in Michigan.[12]

While acknowledging Alliance weakness in Michigan, Benjamin remained optimistic about "very significant progress" in the national organization's relationship with organized labor. Citing recent statements by Green and the *Federationist*, he reported that the AFL was moving towards greater concern and support for the jobless. Even more significant (and especially important for the Michigan movement) was John L. Lewis's strong interest in closer ties with the Workers Alliance. Lewis was determined that the CIO provide more effective support to WPA unions than had been forthcoming from the Hod Carriers, who had denounced Detroit Local 830 in its formative period. Despite this danger signal, Lasser urged cooperation with the Hod Carriers, though he was adamant in maintaining Alliance organizing activities where the two groups competed.[13]

By 1937, however, the Hod Carriers were virtually irrelevant as an organizing force among the Michigan unemployed. In Detroit, the Workers Alliance had emerged as the voice and advocate of jobless workers on the projects and was prepared to serve as lobbyist for WPA employees at the national level. When the Seventy-fifth Congress convened in January 1937, one of its first agenda items was the consideration of a deficiency appropriation for both direct and work relief programs. At the behest of national WAA leaders, state Alliances agreed to march on Washington in a protest against possible congressional cutbacks in WPA funding. On 8 January 1937, four hundred Wayne County WPA workers crowded into a meeting at Detroit's Cass Technical High School to select five local delegates for the Washington "conference against WPA retrenchment." The Wayne County delegation, like the organization they represented, was racially integrated and gender mixed. It was also heavily Communist in composition, if the reports of the Detroit Red Squad can be believed.[14]

Joining the DFL and the American Federation of Government Employees to resist WPA reductions, McMahon and Local 830 persisted in their demands for an expanded federal job program that would meet the needs of all those seeking work. Meanwhile, at the local level both the WPA union and its parent organization, the Wayne County Workers Alliance, confronted a major challenge when in March 1937 welfare mothers on the Health Survey Project faced layoffs without adequate compensatory benefits from other programs. In response to the arbitrary cutback, survey workers staged a sitdown strike at WPA headquarters that paralyzed the administration of Detroit-area projects. The sitdown produced an immediate protest from the Alliance and the union. Before long both the UAW and the AFL had also endorsed the protest, thus exhibiting momentary solidarity on the issue of unemployment. The outcry eventually produced the desired result when 215 women were restored to their original positions with the understanding that dismissals would not occur unless other benefits covered the workers involved. By its resolute action, the Alliance had demonstrated a commitment to jobless women, thus recognizing that unemployment was a problem affecting all workers, regardless of gender. Forced to admit the soundness of the strikers' position, the *Detroit News* lamented the bad precedent set, "under which any group of public employees" was "invited to manifest its disagreement with government policies by refusing to let the Government function."[15]

Out of the turmoil came an impressive display of solidarity. Not to be outdone by the DFL's cooperation with the strikers, UAW supplied two hundred picketers on the scene; later, the auto union's district council endorsed Local 830's full slate of demands. McMahon reciprocated with a promise that his members would "always be ready to help them [auto strikers] in picketing and fighting for a better wage." These unity pledges did not go unnoticed. On several occasions, Detroit Red Squad watchdogs observed McMahon's professions of solidarity, including his militant vow that the jobless would "fight like hell" for the UAW.[16]

McMahon's words reflected the development of a collaborative relationship between the jobless and the nascent auto workers' union that had begun with the landmark strikes of 1936–1937. An advanced concept of solidarity also owed much to the influence of radicals, both Socialist and Communist, on the origins of UAW. The idea of coalition between employed and unemployed workers had long been expressed by Communists. Always an article of faith for CP activists, the concept of class solidarity grounded on a union base assumed new meaning in the wake of the CIO organizing drives that began in 1936. In short, the unemployed movement, industrial unionism, and community organization were all part of a new social and economic configuration in which class interests promised to prevail over the forces of division and disruption.

Many Socialists shared this sweeping interpretation of worker solidarity and the unifying potential of unionism. Disillusioned with the historic tradition of "business unionism," Socialist activists embraced a definition of the union as an extended social family. Accordingly, Socialist union organizers like the socially conscious Reuthers were determined to forge an alliance with unemployed workers. Acting on the conviction that a union was a social institution as well as an economic body, they dedicated themselves to the creation of an inclusive organization that cared for the needs of its members in all circumstances, including joblessness.[17]

The conception of the union as a comprehensive social institution was much more highly developed among the younger, militant wing of the party that centered in SP Branch 2. Whereas Detroit Branch 1 was dominated by the intellectuals and Christian Socialists, Branch 2 expressed the perspective of labor and was composed of workers and their spokesmen, activists who worked to create a vibrant union that encompassed all aspects of workers' lives and ministered to their human needs. Among the prominent members of the labor wing of the Michigan Socialist Party were the Reuthers, Ben Fischer, Emil Mazey, George Edwards, Bob Kantor, Leonard Woodcock, Genora (Johnson) Dollinger, and Alan and Stuart Strachan. Their mission was to create a labor movement imbued with Socialist ideas. Each worker community—Pontiac, Detroit, Jackson, Flint, and Lansing—contained a distinct Socialist community with its own internal dynamics, union culture, and political culture. What united them was a vision of the union as a social organism that incorporated men, women, families, employed workers, and their jobless peers, all of whom claimed the right to survive socially and economically. Because of its commitment to both industrial unionism and the protection of the unemployed, the CIO was their natural home. And no Michigan union interjected itself into the worker community it served more forcefully than did the UAW, which became a powerful instrument for the advancement of the labor Socialists' agenda.[18]

In late 1936 the new concept of unionism as a social force was put to the test. During the Motor Products strike of 1936, labor activists vigorously protested the WPA policy of hiring strikers for the projects as coercion and official strikebreaking. Arguing that thousands of other unemployed could not get WPA jobs, MESA secretary Matthew Smith attacked the policy of forcing strikers off the picket line by denying them relief if they refused WPA appointments. Despite union complaints, administrators denied that WPA was taking sides, and the policy remained a problem for the striking

workers and the union. One response was Frank Martel's cooperation with UAW in the establishment of a joint relief committee to
distribute supplies and provisions to Motor Products strikers. His
goals were to aid strikers and spike the allegation that "CIO is a
'dual outfit' . . . bent on destroying the American Federation of Labor."
Sensitized to the relief issue, the UAW Socialists were ready for
unemployed problems in December 1936 when the Kelsey-Hayes
strike began. The Reuthers and their supporters responded by
developing a union mechanism for delivering assistance to strikers
and the unemployed. Inspired by a sharpened union consciousness,
many jobless workers cooperated by joining the picket lines "because they saw their future well-being related to the struggle to
build the union." In turn, the union adopted a policy that advocated unemployed rights as fundamental human rights.[19]

Meanwhile, in Flint a movement was building that provided
another opportunity to build bridges between employed and unemployed workers. When the nascent UAW took aim at GM, it
dispatched one of its most dedicated activists, International Vice
President Wyndham Mortimer, to Flint as leader of the organizing drive. After deferring to Homer Martin in the presidential
contest as part of the CP's Popular Front peace effort within the
union movement, Mortimer moved on to Flint in June 1936 to
initiate preparations for a strike. In selecting Mortimer for the
job, the UAW executive board had chosen the union's leading
proponent of class struggle in the contest with auto management.
Equally significant was the decision to send Robert Travis to Flint
as part of the same effort. Travis, a veteran of the Toledo Autolite
strike, shared Mortimer's leftist sentiments and was prepared for
a class appeal. The presence of Travis and Mortimer in Flint
reflected the reality that CP organizers possessed the skills and
experience needed in the CIO's drive to organize the unorganized.
Moreover, Travis brought with him prior experience that had
demonstrated that collaboration between the employed and the
unemployed could pay dividends in strike situations. During the
Autolite strike of 1934, the unemployed had been active participants on the picket line, as Musteites and Communists had closed
ranks to support the walkout.[20] Travis and Mortimer came to
Flint prepared to mobilize the jobless as an element in the overall
plan to organize GM.

When Mortimer arrived in Flint, he found willing supporters
among the unemployed. Since the inauguration of WPA, the Flint

Unemployed Workers' Association and later the Workers Alliance and its Hod Carriers affiliate had agitated for the rights of the city's jobless. By most accounts "conscious union-building fellows" who would never scab, the organized unemployed played an important role in the Flint drama. Led by unemployed CP member Charles Killinger, who later headed the Hod Carriers Union, members of the Workers Alliance aided Mortimer in plant organization by identifying union sympathizers. Killinger's Communist ties earned him the enmity of both GM and his local union. Fired by Buick for political activities and blacklisted in Flint, Killinger "had names in every plant," a list which proved valuable to Mortimer in the early stages of the campaign. In addition, he organized sixty jobless Alliance members for a literature and newspaper distribution effort that ensured wide dissemination of union news. Finally, Killinger's group organized the unemployed for picket-line duty. As a result, scab labor never presented a serious problem during the climactic struggle for power and recognition. On the contrary, Killinger and his unemployed group were among the most militant unionists on the line. At the legendary Battle of Bulls Run, for example, they joined workers from Fisher No. 1 and Toledo in fighting the police with bottles and rocks. By April 1937, the WPA union had become so influential that WPA district director Harry Loudon preferred not to antagonize its members "because of the strength" of the group, which was "very troublesome when aroused." To Killinger, the concept of solidarity in crisis was one of the major goals of the unemployed movement.[21]

Another link with jobless workers was forged by Roy Reuther, who had worked in the Flint FERA Workers Education Program. Union activists were convinced that the Workers Education Program could be a force for intelligent, committed unionism and disciplined membership. In one case, for example, a union education chairman argued that the program had been a "training ground for most of the present leadership" of the local. Similarly, President Homer Martin believed that the program had "made history" as workers had been "trained in the principles of unionism." Of immediate significance for Roy Reuther were the contacts with union-oriented workers provided by the program. As city workers education supervisor, he had developed ties with the old Federal Labor Union members, many of them potential UAW recruits. Like Mortimer and Travis with local Communists, the popular Reuther was able to expand Socialist contacts among Flint's most militant auto workers.[22]

Although Socialists were to play an important part in the sit-down, the evidence suggests that because of their small but effective mass base, the CP was an equally significant force in carrying out the strike. Flint Socialist Hy Fish, who headed the Michigan SP, acknowledged that his party entered the picture somewhat late in the game. Nonetheless, many Socialists, including Roy and Victor Reuther, Genora and Kermit Johnson, and Powers Hapgood, were prominent strike leaders, and the Flint Socialists identified with the SP's working-class wing. Moreover, as Fish later asserted, "the work that was done even in the last week or two . . . laid the foundation for the Socialist caucus, the Socialist Auto League."[23] The League not only became a base from which the SP later contested the Communist position, but it also played an important role in the eventual UAW organization of WPA workers.

In the short run, however, the strike raised other questions for temporarily jobless workers. Since November 1936 the unemployed had grappled with an unresponsive and sometimes hostile relief system and welfare bureaucracy. Part and parcel of the repressive atmosphere in Flint during the company-town era was an intrusive paternalism presided over by the Genessee County Emergency Relief administrators. One controversial practice was the local Relief Commission's pressure on the unemployed to accept loans from local employers before applying for relief. And in November 1936 UAW organizers complained that the authorities were administering a questionnaire that dealt with unemployed workers' political views and attitudes towards labor unions and sharing responses with the General Motors Employment Offices. UAW activists Bud Simon, Walter Moore, and Charles Killinger told the La Follette Civil Liberties Committee that unemployed workers were suspicious of the "close relations" between the Relief Commission and the factories because the commission's client records were "part of the blacklisting system employed" in Flint. When the *United Automobile Worker* repeated the charges, state relief administrator William Haber vigorously denied any wrongdoing. However, under union pressure, the offensive procedure was abandoned.[24]

Once the strike began, the relief situation became even more important in view of the increased burden placed upon strikers and their families. On one front, an ad hoc committee solicited food from sympathetic local farmers. In Roy Reuther's words, "we mooched." Another approach was to demand public relief. In December 1936, Michigan CP district organizer William Weinstone emphasized the union's responsibility to actively assist in securing welfare benefits for members. And although he believed that the strike would have succeeded without public assistance, Roy Reuther later recalled that under Haber's leadership, the situation was "not bad." In fact, the UAW exerted heavy pressure on Governor Murphy, who was persuaded to order the Flint Relief Commission to certify strikers for relief. From the beginning, the UAW's welfare committee was "in conference with relief administrators." As the strike wore on, however, tensions increased and the committee became more assertive in seeking preferential treatment for union members; so much so that the welfare office had to declare a policy of equal treatment for clients without preference to strikers. As a result, *Survey* could report that the union committee "showed willingness to accept established routine," while the welfare office exerted itself to "correct mistakes."[25]

Despite the civility, UAW grumbled about the slowness of the intake process. Once again, the leading figure in unemployed activity was the veteran CP organizer Charles Killinger, who served as chairman of the UAW Welfare Committee. To Killinger fell the task of demanding preference for strikers in the relief lines. Supported by strike leader Bob Travis, Killinger urged that striking workers be rushed through the intake procedure to permit their early return to the picket lines. Recognizing that Killinger's committee had "a great deal of influence," the Emergency Welfare Relief Commission asked that relief requests be confined to cases of real need and that the union maintain close cooperation with welfare authorities. Commission field representative Ella Lee Cowgill reported that cooperation from the UAW Welfare Committee was "very much in evidence" and that client attitudes had been constructive and "understanding."[26]

Though its significance was not well understood at the time, the emergence of the UAW Welfare Committee as a militant force for the jobless was one of the critical innovations of the strike. For unemployed unionists, it was crucial. Because of the union's responsible management of member needs and collaborative work with relief authorities, UAW gained credibility not only with the rank-and-file but also with the state bureaucracy. The symbiotic relationship with relief officials that gradually developed during the tense days of January provided a model for the long-term development of the UAW welfare committee as a tool for serving jobless union members. By May 1937, Detroit's innovative west side Local 174 had moved to institutionalize its own welfare committee as its major means for meeting the relief needs of the membership,[27] thus providing the entering wedge in what would eventually develop into a spirited UAW–Workers Alliance contest for the loyalties of the unemployed.

The leadership provided by Local 174 was the product of both necessity and the social vision of Walter Reuther and the west side Social Democrats, whose concept of unionism transcended a restricted collective bargaining model of union responsibilities. Offended by AFL callousness towards the unemployed, Reuther was determined to address "any problem that confronted working people" and "to provide some sort of strike relief." Driven by an image of the union as a social movement, he demonstrated "a great interest in keeping the unemployed members close to the union." Finally, it is clear that the goal of solidarity in strike situations was crucial: Reuther saw that by organizing the unemployed, UAW would be able to neutralize scab labor, strengthen its position, and convert the jobless to the cause of unionism.[28]

To labor journalist Joe Brown, a perceptive reporter for *Federated Press,* the strikes of 1936 were the catalyst that induced UAW to move towards the establishment of a "permanent welfare setup" within the union that separated its activities from the efforts of a "multiplicity of welfare-bound groups." Among the important functions of the committees was agitation at local welfare offices on a massive scale. UAW welfare committees negotiated with government agencies, and the union exerted pressure to get its members certified on welfare rolls. The ombudsman role was crucial in the creation of a permanent bond between jobless auto workers and their union. Union activities included organizational lobbying to protect the union member's property, automobile, and furniture through pressure for extended time payments. By exerting these pressures, the UAW was often successful in preventing foreclosures and winning extensions for the unemployed unionist. Strongest in Detroit, Flint, and southeastern Michigan, the UAW welfare committees played a role for UAW members comparable to that assumed earlier by the Workers Alliance and Unemployed Councils, which provided a model adopted by the union. Given the predominance of the automobile industry in the Michigan economy and the strength of the UAW, it was inevitable that the union would come to dominate the state's unemployed movement.[29]

Although human distress was an important factor in the creation of plant and local welfare committees, Victor Reuther later acknowledged the fact that "large pools of unemployed workers" that might be exploited as scab labor "constituted a threat" that the union could not ignore. Aware of danger in the army of the unemployed, the Local 174 committee consciously worked towards unity. According to Local 174's welfare director Harold Hartley:

> The Committee mobilized members for active strike duty during strikes, for demonstrations, parades, etc. In addition, many leaflets were distributed by the thousands to the unemployed on vital questions affecting them. This propaganda and agitation served to enlighten the unemployed inside and outside the union on the tasks ahead of them and served to strengthen the solidarity of unemployed with employed workers.[30]

The source was new, but the rhetoric of solidarity differed little from the conceptual framework established by the Unemployed Councils in the darkest days of the Hoover years. This connection was not entirely coincidental, since Hartley's personal history in the unemployed movement reached back to his Wisconsin years as state secretary of the Unemployment Council in Milwaukee.[31] His work with the Welfare Committee was also a natural extension of a strong commitment to the Popular Front, which had led him to a leadership position in the Wayne County Workers Alliance prior to his work with Local 174. In short, Hartley had a record of participation in CP organizations, and was at the least a supporter of Party causes.

The origins of an early Wayne County collaboration between UAW and the Alliance may be traced to the welfare crisis in Detroit during the sitdown strikes. Because welfare investigators were handicapped by incomplete information which could be supplied by the union, the Detroit Department of Public Welfare agreed that the UAW might serve as a certifying agency. The Local 174 *GM Conveyor* asserted during the Cadillac strike that "this victory was possible only through the fighting stand of the strikers' Welfare Committee, the solidarity of the Workers Alliance, and the delegation of strikers." The united front was a natural extension of a cooperative agreement between the Alliance and UAW engineered by union organizational director Richard Frankensteen, who had received WAA assurances that its members would refuse to scab in Wayne County auto strikes.[32]

Complementing UAW pressure on the certification issue, in January 1937 both Hartley and the Workers Alliance launched a campaign to win increased relief allowances from Commissioner G. R. Harris and the Welfare Commission. Thus, the broader unemployed movement and the unionized jobless drew closer in the face of common adversity. Although the Alliance received only courteous assurances that its demands would be considered and relief clients serviced on a case by case basis, UAW fared better. The union induced the Welfare Commission to allow direct certification by the UAW Welfare Committees. Harris nervously asserted that this innovation should be considered an emergency measure to handle a burgeoning case load. Although he claimed that strikers were not receiving special consideration, Harris's actions conveyed an alternative message: in hopes of reducing tensions in strike-bound Detroit, the union had been admitted to a participatory role in municipal policy decisions. The right to certify union members for relief benefits implied direct access to authority and a place in the Wayne County power structure.[33] The Detroit decision also foreshadowed the direction soon to be taken by the unemployed movement throughout southeastern Michigan, as the union movement swept over the urban landscape.

During this transitional period in 1937, efforts to forge a close link between UAW and WAA members persisted. There is evidence that the Alliance and the union cooperated to prevent deliveries on the projects in trucks owned by struck firms. And employing a technique used by the auto workers' welfare committees and the old Unemployed Councils, the Workers Alliance also launched sitdown strikes at welfare offices. Calling for solidarity, the Wayne County Alliance reminded UAW workers that "the organized unemployed have aided in the building of unions" and that the labor movement now had "an opportunity to help the unemployed" by supporting the relief strikes.[34] UAW and WAA thus edged closer to a firm solidarity that would soon make both groups more effective lobbyists for the unemployed.

An important aspect of this trend was the developing link between the Workers Alliance of America and the expanding CIO. As early as October 1936, Benjamin had apprised his CP associates of a warm relationship between Alliance leaders and John L. Lewis, who was assumed to be anxious to promote close cooperation. In turn, CIO pointedly reminded the 1937 WAA convention of its own dedication to "the goal of economic security for all working people." Within the Alliance, moreover, strong sentiment existed for a direct tie with the burgeoning industrial union movement. While the WAA Organization Committee acknowledged that cooperation with all labor organizations best served the interests of the jobless, it bent to pressure from the ranks with a recommendation that the incoming executive board develop plans for the "closest possible association with the CIO."[35]

While WAA officials thus attempted to skirt direct involvement in labor's escalating civil war, the UAW moved aggressively to attack the problem of unemployment in southeastern Michigan. As labor activism accelerated with the spread of the sitdowns in 1937, the CIO conscripted many of the seasoned organizers trained in the unemployed movement. A prime example, very significant for the organization of the Wayne County jobless, was the fate of Harold Hartley, who in May 1937 signed on with Local 174 as welfare director. For Hartley, the transition from the Workers Alliance to UAW represented a natural progression that mirrored the gradual evolution of the Detroit-area unemployed movement. Once the Local 174 Welfare Committee was firmly established, the union succeeded in building effective committees in all union plants both inside and beyond the west side local. Pledged to "work in cooperation with the Workers Alliance," Local 174 next urged all UAW and other CIO locals to build comparable committees to process grievances, negotiate with relief officials, and lobby with state and local agencies, administrators, and legislators on behalf of the unemployed. These efforts to expand the scope of union welfare activity culminated in the creation of a citywide General Welfare Council, representing Detroit's UAW, CIO, WAA, and some AFL locals. Through this instrument unionists worked to assist union members and other relief clients in combatting the humiliation and obstructionism often encountered at welfare offices. Especially important was an educational function. It was necessary to promote among auto workers a consciousness of an "inherent right to work" before they would "fight against the miserable relief standards and methods of relief officials." To Hartley, education was the prerequisite for the development of militance: workers could be organized for demonstrations without difficulty, but sustained committee work and steady pressure at relief stations required a "higher degree of union consciousness." He maintained that the union's welfare committee had developed slowly because "only the more developed union members availed themselves of [its] services."[36]

Other committee functions included demonstrations, picket line duty, agitation for the single unemployed, pressure-group activity in support of relief and WPA appropriations, and eventually active organization of WPA workers. Since early 1937, Local 174 had held regular meetings for unemployed members and cooperated in planning WAA meetings. These gatherings later became a "recruiting ground for the WPA Auxiliary," which in April 1938 became the UAW mechanism for organizing project workers. Moreover, the Welfare Committee used the meetings to mobilize the jobless during strikes and thus cement worker solidarity.[37]

Committed to the unemployed movement, Hartley threw himself into his new job. Sounding a prophetic warning against imminent layoffs, he argued in June 1937 that "another unemployment crisis may not be far off," a threat that made the establishment of plant, local, and city committees essential. Echoing the rhetoric of the west side Socialists, Hartley insisted that "to keep our union solidified and strong, we must defend the standards of living of the unemployed members." Radical rhetoric aside, other analyses departed from his view of the committee's work. Community organizer Chris Alston later maintained that a rapidly bureaucratizing UAW often failed to aid the unemployed with the solution of their immediate problems, and was particularly neglectful of the unaffiliated. Alston recalled that union officials sometimes became removed from the jobless and their everyday problems, especially after UAW Welfare Department leaders were integrated into the organizational hierarchy. And a cynical *Detroit Free Press* saw "quite a harvest" for UAW "reaped at the expense of the people of the United States" who were "forced contributors to the support of their union."[38] In some sense, all were correct. More importantly, in differing ways, the remarks of each attested to the close link that had developed between the UAW and the unemployed by summer 1937.

The union's remarkable growth in 1937 was itself an extension of feverish CIO organizational activity. Most veterans of the CIO's organizing drives recall this period as one of extensive, intense, and sometimes chaotic activism. Partly as a result of Roosevelt's active encouragement, including the license granted by the terms of the Wagner Act, industrial unions grew dramatically. In Detroit alone, there were 130 sitdowns in auto factories, retail establishments, and small shops in spring and summer 1937. Socialist organizer Ben Fischer caught the temper of the times when he recalled that workers were ready to organize and they came to join the CIO: in this environment, "an organizer was somebody who knew how to get a hall, pencils, and cards, and bring them to the hall." In Michigan, this collective spirit expressed itself in the rapid expansion of UAW. Although the union failed to organize Ford in its first attempt, Chrysler and GM yielded to the on-rush of industrial unionism. By the end of 1937, nearly 300,000 auto workers had signed union cards, and UAW's future seemed assured.[39] And unemployed workers had lent support to union organizers who had shown interest in their needs during this remarkable period of growth.

The deepening relationship between employed and unemployed workers found expression in the issues emphasized by UAW in 1937. Not the least of these was the insecurity endemic in the seasonal cycle of the automobile industry. Except for highly skilled specialists, Michigan's auto workers were constantly haunted by a lack of job security. As noted in chapter 1, this insecurity had become clear in the 1920s. By 1936, an estimated 90 percent of auto industry employees could expect layoffs at some time during the year, with no guarantee that the same job would be available at the time of rehiring. Chronic insecurity was an important factor in the union's decision to emphasize the thirty-hour week and a guaranteed annual wage in both the GM and Chrysler strikes of 1937. UAW research director William Munger argued in March 1937 that without a price increase, the technologically sophisticated auto industry could realize productivity increases that would permit a guaranteed wage sufficient to enable employees "to master some of the workers' own financial problems."[40] The overriding union objective was to stabilize employment and to annualize income in what had historically been a chaotic industry with an unpredictable employment picture.

On another front, UAW played a role in the origins of the rent strike movement of 1937. The union's interest in the housing issue and rent control reflected the same impulse towards community organizing that had given rise to union involvement in the unemployed movement. The housing problem was an outgrowth of depressed conditions in Detroit, including joblessness, evictions, homelessness, and a shortage of living units. Because of their peculiar vulnerability, unemployed renters were severely affected by the housing crisis. As a result of this crisis, community activists launched the Detroit Renters' and Consumers' League in an effort to aid those workers most squeezed by Depression conditions in the housing market.[41]

Responding to the initiative of the Pontiac local, the union's Detroit District Council moved in June 1937 to create a Tenants and Consumers' Committee. Under the chairmanship of Mort Furay, a UAW organizer also active in Labor's Non-Partisan League, the committee was designed to protest the escalating Detroit area rent scale. Real estate profiteers drew a bevy of criticism at a mass meeting held at Cass Technical High School, where Furay warned the "rent gougers" that they would no longer be permitted to "profit at the workers' expense." Helen Goldman of the UAW Woman's Auxiliary angrily denounced the "greedy landlords" for trying to neutralize the raises won in the hard-fought sitdown strikes. Other speakers, including Walter Reuther, Reverend Horace White, Mary Zuk, and Richard McMahon, echoed these sentiments and pledged solidarity with the Pontiac resistance. Despite an early legal setback with the conviction of one rent striker for illegal possession of property, the Detroit Renters and Consumers' League compiled a list of "fair" and "unfair" landlords and instructed members to withhold rent payments not sanctioned by the organization. RCL also mobilized flying squadrons to protest evictions and replace furniture in worker homes in defiance of local constables. By mid-June, the Pontiac militants claimed that a stabilization in area rents had occurred due to the strike, an assertion confirmed by several local landlords' groups. And Furay later claimed "some degree of success in restraining the landlords," though it took public housing to remove the pressure on renters.[42]

The League, though the product of UAW initiative, was a prototype of the united front organization. Combining UAW, CP, SP, and Polish and black community groups, it remained militant not only in ongoing tenant struggles, but also as a voice for the unemployed of the Detroit area. Active in Hamtramck's Polish community was CP organizer Mary Zuk. *Detroit Saturday Night* noted that her work in RCL was a "natural step" from her leadership of the meat strike movement. As RCL developed, however, black workers on the east side assumed a larger role in its affairs, especially after CP activist Merrill Work and the Consolidated Tenants League opted for affiliation. The organization served the union's needs as a tool for activating previously unorganized workers, and was especially effective in establishing a UAW presence in the black community. Communists, meanwhile, also found RCL helpful in advancing their goals. To Merrill Work, for example, action on the housing problem had become the CP's "principal means of reaching Ford workers." The union's commitment to the League was underscored by Victor Reuther's pledge of support from 300,000 UAW workers. Reflecting Socialist strength on the west side, Local 174 voted in September to affiliate with RCL and "cooperate in every way possible in the drive to enlist our members in the organization." While *Detroit Saturday Night* regarded the organization as the "offspring" of UAW, the Detroit Red Squad observers stressed CP influence.[43] This alignment matched the ongoing collaboration between Socialists and Communists in the UAW's Unity Caucus in 1937.

Cooperation was also evident in the revival of the long-standing campaign to organize Ford, an effort in which the unemployed were soon to play a central role. In January 1937, UAW vice-president Wyndham Mortimer had fired the union's first shot in the war over unemployment at River Rouge by blasting Ford Motor Company for massive layoffs, which he argued had created a "serious social problem" for Hopkins and the WPA. Asking for an investigation of Ford's ability to retain these workers, Mortimer charged that "this rugged individualist [Ford] creates 40,000 ragged individuals." At the same approximate moment, the Local 174 Welfare Committee began organizing regular meetings for unemployed union members at Ford, aimed not only at halting evictions and increasing relief assistance, but also at building morale and promoting social cohesion among the jobless. An important dimension of this work involved collaboration with the Workers Alliance to rally the Dearborn unemployed. According to Hartley, the combined activities in Dearborn were the first open meetings held in that Ford stronghold in several years.[44]

Joint action by the UAW and the Alliance reflected intensified united front activity by Communists and Socialists in the Detroit unemployed movement. When UAW shifted its attention to Ford following the GM and Chrysler sitdowns, the only union members at Ford were Communists organized by CP activist Bill McKie and a smaller group of workers organized by Local 174. Because of mass layoffs, the unemployed, especially WPA workers, became important in the early stages of union activity at Ford. Many Ford workers, including a large number of blacks, gained their first organizing experience on the projects, where Local 830 and the Alliance held sway in early 1937. Subsequently, CP members were crucial in the mobilization of the Ford jobless, and unemployed workers played a pivotal role in the grass-roots organizing that got under way in 1937. Dedicated to building the union, the Alliance provided the names of its most militant WPA stewards to UAW. In addition, unemployed Ford workers were aggressive in persuading their friends at the plants to join the UAW.[45]

As a byproduct of the union's increasing concentration on the jobless, UAW began to strengthen its link with workers long regarded as "outsiders," especially blacks and women. Many of the women on the Detroit sewing projects were laid-off Ford workers at Highland Park, while a disproportionate number of the Dearborn/west side unemployed were black employees. (See figure 10.) And it is significant that Paul Kirk, the UAW's first black organizer, had been a leader in the unemployed movement and maintained a working relationship with the Workers Alliance. Both blacks and women were introduced to the principles of unionism through WPA organizers, and these new recruits formed the nucleus of the Ford local that emerged after the WPA cutbacks of 1937–1938.[46]

The individual who linked the unemployed with the UAW during the Ford drive of 1937 was undoubtedly Paul Kirk. A native of Alabama, Kirk had joined the union in 1936 and been elected recording secretary of the half-black Local 281 at Michigan Steel Casting. By the time of his appointment in April 1937 as UAW's first paid black organizer, he had also become deeply involved in the activities of the leftish National Negro Congress, which enjoyed the covert support of John L. Lewis and the CIO. Together with such Unemployed Council veterans as William Nowell, Walter Hardin, and Joseph Billups, Kirk became a powerful force in UAW's increasingly vigorous effort to attract black workers to the union. However, because of his CP ties, Kirk incurred the wrath of the increasingly suspicious anti-Communist Homer Martin, and was eased out of the organizing staff by late 1937.

Figure 10   A WPA Sewing Project in Detroit, ca 1936 *(Archives of Labor and Urban Affairs, Wayne State University)*

Before his departure, Kirk was instrumental in planning a conference on black-union relationships that embodied the spirit of the Popular Front. The meeting also provided ample evidence of close collaboration between UAW organizers, unemployed organizations, and the NNC. At least one observer, the Reverend Horace White, saw it as a UAW-CIO initiative. Cosponsors included the NNC, Workers Alliance, WPA Union, and International Workers Order. Panel sessions emphasized the benefits of union membership for black Ford workers, as well as the necessity for interracial solidarity as a prerequisite for the development of industrial democracy in America.[47] The problems of the unemployed also received extensive attention, and their role as potential subverters of the Ford order was implied throughout the deliberations.

By autumn 1937, therefore, a promising start had been made at Ford. Recognizing the potential for long-term union growth, UAW had turned to the unemployed worker as an important wedge that might help pry open the Ford gate. Looking to the future, the UAW recognized that "many of these people were not yet in the union, and if you could organize them on the projects, then when they did get a job they would be acquainted with the union and be members of the union."[48] In short, both the Welfare Committee and Workers Alliance functioned as a training ground for unionism. Out of the labor struggles of 1937 came a sharpened awareness of the jobless as a new weapon in the battle to establish UAW hegemony throughout the auto industry. Equally significant was the close cooperation of UAW and the Workers Alliance in the larger task of union-building in southeastern Michigan.

Although the organizational thrust was strongest in the urban centers, unemployed activity also persisted in the remote areas of the Upper Peninsula. By spring 1937 the militance of the sitdowns had rejuvenated the area's Workers Alliance, which in May launched another campaign to raise wages on Region 6 WPA projects. Led by regional president Raymond Rintala and Secretary Frank Walli, the Alliance insisted upon a revision of the district prevailing wage to provide compensation consistent with standards in effect throughout the northern states. Their demands rejected by WPA administrators, UP Alliance leaders staged a mass meeting in Iron Mountain to lay plans for a strike in protest of both wage levels and working conditions described as "terrible." Also at issue were the right to organize and the Workers Alliance bid to become exclusive bargaining agent for WPA workers. Although Alliance stewards were authorized on the projects, authorities refused to grant the organization exclusive bargaining rights or to increase wage levels.[49]

Confronted by unmovable resistance, Rintala, Walli, and CP activist Matt Savola led Alliance workers off the job in a strike that spread into a four-county area encompassing Gogebic, Iron, Houghton, and Dickinson counties, traditional centers of the UP unemployed movement. Reports of the strike's effectiveness varied, but it appears that only Gogebic County workers were able to close the projects. In Iron County some workers struck, while in Dickinson, the movement failed. The strike's success was limited by both the dependent status of WPA employees and the perception that solutions lay outside the district in Washington. The always critical *Marquette Mining Journal* noted that a WPA strike was "no more realistic than a sitdown" and that strikers ran the risk of permanent removal from the rolls "because of the pressure of other men to go on them."[50]

Not all observers agreed. In Gogebic County, where an estimated 800–1,000 strikers had paralyzed WPA projects, the local press candidly reported the Alliance's success. By this time, it was evident that the central issue was the failure to pay prevailing rate, which resulted in an inadequate monthly security wage of $57.00. By 25 July the Alliance could claim significant progress. After a conference in Ironwood with a WPA representative, workers won a higher wage rate, though total monthly wages were not increased. Reflecting the Alliance's view of the result, one Michigan delegate later told the Workers Alliance national convention that the militant Gogebic County Alliance had won the strike.[51]

A parallel movement, linked by many local observers with the Alliance walkout, was the bitter Timber Workers strike that divided UP residents in the spring and summer of 1937. In some respects, the lumberjacks' struggle for union recognition connected UP workers with the aspirations of their brothers and sisters in the urban southeast, then in the process of transforming the state's labor movement. Most notable was the jacks' decision to cast their lot with the rising CIO, thus identifying the cause with the thrust of industrial unionism. Moreover, among the lumber interests they challenged was the timber empire of Henry Ford, the largest operator in the area. Finally, a crucial component of the Timber Workers' new activism was the vital role of the Communist Party, a constant in the statewide unemployed movement, as well.[52]

Several strike leaders and supporters were drawn from the ranks of Workers Alliance militants, including Walli, Savola, Garvey, and Wiita (who, though not an Alliance member, had worked to further unemployed organizing). Thus, the *Marquette Mining Journal* was essentially correct in asserting that "the woods workers strike and the strike of WPA workers tap from the same root." Noting the relationship between the two walkouts, the *Mining Journal* also reported that the Iron and Dickinson County Alliance leaders had "openly identified themselves with the Communist Party."[53]

Perhaps the unemployed movement's most important legacy for the Timber Workers' strike was the leadership provided by one of its number, young Matt Savola. A product of the Finnish working-class experience, Savola joined YCL in 1930 and rose through CP ranks to become section organizer in Iron River in 1937. Blacklisted for organizing miners at the Davidson mine, he soon found himself on WPA, where he worked to build the Workers Alliance.

Employed only eleven days a month on the projects, he "had plenty of time for organization work," which enabled him to establish a reputation for skillful oratory and militant resistance to evictions. As a result, Savola was tapped by Walli and Wiita to assist in the organization of Gogebic County timber workers when the strike broke out. Introduced to the striking lumberjacks, Savola was immediately elected chairman of the Strike Relief Committee,[54] where his experience in the unemployed movement served him and the strikers well.

As the strike wore on, the problem of relief loomed large due to the local authorities' determination to deny strikers access to relief assistance. Under Savola's leadership, the strike relief committee took immediate action, organizing a mass march in Ironwood to demand relief and consolidate the ranks behind the walkout. Complementing Savola's initiative, an old ally of the unemployed, Raymond Garvey, also pledged support for the strikers. Labor insiders recognized that because union strike funds were exhausted, the relief question was "becoming very urgent." With county emergency relief funds low, the increased caseload created severe pressures on an already overburdened welfare system. Responding to the crisis, a UP-wide meeting of Federal Emergency Relief Administration officials decided that preference could not be given strikers. In a solution reminiscent of Flint, they determined that strikers' applications would be investigated according to standing procedure, with relief provided on the basis of need and available funds.[55]

Confronted by government disinterest, Savola and the relief committee fought back on several fronts. As a first step, the union helped workers qualify for relief benefits by aiding in the application process. Moreover, CIO Timber Workers from Duluth provided financial assistance, distributed by the union, which by this time had shifted its affiliation to CIO. Equally important were donations of food from local farmers, whose contributions were channeled through the Workers Alliance. Finally, union members defiantly violated game laws to secure fish and game, so much that in Gogebic County, the sheriff's department gave up on enforcement because the local jail was filled with temporary guests.[56]

Throughout the strike, the union maintained a steady barrage of criticism aimed at the state and local government policy of detachment from the relief crisis. It was not until late August 1937 that food relief was finally granted by Gogebic County, the first such assistance since the strike began. By this time, the assistance was too little, too late; Governor Murphy's inaction and the strikers' vulnerability were important factors in the outcome of the battle. Even after the dust had settled, lumberjacks found themselves in a desperate situation since their transient status often disqualified them for the relief benefits available to more settled workers. By late 1937, Savola and the Timber Workers were again pressuring WPA and FERA to accept "state and federal responsibility to provide relief for the unemployed."[57]

The Timber Workers and Workers Alliance strikes of 1937, linked in the public mind, reflected an extension of union activism well beyond the cradle of the UAW. Both provided evidence of a militancy that reflected the influence of industrial unionism on the labor movement in all areas of the state. From Flint to Ironwood, workers challenged management hegemony as activists on the left harnessed long-suppressed energies on the shop floor and in the lumber camps. And in most places, the sharpened union consciousness grew side by side with a more sophisticated awareness of an identity of interest between employed and unemployed workers. This advanced concept of solidarity found clear expression in frequent collaboration between CIO unions and the Workers Alliance, and sometimes included cross-membership and cooperation between the Alliance and UAW's rapidly expanding Welfare Committees.

During the summer of 1937, the united front in Detroit drew closer as the Alliance and UAW combined to resist WPA layoffs then under way. The immediate stimulus to action was WPA's announcement that 600,000 project workers would be dropped from the rolls on 1 July 1937. In July Richard McMahon of Local 830 and Margaret Riopelle of the Wayne County Workers Alliance called upon UAW to support a major protest parade at WPA headquarters. While McMahon issued a general call for solidarity, Riopelle argued for reciprocity with a pointed reminder that the Alliance had mobilized the jobless during the recent auto and cigarmakers strikes:

> We have taught the unemployed that we are all part of the working class and that what affects one hurts all. Therefore they organize readily to fight for their rights and those of all those who must work for a living.[58]

Responding to the Alliance's appeal, UAW members and leaders endorsed and participated in the mass demonstration. Numerous locals gave support, while international secretary-treasurer George

Addes sent a message of encouragement to the picketers. Among those unionists most prominent on the line were shop stewards from the Cadillac local. The major goal of this protest was to publicize discrimination against Detroit by WPA officials, who had allegedly under-allocated jobs to the Detroit area.[59]

Complementing the local protest, UAW and the Workers Alliance actively lobbied for the Schwellenbach-Allen Bill to prevent WPA dismissals and increase WPA appropriations. On 9 August 1937, Lasser appeared in Detroit to promote the legislation, as well as the Alliance program. He told a Local 830 audience that the Workers Alliance endorsed a permanent WPA and a 30 percent pay increase. When the Alliance organized a national demonstration in Washington to protest the layoffs and support the Schwellenbach-Allen Bill, CIO and AFL unions reportedly subscribed $4,500 to support the Michigan delegation, consisting of marchers from Detroit, Grand Rapids, Jackson, Kalamazoo, Battle Creek, Bay City, and the UP. In Hamtramck, where Mary Zuk led a strong CP element, the city council endorsed the bill and its members contributed $100 to the march fund. Endorsements came in from Governor Murphy, the Timber Workers Union, Central Cooperative Wholesale, Labor's Non-Partisan League, UAW locals, and the Alliance. Following the Washington demonstration, the Local 174 Welfare Committee heard a report that emphasized the need for a renewed commitment to "mobilize the unemployed and the unions in a united struggle to put the unemployed to work and win adequate relief for those who cannot work."[60]

The message was wholly compatible with the west side local's standing program. While McMahon and the militants from Local 830 were engaged in high profile activities, including an August sit-in at Murphy's Lansing office, Hartley, Reuther, and other Local 174 activists immersed themselves in the day-to-day business of serving the union's dislocated members. Particular emphasis was placed on the relief issue, and the union encouraged members to be aggressive in presenting their grievances to Wayne and Oakland County officials. Stressing the importance of continuity in union membership and the availability of a dues exemption for jobless members, Hartley urged unemployed unionists to work through their welfare committees to "win proper aid." The Local 174 Committee warned workers not to "wait until you are dead broke before you apply for welfare." Early action promised to "give the welfare committee a chance" to fight a case, secure food, prevent an eviction, or protect personal possessions. Simultaneously, Local 174 urged all locals to establish welfare and unemployment committees to secure needed "aid for unemployed and needy union members."[61]

Equally significant was the west side joint council's determination that its welfare committee "cooperate with other organizations in their efforts to win adequate state aid for the unemployed." Convinced that a new wave of unemployment was imminent, Local 174 resolved to "support the Workers Alliance of America in its program for an adequate standard of living for the unemployed and WPA workers." Committed to a united front, the joint council directed union welfare committees to collaborate with the Alliance to develop a common program for relief. Moreover, the resolution, which was adopted by the UAW's tumultuous Milwaukee convention in August 1937, urged that the CIO cooperate with the Alliance to hammer out a joint program at the national level.[62] (See figure 11.)

Figure 11   Delegates Confer at the 1937 UAW Convention in Milwaukee, August, 1937 [Left to Right, Richard Frankensteen, Lester Washburn, Walter Reuther, Robert Travis, and George Edwards] *(Archives of Labor and Urban Affairs, Wayne State University)*

UAW's growing interest in the unemployed paralleled an increased interest in the problem within the highest councils of the CIO. Following a September conference with Lewis, Lasser told Norman Thomas that the labor chieftain possessed an "unusual sense of the impending political developments," which included serious concern over an imminent recession. Sharing his alarm, Benjamin and Lasser urged Lewis to commit a large sum of money to a CIO organizing drive among the unemployed and WPA workers. Demonstrating substantial interest in the Alliance scheme, Lewis agreed that the issue would be an agenda item for the October CIO meeting in Atlantic City. He took this step in full knowledge of the fact that a jurisdictional dispute over unemployed workers had been simmering since midsummer. While the CIO's Walter Smethust disclaimed interest in infringement on "the territory of the Workers Alliance," a CIO policy paper asserted that under "certain special circumstances" Alliance locals could affiliate with CIO.[63] By October 1937, then, the CIO outlook on the unemployed worker was becoming an important issue as Lewis edged towards rapprochement with the Workers Alliance.

In Detroit, where the UAW Unity Caucus embraced the Popular Front, union welfare committees had advanced even more rapidly. In October 1937, the west side committee, anticipating imminent layoffs, negotiated a working agreement with Detroit welfare administrator G. R. Harris, which was designed to ease the process of relief application by using plant committees as consulting bodies. Welfare Director Harold Hartley urged all UAW welfare committees to establish working relationships with the city bureaucracy so union members would "receive relief much more rapidly" and the committees could "be of real service" to workers. One month later, UAW closed ranks with the Wayne County Workers Alliance to establish the Detroit Council of Welfare Committees representing UAW, Alliance, and other CIO members. Consistent with the intent of the Milwaukee convention, UAW thus "achieved the unity of the organized employed and the organized unemployed."[64]

On the eve of the CIO national conference, therefore, UAW had taken leadership in the unemployed struggle that had been developing in lower Michigan. Maintaining a collaborative arrangement with the area Workers Alliance, auto workers' welfare committees had seized the initiative to extend the limits of union consciousness through service to unemployed unionists and, in theory at least, the larger community of the dispossessed. The bold *demarche* not only established UAW as the most influential voice of the Michigan unemployed, but also placed it in the vanguard of socially conscious industrial unionism. By October 1937, the Michigan unemployed movement had become deeply intertwined with the rapidly developing union movement. All eyes now turned to the CIO.

The Union Militant
UAW and the
Organized Unemployed, 1937–1938

T he strike wave of 1937 had demonstrated that unemployed workers could play a role in the struggle to create industrial unions. Likewise, the UAW had accepted a responsibility to jobless auto workers, partly due to the social vision of industrial unionism and partly to forestall management manipulation of the reserve army of the unemployed. Confronted by the ravages of the "Roosevelt Recession," the UAW moved to expand its services to the unemployed in an attempt to preserve and build the union in a time of economic adversity. By the time the recession came to an end, the welfare committees were to become institutionalized as the UAW WPA Welfare Department, which developed rapidly as an element in the union bureaucracy. The bureaucratization of unemployed services inside UAW developed side by side with the growth of the CIO's Unemployment Division, which emerged in 1938 to coordinate the unemployed programs of affiliated unions and promote the interests of the union unemployed in the national legislative arena. By so doing, CIO extended a long-standing labor interest in mitigating the problems created by layoffs, seasonality of employment, arbitrary management practices, and relief to the jobless. As David Montgomery and Ronald Schatz have noted, CIO unions moved aggressively to augment the traditional labor emphasis on the closed shop, standard wage rates, and work-sharing with a new drive to institutionalize seniority and secure adequate relief for unemployed unionists.[1] By 1938 some CIO unions were prepared to move beyond this defensive posture to exploit unemployed WPA workers as an organizing opportunity. While this pattern was evident in the activities of the United Electrical, Radio, and Machine Workers (UE) and other industrial unions, UAW established a model for unemployed organizing that was quickly adopted by the CIO leadership.

The growth of CIO organizational activity among the unemployed presented a major challenge to the Workers Alliance, which had long functioned as advocate for the jobless. By early 1939, the Alliance had fallen on hard times in many states. Because of the power of the UAW in Michigan, the Alliance lost the battle for the loyalty of the unemployed, as the union came increasingly to dominate the field. But even as it became a successful union institution, the UAW's WPA Welfare Department was to suffer severe damage as a result of the internal warfare that threatened to destroy auto workers unionism from within.

Mobilizing for Recession

As the first national CIO convention opened in Atlantic City in October 1937, a spirit of optimism prevailed among delegates, who could reflect upon a year of stunning successes in rubber, automobiles, and steel. Although Ford and Little Steel remained unorganized, CIO membership had reached 3.4 million. Lewis's public pronouncements reemphasized his passionate commitment to the extension of collective bargaining and full industrial democracy to all American workers. Beneath the surface expressions of confidence in the future, however, there lay increasing doubts about the stability of an economy soon to lurch into the depths of the "Roosevelt Recession" of 1937–1938. This uncertainty shaped the legislative program hammered out at the October conference. Embracing wage-hour legislation, guaranteed employment, and expanded social security, the CIO announced that the "basic feature of its legislative and economic program" was the assumption that "every worker has a right to a job." Chiding the AFL for its inattention to the unemployed, the CIO demanded employment security and its logical corollary, the assurance that WPA and PWA would absorb all surplus labor. With a work security program in place and a ringing endorsement from Lewis,[2] the organization prepared to confront a recession already taking shape.

The CIO action came not a moment too soon. The ink on the first CIO union contracts had barely dried when the economy veered downward in late 1937. By mid-1938, economic indicators had receded to near-1933 levels. During the last quarter of 1937, steel production dropped 70 percent, while auto production declined to two-thirds of the 1936 rate. The stagnant economy and associated layoffs halted the CIO organizational juggernaut and stiffened management resistance to unionization. Confronted by unyielding corporate adversaries, Lewis and other industrial union leaders feared a repetition of the repression that had devastated labor between 1920 and 1922 after the great strike wave of 1919.[3] An awareness of this danger was undoubtedly a factor in the CIO decision in October 1937 to develop a comprehensive employment security plan. In short, the Lewis program was in large measure the product of a concern for self-preservation, if not the aggrandizement of industrial unionism.

In response to the crisis, CIO leaders began in November 1937 to develop a coherent policy on union service to the unemployed. While anxious to minimize layoffs, CIO leaders focused their main efforts on a drive to ensure that union members had access to adequate relief benefits. Recognizing the path-breaking work done by the UAW Local 174 Welfare Committee, Lewis aide John Brophy contacted Harold Hartley for information on the committee's work with relief agencies and unemployed members. At this time, Brophy and CIO secretary Katherine Ellickson were engaged in the process of formulating a plan for the jobless that might be implemented by all local industrial unions. The result was a directive issued on November 27 urging all CIO affiliates to establish unemployment committees and uniform machinery to guarantee that union members would be placed on WPA projects and receive all unemployment compensation and other benefits to which they were entitled. In Hartley's view the CIO program "correspond[ed] precisely with the Welfare Committee and the program already established" in the Detroit west side local. He later asserted that the UAW effort had constituted "genuine pioneer work" which aided the CIO in formulating a progressive national policy to serve its unemployed members, thus departing from the "traditional AFL total neglect of its unemployed."[4]

Always with an eye to the main chance, the Workers Alliance national office reacted with enthusiasm to the quickening of CIO activity on behalf of the jobless. In early November, Alliance secretary Herbert Benjamin applauded the stand taken at the October CIO Conference as "a landmark for the whole labor movement." More to the point, he urged Lewis to explore with the Workers Alliance an "entirely new approach" to the manner in which unions dealt with the problem of unemployment, which would require a "fundamental change" in the Alliance's "organizational forms." Benjamin's goals became clearer when he advised Alliance locals against insisting on "any particular organizational form" and recommended that the wishes of established unions guide their efforts to organize jobless union members.[5] In short, the national Workers Alliance hoped to cooperate with CIO in meeting the needs of unemployed unionists and by so doing, solidify its own link with industrial unionism.

CIO was willing to collaborate with the Alliance, but only on its own terms. In early December Brophy explained the CIO unemployment policy to both Lasser and Benjamin. Their conversation preceded by one day the CIO's definitive policy statement, which made it very clear that the major vehicle for unemployed organizing would be existing industrial unions. On 7 December 1937, Lewis declared that it was the "duty of American labor to face with courage and realism" the reality of "unemployment more bitter than ever before in our history." Accepting responsibility for the jobless, CIO launched a nationwide drive to establish local unemployment committees within industrial unions, protect unemployed unionists, represent them before welfare authorities, and lobby Congress for legislation to ease their plight. Resting his case on the citizen's right to work, Lewis concluded with a flourish that if the great corporations failed to provide work, "then there must be some power somewhere in this land of ours, that will go over and above and beyond those corporations" to ensure the workers the "right to live."[6] Beyond the lofty rhetoric was a hard-headed determination to exploit an organizing opportunity and to steal a march on the AFL with an appeal to the jobless.

Brophy followed the Lewis manifesto with a detailed memo to local industrial unions and the industrial union councils spelling out the unemployment compensation systems soon to be operating, together with instructions for speedy worker registration. Locals and councils were to discuss the "essential facts about unemployment compensation" with union members and encourage full use of the new system. He later instructed field representatives and regional directors to assist unemployed union members in securing both WPA jobs and relief benefits. The Brophy memo took seriously the CIO's "responsibility for seeing that the unemployed are properly cared for."[7] It also reflected an awareness that it was in the interest of CIO unions to retain unemployed members as a safeguard against future membership losses.

The scope of the CIO program impressed the Workers Alliance as a "notable step forward." Nonetheless, the Alliance quickly grasped the competitive aspect of union-based unemployment committees. Lasser and Benjamin warned the CIO's Ralph Hetzel Jr. that as a result of the union committees' inexperience, delays in securing benefits might occur, resulting in discouragement or resentment against the union. Moreover, because the CIO initiative focused primarily on unionists, the nonunion unemployed, who constituted the majority, could easily be ignored. Consequently, the Alliance claimed jurisdiction over the organization of the estimated 80 percent of the unemployed who were not union members, while urging the CIO to work cooperatively with it to help reach the unorganized. Benjamin and Lasser recommended the establishment of citywide joint unemployment committees that would include CIO unions, Workers Alliance representatives, and non-CIO unionists, all working to serve the needs of the jobless through direct action at the local level, including client advocacy, political activity, and publicity work. While asking for CIO support, the Alliance was careful to remind its members to "help build the unions" by encouraging jobless unionists to remain loyal to their home unions and exhorting the unorganized to affiliate with one.[8] It is clear that the CIO *demarche* had created both a problem and an opportunity for the nation's largest unemployed organization as Americans entered the economic downturn of 1938. While a closer tie with CIO might bring the Alliance access to the larger organization's greater resources, industrial unions would now compete with WAA for the allegiance of the unemployed.

In no state was the impact of the slowdown more evident than in Michigan, where cyclical unemployment had long been a serious problem. As early as November 1937 automobile production began to decline as demand softened, and by the end of the year production had dropped precipitously. One month later, the UAW estimated that out of 517,000 automobile workers, no less than 320,000 were jobless and 196,000 partially unemployed. By May 1938 unemployment in the industry was to approach 70 percent. Summarizing the human impact of the 1937–1938 recession, the Michigan Emergency Welfare Relief Commission concluded that in terms of both unemployment and total relief load, the crisis was "more severe and more devastating" than the long depression of 1929–1935.[9]

While the national Workers Alliance worked to establish a direct tie with industrial unionism, in Michigan the UAW acted independently to deal with the state's escalating unemployment crisis. The union's direct engagement in this effort was not only consistent with the relief work previously undertaken by Local 174, but was also a matter of necessity because of a sharp drop in union membership. With dues payments in decline and without its own relief fund, the UAW survival instinct led it to embrace welfare rights and service to the unemployed as critical union concerns. Ethel Polk, a key staffer in the UAW Welfare Department from 1938 to 1941, later recalled that the union was forced to organize its unemployed members because "you could hang on to them that way." By November 1937 many Wayne County locals had protested the impending layoffs and over twenty had established their own welfare committees or appointed welfare directors on the Local 174 model. Local committees moved quickly to halt evictions as "the employed rallied to defend the unemployed."[10]

In the Detroit area, a crucial function of the UAW welfare committees involved certification of welfare recipients and WPA workers. To relieve pressure at crowded welfare stations, the Detroit Welfare Department permitted clients to be certified eligible for relief by the UAW Welfare Committee, which provided valuable information to officials and saved time for applicants. Critics noted that it also enhanced union prestige by suggesting that relief could "more easily be obtained by belonging to the union." Welfare Commissioner Fred H. Cole later wrote Mayor Richard W. Reading that the system might increase the case load and contribute to the likelihood of strikes as a result of union involvement, results which he viewed as "the undesirable part of the plan."[11]

Cole's concern was the union's great opportunity, and the UAW was prepared to exploit it. As a first step, Homer Martin urged all locals to retain their unemployed members through "out of work" stamps that would hold them within the union. He promised that by so doing, jobless unionists would retain the "advantage of the collective voice and collective power of the automobile workers." It was essential for the union to maintain contact with jobless workers, a goal that was paramount, especially for Reuther and the west side Social Democrats. In Reuther's mind the union was an extended social family, a concept that implied concern for all constituent members. Equally significant as a goal, however, was the UAW's survival as an institution. As a result, Martin insisted that no member leave his local for any other unemployed organization because no other group could serve an autoworker better than his own union.[12]

To strengthen the bond between workers and the union, the International now moved to coordinate unemployed work through a new unionwide UAW Welfare Department headed by Richard Leonard, president of the De Soto local. A welder by trade, Leonard had risen through the ranks to leadership at De Soto. His appointment as welfare director guaranteed that a strong Reuther ally was to head the new department. Designed to supplement the work of existing local committees, the new central office increased the union's visibility in providing relief services, grievance processing, and lobbying for unemployed benefits. Leonard's appointment coincided with the announcement that in Flint and Lansing, plans were under way for expanding and streamlining UAW welfare activities in Genesee County and in western Michigan. These developments, together with Richard T. Frankensteen's appointment to the Michigan State Emergency Relief Commission in the same week, underscored the union's renewed commitment to the struggle on behalf of its jobless members. The Frankensteen appointment meant that the CIO perspective on unemployment would be heard at the policymaking level.[13]

The UAW Welfare Department worked in cooperation with a new citywide coordinating committee, which included members of UAW, WAA, the United Rubber Workers, Steel Workers Organizing Committee, United Dairy Workers, and the State, County, and Municipal Employees Union. Its membership marked it as a thoroughly integrated united front organization. Moreover, through the presence of the public employees' union, the council was well connected with Detroit relief workers, whose representative promised to keep labor informed of "the inside dope on the Welfare Department." The coordinating committee planned a visit to Governor

Murphy to appeal for greater relief funding, as well as ongoing local lobbying on behalf of unemployed Detroiters.[14]

Side by side with the coordinating committee stood the new UAW Welfare Department and the UAW City Welfare Council, chaired by Harold Hartley of Local 174. At the outset, the new department's principal task was to assist relief clients in coping with the contempt and obstructionist behavior encountered at welfare offices. Because the department was new, there were few set rules and no experienced relief workers upon whom the union could rely. Young Ethel Polk, who came to the Welfare Department as a clerical worker in early 1938, soon received more extensive duties:

> We became the liaison with the social agencies, which no one else was doing. I had no background as a social worker. I became the liaison. I talked with clients and city officials. I had no final authority. I would recommend . . . But we also put pressure on the agencies.[15]

Equally important was an educational function. It was necessary to promote among workers a consciousness of an "inherent right to work." To Hartley, effective worker education was an essential prerequisite to the development of militance and union consciousness.[16]

On the political front, the new Welfare Department took a leading role in the planning and execution of a major unemployment conference at Lansing on 19 December 1937. The statewide meeting, sponsored by ten CIO unions and the Workers Alliance, urged Governor Frank Murphy to call a special legislative session to provide for immediate aid to the unemployed. CIO regional director Adolph Germer asked Murphy to advance the effective date of the new Michigan unemployment compensation law, while delegates agreed to conduct systematic surveys of the state's industrial communities to accelerate the process of obtaining further state and federal funding for jobless benefits.[17]

Behind the intense union activity on behalf of the unemployed lay a complex internal struggle that threatened to disrupt the UAW and fragment the movement to aid the victims of the faltering Michigan economy. Central to the conflict was the growing influence of CP outcast Jay Lovestone on Martin and a small group of his followers. The Lovestoneites, a dissident Communist group that since 1930 had opposed the Stalinist line, were committed to work within established unions. The significance of Lovestone, who had been expelled by the Communist Party, lay in his relationship with Martin, who became increasingly enamored of his mentor's peculiar brand of "anti-Communist Communism." Most accounts have concluded that while a brilliant orator, Martin lacked leadership ability. Especially damaging was his tendency to be unpredictable. Martin's instability and erratic behavior were themselves a problem for the union, but his alliance with the Lovestone group proved to be absolutely destructive. Not only did Martin place Lovestoneites in key staff positions, but he also proceeded to purge alleged "Stalinists" from the UAW leadership. To achieve this objective, Martin was willing to work with what some observers recall as the "thuggish" or "unsavory" elements in the union. Together with a few Trotskyites and the more numerous followers of Vice-President Richard Frankensteen, especially from the Chrysler locals and plants outside the Wayne County area, the Martin-Lovestone clique constituted the Progressive Caucus within the union. Communists, Socialists, independent leftists, and a large nonaligned group cooperated to create the anti-Martin Unity Caucus, which included the rising leader of Local 174, Walter P. Reuther, and his followers. While the Progressive group was united by anti-communism, the Unity Caucus was a rather uneasy coalition formed in self-defense against Martin.[18]

From the beginning of the recession, the Lovestoneites saw the unemployed organizations as a critical battleground in their struggle against Stalinism. In December 1937, *Worker's Age*, the national voice of the Lovestone Group, applauded the CIO's decision to create unemployment committees as a step "of vast significance" that indicated a new sense of social responsibility in the union movement. More to the point, it warned against leaving the unemployed to "outside organizations" that might "take over" their organization and "open the way for the deunionization of the jobless unionists." In a letter to his ally in the Progressive Caucus, Richard Frankensteen, Lovestone was more explicit:

> the Union *itself* should organize, direct, and control all unemployment activities. Any organization offering the Union assistance should be thanked for the same and told that the Union will call upon it whenever the UAWA finds such an aid necessary. This is in line with the CIO policy of which you

have been apprised two weeks ago, in a communication signed by Brophy. You will recall that the communication and the policy therein *centered solely on the CIO affiliates themselves handling their unemployed problem,* and not calling in or relying upon self-styled expert organizations, specialized outfits with Messianic missions arrogated by themselves to themselves. The latter organizations, while proposing to render service to the Union, actually tend to devitalize the UAWA by seeking to share workers' loyalty with the Union, or by seeking to shift the loyalty of the individual member or local from the International to the so-called special outfit.[19]

The union's initiative, in Lovestone's view, was intended to make it the agency the jobless auto worker looked to for service and to thereby "hold the loyalty of the union members" and "win the loyalty of unemployed auto workers hitherto not organized." Upon close examination, the detailed program laid out for UAW by the Communist Party Opposition (Lovestone Group) conformed very closely to policies already initiated by the union's own welfare committees and the CIO's sweeping plan for organizational activity among the unemployed.

Taking credit for having influenced the CIO's December policy statement through an earlier discussion with CIO economist Jett Lauck, Lovestone reiterated the importance of handling all unemployment activities through the unions. In January 1938, he told Lauck that the CIO statement had "prevented, particularly in Michigan, the CP, through its stooge organization, the Worker's Alliance, from devitalizing the UAWA and other CIO unions." These comments suggest sharp competition between the UAW Welfare Department and the Alliance for the support of the unemployed. Sensitive to the rivalry and determined to give "direction" to the CIO initiative, UAW vice-president Wyndham Mortimer urged the adoption of a UAW anti-unemployment program that urged locals to "work in conjunction with the Workers Alliance to fight for adequate and immediate relief." Mortimer argued that corporate America was "sabotaging" recovery in order to "destroy the great wave of unionism inspired by the CIO" and "throttle the ever-increasing militancy of workers" so that the "slavery and impoverishment" of the open shop might be reestablished. Mortimer's diatribe, although it galvanized the Unity Caucus, was characteristic of the CP's "shrill" approach to the unemployment crises that UAW welfare director George Edwards later insisted "did not wash with the average auto worker."[20]

Consequently, on 15 December 1937, when the Unity Caucus finally agreed on a comprehensive program, including a plan to deal with massive layoffs, some of Mortimer's inflammatory rhetoric had been removed. As amended by Edwards and Walter Reuther, both committed Socialists, the program embraced the CIO policy declaration and set out two primary objectives: first, to force the corporations to shoulder responsibility for causing layoffs; and second, to secure expanded work relief and adequate relief payments. These goals were to be achieved through a combination of mass protest, militant demonstrations, sitdowns, picketing, and union publicity. The primary participants in the mass actions would be unemployed UAW members, working through local union welfare committees and cooperating with the Workers Alliance in a show of solidarity.[21] In short, the various groups in the Unity Caucus closed ranks behind the unemployed.

In January 1938 the UAW and its new Welfare Department were sorely tested when the layoffs began to hit home. With two-thirds of Detroit's auto workers idle, the union mobilized for action, starting with political pressure at state and national levels. Reacting to Chrysler's layoff of 25,000 workers, UAW vice-president R. J. Thomas protested to Roosevelt, Hopkins, Governor Murphy, and James Byrnes, chairman of the Senate Unemployment Committee, and insisted that "drastic measures" were necessary to secure adequate relief for Detroit's unemployed, who were in "desperate need." As a followup, Martin testified before the Byrnes Committee that fully 50 percent of all American auto workers were unemployed and destitute. Two weeks later, the International Executive Board adopted a five point anti-depression program. Protesting layoffs, wage cuts, and inadequate relief programs, the board urged locals to strengthen their machinery for handling relief cases, securing adequate relief appropriations, and promoting effective administration of relief.[22]

In Detroit an important part of the administrative system was the UAW's role in certifying union members for relief. In January 1938, however, the new mayor, conservative Richard Reading, ordered a review of the established union certification procedure, which he opposed. Reading had defeated the CIO-backed mayoral candidate, Judge Patrick O'Brien, in November 1937 after a bruising campaign that had also featured a five-man labor slate of Common Council candidates, including the UAW's Walter Reuther, Richard Frankensteen, R. J. Thomas, and Tracy Doll, as well as labor attorney Maurice Sugar. One of the new mayor's first official acts was the termination of the cooperative working relationship between the UAW and the Detroit Welfare Department.[23] Detroit welfare director G. R. Harris defended the "understanding" with the UAW Welfare Department as an emergency measure that had been "very helpful" in handling the avalanche of applications produced by the recession layoffs. Noting that a union investigation did not mean automatic eligibility for relief, Harris asserted that the agency had been able to depend on the union's judgement. Detroit Welfare Department staff members were convinced that Reading's antagonism was blatantly political in that he interpreted his mayoral victory as a mandate to "curb union activity" and "oppose unions on every front." According to one case worker, the mayor felt that "union members should be chastised."[24]

Infuriated by Reading's attack, UAW welfare director Richard Leonard shot back a sharp protest asserting that the union's sole purpose in cooperating with the Detroit Welfare Department had always been "to facilitate the work of taking care of the thousands of unemployed." Leonard denied that preference was given UAW members, and reminded the mayor that the citywide welfare council established by the CIO encompassed most labor and unemployed organizations in the city. Escalating the union attack, he argued that if UAW had not assumed responsibility for relief services, "thousands of automobile workers would be starving." Likewise, Richard Frankensteen blasted Reading for his "lack of social understanding." CIO regional director Adolph Germer added his own conviction that Reading was simply not familiar with the community's relief needs. Germer succeeded in persuading the city welfare commission to delay final implementation of the mayor's policy on certification until CIO officials could discuss the matter with Reading.[25]

On 19 January Germer and Leonard called for a conference with the mayor on the unemployment crisis. Adding fuel to the fire, Martin attacked Reading for his criticism of CIO's sit-down tactics, asserting that the mayor's time would be better spent getting men back to work. After citing Detroit's dismal unemployment figures, Martin asserted that "the only sit-down the mayor will have to worry about in the near future is a sit-down on his doorstep of unemployed demanding food." Despite a UAW appeal to the Detroit Common Council, the mayor had the last word when a new certification system involving police department investigations of welfare recipients was instituted. Ironically, Reading's reform cost the city more than it was able to recover because the special investigations revealed many cases in which benefits increased.[26]

Although the union lost its certification function, the concrete results of UAW Welfare Department activity were substantial. In January 1938 Leonard reported that the department had already served 10,000 union members. And by June, Local 174's Hartley asserted that another 10,000 had availed themselves of his services. Staff worker Ethel Polk asserted that "people had advocacy" and that all people received representation, union and nonunion alike. Although relatively few union members relied upon the services of the local welfare committees, when crises occurred it was the UAW Welfare Department that interceded for workers confronted by an impersonal bureaucracy. For example, in January 1938, when 1,000 Detroit WPA workers were dismissed because of their eligibility for other Social Security and Aid for Dependent Children benefits, the UAW Welfare Department was on the doorstep of Michigan state WPA director Abner Larned with a demand for reinstatement. At another level, UAW took advantage of Frankensteen's strategic position on the Michigan Emergency Welfare Relief Commission. On motion by Frankensteen, the Commission decided in March 1938 to "put all possible pressure on counties" to make local funds available. Complementing these efforts, Nat Wald of the Wayne County Workers Alliance prodded Michigan senator Prentiss Brown in Washington to help reverse the Detroit dismissals.[27] Though the plea was unsuccessful in this instance, such collaboration reflected the UAW's pragmatic policy of cooperation with all groups in support of the jobless.

More productive was UAW's leadership in the effort to increase the number of WPA jobs in Michigan. Not only did the UAW Welfare Department work to streamline the certification process, but union leaders also headed an active Michigan lobby for larger state quotas. In February 1938, for example, Frankensteen and Martin pressured Roosevelt to provide massive aid to hard-hit Michigan, including $100 million in new WPA funding. And together with eight other cities, Detroit was granted an unlimited quota of WPA jobs. Following their mission to Washington, the UAW called for a mass demonstration in Detroit's Cadillac Square to dramatize the unemployment problem.[28]

As early as 3 December 1937, George Edwards of Local 174 had predicted "unemployed demonstrations such as 1931 never saw." In January 1938 he wrote that the planned demonstration in Cadillac Square would center around the right-to-work slogan, "late the property of the chambers of commerce," but "now ours." Edwards saw the public show of union strength as essential as a counter to the "determined reactionary drive against WPA appropriations." Determined to make the event the most impressive ever held in Detroit, Leonard and Germer exhorted all locals to turn out the troops as a union response to the antilabor attitude of Mayor Reading and as a message to Congress, then considering a supplementary WPA appropriation. Leonard also urged unions to demand the $600 million proposed by the CIO rather than the $225 million approved by the House of Representatives. Citing "great dissatisfaction" among Detroit workers, he defended UAW's concentration on an unemployed demonstration as a response to jobless workers who "had indicated that they wished their situation to be graphically shown." Finally, Germer and Leonard emphasized the breadth of support for the undertaking by soliciting the participation of the Workers Alliance, AFL, and nonunion unemployed.[29]

The projected mass meeting was intended to be what Local 174 termed "one of the most important demonstrations held in the city of Detroit." The *West Side Conveyor* published a full statement of UAW demands, including an increase in WPA jobs, adequate relief, restoration of the union Welfare Department's certification role, a moratorium on debt payments, and a halt to industry wage cuts. The militancy of the west side local was evident in a defiant editorial that appeared on the eve of the rally:

> Okay Wallstreet! If you won't run your plants, we'll get jobs from the government through WPA and other ways. And we'll have the government send you the bill in increased taxes and inheritance and profit taxes.
>
> To show you we mean business, we're giving you a sample of our strength in Cadillac Square this Friday. Come down and give us the once over. Then make up your mind whether

you'd rather pay wages and rake in the profits, or pay taxes and move toward the red ink. . . .

Cadillac Square . . . we'll be seeing you there-you, Mayor Reading, and your Wall Street bosses.[30]

The confrontational mood in Detroit worried even the friends of the union, most notably the pragmatic Germer and the unpredictable Homer Martin. On separate occasions, Germer warned both Wyndham Mortimer and Henry Kraus of another Haymarket Square massacre. George Edwards Jr. later recalled that Germer "feared police action and violence in the streets" and thus did what he could to control the demonstration. The anxiety reached as far as Washington, which according to James Dewey of the Labor Department was "jittery" about the union's plans. Arguing that the "eyes of the whole country" would be on Detroit, Leonard urged John L. Lewis to be present. Aware of Germer's reservations, Lewis endorsed the demonstrations but chose not to attend.[31]

With the cooperation of the Workers Alliance, AFL, and WPA workers, the union was able to mobilize over 100,000 demonstrators, who shouted their approval of Frankensteen and Martin's earlier request for more WPA jobs, as well as the union's program for relief and a debt moratorium. Always eloquent before a crowd, Martin maintained that the "test of any nation is the standard of living for the majority of the people." Rejecting poverty and insecurity as "inexcusable," he demanded "immediate, substantial, direct government relief" and called for a new "back to work movement." Other speakers attacked the Detroit welfare system and the antilabor policies of "Mayor Reading and his overlords."[32]

Reaction to the event on the Left and within the labor movement was enthusiastic. A relieved Germer, a reluctant participant, told Lewis that he had "missed a great treat by not coming." Communists inflated the crowd estimate to 250,000, while the *Socialist Call* described the rally as "the largest demonstration in U.S. labor history." Similarly, the UAW Welfare Department later asserted that Cadillac Square was "probably the greatest demonstration that was ever staged by one union."[33] (See figure 12.)

For the UAW and organized labor, the mass meeting had a deeper meaning. In a major address in Indianapolis, John Brophy cited the work of the UAW in Detroit as a model for CIO unions everywhere. He warmly endorsed the UAW Welfare Department's work

Figure 12 The UAW Cadillac Square Demonstration, February 4, 1938
(Archives of Labor and Urban Affairs, Wayne State University)

on behalf of the unemployed, especially its establishment of a cooperative relationship with the city welfare department. Brophy's greatest enthusiasm was reserved for the Cadillac Square demonstration, which he regarded as a breakthrough for the labor movement. He noted that not long after the event, "wheels began to turn." While Washington promised more funds for relief work, Michigan actually enacted a large relief appropriation. Brophy's entire speech was a call to action by CIO unions on behalf of the jobless, in keeping with the spirit of the Atlantic City economic security program.[34]

On one level, Cadillac Square marked the UAW's full commitment to the concept of unemployed organizing. UAW welfare director George Edwards Jr. later saw national political implications in the massive outpouring of support for the jobless. To the Federated Press, it meant that "union labor means business in Detroit," while Wyndham Mortimer believed that Cadillac Square "demonstrated beyond a question the power of labor in Michigan." And Richard Frankensteen was certain of the rally's importance in helping the UAW to convince Roosevelt of the "gravity of the unemployment situation in Detroit."[35] The profound effect of the day's events clearly demonstrates that the significance of the unemployed movement transcends the matter of paid-up memberships in jobless unions.

One thing is clear. By 10 February Roosevelt had earmarked additional WPA jobs for the Detroit area and by April WPA quotas for selected areas were lifted, thus creating thousands of new jobs in Michigan. And as early as 18 February, Martin asserted that "the pressure we have been able to bring to bear has resulted in a changed situation on relief." By May 1938 Wayne County WPA employment had risen to 67,252, a 434 percent increase over the 13,598 employees on WPA rolls in October 1937. Union power had made a difference. *Workers Age* spoke for many workers when it concluded that the UAW had "come of age."[36]

Solidarity Redefined: UAW on the Projects

Intent on pressing its advantage, UAW next moved to organize project workers into a new WPA Auxiliary. On one level the union maintained high visibility with jobless workers by attacking the Reading administration's relief policies and disinterest in WPA expansion. Cooperating with the Workers Alliance and the Mine, Mill, and Smelter Workers Union, for example, Local 174 led picketing of the Fort Street Welfare Station to protest relief cuts and the failure to recognize a grievance committee. Similarly, the UAW sponsored a unity meeting at the Packard Local Hall, designed to support a demand for more WPA projects, increased relief benefits, and a debt moratorium. This gathering displayed united front tactics by including presentations by the UAW, the CP, the Renters and Consumers League, the Workers Alliance, and one of Detroit's most liberal councilmen. While the union pressure escalated, west side welfare director Harold Hartley also worked to educate WPA employees on the "best way to organize on projects."[37]

The way became clearer for the UAW leadership in March 1938. With Cadillac Square behind them and cognizant of rapidly expanding WPA rolls, the union now assumed responsibility for spreading the message of unionism to WPA workers. With one eye on the Workers Alliance, Martin told all UAW locals in February 1938 that members who had taken WPA jobs should be "organized as part of our regular UAW welfare set-up and not in any special union of the unemployed."[38]

Given the fact that auto workers dominated the WPA constituency in Michigan and in view of the UAW's previous activity on the relief issue, it was a logical step. To Ethel Polk, it was "implicit in the operation." As noted by President R. J. Thomas in 1939, "with tens of thousands of automobile workers on WPA, the welfare department of the UAW-CIO had to be extended to include WPA workers." The idea of organizing WPA workers under the aegis of the state's predominant international union was a new one—an innovation necessitated by a collapsed industrial economy in Michigan. In the large west side local, for example, 20,000 of 32,000 members were laid off in late March, which forced Reuther and the union to step up activity among the unemployed and to fight for increased relief benefits and WPA employment.[39]

The WPA initiative was in part the result of a proposal by Homer Martin to dramatically expand the scope of CIO organizational activity on WPA projects. Referred to by Lewis confidant Adolph Germer as "Martin's WPA brainstorm," the plan called for an aggressive UAW drive to organize *all* WPA workers. On 22 March UAW vice-president Wyndham Mortimer alerted John Brophy in Washington to Martin's scheme to extend UAW jurisdiction over "all WPA workers who wish to avail themselves of its services." To Mortimer, whose CP ties predisposed him to safeguard the interests of the Workers Alliance, the proposed program seemed to be a "dubious undertaking" that would embroil UAW in numerous disputes. While Mortimer saw the need for such an organization, he argued that to be successful, it must be restricted to the organization of former auto workers on WPA. Two days later, the CIO's unemployment director, Ralph Hetzel Jr., was in Detroit to discuss WPA matters with Germer, Walter Reuther, Wyndam Mortimer, Richard Leonard, George Addes, and Martin aide Francis Henson. Hoping to head off further internal feuding over unemployed organizing, Hetzel promised to send a clear policy statement from CIO headquarters following his return to Washington.[40]

By 1 April 1938, Martin's expansive program had generated substantial debate over union jurisdiction in unemployed organizing. Not only had his "brainstorm" energized Workers Alliance sympathizers like Mortimer, but it also posed a challenge to the interests of other CIO Internationals. So broad was Martin's reach that CIO was forced to clip his wings with a policy statement that called for WPA workers to be organized by their respective unions. In short, CIO was moving to protect traditional CIO union jurisdiction while adopting a more aggressive stance towards WPA organization on a national scale. For all practical purposes the restriction meant little in Michigan because of UAW dominance on the union scene. By the end of March 1938, 80 percent of WPA workers in Michigan were UAW members, and UAW grievance committees were functioning on twenty projects. Ultimately, at a meeting of thirteen Detroit Internationals, eleven of the participating CIO unions waived jurisdiction and agreed to recognize the UAW WPA Welfare Department as the area's legitimate unemployed organization for their members.[41]

The immediate outcome was promising. Within one month 43,000 application cards had been signed by project workers. Absorbing the unemployed members of those CIO unions that had waived jurisdiction, the UAW WPA Welfare Department soon became the "recognized organization of workers on WPA in Michigan." The union's vigorous campaign reflected Martin's conviction that WPA organizing was "one of the most important jobs in Michigan" for the UAW, which was determined to "lead the field in the CIO" in its commitment to the jobless. Others were alarmed by the union initiative. The *Detroit News* saw "several regrettable aspects" of the UAW plan to organize on the projects, including the reality that there was "no such thing as collective bargaining with a Government." More to the point, the *News* charged UAW with "transparent greediness" for allegedly responding to reduced employment in auto plants by focusing on an "industry" where employment was booming, thus grasping a "rather obvious opportunity" in a "repulsively cynical" maneuver.[42]

In an angry rebuttal, the UAW Auxiliary's national director, Richard Leonard, attacked the *News* itself as "cynical" in attempting to deny workers the right to organize and alleviate the many abuses WPA workers endured. Leonard pledged that UAW would organize project workers "no matter who gets annoyed by it." In fact, Michigan WPA administrators welcomed the UAW organizational drive. Not only was unionization of project workers consistent with government policy, but as Victor Reuther later recalled, public officials "breathed a sigh of relief when a major trade union established a formal structure for dealing with the problems of the unemployed." No longer could conservatives use leftist elements within the Workers Alliance as a "club" to crush "any activity that was in support of the unemployed." The UAW initiative and the CIO endorsement were consistent with the broad social emphasis of industrial unionism, which was evident in the CIO unions' commitment to serve unemployed members.[43] It is equally true that unemployed organizing served the self-interest of unions reeling from the job losses occasioned by the recession.

Unemployed organizing was clearly a two-way street. From the beginning UAW leaders understood that the retention of union ties was essential to the overall health of the union as well as the interests of the unemployed auto worker. Martin defended his plan for WPA organizing as insurance that UAW members would not be "de-unionized," as had been the case in 1937 when the first wave of layoffs had occurred. UAW was convinced that if WPA workers could be organized, "then when they did get a job they would be acquainted with the union" and "you would get additional membership into the Ford plants and other unorganized plants." In this vein, Local 174 welfare director Harold Hartley asserted that his local committee always "felt responsible for the development and training of rank and file union members." As a result, new union leaders took their experience from the unemployed organization into such plants as Cadillac, Ternstedt's, Bowen Products, Detroit Brass and Malleable, Timken, Federal Screw, Universal Products, Kelsey Hayes, American Brass, Michigan Malleable, O & S Bearing, and Federal Truck. The potential value of grooming unionists in the WPA organization was summarized by an unidentified observer who noted that "when Mr. Ford, who throws fifty thousand men out of work without winking, comes to take them back, he will find them organized into the UAW."[44]

Emphasis on union consciousness promised another benefit for UAW, protection against the reserve army in time of crisis. Martin reported to the International Executive Board in May 1938 that the WPA Auxiliary had been "insurance against splitting of members" into "those employed in private industry as against those on relief." Worker morale was high because WPA workers knew they "had not been forgotten" by the union and that behind them stood the "organized support of workers in private industry." All Michigan locals were instructed to hold organizational meetings to explain the new WPA Auxiliary to their unemployed members. At the same time, Leonard advanced a program that demanded a 75-cent-per-hour minimum wage for WPA workers, the thirty-hour work week, improved working conditions, adequate clothing for employees, the employment of single men and women on the projects, and an established grievance procedure that incorporated union stewards as worker representatives.[45]

On the projects, the UAW's presence made a difference for workers. WPA administrators recognized the steward system and established a formal grievance procedure, at least in Wayne County. The most significant gains were made in the improvement of working conditions and the reduction of arbitrary decision-making by supervisors. These improvements were especially noticeable after May 1939, when the Michigan WPA responded to union pressure by issuing a blanket labor relations policy. The policy promulgated by WPA state administrator Abner Larned outlined a grievance system, forbade discrimination on the basis of union membership, and established liberal provision for publicizing union activities. And occasionally, the union was able to win wage concessions, though such gains were limited by federal authorizations and legislatively mandated wage scales. Because of these limitations union organizing on the projects could sometimes be "a frustrating and not very rewarding effort," according to organizer John W. Anderson, who acknowledged that there was precious little to be bargained for. Although the union won only limited gains on the traditional wage-hour issues, Anderson maintained that the effort was "worthwhile" in that organizers were able to "talk unionism to the workers."[46] In short, the WPA Auxiliary was a valuable teaching tool in the school of unionism.

To Martin, however, the clearest indication of the Auxiliary's success was the CIO's adoption in April 1938 of a national program for unemployed organization, based largely on the UAW program in Michigan. After Lewis had extolled the recent accomplishments of CIO unions in the battle for the jobless, a CIO national conference in Washington moved to institutionalize the modified Michigan plan, which provided that CIO affiliates redouble their efforts to organize their own unemployed members on the WPA projects. Placed in charge of CIO's effort to organize and serve the jobless, national unemployment director Ralph Hetzel went beyond the standing CIO policy to urge local Industrial Union Councils to cooperate with organizations whose members were not eligible to join CIO unions by establishing special unemployment subcommittees on the WPA projects to represent workers. At the Washington conference, the UE's James Carey, who was named chairman of the new CIO Unemployment Committee, argued that the "greatest work" that could be done was to organize workers, "whether employed or unemployed." In agreement with Carey's analysis, Frankensteen (also a member of the CIO Unemployment Committee) added that the Michigan experience had shown that WPA organization meant more than merely taking care of unemployment, because it constituted "organizing the unorganized in a real sense." Hetzel concluded that the unemployed initiative had been a "bulwark of the CIO's strength in time of depression." The program had maintained membership and, in some locations, become the "dominant activity of the union." Seasoned observers Joseph Alsop and Robert Kintner saw the CIO program as evidence that Lewis had discovered in unemployed organizing a "device for upsetting the old maxim that hard times are harder on labor organizations than anything else." Likening the CIO unemployment committees' services to those of the nineteenth-century Tammany district leaders, Alsop and Kintner noted that Lewis could count on the loyalties of their unemployed legions in the future.[47]

Moving in May 1938 to exploit the opportunity, Lewis declared war on unemployment with a bold demand for 3.5 million new WPA and PWA jobs by the end of the year. Not only was a massive government employment program defensible "on all grounds of humanity and decency," but also it was essential as a stimulus to the weakened economy. CIO demanded work projects that would conserve worker skills and meet important social needs without pauperizing and demeaning job recipients. As a complement, Labor's Non-Partisan League published a statistical brief that documented the expanded relief needs created by the recession. Both Lewis and CIO's political arm made support for Roosevelt's relief program the litmus test for support of incumbent congressmen in the upcoming elections. These efforts were rewarded in May when the administration's $1.5 billion relief bill passed by a wide margin in a clear victory for House liberals and a politicized labor movement. The CIO was especially gratified by the "express statement" in the law that confirmed the right of WPA workers to labor union membership, a provision which Hetzel urged local CIO Unemployment Committees to rely on in their dealings with WPA authorities at the local level.[48]

As a supplement to its exertions on the political front, CIO also swung into action on the local organizational scene with a survey of its Internationals to assess then-current efforts to serve the jobless. In June the CIO national Unemployment Committee launched a comprehensive program for the organization of WPA workers outside the locals' jurisdictions, beginning with the CIO chartering of Project Workers Local Industrial Unions. These independent project workers' unions were intended to function side by side and in cooperation with the existing unemployment committees of local unions or Industrial Union Councils. Moreover, CIO pledged to cooperate with the Workers Alliance through joint committees where the Alliance was already established. Finally, as a practical matter, CIO targeted the hard-hit states of Michigan, Ohio, Illinois, Indiana, Missouri, Wisconsin, and New York, where high levels of unemployment promised the greatest successes.[49]

Even before the CIO program was in place, UAW had plunged aggressively into the field of unemployed organizing on the projects. Claiming broad jurisdiction, its WPA Auxiliary had accepted auto workers, former CIO unionists whose unions had deferred to UAW, and other project workers who sought UAW representation. UAW's first step was to replicate for WPA workers the steward system that existed in the plants and to establish a workable grievance procedure. Occasionally, when supervisors became dictatorial or arbitrary, the union staged sit-downs or demonstrations that in the words of John W. Anderson, showed "what economic power could do," though they usually produced "results of a very limited type." For Martin, a strong WPA Auxiliary meant that locals would "hold their members" so that UAW could "remain intact," preserve "gains made in better times," and "protect steadfastly the living standards of all its members."[50]

Early results were impressive. Young Socialist George Edwards Jr., a Reuther ally assigned by the International to organize unemployed west side workers into the WPA Auxiliary, remarked that auto industry layoffs had made WPA "the biggest industry in Michigan." By the end of May 1938, 60 percent of Michigan's 500 projects had been organized and over 50 percent of all WPA workers had joined UAW. Moreover, a grievance procedure was in place, the steward system was recognized, wage discussions had been opened, sanitation on the projects had improved, discriminatory hiring practices had been removed, and intimidation of union workers no longer occurred. Finally, significant numbers of black workers began to respond to the union message when they encountered UAW organizers through the WPA Auxiliary.[51]

And ironically, the massive layoffs of 1938 now brought the most important prize within the union's grasp. *West Side Conveyor* reported that so many Ford workers had been laid off that the projects were "crowded with them," and Edwards told the Local 174 Joint Council that "the most militant and active people on the WPA projects are former Ford workers." The UAW's strategy was to use unemployed Ford workers to lay the "groundwork on the outside" as the first step in reaching those plants. After years of exposure to the "brutality of the Ford service system," the speed-up, and "utter lack of freedom" in the Ford domain, many workers responded to the WPA Auxiliary with enthusiasm, especially after it became clear that the union had been able to remove Ford service men from supervisory positions on the Wayne County projects. To Local 174 leaders, the joke was on Henry Ford, who was to find trained and committed unionists returning to the Rouge plant. Indeed, the entire industry was destined to confront more dedicated unionists because the union had stood with its members through the recession and fought for their interests in the darkest of times. The *Conveyor* concluded that "the CIO overlook[ed] no bets" and had "contrived to turn even the WPA into a useful builder of unionism."[52]

In June 1938 the union took the battle to the enemy in a rally at Baby Creek Park, intended to "condemn Henry Ford," in the words of the Red Squad's observers. Sounding a theme that was already becoming the WPA Auxiliary's stock-in-trade, one UAW unemployed organizer called for full organization of WPA workers so that when the economy recovered, "King Henry" would confront 80,000 men, "all wearing the union button." He argued that despite a management conspiracy to use the recession to break the union, UAW "beat them to it by organizing the WPA workers." As a followup, a black organizer reminded the audience of a discriminatory lay-off system that made blacks the last hired and first fired. The solution, he insisted, would be found when white unionists "put out their hand of comradeship to the negro," which would result in the organization of Ford.[53] (See figure 13.)

By this time the WPA Auxiliary had become embroiled in UAW's increasingly acrimonious factional struggles. When Leonard was elected secretary-treasurer of the newly established Michigan In-

UAW Ford Rally

SPEAKERS:

HOMER MARTIN, President U.A.W.A.
WALTER REUTHER, U.A.W. Executive Board Member
Z. DOBRZYNSKI, Detroit Director U.A.W. Ford Com.
WM. TAYLOR, Director U.A.W. WPA Auxiliary.
EVE STONE, Nat'l Director UAW Women's Aux.
MORRIS FIELD, UAW National Educational Director.

Sunday, June 5, 2 p. m.

Baby Creek Park

West End at Dix Avenue and Vernor Highway
Baker Car Stops at Meeting Place

These nationally prominent speakers
will deal with such pressing problems as

ORGANIZATION OF FORD'S
UNEMPLOYMENT AND WPA
CIVIL LIBERTIES
HUNGER-MISERY-POLICE BRUTALITY

The workers of Detroit and Dearborn must rally at this meeting to protest the brutality and discrimination against Labor by
the employers and their agents.

EVERYBODY OUT ! ! !

Under the auspices of
Ford Organizing Committee
United Automobile Workers
of America.

 35

Printed by Baker   Distributed Under Dearborn License No. 18

Figure 13   The Employed and Unemployed Rally Against Ford, June 5,
1938 *(Archives of Labor and Urban Affairs, Wayne State University)*

dustrial Union Council with Communist support, Martin moved
his own close ally, William B. Taylor, into the position of welfare
director and director of the WPA Auxiliary. Recording secretary of

Chrysler Local 7 and a former member of the Ford organizing committee, Taylor was a trusted Martin backer with ties to the Lovestoneites in the union's Progressive Caucus. His appointment in May 1938 coincided with the UAW Executive Board's decision to intensify the WPA organizing campaign in keeping with the CIO's new policy on the organization of project workers.[54]

Almost immediately, internal conflict erupted over the activities of the WPA Auxiliary, as Taylor began to "use the Department as a factional weapon." These developments parallelled the rapid disintegration of the Progressive Caucus, which produced a twenty-point program to end factionalism, adopted by the Executive Board on 26 May 1938. An important provision of this plan was a commitment to intensify the organization of WPA workers. The program reflected strong pressure from Reuther, Local 174, and the Unity Caucus, which urged a united front in cooperation with the Workers Alliance and "any other organization working in the best interests of the unemployed." Equally active as a proponent of an aggressive WPA organization was Martin's former ally, Richard Frankensteen, who by May had drifted towards the Communist camp within the union. Because Frankensteen's defection deprived Martin of a majority on the Executive Board, an angry Martin responded by denying Frankensteen his position as assistant to the president. Moreover, convinced that Frankensteen's pursuit of personal power reflected a Communist conspiracy to control the union, Martin drew even closer to the Lovestoneites, who had become a significant influence on his stewardship of UAW affairs. When on 6 June 1938 the Executive Board censured Martin in his absence, he responded with the suspensions of Frankensteen, Mortimer, Addes, Ed Hall, and Walter Wells, all officers identified with the Unity Caucus.[55]

Martin later argued that the "Lewis–Communist Party conspirators on the Board" had attempted to defeat his plans for organizing the unemployed. Despite Martin's protestations, it is a fact that UAW had taken extraordinary steps to make the union a voice for the unemployed in Michigan. A CIO national Unemployment Committee report concluded that UAW had been unique in its approach:

> In one case, notably the automobile workers, special provision is made for WPA workers to pay 50 cents monthly dues to a special WPA Department, at the same time that the member continues in good standing in his local, which issues "unem-

ployment" receipts to him without charge. This union is put-
ting on an active campaign to bring into its ranks workers in
the industry who are on WPA, and to keep active those members who have already left the industry because of unemployment and are on relief or WPA.[56]

Without a doubt, the WPA Auxiliary had been a factor in the
lives of unemployed workers on a day-to-day basis. The Auxiliary's
activities ranged from organizing street demonstrations and protests at welfare stations to the direction of intensive lobbying campaigns in Washington to promote legislative and administrative
changes relating to the WPA program. The organization was also
vigilant in urging aliens to file declarations of intent to become
citizens in order to qualify for WPA employment. Moreover, the
Auxiliary lobbied in Lansing for the development of youth programs and special attention to the needs of the single unemployed.
And to better serve the thousands of jobless women in Michigan,
Taylor established a WPA Auxiliary Women's Department in May
1938. This group, headed by Lovestoneite Eunice Crooks, was
intended to ensure that proper hospitalization, medical care, and
family welfare benefits were available to the unemployed. It also
addressed the wages, working conditions, and other problems of
female WPA workers.[57] Critics argued that, in practice, the Crooks
appointment was primarily significant as another effort by Martin
to entrench his Lovestoneite supporters in positions of influence
within the union hierarchy. But the creation of the Women's Department also demonstrated that union activists in the unemployed
movement perceived joblessness as not simply a men's issue, but
rather as a women's issue with serious family implications.

While factional rivals sparred within the UAW hierarchy, the
union's unemployed activists concerned themselves with militance
in the streets and on the line. One important issue that drew their
attention in 1938 was the unrelieved plight of the single unemployed, particularly the question of inadequate housing for homeless workers. The UAW's rising interest in the problem resulted not
only from the trend towards union engagement in unemployed
organizing, but also from enlightened self-interest.

The focal point for this activity was Fisher Lodge, a city-oper-
ated lodging house for twelve hundred jobless single men. By early
1938 the residents had organized themselves into a Single Men's
Unemployed League, which functioned as a union-like grievance

committee. It also served as an organizing body when UAW or other worker groups sought to mobilize crowds for demonstrations or other pressure activities. Such residential facilities were to be found in several Detroit locations, some of them partially subsidized by UAW. The union-backed dormitories housed workers from the Chrysler, Hudson, Briggs, and Motor Products plants, who were readily available for strike duty, sit-downs, or other demonstrations. The Detroit Red Squad's concern about these facilities escalated when it received reports that the buildings were stocked with 2" × 2" clubs that could be used for picketing purposes, as were the residents. Red Squad reports asserted that the dormitories were indeed maintained by the UAW,[58] which appeared to be raising its own reserve army. With the union's blessing, collective action was supported by collective living arrangements that drew the homeless together and provided UAW organizers with mobilizable troops.

Aware of the union's increasing involvement in unemployed organizing, the Red Squad kept a watchful eye on its activities elsewhere. In early June, when an effort was made to organize WPA workers through east side Local 203 (Motor Products), police observers monitored the proceedings. The union reportedly believed that once district councils and WPA units had been organized, UAW would "be in a position to turn on the heat" at will. The Local 203 president therefore exhorted his unemployed brothers to come to the local for help and join the WPA Auxiliary if employed on the projects. His argument rested on the assumption of firm solidarity among employed and unemployed workers. It also supported a clear attempt to hold the union together in the face of adversity and layoffs.[59]

Even more ominous to the Red Squad was mounting evidence that the union's reserve troops would act. During the American Brass Company strike, for example, two unemployed pickets assaulted a policeman, an action which earned them special union recognition for their "bravery." So alarmed were the authorities that the Detroit Welfare Department swung into action against unemployed unionists. Not long after the altercation, those American Brass strikers who were on welfare received notice that there were jobs for persons who wanted work. UAW's Richard Leonard told Governor Murphy that the company's ploy constituted "collusion" between local government and management in "a strike-breaking activity." Murphy responded with a pledge to investigate the problem.[60]

Meanwhile, in June and July 1938 Taylor worked to strengthen his hold on the WPA organization and to broaden its reach. Now the UAW reached thousands of workers who had not previously been affiliated with labor unions, while "maintaining the spirit of unionism among the unemployed auto workers." The major weapon in the ongoing union assault was the UAW's insistence on a 75-cent-per-hour minimum wage on the projects for a 100-hour month. The UAW WPA Auxiliary assumed that "WPA is an industry and should be considered as such by UAWA." Taylor and the union understood full well that the WPA's 60-cent hourly minimum threatened existing pay scales because it provided a "continual excuse for manufacturers to cut wages."[61] In this respect UAW shared the concerns of the AFL unions over the WPA's downward pressure on prevailing wage levels. But for Taylor and the auto workers, an additional problem loomed large: not only were hard-won wage concessions in jeopardy, but massive layoffs also posed the threat of unacceptable membership losses. It was these fears, coupled with Martin's factional objectives, that lay behind Taylor's frenetic activity in the summer of 1938.

While Taylor and the Lovestoneites intensified their unemployed work, their factional opponents were not idle. Consistent with the history of its concern for its unemployed members, Local 174 increased its effort to serve the jobless. The local's welfare director, Harold Hartley, reported in June 1938 that the department's offices were constantly "over-crowded" with union members seeking assistance in dealing with the Detroit and Wayne County welfare bureaucracy. While some were disappointed, Hartley argued, demands could be won by "constant, uninterrupted hammering at relief officials." In mid-June the west side local sponsored a victory meeting to celebrate the enactment of Roosevelt's relief bill, which it claimed some credit for enacting. And two weeks later Local 174 reemphasized its policy of cooperation with the Workers Alliance by sponsoring an address by black activist and Alliance leader Merrill Work. As Hartley noted in July 1938, the Local 174 Welfare Department meetings had always invited "the freest and most democratic expression of opinion" that did not "exclude the expression of any point of view."[62]

As of August 1938 several obstacles to the achievement of the UAW-WPA Department's objectives remained, including the problem of educating the UAW membership. First, union members needed to see WPA work as a job rather than charity, thus legitimizing labor organization on the projects. Even more important was the education of local unions that had not always understood the value of unemployed organizing and had therefore not given full cooperation to the UAW-WPA Department. Beset by shifting personnel, changing job locations, and an unstable membership base, the union's WPA Department confronted serious organizational problems by its very nature.[63] Unmentioned, but certainly a factor, was the debilitating influence of factional strife on the union's efforts to build the WPA Department into a bulwark against the open shop. By summer 1938 the Lovestone group had completely captured Martin's sympathies, which meant a new assault on the Workers Alliance. Following the expulsions from the Executive Board in June, Lovestoneites charged that the CP had been "striving to breakup the UAW-WPA Auxiliary" so that the "Communist-controlled" Alliance could "gather in the members to be milked for the benefit of the Stalin stooges." In fact, heightened factionalism, Martin's paranoia, and Lovestoneite meddling had undermined the WPA Auxiliary more dramatically than any Alliance activity could have. Always underfunded, the union's WPA Department nearly fell victim to an economy campaign foisted on Martin by Lovestone supporter Fred Pieper. Pieper persuaded Martin to fire the entire WPA staff after Martin had promised Taylor that no WPA organizers would be laid off and after the Lovestone caucus had gone on record in favor of a major organizing drive on the projects. Although Martin then reversed himself, his erratic actions raised some serious doubts about his widely publicized claims to be the leading advocate of the unemployed within the union. Martin's impulsive action was so damaging to the WPA Auxiliary's morale that Taylor confided to a family member that the threatened staff layoffs seemed to confirm the critics' charges "so clearly" that "I am beginning to feel as though I am one of them."[64] By August 1938, therefore, the WPA Department, like the UAW, was rent asunder by the internecine struggles that threatened to destroy the union and wipe out the hard-earned gains made since the anxious days of 1937.

The advances had been substantial. In the August issue of the *WPA Department Bulletin* Taylor reflected upon the UAW's attempt to retain its jobless members and prevent the union's dissolution. He found much that was encouraging. Not only had several thousand nonunion workers been brought within the CIO fold, but wage increases had also been won in most Michigan counties. UAW had become a model for the CIO initiative in the field of WPA organization, which had spread significantly in many states. In Detroit, "anti-unionism on WPA" had "almost been wiped out," while working conditions had improved. Indeed, Taylor boasted that in Wayne County no major demand or grievance had been lost. Moreover, the union had projected itself into the community through social events for WPA families that "brought workers closer together as friends and brothers in the labor movement." And the WPA Department had "performed a work of education" that would be "of inestimable service to the International," in that it had trained thousands of stewards who would become the future officer corps that would "hold the union safe and strong." In sum, full WPA organization was certain to demonstrate that the UAW was pioneering in "constructive unionism" and "progressive social achievement."[65]

But the cup was half empty. Not only were wage levels inadequate, but the WPA program had not completed its task. Taylor called for a federal jobs program that would develop worker skills and focus on public projects of social value, such as housing projects. More than this, the federal government was obligated to "absorb the unemployed" so long as management failed to "live up to their responsibility to provide jobs." In effect, Taylor argued for a permanent WPA program, which he saw as a "vital necessity to the labor movement." Because the job of recovery was unfinished, the organization of the unemployed remained a UAW priority, as was ongoing propaganda that would stress the "far-going nature of the UAW program for WPA."[66] But before the union could look to the future, it had to heal the wounds left by the internal struggles of the past.

The Other Activists
Alternative Approaches to Unemployed Organizing, 1937–1938

A major factor in the factional struggle within the WPA Auxiliary was the role played in the Michigan unemployed movement by the Workers Alliance, which by 1938 had been forced into a subordinate position by an activist UAW. In Wayne County, where both groups maintained correct relations on the surface, cooperation was substantial. In an expression of Popular Front unity, UAW, WAA, and the Wayne County CIO Council had arrived at a working formula which favored established unions. Consistent with CIO policy, unionists were to stay in their home organizations, while nonunionists were to join the Alliance. The Wayne County Alliance pragmatically accepted the arrangement, but although UAW agreed to direct non-CIO workers into the Alliance, the concession was of dubious value. As early as January 1938, the ubiquitous Jay Lovestone told CIO economist Jett Lauck that channeling unemployment activities through the unions was the key to success in Michigan. By utilizing this approach, he argued, the Welfare Department and the CIO had prevented the CP from "devitalizing the UAWA." Although Lovestone exaggerated his own influence, his analysis of the situation had some validity. Socialist Party organizer Ben Fischer later recalled a widely held concern that the unemployed would "become a focal point for CP activity and potentially slop over into union politics."[1]

While it was union initiative rather than Lovestone's pronouncements that produced UAW's gains among the unemployed, he was prescient in forecasting the impact of a bureaucratizing institution such as the Welfare Department–WPA Auxiliary on the fortunes of the Alliance. It became increasingly difficult for the WAA to compete with the power of the popular UAW in a state where the auto workers' union was the dominant labor organization. Moreover, the Alliance's experiences in Michigan parallelled an unsuccessful attempt by its national officers to develop a direct tie with the CIO, which was then intensifying its own activity on behalf of the jobless.

The National Context:
Industrial Unionism and the Unemployed

Never one to miss an organizing opportunity, John L. Lewis had become an outspoken advocate for the unemployed. Since the Atlantic City conference of October 1937, Lewis had prodded CIO unions to embrace the cause of displaced workers. The CIO program for the jobless resulted from a combination of self-interest and social commitment. The fact that organizational initiative came from Washington does not, however, mean that worker activism was absent. From the early Depression years onward, the jobless had organized as a matter of self-preservation, and members of unemployed organizations had actively sought a connection with the industrial union movement once the CIO had burst upon the scene. Consequently, the trend towards affiliation in 1938 was the logical outcome of a long-standing interest, certainly among Workers Alliance rank-and-file activists, in closing ranks with the CIO. At the same time, Lewis and Brophy had been scrupulous in their effort to maintain a cordial, if institutionally distinct, relationship with the Alliance.

One of the key issues addressed at the April conference of CIO leaders in Washington was the problem of mass unemployment and the appropriate response to the crisis by labor. On 12 April 1938, the CIO leaders considered a letter from David Lasser, who praised Lewis and the industrial unions for their cooperation with the Workers Alliance in meeting the needs of the jobless. Sensing the temper of the times, Lasser underscored the "bond of solidarity" that had been established between the union and nonunion unemployed and reminded Lewis that WAA had long advocated active union participation in the unemployed movement so that unions could hold their jobless members. He then tactfully reminded the CIO that the role of the Alliance was to organize those unemployed who were ineligible for union membership, to agitate on their behalf, and to make them more "union-conscious." The WAA house organ, *Work*, nervously welcomed the CIO into the field of unemployed organizing and ostensibly saw no conflict between Alliance activities and those pursued by the unions. More likely, it thought, was the replication of the "close working relationship" already established between the Alliance and the industrial unions.[2]

Behind the cooperative rhetoric lay an active effort by the Workers Alliance to forge a direct link with CIO through formal affiliation. The first step in this courtship was an Alliance proposal in March 1938 to cooperate with CIO in a nationwide organizing campaign among the jobless, with WAA responsible for the nonunion unemployed. Jay Lovestone gleefully noted in a letter to David Dubinsky that when the left-leaning Lee Pressman urged that the Alliance be given office space at CIO headquarters, Lewis followed Brophy's advice in rejecting the idea, a decision "of considerable significance." Later, at its 1938 convention, the Workers Alliance weakly argued that in April the CIO had not been "ready for any national plan." The CIO's reluctance to fully commit itself to an organic relationship with the Alliance did not prevent the *Daily Worker* from announcing that the April CIO conference had worked out a plan for cooperation between CIO unions and the Workers Alliance. And Herbert Benjamin asserted that "responsible leaders in CIO" recognized that although the unions had a responsibility to represent their unemployed members, there was "still need for organizations such as the Workers Alliance" and that "each recognizes the role and the rights of the other."[3]

Benjamin's insistence on autonomy did not, however, mean that the Alliance ceased advocating integration into CIO. In June, Lasser and the WAA National Executive Board advanced several proposals for the unification of the two organizations. Although the Alliance preferred to maintain its independent identity, it was willing, if required to do so, to demobilize its national organization and allow CIO to charter the former WAA locals separately. In short, it was ready to sacrifice full autonomy to "weld a firm bond of solidarity between the unemployed and the employed." There is some evidence that an anxious Lasser pressed for unity at all costs, and despite its preference for independence, the Alliance's National Executive Board was willing to "accept any plan which might finally be devised for improved relationship and cooperation."[4]

On 6 June the CIO Unemployment Committee discussed the idea of creating its own WPA and Relief Division, which would encompass the Workers Alliance and place two Alliance representatives on the CIO's National Unemployment Committee. Benjamin and Lasser were to assume executive positions within the new WPA and Relief Division when the national and state Alliance organizations were dissolved. Although the Alliance board was "not entirely satisfied" with this approach, Benjamin and Lasser appeared before the CIO Unemployment Committee to discuss the proposed merger. While they reluctantly accepted the CIO terms, they "were not given any satisfaction by the committee."[5] It is clear that there was CIO resistance to an open link with the Workers Alliance, an attitude rooted in the supplicant organization's leftist image.

Ten days later, Benjamin and Lasser met again with the Unemployment Committee and the CIO regional directors to work out the remaining differences over organizational structure. Benjamin found the CIO regional directors "much more amenable" and "practical" than the committee had been, which led the Alliance to resurrect its preferred plan for an independent semi-autonomous organization affiliated with CIO. However, the CIO representatives rejected this proposal and resolved to organize local industrial unions of unemployed workers without any direct collaboration with the Alliance. Many union leaders saw a major obstacle in a close tie because some workers flatly refused to go into the Workers Alliance. At the same time, the group did agree to consider the use of Alliance personnel and machinery in order to facilitate the organization of WPA workers. Finally, the regional directors recommended that CIO quietly absorb the Workers Alliance without any public declaration that such a step was being taken. In short, CIO refused to risk explicit public identification with WAA, but wanted its "complete cooperation" in carrying out its own plan to organize WPA workers into the new CIO Unemployment Division. But even these plans were unacceptable to the CIO leadership, and Alliance spokesmen had to content themselves with a promise of further discussion of cooperation and affiliation.[6]

All of which was disconcerting to Benjamin, who complained that CIO was rent by internal rivalry between the Internationals and generally unaware of the Alliance's proper role in labor's efforts to organize the jobless. To Benjamin and his CP allies, CIO maintained an "entirely incorrect attitude as far as the unemployed are concerned." He saw the crux of the matter as CIO's excessive concentration on WPA workers to the exclusion of the larger jobless community, including relief recipients, transients, unemployables, and others unreached by government job programs. Relations between CIO and WAA remained friendly, but no immediate affiliation was on the horizon. Such a relationship would have implied the strengthening of the Communist element in the CIO, which would have been, in Victor Reuther's words, "a little too raw" to merit the approval of Lewis. It is significant that in his report to the CIO Constitutional Convention in November, Lewis provided an extensive and detailed report of the year's unemployment activities that omitted any reference to the controversial Worker's Alliance.[7]

Undaunted by the rebuff, Lasser doggedly pursued an agreement with Lewis, the CIO, and the industrial union movement. The last thrust in his drive to link the two organizations came in August 1938 when he responded to Hetzel's request for a clear proposal for a cooperative program to create a new CIO WPA and Relief Division. Lasser's memo was essentially a capitulation to all of the demands made by CIO in June, including the dissolution of the Alliance's state and national organizational structures and the absorption of its executive officers and board members into the new division's administration and board. Yet even this arrangement was unacceptable, and as the summer came to an end the CIO was "not ready to go ahead on any general policy and plan."[8]

By September the Alliance Executive Board had abandoned all hope of an immediate deal with CIO. Meeting at Cleveland, WAA convention delegates instructed their board to continue negotiations in the hope that unity might be achieved. While the rank-and-file hoped for a link with CIO, the Executive Board realistically concluded that for the foreseeable future the Alliance must remain an independent national body, and that its efforts would be best directed towards building the organization. Nonetheless, Lasser stressed progress towards unity when he told the delegates that as a result of CIO actions during the recession of 1937–1938, the Alliance had found that "for the first time we were not standing alone, but had the backing of millions of union members." He insisted that the "urgencies of the times" mandated "close collaboration between the organized employed and the organized unemployed."[9]

Despite the Alliance's willingness to make concessions, CIO resisted its overtures, and the elusive tie with industrial unionism never materialized. Instead, Lewis and the CIO followed their own path towards the incorporation of unemployed organizing into the union movement. By so doing, the organization believed that it had accepted the labor movement's "full responsibility" for the unemployed "for the first time in American labor history." James B. Carey told the 1938 CIO convention that their unemployment program was based on the assumption that unions were obligated to serve their members "in their time of greatest need." Linked with the CIO's extension of service to the unemployed was a vigorous demand for a federal works program that would guarantee a job to every able-bodied worker. Carey also argued for projects that were "socially necessary" and suited to the needs and skills of unemployed workers. While CIO took responsibility for aiding the casualties of the Depression, it stressed the importance of restoring a full production economy, a goal that could only be reached through increased worker purchasing power.[10]

By late 1938, therefore, the CIO had charted its own course in an attempt to make unemployment a priority issue and to serve the nation's jobless. Lewis's decision to organize and serve the unemployed promised to preserve and even enlarge CIO unions while it aided displaced workers and their families. Although industrial unionism was likely to benefit from this policy, the new departure spelled trouble for the Workers Alliance, which already found itself under attack because of its Communist ties. As the year came to an end, the Alliance's future was very much in doubt.

An Uphill Battle:
The Workers Alliance and the Michigan Unemployed

From the national Alliance's perspective, Michigan and the UAW had become a major problem, especially after the WPA Auxiliary began to spread beyond Detroit to other automobile centers. In July 1938 Benjamin reported to CP authorities that a "bad situation" existed in Michigan. Although WAA was growing in the state, UAW had complicated the situation, and in the crucial Wayne County area, there was "an overeagerness to go into the CIO." In the words of Harold Hartley, fraternal delegate to the Alliance's Cleveland convention, a "fog of confusion" had developed since the UAW had embarked on a program of unemployed organizing. Benjamin frankly noted a tendency in the Detroit area to "completely liquidate our organization."[11]

Despite Benjamin's concerns, the Workers Alliance had demonstrated significant growth during the recession of 1937–1938. By September 1938 the Alliance was organized in thirty Michigan counties and thirty-seven cities, and the organization claimed 7,600 dues-paying members, a 600% increase over the 1937 figure. State organizer Frank Ingram asserted that the Michigan Alliance had emerged as a "progressive power in the state" with close ties to organized labor. A veteran unemployed organizer with experience in the Wisconsin Workers Committee (later Workers Alliance), Ingram was a dedicated Popular Fronter. After a brief stint as a CIO organizer, he devoted his efforts to the revitalization of the Michigan Workers Alliance in 1938. Although Ingram was proud of the Alliance's strong presence in Detroit and Flint, he noted that recent growth had been especially evident in rural, small-town areas, which he regarded as a "real forward step in building farmer-labor unity." On balance, however, Benjamin's assessment seems more accurate than Ingram's assertions. Throughout its history the Alliance had faced great difficulties in mobilizing the Michigan work force,[12] and UAW competition increasingly limited its options and opportunities for growth.

Despite the obstacles, however, the Michigan Communist Party had seen the Workers Alliance as its key link with the state's unemployed. Yet it was realistic enough to recognize the power of the UAW and to seek a collaborative arrangement with the CIO. When WAA and UAW were able to cooperate, as they did in Detroit in 1938, they became a formidable and effective lobby for the jobless. And although the Alliance was widely regarded as heavily influenced by Communists, its radicalism was directed towards demands that were, in the words of Michigan WPA administrator Abner Larned, "entirely justifiable."[13]

As the UAW became more deeply engaged in unemployed organizing, the Workers Alliance and the union came to share the spotlight, each as a distinct strand in a web of advocacy organizations that emerged to champion the rights of those most vulnerable to the vicissitudes of a slumping economy. While the union increasingly dominated project organizing, the Alliance led the resistance to WPA's policy of dismissing aliens, maintained street-level agitation on behalf of relief clients, and exerted pressure for the improvement of living conditions in the unemployed lodging units. One of the leading organizations in this effort was the Single Men's Unemployed League, formed in January 1938 to assert the "right to WPA work." In February 1938, chairman Rudolph Schware claimed that with the support of both UAW and the Workers Alliance, conditions in Fisher Lodge had already improved and the right of single persons to WPA employment had been asserted. By June, over one thousand WPA jobs had been won for single men in Detroit. Similarly, UAW, WAA, and CP activists had participated in the work of the Renters and Consumers League, which fought against evictions and efforts by landlords to extract back rent from unemployed workers. This organization had successfully united Detroit tenants for picketing, negotiations, and occasional successes in stabilizing rents. More dramatic were the league's use of "flying squads" to halt evictions, which gained it a loyal following among the destitute.[14]

Communist Party activists took a leading role in promoting the street protests of 1938. The Party's emphasis on unemployed activity was evident at one CP section meeting in February 1938, at which several organizers stressed the importance of intensified work within the Workers Alliance. At this meeting, a well-known black Party member urged black Detroiters to improve their situations by becoming active in union affairs. He insisted that "every Party member must be a member of the UAW or the Workers Alliance." Two weeks later, the same militant implemented his own idea by leading 250 WPA workers off their project to picket and present demands to the authorities at the Grand Army of the Republic building. Many such activities reflected grass roots initiative to improve living and working conditions on the job and in the neighborhoods. For example, in April 1938 Workers Alliance organizers worked with neighborhood churches, trade unions, language groups, women's organizations, and black organizations to issue a call for the creation of an east side unemployed federation, christened the East Side Unemployed Council in an effort to establish continuity with the militancy of the early 1930s. This group focused especially on the inadequacies of the relief system and included the larger community of the nonunion unemployed.[15]

The Alliance's drive to highlight "peoples' issues" was also evident in Dearborn. In the home of the Ford empire it played a unique role as the most militant workers' organization in a nonunion environment. Claiming CIO endorsement, the Communist-led Alliance embraced the causes of unemployed single men, direct relief clients, and laid-off alien WPA workers. In April 1938 a series of protests resulted in ameliorative action by the authorities. Not long after a single men's planning meeting had occurred, a bevy of new WPA positions were announced. Similarly, when several relief recipients in an Alliance delegation spoke on their own behalf before Dearborn Welfare Commissioner L. N. Hutchinson, most grievances were promptly adjusted. CP observers asserted that these successes had led the Dearborn unemployed to join the Workers Alliance "by the flock."[16]

Although Communists led in these activities, the UAW consciously lent its support to the "peoples' organizations," and in the case of the Renters and Consumers League, union financial support was essential to the gains made. Likewise, when in February 1938 protests were lodged with Mayor Reading on behalf of the single unemployed, the lobbying was the work of a united front composed of the Workers Alliance and UAW Locals 174, 155, 157, and 208. Similar pressure campaigns in March, aimed at Governor Murphy and the Detroit Welfare Commission, reflected the interest of both the union's west side local and Briggs Local 212 in the plight of single persons.[17] Although the UAW and its welfare committees were deeply involved in these initiatives, the important role played by Harold Hartley and Nat Wald confirm the cooperation that occurred between the Alliance and the union in early 1938. The drive to organize and serve the unemployed was, at this stage, a combined effort in the spirit of the Popular Front, especially in locals sympathetic to the Unity Caucus. It was such worker unity that brought the greatest successes in aiding the Wayne County jobless.

These developments were consistent with the national Alliance's courtship of the CIO in April 1938. Exploratory negotiations had laid the basis for solidarity between the unionized and the nonunion unemployed. In Michigan, these tentative arrangements were best exemplified by the efforts made by Reuther and the west side Socialists to arrive at a cooperative relationship with Hartley and the CP element in the union. In April, CP activist Rudolph Schware of the Wayne County Workers Alliance told Reuther that the Single Men's Unemployed League regarded Local 174 as "one of the strongest forces in helping the single men at Fisher Lodge" and in "ending the discrimination against single men and women" by the Detroit Welfare officials and the WPA. Schware and the Alliance proposed a division of organizing jurisdiction based on the CIO's plan of organizing the union unemployed and leaving the nonunion jobless to the Alliance.[18]

For a moment it seemed that the marriage would be consummated. Two days after Schware's proposal, Lasser was in Detroit to speak on the WAA relationship with the AFL and CIO. And not long thereafter Alliance leader Frank Ingram asked Germer for a subsidy from the CIO to supplement his Alliance salary for Michigan unemployed organizing. Germer withheld salary support, and instead explained the CIO's policy of organizing all potential union members into their respective unions. Although Germer was cautious about a financial commitment from CIO, Benjamin later acknowledged to HUAC that in 1938, the Workers Alliance had received a $7,000 contribution from UAW. And in June 1938 Hartley maintained that one of the "immediate jobs ahead" for the Local 174 Welfare and Unemployment Committee was collaboration with the Workers Alliance to organize all non-CIO unemployed into the Alliance.[19] In short, cooperative unemployed work, including the mobilization of both relief recipients and project workers, went on simultaneously with UAW's major effort to organize WPA employees in spring 1938.

Other Responses to Adversity:
A Statewide Unemployed Movement

Beyond Detroit, unemployed organizations grew more slowly, but despite less favorable local conditions several centers of activity developed during the "Roosevelt Recession" of 1937–1938. In these peripheral areas, the Workers Alliance was a strong partner in the front against joblessness, and in some localities it became the leading unemployed group in 1938. Michigan WPA administrator L. M. Nims reported persistent difficulties with the Workers Alliance over routine grievances, especially in Pontiac and Oakland County. Official responses to Alliance initiatives suggest that WPA was sometimes able to remedy minor problems, but very often found itself either swamped with nuisance complaints or hamstrung by legislative and policy guidelines. One important reason for the Alliance's active presence in Pontiac was the destructive factionalism that threatened to destroy the UAW's Welfare Committee in Local 159. By August 1938 complaints about Martin's disruptive influence were pouring into Lewis's office in Washington, most of them pleading for CIO intervention to save the union's unemployed organization. Typical was a letter that endorsed the WPA Auxiliary as essential to "keep the spirit of unionism among our WPA workers," but argued that Martin's organizer had "made a mess of every committee on which he served." Another critic reported that because of the "fratricidal conflict" in the union, the Local 159 Welfare Committee had been abolished. Finally, one frustrated unionist recounted the successful organization of WPA workers in response to the UAW Executive Board's twenty-point program. When Martin's lieutenant, William Taylor, dissolved the Auxiliary, Pontiac workers regarded the move as an unwelcome "attempt to insert factionalism into the WPA organization."[20]

Much less volatile was the situation in western Michigan, where there was relatively little industrial concentration, and where conservative social attitudes undercut militant unemployed activity. A Workers Alliance functioned in Kalamazoo, for example, but it confined itself to modest requests concerning work rules and working conditions. Another local organization, the American Federation of Unemployed, advanced a polite inquiry into wage rates and maximum hours, which drew an equally pleasant referral to state WPA officials. From Benton Harbor came a plaintive expression of concern from the Workers Alliance over the plight of the single unemployed, who were "walking the streets" after being refused jobs because of their single status. The response from Washington was a clinical recitation of WPA policies that deferred to state prerogative on certification, which meant that some states gave preference to those jobless with dependents. In one instance the Kalamazoo Alliance, working through Benjamin, did succeed in reversing sixty-five dismissals at Camp Custer. More promising was the brief spurt of organizational activity occasioned by a CIO foray into Kalamazoo in April 1938, when veteran unemployed organizer and CIO representative Frank Ingram joined the United Paper Mill Workers to import John Brophy for an inspirational message. Designed to stimulate CIO activism in hostile territory, Brophy's speech dwelt heavily upon the commitment of Lewis and the national organization to the protection of unemployed union members and the promotion of expanded relief and WPA programs. Brophy implied that paper workers should organize in self-defense, with an eye to protection in the event of layoffs.[21]

Brophy's remarks injected an element of energy into a debate that had produced little sharp conflict. Economically diverse and culturally conservative, southwestern Michigan was not fruitful ground for the growth of militant unionism. The tepid responses to the few organizational drives mounted by the Alliance and the CIO mirrored the values of an area geographically and ideologically distinct from the urban southeast. In general, unemployed organizing and agitation in the southwestern district was marked by an air of civility quite different from the acrimonious interaction that characterized labor-management discourse on the projects in the urban centers of southeast Michigan, where relief clients and WPA workers displayed greater militance in asserting their conception of worker rights.

Similarly, the Grand Rapids area was slow to respond through organization to the recession crisis of 1938. Reflecting the area's strong support for self-help, Mayor George W. Welsh wrote Senator Prentiss Brown in April 1938 that he detested direct relief and intended to give able-bodied citizens an opportunity to work. He pledged that Grand Rapids would "obligate itself to the limit" if federal loans were made available to fund public works programs. His willingness to consider government spending suggested that an undercurrent of public impatience made fiscal restraint difficult for even dedicated conservatives. As early as March 1938, a group of Grand Rapids relief clients calling themselves the WPA-Relief Auxiliary organized to demand an expansion of the WPA program and a guarantee of humane treatment of relief recipients. The group pledged to organize all Grand Rapids workers, who were "awakening at last and *will be* heard." Among the leaders of this body was the veteran Socialist and unemployed agitator, D. B. Hovey, who had been one of the leaders of organizational efforts during the

Hoover administration. Even more significant was the sponsorship of the CIO Relief Committee, which meant that at last a formidable labor organization had committed itself to the struggling unemployed movement in Kent County.[22]

By April 1938 labor's involvement had generated widespread support, at least by Grand Rapids standards. On April 13 the UAW joined with Labor's Non-Partisan League to sponsor a mass meeting to demand that the Kent County Welfare Commission release all available funds so that relief benefits could be expanded. In addition, the group adopted resolutions calling for improvement of working conditions on WPA projects. UAW welfare director Richard Leonard urged a crowd of one thousand to pressure the commission for action on the relief issue, while Tracy Doll of LNPL told them that they would have only themselves to blame if their representatives "[made] suckers of [them]." Doll insisted that "labor must take for itself what the American system originally intended it to have." By June an active UAW WPA Auxiliary organization was firmly established in Grand Rapids, based in Kelvinator Local 206.[23] The ravages of unemployment had produced militance even in the home territory of the cautious Christian Labor Association.

A similar restlessness was evident in widely scattered parts of the state by mid-1938. UAW, WAA, and independent unemployment groups were emerging in previously quiescent communities such as Ludington, Elsie, Bay City, Saginaw, and Mount Clemens. The critical issues ranged from inadequate relief to WPA working conditions and inadequate compensation on the WPA sewing projects, which primarily affected women workers. In most instances these efforts produced orderly protest, though in the Bay City–Saginaw area several WPA strikes halted work on the projects and resulted in modest gains for jobless workers.[24]

Closer to the urban centers of the southeast, the UAW was even more active and competition with the Workers Alliance more intense. When the UAW launched its major WPA organizing initiative in March 1938, Leonard moved aggressively into the Lansing area, where Lovestoneite influence was substantial. Because of the Lovestone group's interest in mobilizing the unemployed as a bulwark against the CP, Leonard's WPA initiative produced a sympathetic first response. By April, however, the Unity Caucus was encountering heavy opposition from the Martin forces as factionalism intensified. One Reutherite reported that some Lansing workers were "out to organize the unemployed in the Workers Alliance in order to keep them away from the UAW and Martin." As a result, a small but active Workers Alliance competed with Martin's backers for hegemony among the jobless in Lansing, which remained a heavily contested area until the late 1930s. By 1939, however, the Lovestone group had gained control of the Lansing UAW and the WPA Welfare Department dominated unemployed organizing in the area.[25]

The competition for the loyalty of the unemployed in Lansing was surpassed by the dramatic struggle that unfolded in Flint, where the activities of Communist Charles Killinger had given the Workers Alliance a foothold by 1938. While the CP had actively colonized in Flint, the SP also had a strong toehold, due to the ongoing efforts of Reuther loyalists such as Kermit and Genora Johnson, Tom Klasey, Roy K. Lawrence, and Ted LaDuke. Consequently, the stage was set for conflict when the massive layoffs of 1938 triggered a spirited battle to represent the Flint jobless.

The recession of 1937–1938 brought the rapid expansion of the Flint labor movement to a temporary halt, although the militancy of the sitdowns remained. The massive unemployment of 1938 marked the first half of that year as the nadir of the Great Depression in Flint. By April 1938, 65 percent of Buick and Chevrolet workers had been laid off, while early in the year some 20,000 Genessee County families received public assistance. Never very sympathetic to the needs of the local underclass, area relief officials exacerbated tensions with an undisguised verbal attack on their clients. Historian Ron Edsforth concludes that their ill-advised criticism of the needy backfired in that it further solidified working-class consciousness by uniting the employed and unemployed.[26]

In the short run, mass unemployment meant that it was a major challenge just to keep the union intact. UAW veteran Tom Klasey later recalled the development of the union's unemployed organization as a matter of self-preservation that would enable unionists "to hold [their] people together." Complicating the task was a competitive initiative by the remnants of the old Unemployed Councils, now operating through the Workers Alliance. When UAW acted to hold its unemployed members by cutting dues to 50 cents per month, the Alliance forces countered by slashing dues to 25 cents. Because the Alliance was not as strong as the union, it was less able to aid jobless workers, and eventually most unemployed unionists sided with Klasey and the UAW WPA Welfare Auxiliary. The reputation of a union that had only recently brought General Motors to its knees was a significant deterrent to the growth of the Workers Alliance as an effective unemployed organization in Flint.[27]

In contrast to the frustrated Workers Alliance, UAW made a major contribution to the effort to meet the needs of the economic casualties of 1938. By January 1938 the Flint Local 156 Welfare Committee was providing increased advice, instruction, and encouragement to potential relief registrants, who received counseling in a series of local neighborhood meetings. But the clearest expression of this new militance was the fledgling UAW WPA Auxiliary organized in March 1938. Led by such militants as Gilbert Clark, Claude Workman, and Roy K. Lawrence, the Flint Auxiliary immediately demanded that government "start the wheels" where "private industry is on a sit-down strike." Addressing the Flint Auxiliary's organizational meeting, UAW legal counsel Larry Davidow blistered American industry for its withdrawal of capital investment and insisted that government "take over the wheels of industry and move on." Clark argued that since the auto industry had "taken its present position to defeat our [UAW] movement," it was necessary to "organize on the outside [WPA]." He maintained that because politicians loved votes, "all the people on the WPA have to do is to organize and they can get anything within reason." Clark denied that strikes would be needed because the WPA Auxiliary could "just turn on the steam" and "Senators and Congressmen will listen."[28]

Once organized, the Auxiliary worked to modify working conditions on the Flint projects and to raise WPA wage levels. Moreover, pressure from the unemployed brought the work-sharing issue to the fore within the union. Klasey noted that "the unemployed question went all the way through this organization," and because many employed workers resisted wage reductions to spread the work, the UAW had "one hell of a fight." Despite these tensions, an awareness of class interests held Flint workers together in an expression of a tenuous solidarity. For example, the celebration of the sit-down's first anniversary had a second purpose: to "demand adequate relief for the thousands of unemployed workers in the automobile industry."[29]

This overriding unity was evident in April 1938 when Flint labor planned and carried out a major mass demonstration to focus

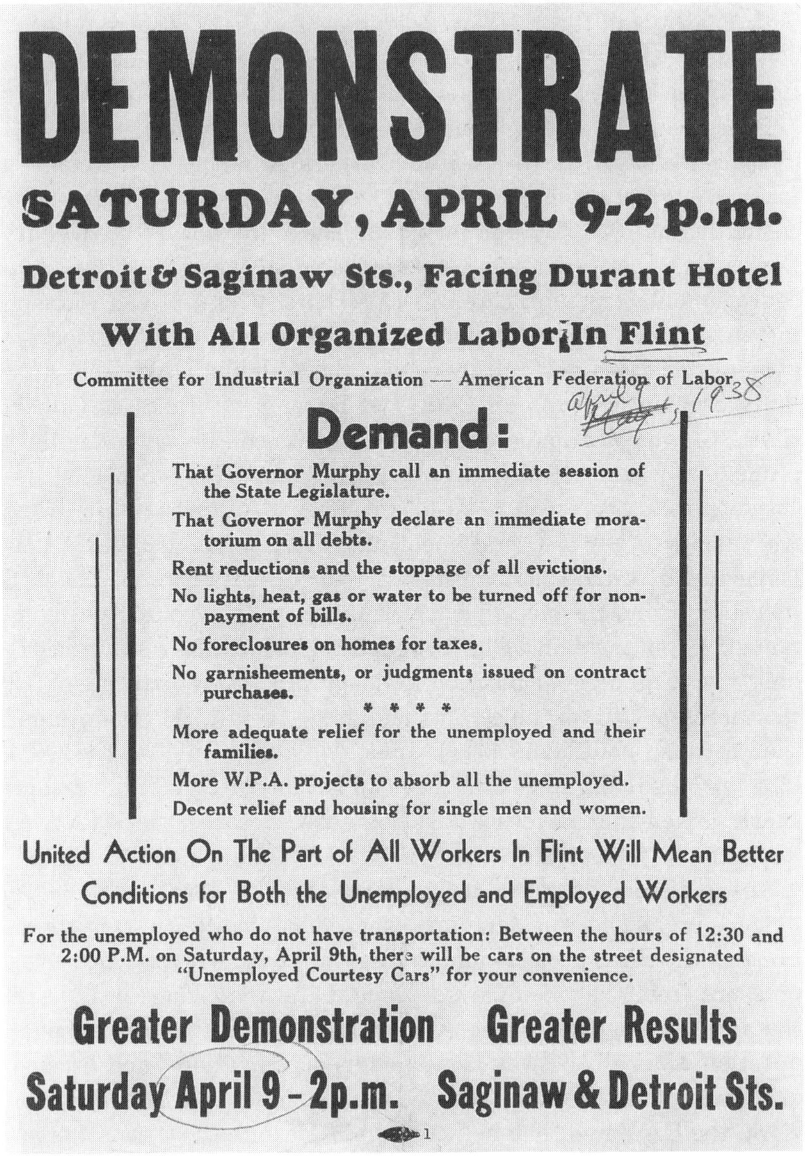

DEMONSTRATE

SATURDAY, APRIL 9-2 p.m.

Detroit & Saginaw Sts., Facing Durant Hotel

With All Organized Labor In Flint

Committee for Industrial Organization — American Federation of Labor

Demand:

That Governor Murphy call an immediate session of the State Legislature.

That Governor Murphy declare an immediate moratorium on all debts.

Rent reductions and the stoppage of all evictions.

No lights, heat, gas or water to be turned off for non-payment of bills.

No foreclosures on homes for taxes.

No garnisheements, or judgments issued on contract purchases.

＊ ＊ ＊ ＊

More adequate relief for the unemployed and their families.

More W.P.A. projects to absorb all the unemployed.

Decent relief and housing for single men and women.

United Action On The Part of All Workers In Flint Will Mean Better Conditions for Both the Unemployed and Employed Workers

For the unemployed who do not have transportation: Between the hours of 12:30 and 2:00 P.M. on Saturday, April 9th, there will be cars on the street designated "Unemployed Courtesy Cars" for your convenience.

Greater Demonstration   Greater Results
Saturday April 9 - 2p.m.   Saginaw & Detroit Sts.

Figure 14   The Flint Unemployed Organize, April 9, 1938 *(Archives of Labor and Urban Affairs, Wayne State University)*

national attention on the city's critical relief problem. (See figure 14.) Even the AFL cooperated for this purpose through the participation of John Reid, secretary of the Michigan Federation of Labor, who spoke on the relief problem as a legislative issue. Challenged by William Green, the Michigan craft unionists argued that their presence was vital to the reelection effort of Governor Frank Murphy, the featured speaker at the rally. AFL and CIO organizers were committed to "united action on the part of all workers in Flint" as a means to achieve better conditions for both unemployed and employed workers. The depth of solidarity was underscored by the participation of both Homer Martin and Rudolph Schware, CF activist and president of the Wayne County Workers Alliance.[30]

The mass meeting brought out over 10,000 demonstrators, who gathered at Flint City Hall to protest unemployment and plead for a debt moratorium. Murphy told the crowd that he had spoken to White House officials, who promised a supplementary relief assistance program. Murphy declared: "You want action and you are going to get it." The governor also pointedly complimented Flint's AFL and CIO leaders for joining in a united front demonstration, a matter of no little significance for a liberal incumbent seeking reelection. (See figure 15.) A parade of labor leaders echoed Murphy's enthusiasm for programs to aid the jobless in Flint, where a reported 60,000–75,000 were on relief.[31] The severity of the job crisis predisposed workers to coalesce for an event symbolic of a new class awareness.

By April 1938 the Flint WPA Auxiliary was emerging as the strongest of the city's unemployed organizations. While the Auxiliary had invited Workers Alliance members to join the UAW unemployed group, the Alliance was unwilling to abandon the gains it had made before 1937. Despite declining influence, the Alliance continued to speak out on the unemployment issue and lobby for its dwindling membership. More significantly, it attempted to meet the UAW challenge with an erroneous claim of sole collective bargaining jurisdiction on WPA projects, which was denied by WPA administrator David K. Niles in Washington. Assured of an open field, Flint WPA organizer Gil Clark moved aggressively to establish UAW's position on the projects. A major breakthrough occurred when Clark, union welfare director Paul Treadway, and Local 156 president Jack Little journeyed to the capital at Lansing, where state WPA officials confirmed their charges that Genessee County WPA supervisors were violating the law by denying UAW bargaining rights on the projects. The effective result of the conference was recognition of the union's WPA Auxiliary as bargaining agent for Flint's project workers. Little proclaimed a WPA victory that meant "organization benefits and protection for the workers outside the

Figure 15 Governor Frank Murphy Pledges Aid to the Jobless, April 9, 1938 *(Archives of Labor and Urban Affairs, Wayne State University)*

shop as well as in." Promising an accelerated organizational drive, he argued that WPA foremen and supervisors would now be forced to "deal with the abc's of collective bargaining and how to treat a union man."[32]

By June 1938 the WPA Auxiliary's prestige had risen as Gil Clark became more effective in meeting worker demands. Although it continued to function on a reduced scale, the Flint Workers Alliance experienced the same decline that affected the organization elsewhere in the state. Symptomatic of the union Auxiliary's hegemony was CP activist Wyndham Mortimer's firm insistence in June that "dual organizations" among the unemployed be avoided and that the UAW jobless "not be segregated as a result of the unfortunate condition of unemployment."[33] With leftists like Mortimer backing the Auxiliary, the Alliance simply had nowhere to turn, and the UAW rapidly filled the power vacuum thus created. Moreover, these developments must be viewed in the wider national context of the negotiations then under way between Lasser, Benjamin, and the CIO Unemployment Committee. Since the national discussions seemed likely to end in the quiet absorption of the Alliance into the CIO's proposed WPA and Relief Division, dual unionism served no group's interest in June 1938.

As the year wore on, the WPA Auxiliary functioned successfully for the Flint unemployed. As early as April 1938, a united front labor sit-in at the Genessee County relief office forced the revocation of cuts in county food allowances. And later in the year, united protests also resulted in the removal of an especially offensive local relief official, Louis Ludington. Perhaps most dramatic was a July sit-down that idled an estimated 1,500 WPA workers and ended in altered work schedules and higher hourly rates through a cut in working hours. The UAW expressed the conviction that the successful work stoppage would "convince the proper authorities that collective bargaining is here to stay."[34]

Union power also began to make a difference in another area far removed from the industrial heart of Michigan. In the remote areas of the Upper Peninsula, the timber workers strike of 1937 had left the mark of the CIO in an area long hostile to any form of unionism, let alone the industrial variety. Although the strike had resulted in the organization of one-third of the UP's timber workers, the union never reached its goal of "unionism 100 percent throughout the Upper Peninsula." The opposition to labor generated by the events of 1937 only intensified the UP power structure's hostility to the Left. In an attack on government spending for job programs, the *Manistique Pioneer-Tribune* summarized the area's antagonism by arguing that the state needed to "stop financing radicals, communists, labor agitators and plotters."[35] All of which presaged hard times for the UP unemployed movement.

Despite the handicaps, however, Timber Workers Local 15 had made an impressive start against great odds. Plagued by seasonal unemployment and curtailments in production, lumberjacks and their union embraced the CIO's new departure in unemployed organizing in November 1937, when the first drive to create unemployment committees began.[36]

Matt Savola and other union activists soon settled on a solution to the problem of unemployment, specifically attuned to the needs of the UP. In Lansing for a CIO legislative conference, Savola conferred with state relief administrators to press the case for an immediate relief appropriation to meet the needs of jobless timber workers. His plan became clearer on 14 January 1938 when he met in Bessemer with FERA administrator Walter Berry to urge the establishment of relief camps where the jacks might at least exist at a subsistence level. Helvi Savola later recalled that "the camps were their homes and without their homes the workers had no place to live." To the union, the answer was the relief camp to house the unemployed, a conclusion concurred in by Berry and Michigan relief officials, but which meant that the jobbers and companies would have to agree to their use. An alternative advanced by Matt Savola and Local 15 was the use of abandoned Civilian Conservation Corps camps, which Berry also thought feasible. Savola argued that the lumberjack had "never been given a square deal" because he had been "considered apart from society, living in a separate world," but that his "voice must be heard."[37]

The results were encouraging. Federal officials at the Bessemer conference agreed to investigate the problem and by March 1938 several cooperative relief camps had been opened, including facilities in Iron River, Ontonagon, and Munising. Both government and industry sites were used, while under union pressure, counties and municipalities supplied provisions. Savola urged Timber Workers locals to keep the pressure on the companies and the relief authorities for more assistance. The union's first priority was to fill the camps and get more opened, but it is also true that the jacks in the camps provided a ready supply of picketers for strike duty, when needed. Finally, on 1 March a delegation from Local 15 and other jobless lumberjacks secured a major concession from Walter Berry, who agreed at a conference in Munising that all eligible workers would either be employed by WPA or placed in relief camps. A report in *Midwest Labor* noted with pride that the agreement marked "the first time that the jacks are receiving any aid and being eligible for WPA."[38] Even in unfriendly territory, CIO and union power had scored a victory for a forgotten element in the underclass.

The energetic work of the Timber Workers Union complemented the ongoing activities of an aggressive Workers Alliance that had long dominated UP unemployed activity. Always a formidable force in Gogebic County, the Alliance again flexed its muscles in July 1938 when its Ironwood chapter launched a petition campaign to remove county road commissioner George Karonsky, who refused to approve a major WPA construction project then pending. Simultaneously, Savola, who maintained close ties with the Alliance, appealed to the county board for an increase in relief allowances to offset cuts sustained in May and June. In response, the Alliance's old ally, Commissioner Ray Garvey, pushed through a resolution calling for an investigation of Savola's charges and allowing for a possible expansion of relief benefits. Finnish leftist George Rahkonen concluded that the board's acceptance of Garvey's resolution confirmed the power of organization and of labor support for the jobless, who would be motivated to embrace the labor movement.[39]

This collaboration between the Timber Workers Union and the Alliance reflected the pervasive influence of Finnish radicalism in the UP, which was evident in the ethnic composition of both the rank-and-file and leadership of both organizations. Equally important was the CIO's demonstrated interest in the jobless. Indeed, when CIO regional director Adolph Germer toured the region in August 1938, one of his major purposes was to clarify and promote the organization's policy of organizing unemployed workers through existing unions. Following Germer's meeting with Workers Alliance representatives in Iron River, for example, local WPA workers immediately proceeded to elect project stewards and committeemen to conform with CIO policy.[40]

Beyond its Gogebic County stronghold, the Workers Alliance remained a dynamic force in economically devastated Houghton and Keewenaw counties, where the percentage of families on relief hovered near 40 percent. Active Alliance chapters were operating in Toivola, Hancock, Calumet-Laurium, and Ahmeek. Here the CP and its supporters in the Alliance reached the peak of their influence in the late 1930s. Because there were still no miners' unions in existence, the WAA became doubly significant as the sole voice of organized worker protest. And with over 20 percent of the male work force on the WPA rolls, its basic constituency was large. Without initial direction, the organization found natural leaders, such as young Ed Spiegal, a CP activist upon whom leadership was thrust. At a meeting in Calumet, Spiegal found himself before a large crowd and responded to pressure from the crowd by accepting the Alliance presidency, which he held in 1938 and 1939. In Spiegal's words, he "learned to become a leader."[41]

But who were the mentors? One key missionary to the UP was the ubiquitous Frank Ingram, who made several trips to Houghton to aid in the organization of the Copper County Workers Alliance. In 1938 Ingram came to Hancock and Calumet to "raise hell" with

Alliance organizers. Ingram wondered why, in view of the massive unemployment in the UP, the Workers Alliance was not even bigger than it was. When Spiegal noted the difficulty created by the dues requirement, Ingram showed him the "angles" that could be used to expand the membership without full dues payment. To Spiegal and the inexperienced Alliance leaders, Ingram was a "good organizer" who "could teach."[42]

And his students were apt learners. When an Alliance-sponsored WPA Workers Conference brought unemployed leaders from Houghton, Ontonagon, and Keewenaw counties together in Hancock on 29 July 1938, the result was a petition for a wage hike that drew not only Alliance support and public backing, but also the endorsement of UP merchants, business, and professional men. The local establishment argued that its "welfare [was] dependent to a large extent on that of the WPA workers" and that therefore the increase should be granted.[43] While the entreaty failed to produce the desired result, the broad local support testified to the Alliance's effectiveness in building a consensus behind a humane work and relief program that served the interest of the wider community. It also revealed the dependency on government investment characteristic of an area in sharp economic decline. Finally, the influence of the Workers Alliance in the Copper Country provides an important reminder that the unemployed movement's impact must be evaluated by many measures, including the development of social consensus on the goals it pursued.

The wage issue was the major unifying force elsewhere in the UP, especially in Escanaba and Delta County, where CP militant Carl Anderson led an active Workers Alliance. Anderson later stressed the multiplicity of concerns that drew the organization's attention, including intervention with welfare officials, eviction actions, food and fuel supply, and the "good government" movement. A WPA employee from 1935 to 1940, Anderson served as Alliance president in 1938 and 1939 when WPA came under increasing attack from the Right. Under his leadership, the Escanaba Alliance struck for an increase in the monthly WPA wage from $44 to $63 and a 20 percent boost in direct relief allotments. Like most other Alliance actions, the strike failed to alter the legislatively determined wage structure, but the unemployed union did make headway on working conditions and fuel assistance after Governor Murphy came to Escanaba and mediated the dispute. Cold weather work was henceforth limited with no loss of income if working days fell below ten days per month, and local officials agreed to permit the jobless to cut city wood and work off their utility bills in compensatory labor.[44]

The presence of Murphy reflected one unique feature of the Delta County Alliance: its political sophistication. Under Anderson's leadership, the Escanaba-area Alliance developed into a politically conscious organization of 450 members. Anderson, later UP Communist Party secretary and 1940 congressional candidate, moved the unemployed into local politics by creating the Escanaba Good Government Forum, later known as the Voters Labor League. This group united Socialists, Communists, Democrats, the Workers Alliance, and several local labor unions into an active citizens' organization that rooted out graft in local government, endorsed candidates, and pressured the city council. Although never very successful in its endorsement policy, the League did collaborate with the Central Labor Council to pressure the Escanaba City Council into hiring a Milwaukee Socialist, George E. Bean, as city manager, which meant that a crucial local official was very sympathetic to the needs of the unemployed.[45]

An important issue that energized Finnish leftists in the UP was the federal ruling in 1937 that aliens be dropped from the WPA rolls unless they took out citizenship papers. The new regulation created a work relief crisis in those counties most heavily populated by Finnish immigrants, such as Gogebic and Iron. In response to the government action and with the encouragement of CP workers and Alliance organizers, aliens began to flock into the UP county clerks' offices to apply for citizenship. In Iron County, for example, where 1,150 noncitizens worked for WPA, the "notoriously radical Workers Alliance" drew criticism for its efforts on behalf of aliens.[46] The entire controversy underscored the importance of cultural heritage as an explanation for the predominance of the CP and the Workers Alliance in the region's active unemployed movement.

In the Upper Peninsula, the absence of a strong labor movement had created a vacuum quickly filled by the CP, which enjoyed a firm if somewhat narrow base within the Finnish immigrant community. As in the desperate years of the early Depression, the Left worked tirelessly to advance the interests of unemployed workers who, isolated from the centers of power and population, were truly the discards of modern industrial society. While the Timber Workers Union and Workers Alliance had supplanted the miners unions, Unemployed Councils, and United Farmers League as the instruments through which jobless workers expressed their anger, Communist initiative and cultural determinants remained as clear lines of continuity with the unemployed organizations of the early 1930s. If the UP's jobless respected Communist leadership, their decision was a rational choice in view of the bleak outlook they faced, confronted as they were by the overwhelming influence of the lumber interests and mining corporations. Doomed though it was, theirs was a genuine grass-roots response to consolidated power in an age of industrial concentration that had left them as casualties of a crippled economy.

Climax: The Last Days of Summer

As the summer of 1938 drew to a close, the Michigan unemployed faced a new crisis. In mid-August, Governor Frank Murphy announced that the state's relief reserves had been exhausted and that a special legislative session would be needed to enact an emergency relief allotment. Reacting to Murphy's proclamation, Frank Ingram and the state Workers Alliance moved in late August to build a consensus behind the governor's position by calling a Michigan Conference on Work and Security to coincide with the special session. The conference was intended to unite AFL, CIO, farm, church, and ethnic organizations in a drive to force the enactment of a supplemental relief appropriation. While William Taylor and the UAW WPA Auxiliary called upon all Michigan locals to pressure their representatives to support Murphy's $10 million plan, Frank Martel coolly told Ingram that he would not be in Lansing with the Alliance "for obvious reasons."[47] Martel's remark reflected the AFL's continuing suspicion of CP influence in the unemployed movement.

The Alliance conference drew over two hundred delegates to the capital on the day of Murphy's address to the legislature. Meeting with the Alliance, a friendly governor promised to force the lawmakers to stay in session until the appropriation was assured. He was, however, embarrassed by the Alliance throng that packed the gallery for his speech. Murphy insisted that he had not invited the group and had actually discouraged labor groups from making a mass appeal for relief monies. Surprised liberals became increasingly uneasy when Representative Philip Rahoi of the UP commandeered the microphone during a recess to introduce Alliance national president David Lasser.[48]

In sweeping terms, Lasser endorsed both Murphy and his relief program, which he regarded as a "minimum program" that would merely keep the needy alive. Lasser's remarks prepared the way for an intense lobbying effort by Alliance delegates, directed by Ingram. Other lobbyists involved included Alan Strachan of the Michigan Non-Partisan League, Mort Furay of the Wayne County NPL, and John Reid of the MFL. The Alliance's national organ, *Work*, insisted that pressure from the gallery had shown the legislators "in no uncertain fashion, what the underprivileged of the state desired and expected from the special session." And when the bill passed, the Alliance was quick to claim credit for the outcome.[49]

Not long after the Alliance's assault on the Michigan legislature, the UAW WPA Department countered with its own lobbying effort in Washington, which focused on increased wages and improved grievance procedures on WPA projects. Coordinated by the UAW's William Taylor and CIO unemployment director Ralph Hetzel, this pressure campaign went to the highest levels of the Roosevelt administration with a demand for a substantial increase in compensation on WPA projects. On September 23 a delegation of twenty representatives from the UAW WPA Department, led by Paul Silver of Taylor's office, presented Roosevelt and the WPA's Aubrey Williams a detailed brief recounting unemployment and living conditions in the industrial states of Michigan, Indiana, Ohio, and Wisconsin. The delegation urged an increase in WPA wages and hours that would yield a monthly income of $90, a continuation of surplus commodity distribution, the elimination of urban-rural wage differentials, medical care for WPA workers, negotiation of job reclassifications, and a prohibition of discrimination against stewards and workers for organizational activity. The project workers argued that there was "every good reason for the extension of WPA in order to achieve its objectives" and save many American citizens from "pauperization and demoralization."[50]

To complement the effort in Washington, Taylor mobilized Michigan locals for a lobbying campaign in support of the September demands. Taylor unleashed a torrent of letters and telegrams to

Roosevelt, Hopkins, and the WPA bureaucracy, all backing his department's longstanding call for a 75-cent hourly rate and a thirty-hour week on the projects. Union leaders understood that their demands could not be met at the time, but the lobbying campaign successfully demonstrated the vitality of the WPA Department as a powerful alternative to the Workers Alliance. Moreover, the Washington pilgrimage gave wide publicity to a program that UAW fully intended to be a major legislative priority in the Seventy-sixth Congress in 1939.[51] The union understood full well that the project workers' battle would be won or lost in the nation's capital.

Before the battle could be joined, however, the Michigan unemployed movement was to suffer a serious setback as a result of the political and factional strife that threatened to devour the UAW. The blow was devastating because by September 1938, the union had become the voice of the state's unemployed in the heavily industrialized areas of the southeast. Staff worker Ethel Polk recalled clearly that the UAW Welfare Department literally "became the establishment for those people."[52] Meanwhile, the Workers Alliance was seriously weakened by escalating charges of Communist domination and the resulting deterioration of the political climate that had nurtured its earlier growth. Michigan's gubernatorial politics, together with vicious union infighting, combined to make the campaign of 1938 and the legislative battles of 1939 a mean season for liberalism and a period of great danger for the organized unemployed.

8

Troubled Times
Political Conflict and Factional Strife, 1938–1939

The intense factionalism that had paralyzed UAW by August 1938 was in part the product of open warfare among Michigan Socialists, Lovestoneites, and their Communist adversaries, all of whom fought for the heart of the union against the backdrop of recession. Between the summer of 1938 and the UAW split of March 1939, these political battles paralleled a related struggle between unemployed organizations, as ideologues vied for leadership of Michigan's jobless legions. The result of these conflicts was the disruption of the union and the eventual weakening of the unemployed movement in Michigan.

Warfare on the Left

In late 1937 and early 1938, the Communists had gained grudging acceptance as an element in the emerging Unity Caucus within UAW. This rapprochement was made possible by the cooperation of the more pragmatic Socialists, many of whom had been willing to work with the CP in a united front alliance. In turn, the growth of the Unity forces had occurred side by side with an important internal revitalization in the Socialist Party itself.

The most striking development for the SP was the emergence of an aggressive labor-oriented wing spearheaded by the energetic members of Detroit's Branch 2. Led by such activists as the Reuthers, Ben Fischer, Emil Mazey, George Edwards, and Leonard Woodcock, the union-based Socialists brought a new vitality to the party's activities in Michigan, including a strong commitment to unemployed organizing. Symptomatic of this revival was the growth of the Socialist Auto League under the direction of its national secretary, Ben Fischer. The League was a coordinating committee that united Socialist organizers in the major auto centers of the midwest. The Auto League's activism reflected the conviction that Socialism could only prosper if its adherents diverted their energies away from the party's traditional emphasis on electoral politics towards vigorous and sustained grass-roots organizing through the union movement. As a result of the party's new emphasis on the union, Fischer, who was also state party secretary, could report in July 1938 that significant SP growth had occurred in Michigan's industrial centers, especially Flint, Detroit, Lansing, Pontiac, and Bay City.[1]

Working to strengthen both the SP and the union, Fischer had to maneuver his way through an ideological minefield. He found himself caught between the Communists, who had been effective unionists, and the Lovestoneites, who were working with the most conservative and unsavory elements in the Michigan labor movement. His task, then, was to pry the Socialists away from their flirtation with the CP, while keeping them independent of the Lovestone clique that had become such a significant influence on Homer Martin. If he could strengthen the labor Socialists, it would be possible to advance the SP cause in Michigan; to Fischer, the "purpose of the union was political."[2]

The Michigan Auto League and the state party thus placed a high priority on the preservation of the union in the face of its escalating internal crisis. The League struggled to find a middle ground between the Communist-Frankensteen coalition and "reactionary administration elements" led by Fred Pieper and identified with Homer Martin. Basing their hopes for unity on the 26 May twenty-point program, Socialists worked to prevent the rupture of the union through the reinstatement of the five suspended officers and reliance upon CIO guidance. For their part, the Communists argued against destructive factionalism. Denouncing the Lovestoneites as the primary source of faction, Communist spokesmen William Weinstone and B. K. Gebert insisted that "the great body of leaders within the UAW are constructive and that it is necessary for them to get together by eliminating factions and work for the best interests of the union." The CP called for a return to the "real issues before the union," such as the Ford drive, union unity, and Murphy's reelection. Party protestations to the contrary, however, Weinstone bore heavy responsibility for the disruption.[3]

Since the factional dispute unfolded against the background of the devastating recession of 1937–1938, one of the central issues to be confronted was the UAW's activity among the jobless. In June 1938 Socialist UAW organizer George Edwards noted that the UAW's objective, as "the dominant CIO union of this area," was "to organize them all as fast as we can." The full mobilization of the unemployed was essential to "prevent the creation of a tremendous scab labor supply." His enthusiasm reflected the consensus view within the Socialist Auto League that "more and more, the center of union attention and activity in Michigan [was] becoming WPA and relief." This organizational work focused on such auto centers as Detroit, Pontiac, and Flint, but as of June 1938 Socialist activity among the unemployed had not yet "crystallized."[4]

At this point, there was evidence of a rapprochement between Martin and the SP organizers active in the WPA Auxiliary. Martin had always supported aggressive union involvement in unemployed organizing. With the Progressive Caucus in ruins, he now sought allies among the union Socialists. His attitude towards the SP had become "extremely friendly," and by June Socialists George Edwards and Kermit Johnson had been offered positions in the Detroit and Flint Auxiliaries. Moreover, the Auto League reported that Martin lieutenant William Taylor, UAW's national welfare and WPA director, was "beginning to agree that the SP position is correct." The League saw "real progress" in the WPA Auxiliary, but complained that its work was still "too much like routine factory business." Dedicated Socialists fretted because unemployed organizing had "not yet assumed political character."[5] In short, the new Socialist commitment to unemployed activity had not translated into ideological gains among the jobless.

As the summer dragged on, the Auxiliary intensified its activities and scored some successes. In July 1938 pressure from the organization resulted in a statewide wage increase, which included the equalization of wage rates in Detroit, Flint, Pontiac, and Grand Rapids. UAW stewards became an accepted feature of the WPA labor relations scene and occasional strikes and demonstrations produced modest gains. More troublesome to the WPA Auxiliary were reports of unauthorized strikes and sit-downs on the projects. Now bureaucratized, the Auxiliary looked with disfavor on wildcat strikes, which made settlement of legitimate grievances more difficult for all concerned. A testy Taylor warned that there were subversive forces within UAW bent on sabotaging the WPA Auxiliary's program. The Lovestone group had become increasingly apprehensive over disruptive activities, which they often attributed to militancy induced by Communist influence within the UAW. It is also clear that as the unemployed found work on WPA, their union came to view them more and more as employed workers subject to traditional union sanctions.

From a Socialist perspective, the Communists' behavior reflected increasing frustration over the CP's inability to compete successfully with the WPA Auxiliary in the auto centers. By October 1938 the Socialist Auto League regarded conditions on WPA as highly favorable, every request of the Auxiliary having been met, save the demand for a 75-cent per hour wage, which had been softpedaled by UAW in order to prevent embarrassment to Murphy and Roosevelt. On the eve of the election, an exaggerated Auto League report claimed that the WPA Auxiliary's success had "virtually eliminated" the Workers Alliance in areas dominated by UAW.[6]

By this time the WPA and the CP's influence in the unemployed movement had emerged as a divisive issue in the election of 1938. This development mirrored a national trend towards vigorous Redbaiting, which marred the congressional elections then under way. In perhaps the most important state race, Frank Ingram and the Michigan Workers Alliance threw their enthusiastic support to Governor Frank Murphy, as did *Daily Worker* editor Clarence Hathaway. In this instance, Lasser, Ingram, and Hathaway overplayed their hand. Lasser's and Ingram's lavish praise for Murphy and the Michigan Alliance's extravagant claims of influence on the governor damaged liberal prospects in the November election. Especially unfortunate were Hathaway's endorsement of Murphy and Ingram's attack on Representative Clare Hoffman, a leading critic of the CIO, as "an enemy of the common people." The Republicans used the Hathaway endorsement with great effect, and many observers attributed Murphy's loss to the CP's open support. After Murphy went down in the general liberal electoral disaster of 1938, a bitter Alan Strachan of Labor's Non-Partisan League noted that the Michigan Communist Party tactics "bordered on insanity."[7] His view was widely shared.

During the campaign, alleged Communist influence was often linked with the unemployed movement, WPA, and the Workers Alliance. Meanwhile, Murphy walked a political tightrope, extolling his personal commitment to expanded relief and WPA programs while denying that his occasional cooperation with the Alliance and support for a broader relief and public employment program implied Communist influence or personal sympathy with radical solutions to Michigan's economic problems. In some instances, Murphy made his relief and public works record an important aspect of his campaign appeal. He defended his record on relief spending as mayor of Detroit and reminded voters that in 1938, under pressure from his administration and the UAW, Roosevelt had lifted the ceiling on WPA jobs in Michigan. Rejecting welfare cutbacks and budget-balancing for expediency's sake, he insisted that such a policy was not the "act of a responsible government that practices the principles of democracy and Christianity."[8]

While Murphy brandished his firm support of WPA in Detroit, UP Republican congressional candidate John B. Bennett launched a major attack on the program in his effort to dislodge liberal Democrat Frank Hook. Conservative forces in the region had long decried politics in relief administration. During the 1938 congressional campaign, Bennett insisted that in the UP "too much relief money was going into politics" and that Hook and the WPA organization in Gogebic County had fashioned "one of the rottenest and most corrupt political organizations that exists anywhere." After blasting Hook for allowing WPA workers to campaign for him, Bennett engaged in some political acrobatics of his own by promising WPA workers that he would secure a higher wage on the projects than Hook had been able to deliver. WPA had become a crucial element in the vulnerable economy of the UP by 1938, and even Republicans knew it. Recognizing the political popularity of the program, Matt Savola struck back at the Republicans with a sharp attack on gubernatorial candidate Frank Fitzgerald, big business, and other opponents of the New Deal, who had "carried on a vicious sabotage against WPA." Although nothing could save Murphy, the popularity of WPA was a factor in Hook's reelection to a third term in Congress.[9] The economy was not yet strong enough to sustain a conservative campaign against excessive power in Washington, which still supplied an important stimulus to the area's depressed economy.

Postelection analyses from labor and unemployed groups revealed frustration over the Communist role in the campaign, its exploitation by conservatives, and the general politicization of the WPA question. Mort Furay of the Wayne County LNPL unit bitterly noted that the juxtaposition of "private industry versus the WPA" occurred "only when no WPA workers were around." Similarly, Alan Strachan later stressed the negative effect of the CP endorsement on Murphy's prospects, as well as several congressional races. Even more short-sighted was the Communist Party's decision to place Phil Raymond in charge of the Berrien County Workers Alliance, where he could actively campaign against the militant anti-Communist Clare Hoffman.[10]

Strachan's criticism had considerable merit, but it was an incomplete analysis of the result, especially Murphy's defeat. The CP's action was only one of many factors that influenced Republican Frank Fitzgerald's victory over Murphy in November 1938. The campaign of 1938 was a disaster for liberal congressional and gubernatorial candidates throughout the United States. Moreover, the rise of anti-Communism nationwide further complicated Murphy's reelection bid. By autumn 1938 the first House Un-American Activities Committee had focused attention on Communism, including its influence on the Workers Alliance and the entire unemployed movement. In October, Congressman Martin Dies brought his traveling show to Detroit, where HUAC devoted special attention to CP involvement in the CIO and the sitdowns of 1937. Because of Murphy's direct intervention in the General Motors strike, his identification with the CIO was inevitable. Less significant but still a factor in the outcome was warfare on the left, which surfaced in the form of a bitter struggle within the SP over a Murphy endorsement, which was favored by many union Socialists but opposed by the Branch 1 intellectuals. Both Reuther and Fischer urged full support for Murphy, but were unable to deliver strong union and party backing for the governor. Combined with factionalism within UAW, which focused attention on the importance of the Left in the CIO, this ideological bickering contributed to a public perception that Murphy was embroiled in radical political controversy. The conservative attack on WPA and the unemployed, the effect of the Dies Committee's charges, the exploitation of the Communist issue, the Socialist Party split over support for Murphy, Murphy's failure to build a strong Democratic organization, and escalating internal tensions within UAW were all factors in the Democratic setback of 1938, which was also part of a nationwide conservative trend that checked the tide of liberalism throughout the United States.[11]

The WPA Auxiliary in Crisis:
A Change in Direction

Throughout the hard-fought campaign of 1938, the UAW WPA Auxiliary continued to press for solutions to the problems of the Michigan unemployed. While the union welfare office continued to assist both union and nonunion families with direct relief problems, the UAW as an institution began to concentrate organizational efforts on the jobless workers who had found temporary employment on WPA. In October 1938 the focal point of the Auxiliary's effort was its demand for a 32-hour week, a work-sharing device supported by most Michigan locals and endorsed by the UAW Executive Board. Although many locals were behind the plan, Emil Mazey and Local 212 maintained that without a 40-hour wage, it would not work. Mazey pointed out to the International Executive Board that Chrysler's acceptance of the proposal had resulted in cutbacks as far as 20 hours per week in the Briggs Mack Ave plant and a walkout at Dodge.

Despite these concerns the Executive Board, in an act of impressive solidarity with the unemployed, succeeded in forging a largely united front behind the demand that Chrysler honor its contract provision for the 32-hour week. The UAW insisted that because most employees wished to share the work and because technological advances mandated shorter hours, management should work with the union to solve the social problem created by enforced idleness. By the end of October Chrysler had capitulated and its decision was being implemented. To the Socialist Auto League, the settlement of the issue not only addressed a fundamental social problem, but also accomplished a crucial union goal: "unemployed auto workers and WPA workers feel that the union has done a good job in their behalf."[12]

Beyond the work-sharing issue, UAW's other major concern with regard to the unemployed was the inadequacy of WPA wage levels, a problem complicated by its political sensitiveness. Although the union was cautious in pressing this demand, the Welfare Auxiliary, supported by the Wayne County Social Workers Association, was persistent in its work to raise the wage standard. In a followup to the union's September meeting with WPA officials in Washington, the Auxiliary prepared a detailed brief justifying its demands. The UAW documented changes in prevailing rates and cost of living that justified an increase in WPA wage levels to 75 cents per hour in Michigan, Ohio, Indiana, and Wisconsin. Acting as director of the UAW WPA Welfare Department, Richard Leonard argued that prevailing wage rates had not been surveyed since 1935 and that 1938 levels had increased.[13]

Following the 1938 election, the WPA Department renewed its campaign for a wage increase on the Midwestern projects. Relieved of the need to defend Murphy and the Democrats, Leonard and the WPA Department turned up the heat on the Roosevelt administration by insisting that a WPA representative from Washington be sent to Detroit, as provided for by the September conference agreement. Again claiming that WPA wages in Michigan were well below the prevailing rate, Leonard angrily demanded that Hopkins respond to the UAW's repeated requests for a full investigation of the problem and threatened to take the issue directly to Roosevelt. Two days later, Leonard contacted the president's office. His demand drew an immediate reaction from WPA authorities in Washington. Assistant Administrator David K. Niles assured Leonard that every effort would be made to avoid layoffs, while Deputy Administrator Aubrey Williams sent a detailed and conciliatory response to the UAW's exhaustive 6 October brief on work relief needs. Although he questioned the validity of the demand for a 75-cent-per-hour minimum, Williams pledged to send a representative to Michigan to further investigate the prevailing wage question, as well as other disputed points.[14]

Potentially more dangerous to the jobless was the threat of a WPA cutback necessitated by a limited appropriation requiring that funds last until 1 March 1939. As early as October 1938, Ralph Hetzel had warned CIO affiliates of a contemplated slash in WPA rosters and urged that political pressure be applied in hopes of forestalling the cut. One of the first to protest the rumored layoff was Harold Hartley of the west side local, who in late October urged Hopkins to provide WPA workers "assurance" that "none will be laid off until they are certain of work in private industry." Meanwhile, Leonard and his lieutenant, George Edwards, reported to Hopkins the rumored decision to completely halt WPA intake. Leonard and Edwards argued that any such cut would create "untold misery and suffering" because there was "no indication private industry will begin to absorb [the] burden being created by WPA." Finally in December 1938 both Leonard and Michigan's WPA administrator L. M. Nims urged that the hold on new assignments be relaxed, all to no avail since the WPA was hamstrung by the terms of the appropriation that funded its program.[15]

The joint statement resulted from a surge of grass-roots militance that ended in a general strike to protest the halt in intake, as well as alleged WPA discrimination against union members. The strike vote by three hundred UAW-WPA stewards drew the immediate support of a large number of Detroit area UAW locals. On 10 December Germer joined Leonard in an effort to persuade WPA officials to reconsider some of the policies that had led to the impasse. As hundreds of pickets circled Detroit WPA headquarters, WPA administrators agreed to stop firing UAW union stewards and to urge that Washington return to the rolls large numbers of workers who had been removed when they accepted unemployment compensation payments.[16] A modest victory had been won, but the ultimate outcome was still dependent on decisions made in Washington.

Even more significant for the Michigan unemployed movement was the escalating internal struggle for control of the UAW WPA Department. Once Lewis sent Philip Murray and Sidney Hillman into Michigan in September 1938 to reestablish order within UAW, the Martin forces began to retreat. After the suspended officers were reinstated, Martin became progressively more irrational, finally opening negotiations with both the AFL and Ford Motor Company as a first step towards a return to the Federation and the negotiation of a contract with Ford. One important dimension of Martin's desperation politics was an intensification of his fight for the WPA Department against the increasingly influential Reuther group that dominated the unemployed organization. In October 1938 the Trotskyite Martin loyalist, Bert Cochran, who had headed the Detroit UAW WPA Department, was fired and replaced by George Edwards, while William Taylor formally gave way to Leonard, who was again made the union's national welfare director. Edwards stated simply that Cochran had been both installed and ousted for "factional reasons." As the Executive Board carried out its plan to undermine Martin, it was the fate of the WPA Department to be caught in the crossfire. The end result was the board's decision in November 1938 to reorganize the WPA Department. WPA organizing became the responsibility of the separate regional directors, with the Detroit and Wayne County WPA Department reorganized under the authority of the five directors.[17]

The Executive Board's *demarche*, part of a broad attempt to limit Martin's authority, enraged the erratic UAW leader, who henceforth made the Board's "attack on the WPA Department" an important part of his effort to control the union. Martin's supporters, still influential in outstate districts such as Lansing, Flint, and Jackson, argued that the Executive Board's decision to "split up the WPA Auxiliary" was essentially a "decision to destroy it." Raising the Communist issue, the Martinites blistered the Mortimer-Hall-Addes bloc for the board's "disgraceful ruling" and insisted that only Martin could "preserve the WPA Auxiliary . . . and other Progressive union features" that were essential if UAW was to remain "an American union for American workers."[18]

Although it opposed Martin on most issues, the Socialist Auto League agreed that the restructuring of the WPA Department was a retrogressive step. Ben Fischer reported that the CP was ready to abolish what had been an "effective WPA organization" that had previously "succeeded in defeating the CP moves." Martin attributed the decision to an attempt by a conspiratorial board clique to "turn over the task of organizing the unemployed to the Stalinist-controlled Workers Alliance." It is true that the national Alliance was still desperately pursuing a cooperative relationship with the CIO, but it is equally true that CIO had held the Alliance at arm's length. By 1939 the WAA was ready to acknowledge that in some industrial centers, where there was "one dominant union," it would "prove practical" to have that single union "servicing the unemployed." In no district was this approach more relevant than in Michigan, where despite internal bickering, UAW had successfully occupied the organizational vacuum created by the massive unemployment of 1938.[19]

At the national level, meanwhile, CIO remained engaged in a struggle with the Workers Alliance, which Ralph Hetzel admitted had "considerable strength" in some areas, although urban Michigan was not one of them. In a December memorandum on the WPA issue, Hetzel urged Lewis to launch a new campaign for the expansion of WPA as a long-term public works program. Accepting Hetzel's recommendation, Lewis recommitted the CIO to the extension of WPA. On December 23, 1938 all national and international unions received instructions to exert pressure on their congressmen for support of funding for a strong WPA program. And on 9 January 1939 the CIO came out in support of a $1 billion deficiency appropriation that would reverse the effects of the halt in intake implemented in November 1938.[20]

Spontaneous protests and sit-downs continued to occur, and in early January the UAW settled on a dramatic demonstration to emphasize solidarity with the position taken by Hetzel, Lewis, and the CIO. *West Side Conveyor* exhorted its readers to action on behalf of the unemployed, urging their participation in a mass rally at Cadillac Square on January 20. Convinced that the February 1938 Cadillac Square demonstration had forced an end to the last major attack on WPA, the west side local prepared to "give the government another shot in the arm so that WPA slashes will stop." Planning for the January event was placed in the hands of George Edwards, who had risen to prominence as a leader in the UAW WPA Welfare Department prior to the Executive Board's decision to decentralize the organization.[21]

Edwards's task was complicated not only by the WPA Department's "bitter fight with the WPA Administration," but also by the reality that the "war in the UAW" between the board majority and Martin was now "wide open." In early January it became obvious that Martin planned to make preservation of the WPA Department as an independent entity a central issue in his drive to take UAW into the AFL. On 5 January he informed George Addes of his unilateral decision to reassign Taylor, who had worked in the Murphy campaign, as director of the Wayne County WPA organization, which constituted an open challenge to Edwards and his supporters on the board. Five days later, Martin blasted the board's decision to reorganize the WPA Department as a serious blow to the union's efforts to organize the jobless. Martin maintained that by destroying the Department's national coordination, the decision had "reduced the effectiveness of the organization in coping with the problems of the unemployed." The only solution, he insisted, was for the I.E.B. to rescind its action abolishing the WPA division as a national department.[22]

Taylor wasted no time in assuming the offensive. On 11 January he contacted the Michigan congressional delegation, House Appropriations Committee, and President Roosevelt to protest the Appropriations Committee's decision to cut Roosevelt's WPA request. The union's WPA Welfare Department claimed that thousands of Michigan workers faced starvation as a result of the recent WPA cuts and that according to local authorities, further reductions would bring the "complete breakdown" of the state's welfare system. Meanwhile, Edwards proceeded with his plans for a mass rally on 20 January. He blanketed the projects, shops, and union halls with leaflets and posters urging a large turnout so that Congress would be "forced to extend rather than cut WPA." Because of the seriousness of the layoffs, Edwards and his backers had little difficulty building support for the event, which drew the endorsement of Detroit city council president Edward Jeffries and other city officials.[23]

Behind the scenes, Martin worked to undermine the Cadillac Square demonstration, first by limiting publicity in the *United Auto Worker*, then by encouraging planners to postpone the event, and finally by diverting the UAW WPA Welfare Department's funds during the week before the rally. This infighting reached a climax on the morning of 20 January, when Martin supporters occupied the International offices in the Griswold Building while the demonstrators gathered, a step intended in part to discourage union members from attending the event. The Martin "blitzkreig" was completed when his backers took over the WPA Welfare Department central office and confiscated all records and equipment. To Emil Mazey, the Martinites' "splitting tactics" had "betrayed the best interests of the unemployed workers."[24]

Despite the theatrics, the Cadillac Square demonstration was a success, as a crowd of 20,000 stood ankle-deep in slush to protest the WPA wage cuts. Reflecting the escalating ideological struggle over the jobless, the *Socialist Call* viewed the rally as evidence that real progress was possible once an aggressive organization like UAW had supplanted the "now over-mild Workers Alliance." A tribute to the union's successful coalition-building was the involvement of other CIO unions in the Cadillac Square program. Although it clearly played a supporting role, a frustrated Workers Alliance quickly claimed joint sponsorship of what it called "one of the most impressive mass protests ever staged in the city."[25]

Labor journalist Joe Brown recorded his impression that this demonstration was significant as evidence that workers, asserting a "right to live," were turning their eyes towards Washington. From the platform, Common Council president Edward Jeffries readily endorsed the UAW argument that continued federal work relief was the answer to Detroit's woes. He declared that "if this is a Christian government, then the Government must participate in this plan to give people work." The news that Senator Arthur Vandenberg had not replied to a request for a statement was roundly booed. In contrast, the crowd was thrilled by Michigan senator Prentiss Brown's attack on the House cuts as "not justified." Presiding at the meeting, Edwards concluded by reaffirming the original CIO demand for a $1 billion appropriation.[26]

In the wake of Martin's failed coup, the board appointed Edwards director of the WPA Welfare Department. Although the campaign to restore WPA funding was a matter of urgent concern, Edwards and his organization were hampered in their efforts by the ongoing internal struggle with what remained of the Martin group. By this time Martin had expelled fifteen of the twenty-five Board members, including Reuther, Frankensteen, Addes, Mortimer, and Ed Hall, while retaining the support of only three.

Within a month it became clear that the suspended members commanded the loyalties of the UAW's largest locals and most of its second-level leaders. On 23 January the board responded to Martin's seizure of the offices by immediately voting $1,000 for Edwards to use in organizing WPA workers under the aegis of the regional directors. With the support of other CIO unions, the WPA Welfare Department was firmly reestablished. When Martin resigned as UAW president, he charged John L. Lewis's "agents" with planning an organizing convention that would "disenfranchise" those unemployed auto workers who had joined the WPA Auxiliaries.[27] By February 1939 no basis for an accommodation remained.

As the contest intensified, it became clear that while compromise was unobtainable, it was also unnecessary. WPA officials maintained relations with both the Martin unemployed group and the CIO WPA Welfare Department, now headed by a new welfare director, George Edwards. However, before long Edwards became the key union contact on unemployment questions and, in his words, "the dual union efforts of the Martin forces died at birth." Edwards exaggerated. Although the board majority held the allegiance of most autoworkers, Martin's unemployed organization was not yet moribund. In February 1939 the rump group condemned Edwards and his supporters for "splitting tactics" that would result in "great harm" to the unemployed movement and proceeded to reestablish the old WPA Department's grievance machinery. Finally, on 21 March Martin's organization issued a charter to a new autonomous union, the United WPA and Unemployed Workers of America, which was to be affiliated with the rump union that Martin took back into the AFL. The new unemployed union, headed by Martin ally William Taylor, planned a nationwide campaign to organize WPA and unorganized workers and to become the accepted bargaining agent for these groups with WPA authorities.[28]

While the dwindling Martin group postured and maneuvered, Edwards and the board organization maintained the pressure on WPA. From 30 January on, Edwards and his department maintained stewards on all projects and a citywide stewards governing body. On 11 February when WPA administrator David K. Niles announced the end of the intake restriction policy, the board group was quick to assert that the Cadillac Square demonstration had been a major factor in Washington's decision. Two days later Edwards demanded that 1,000 firings of female and elderly WPA workers be reversed as contrary to government policy. By mid-March 1939, thousands of laid-off WPA employees had been reinstated in Wayne County alone.[29]

These vigorous efforts won substantial support for the UAW-CIO Welfare Department from most WPA locals. Edwards understandably enjoyed the endorsement of his home local, Local 174, from January on, but before long other WPA units moved to affiliate with the CIO unemployed organization. By 20 March Edwards was so swamped with welfare applicants that his staff secretary was desperate for help. Requesting additional support staff, Ethel Polk noted that "it doesn't do much good to keep an organizer in the office to talk to welfare cases because they don't know all the ins and outs." Assistance was essential because "doing the best we can is not good enough—and the situation must be handled."[30]

As the UAW-CIO convention in Cleveland drew near, the CIO group had consolidated its position among the jobless in Wayne County. Meanwhile, Martin's strength dissolved, except for loyal enclaves in Lansing, Jackson, Flint, and some other outlying districts. Edwards and the Local 174 group were in the process of developing an ongoing program to organize the unemployed and call attention to the inadequacy of current WPA levels. He did not preclude cooperation with other union unemployed committees and jobless organizations, even the declining Workers Alliance. In March 1939 the Wayne County CIO activists proposed that the Cleveland conference ratify their views by continuing appropriations to the WPA Welfare Department and adding an adequate staff.[31]

Meanwhile, Martin's new United WPA and Unemployed Workers of America worked to establish its own credibility. In April Taylor sent out an open letter to public officials calling for an expanded public works and housing program that would provide employment and serve the national interest. The plea fell on deaf ears in cost-conscious Washington, where WPA officials could only express regret that no state could expect an increase in its employment authorization, regardless of need. Unable to deliver as much as the UAW-CIO WPA Welfare Department, Martin's organization continued to struggle until summer 1939, when it died a natural death after Taylor's resignation.[32] The CIO had proven to be too powerful an adversary, especially on its home ground in Wayne County. Martin's defeat was complete, and the unemployed looked elsewhere for leadership.

The "Other Michigan": Competition for the Jobless

Beyond the UAW's base area, a spirited competition developed for the allegiance of the jobless. In Flint, for example, a small but active CP organization continued to work with the unemployed through the Workers Alliance. Especially active among Polish, Hungarian, and Russian immigrants on Flint's north side, the Alliance expressed its own "ideas on socialism." Bucking the UAW's larger organization in the city, the Alliance organized at the local and neighborhood level, paying particular attention to the non-union unemployed, relief clients, and the "unemployables." Occasionally, as in December 1938, the Flint Alliance called on Lasser and the national organization to protest arbitrary WPA layoffs, but they were no more successful than the UAW in reversing the trend of federal policy. Genora Dollinger later recalled that the Flint Workers Alliance was a "shell organization" by 1939, so weak that it eventually lost its position on the local Industrial Union Council.[33]

The key to the Alliance's decline in Flint was the emergence in 1939 of a powerful Project Workers Union, affiliated with the UAW. Although a few Flint auto workers followed Martin out of the CIO in March 1939, the vast majority were solidly behind the board in the union's internal crisis. The PWU was an expression of CIO and Socialist initiative in the organization of the unemployed. Its leaders included such CIO stalwarts as Genora and Kermit Johnson, Roy Lawrence, Claude Workman, Pat Murray, and Ed Webber. Among the most active project stewards were Jack Lawrence, Alvin Murray, Harlan Murray, and Eugene Johnson. Once the Project Workers Union was organized in 1939, the Workers Alliance faded into the background because of the power conferred on PWU by the UAW identification.[34]

The PWU concentrated primarily on local issues, grievances, working conditions, and adequate relief assistance. There were occasional sit-downs that shut down the Flint projects and sometimes produced modest victories. In March 1939, for example, the PWU successfully organized the Flint sewing project, and soon thereafter six hundred laid off WPA workers were reinstated. In addition, it forced the removal of the sewing project administrator after workers had objected to her policies. These victories earned the PWU a loyal following among Flint's unemployed workers, but the organization's greatest contribution to the area's labor movement lay elsewhere. As was true in Wayne County, the UAW's unemployed affiliate in Flint reinforced the local commitment to industrial unionism. A leading unemployed activist, Genora Dollinger, remembered PWU as an important "training school for the unions."[35]

The UAW identification was also critical in Kent County, where a weaker unemployed movement struggled to protect the jobless. Because the UAW was considerably less influential in Kent County than in the Detroit area, these low-key efforts produced fewer dramatic results. In December 1938 Leonard prodded the Grand Rapids City Council to protest the statewide cutoff in WPA intake, and the Kent County WPA Auxiliary protested age discrimination in WPA assignment with little apparent effect. In general, unemployed agitation was a lonely task in conservative Kent County. Veteran Socialist and union activist D. B. Hovey again worked to organize and aid the jobless. Protesting the curtailed intake on WPA projects, Hovey and the UAW's WPA Auxiliary urged an "enlargement rather than restriction of the government's efforts" to aid those on the "margin of starvation." In short, because of the UAW's organizational initiative, Grand Rapids workers raised a clear though futile voice of resistance against a national policy that promised to increase human distress in Michigan. A similar and equally unproductive protest emanated from the Kalamazoo Trades and Labor Council and the United Paper Mill Workers.[36] Yet no amount of protest could alter the hard fact that limited appropriations meant a cap on WPA employment, which by January 1939 had been imposed throughout the state.

As the distance from Detroit increased, the sources of protest became more diverse. Most notable was the tireless organizational work carried on by the Workers Alliance, especially in areas where the UAW was not a major presence. (See figure 16.) Between November 1938 and January 1939, WPA officials in Washington received numerous protests and petitions on wage levels, working conditions, dismissals, and hiring procedures from widely scattered Alliance locals in such places as Adrian, Battle Creek, Benton Harbor, Monroe, and Buchanan. An important theme in this correspondence was concern over the imminent cutoff in WPA hiring and uncertainty over the future of the entire program. In an attempt to clear the air and assert the strength of the Alliance, Frank Ingram took the complaints of the Michigan organization directly

Figure 16   Delegates to First Convention of the Michigan Workers Alliance in Lansing, November 19–20, 1938 (*Archives of Labor and Urban Affairs, Wayne State University*)

to WPA administrator David K. Niles in Washington. On 13 December 1938, Ingram and a delegation from the state Alliance presented Niles with a litany of complaints that centered on two issues: layoffs and ongoing labor relations on the Michigan projects. Their overriding concern was a strong conviction that WAA members were being discriminated against in Michigan because of their organizing activities, especially in the cities of Kalamazoo, Lansing, and Bangor.[37]

The Alliance's protest induced Niles to inform Michigan WPA administrator Louis Nims of the concerns expressed over the administration of the state WPA program. Both the Niles letter and the response from Michigan WPA officials reveals that the agency was helpless to deal with the cutoff of intake, but remained willing to adjust grievances. They were intent upon protecting the right to organize on the projects and stood ready to deal with the Workers Alliance despite its increasingly leftist image. In most cases, the typical problem involved arbitrary treatment of workers by project supervisors, and the Alliance frequently received satisfactory responses to its inquiries. In short, by 1939 the Workers Alliance had come to function as a legitimate labor union, especially in non-UAW locales. At the same time, it helped WPA to dramatize the needs of the unemployed.[38]

Outside Lansing and Kalamazoo, the major Workers Alliance stronghold was still the UP, where the economy remained deeply depressed. Centers of Alliance strength were Gogebic and Delta counties, where CP organizers Frank Walli and Carl Anderson continued to agitate for unemployed benefits. In Gogebic County a large Alliance organization devoted its attention to raising grievances and interacting with local welfare agencies, while in Escanaba Anderson and the "Forum" group pressed for civic improvements and local solutions to the problems of the jobless. In both communities, a critical issue was the long-standing dissatisfaction of WPA workers with the inadequate $44 monthly wage. Typical was the Marenisco Workers Alliance's plea for a wage hike. On the heels of the Alliance letter came a similar request from the Timber Workers Union, which argued that $44 per month did not allow the average family to "live in any degree of security." The Alliance and the union received support from the Wakefield Democratic Club, which dismissed the current wage as a "bare subsistence" income that failed to provide family security. Despite the best efforts of Gogebic

County Democrats and radicals, WPA officials in Washington rejected their demands as contrary to the existing policy of spreading the work to as many needy workers as funds would permit.[39]

Like unemployed workers elsewhere in Michigan, UP workers expressed alarm at the prospect of impending WPA cutbacks. As always, the Houghton-Keeweenaw County jobless were among the most active due to the severity of unemployment in the Copper Country. In December 1938, Matt Bari and John Spiegal of the Toivola–Misery Bay Workers Alliance protested contemplated layoffs as potentially disastrous for their communities, in which the projects were the "only means of a livelihood" because there was literally no private industry.[40] UP workers approached the year 1939 with a deep sense of foreboding produced by the impending crisis in WPA funding.

As the new year opened, uncertainty haunted the struggling Michigan unemployed movement. The UAW, which harbored the state's largest and most successful unemployed organization, was entering the final stage of a bitter factional fight that had increasingly complicated its battle for the jobless. Meanwhile, the Workers Alliance, chastened by the Murphy disaster, was increasingly handicapped by the image of radicalism it had itself helped create. With the WPA under congressional attack, 1939 began on an ominous note for Michigan's dispossessed. It was to be a year of decision.

A Movement in Decline
The War Economy, Job Opportunity, and the "Unemployables," 1939–1941

With the emergence of the new, strengthened UAW in mid-1939, the union's WPA Welfare Department stood poised to advance the cause of the unemployed in response to the WPA cutbacks that threatened the existence of men and women living on the margin of society. Meanwhile, a struggling Workers Alliance was prepared to contest the UAW position, especially among the most desperate elements of the underclass. Neither organization was ready for the intensity of the attack on WPA by conservatives and Red-baiters that was to destroy the unemployed movement's organizational base. And simultaneously, an economic revival began that promised to make jobless organizations superfluous. For leftists, social activists, and liberal bureaucrats, it was the end, not the beginning, of a movement.

Crisis in the Unemployed Movement:
UAW, CIO, and the Assault on WPA

Against the background of WPA cutbacks and congressional hostility to leftist elements in the unemployed movement, the UAW moved in March 1939 towards a resolution of its internal disagreement. When the board group assembled in Cleveland to consolidate its position among auto workers, the issue of WPA organization was one of several important problems that drew its attention. The result was the special convention's call for a new unemployed union affiliated with the CIO and organized on a national scale. Aware that the UAW's own WPA organization could not adequately service a nationwide constituency, the delegates petitioned CIO to inaugurate a campaign to organize WPA workers through a separate project workers organizing committee.[1]

As a first step, the new UAW resolved to assist the CIO effort by forming WPA locals from its own WPA Auxiliary. The union adopted a constitution that reauthorized UAW regional WPA Auxiliaries under the direction of a national WPA coordinator. These bodies were expected to evolve into the new project workers union. Three weeks later the UAW executive board followed through by endorsing an immediate organizational drive and instructing all regional officers to survey their regions to prepare for the establishment of new WPA Auxiliaries. The UAW approach drew the endorsement of Michigan Socialists, whose leaders saw the proposed CIO-affiliated unemployed union as an effective counter to the fading Workers Alliance.[2]

Meanwhile, Martin's United WPA and Unemployed Workers of America struggled for life. Although it chartered several new locals in April 1939, the independent union, headed by Taylor, was largely a paper organization, with the exception of some active locals in outstate areas such as Lansing, Jackson, and Muskegon, where the Lovestoneite Martin loyalist, Lester Washburn, remained a significant influence. (See figure 17.) Addressing delegates from seventeen western Michigan locals at Niles on 16 April, Taylor was forced to admit that little concrete progress had been made and that funds were short. When they did take action, Taylor and his Wayne County operative, Paul Silver, seemed bent on dramatic confrontations with WPA authorities designed to attract maximum public attention; but the protests were not very productive if measured by concrete gains for workers. On 22 April, for example, Silver's followers staged a sit-down at the office of Michigan WPA administrator Abner Larned to protest a recent cutback of 4,000 Detroit project workers. The demonstrators disappeared quickly when the Detroit police appeared. While Silver and his small band of followers were

Figure 17   Martin Ally William B. Taylor, 1940 [Second from the left]
(Archives of Labor and Urban Affairs, Wayne State University)

demonstrating, Edwards and a delegation from the WPA Welfare Department were inside, pressing the case with WPA personnel director Allen Selmin for expending all available funds.[3] The entire incident illustrated the fact that Edwards and the CIO group had already established their position as the largest and most significant of the two competing organizations.

Edwards and the UAW-WPA Auxiliaries fought for the interests of the jobless on a day-to-day basis. In April, their efforts produced a clear WPA labor relations policy and in May, the WPA Social Service Department created an Information and Adjustment Service to improve personnel relations and aid project workers in dealing with employment, reclassifications, and reinstatements. During these months, Edwards and his department also handled welfare, unemployment compensation problems, and other member grievances that could not be resolved by project stewards.[4]

By June 1939 Edwards could proudly cite the UAW WPA organization's achievements, including the return of 1,000 fired WPA workers to the projects, the authorization of 3,000 new jobs, and several improvements for direct relief recipients. UAW president R. J. Thomas asserted that the department had not only won WPA jobs for auto workers, but also had become a leading defender of WPA as a "national institution." Through collective bargaining, the union had won improved working conditions and some wage hikes for WPA workers. And as a service organization, the WPA Welfare Department had handled thousands of relief and unemployment compensation cases for union members and lobbied for adequate relief benefits for all unemployed workers. Perhaps most important, from the UAW's point of view, was the Department's crucial role in building the union. Thomas reported that it had "maintained the spirit of unionism" on the projects and among the unemployed. Already thousands of trained unionists had returned to the shops, where they would "give active help rather than opposition" to further organization drives.[5] While UAW leaders took satisfaction in the department's successes, they were equally gratified by the collapse of the Martin-Taylor WPA organization, which was confirmed on 8 June when Alex "Scotty" McKay and two hundred Detroit officers, stewards, and members of the rump union returned to the UAW WPA Department. Announcing his defection from Martin's UWPAUWA, McKay proclaimed that the organization had been "a phony from the start." The conflict reached a climax when Taylor severed his last ties with the hapless UWPAUWA, which was headed toward reintegration into the AFL, along with Martin and the remnants of his organization.[6]

While the rump organization's unemployed union floundered, the UAW-CIO WPA Auxiliary Department grew rapidly. Led by Edwards and supported by the UAW WPA Committee, which included President R.J. Thomas and Secretary-Treasurer George Addes, the WPA Auxiliary worked to unite the "organized workers in the plants with the organized workers on the WPA projects." By August 1939 the union's WPA organization had chartered units in Detroit, Pontiac, Flint, Jackson, Grand Rapids, Bay City, and Muskegon. Moreover, WPA Auxiliary locals were active in other UAW cities throughout the Midwest, including Racine, Kenosha, Milwaukee, Anderson, Evansville, South Bend, and Toledo. In many Michigan communities, the organization focused on efforts to cope with the relief crisis of 1939. In Pontiac, where William McCauley and Roy Reuther rebuilt the WPA unit, the unemployed organization was regarded as "one of the factors in the recent amazing comeback of the UAW-CIO."[7]

Table 3 Membership of Workers Alliance of America, by States, as of 1 April 1939

Membership		Membership	
Alabama	6,962	New Jersey	9,286
Arizona	580	New York	39,131
Arkansas	400	North Carolina	791
California	24,000	North Dakota	1,212
Colorado	619	Ohio	22,467
Connecticut	406	Oklahoma	2,002
Delaware	2,214	Oregon	3,000
Florida	1,436	Pennsylvania	19,274
Georgia	1,343	Rhode Island	153
Idaho	15,685	South Carolina	565
Illinois	4,443	South Dakota	306
Indiana	3,120	Tennessee	967
Iowa	1,605	Texas	1,812
Kentucky	3,836	Utah	2,990
Kansas	1,104	Vermont	64
Louisiana	357	Virginia	771
Maryland	10,310	Washington	16,292
Massachusetts	333	West Virginia	2,234
Michigan	1,044	Wisconsin	11,400
Minnesota	29,800	Wyoming	1,135
Mississippi	184	Dist. of Columbia	668
Missouri	6,875	Alaska	55
Montana	5,700	Puerto Rico	100
Nebraska	1,284		
Nevada	35		
New Hampshire	300	Total	260,640

Source: U.S. Congress, House, Subcommittee on Appropriations, *Investigation and Study of the Works Progress Administration*, 76th Congress, 1st Sess., 1939, p. 37.

Despite the strong growth that occurred within the UAW-CIO WPA organization, it did not go unchallenged in the battle for the loyalty of the Michigan unemployed. During his testimony before a House investigation of WPA in April 1939, David Lasser reported that the Michigan Workers Alliance was among the "largest organizations" in the beleaguered WAA. (See Table 3.) Despite his claims, however, membership data for April 1939 revealed that Michigan's totals did not compare favorably with those in other industrial states.[8] Through aggressive organizational work, UAW had clearly outflanked the Alliance, though the weaker organization remained a force among the Michigan jobless. It is also true that, as previously noted, membership statistics consistently underestimate support for an organization that appealed to the outcasts on society's bottom rail.

Much more destructive to the Alliance was a barrage of negative publicity stemming from the Dies Committee report, *Investigation of Un-American Activities and Propaganda*. The report alleged that Communists had penetrated several labor unions and other organizations, including WAA. It also claimed that the "unemployed leagues" and "unemployed councils" were led by Benjamin and Lasser and that the 1936 merger had given the CP a vehicle for financing "front" organizations.[9] The Alliance faced an increasingly hostile public as it entered 1939, which proved to be a year of decision for the organized unemployed nationwide.

Frustrated by federal intransigence and WPA cutbacks, the Alliance now targeted the Michigan legislature and Republican governor Luren D. Dickinson, both stalling on a proposed $20 billion relief appropriation. Led by State Organizer Frank Ingram, the Alliance demanded the full appropriation on behalf of the 140,000 Michigan unemployed whose plight had been aggravated by WPA retrenchment. Aware of Dickinson's inflexibility on the relief issue, Ingram next turned up the heat in a brief address to the legislature. He blasted the Republicans for their inaction and warned that a slash in relief funding would mean a return to "Hooverism." Both Ingram and State Senator Stanley Novak promised that the Alliance would return to Lansing with thousands of demonstrators, a prospect unappealing to the solons who recognized the potential power of the organized unemployed. To dramatize the issue, the Alliance also orchestrated a 72-hour "death watch" demonstration featuring mass picketing around the state house with a huge coffin symbolic of layoff and relief cutback victims. While no comprehensive solution to the relief problem was found, the committee did manage to approve an immediate appropriation of $1 million to ease the relief crisis in Detroit.[10]

CIO efforts complemented those of the Alliance. After a fruitless appeal to Dickinson, the UAW-CIO leaders moved in mid-May to the friendlier environs of WPA administrator Abner Larned's office, where their complaints against the combination of WPA layoff orders and relief cutbacks drew a more sympathetic response. Larned responded by telling Governor Dickinson that the $9 billion relief appropriation then under consideration in Lansing was "very inadequate to meet the serious situation" and urging that welfare policy "not be blind to the real need which may exist, particularly in the industrial areas." After the Michigan Industrial Union Council endorsed a higher relief appropriation, a special legislative session finally increased the allocation, although not as dramatically as the Workers Alliance had originally proposed.[11]

While the UAW and WAA responded to the welfare crisis in Lansing, the relief problem was generating intense local protest activity. A tense situation developed in Flint, where relief cuts fell with brutal impact on the jobless. A combination of the UAW Welfare Department and the WAA moved in March and April 1939 to combat the policies of Flint city manager James R. Pollock, who had been instrumental in denying sponsor's funds to keep the city's WPA program intact. The result of Pollock's intransigence was immediate layoff for five hundred project workers, which ignited protests from both William Taylor and the local UAW-CIO unemployed organization led by Claude Workman, Genora Johnson, and Roy Lawrence. Charging that Pollock and the "labor-hating forces in Flint" had "declared war against the unemployed," the Flint WPA Division insisted that it stood for "a job on WPA for every able-bodied worker at a living wage."[12]

No sooner had the layoffs been announced than the Flint Welfare Office cut off nine hundred relief families on 1 May. Genora Johnson, Claude Workman, and the UAW-CIO WPA Division responded by organizing a "death watch" in a city park opposite the relief office and adjacent to the Buick plant. Johnson later recalled that workers in the plant kept watch over the pickets and were "ready to crack heads" if the demonstrators were disturbed. Flint's WPA Division Local 12 augmented the "death watch" with demands that the Genessee County Tax Allocation Board furnish the required sponsor's funding to cover the hiring of all relief clients by WPA, a solution it maintained would be cheaper and more humane than keeping relief clients on the welfare rolls.[13] While the Workers Alliance supported the "death watch," Charles Killinger and the fading Alliance attempted unsuccessfully to undermine the UAW project workers union, which by summer 1939 had become the driving force in the Flint unemployed movement.

In one other area—the UP—the Workers Alliance remained an active force in the struggle against WPA layoffs. Always a bastion of Alliance strength among the unemployed, the Gogebic County jobless again mounted militant resistance to the retrenchment in relief and public works programs. Consistent with traditional UP concern for the rights of immigrant workers, the CP worked through the Workers Alliance to mitigate the worst effects of the WPA's alien registration provisions. In March 1939 the UP WPA administration dropped nearly eight hundred aliens from the work rolls in an action that had an especially harsh impact in heavily Finnish Iron, Gogebic, and Houghton counties. In Iron River, CP activists such as Rachel Kangas worked with immigrants to encourage them to take out citizenship papers. Communist leaders often aided aliens to complete night school programs that made it possible for them to secure citizenship papers, which in turn kept them eligible for WPA employment.[14]

Combined with the implementation of alien dismissals, the sharp cutbacks in WPA employment galvanized the Gogebic County Workers Alliance in opposition to federal work relief policy. Marenisco Alliance leaders urged every WPA worker to organize "to hold your job," while Iron River Alliance secretary Paul Henley combined with the Iron County Board and Democratic congressman Frank Hook to attack the imminent layoffs. Responding to Hook's protest, WPA authorities cited congressional limitations as the cause of the current employment crisis and noted that implementation of federal policy remained in the hands of state WPA officials.[15] No one, it seemed, was responsible for the plight of the jobless, save the Congress that had limited funding.

The layoff crisis produced an even more aggressive counterattack in Wayne County, where Edwards and the UAW-CIO WPA Department trained their guns on the Roosevelt Administration, the WPA, and Detroit city officials. UAW Secretary-Treasurer George Addes launched the barrage with an Executive Board protest to Roosevelt charging that the curtailment of WPA had spawned a "serious relief crisis" in Michigan that threatened to produce "much suffering, actual starvation, and great social unrest." Addes and the board insisted that the gravity of the situation justified an immediate reallocation of WPA jobs for Michigan. Edwards followed up with a telegram to the president urging quick action to alleviate the "suffering of unemployed workers," whom he described as close to the "breaking point." In a companion protest to Harrington at the WPA office, Edwards declared that children faced "slow starvation" and that those few families that succeeded in securing welfare assistance were provided budgets "far below danger levels." Harrington's cooperation was deemed "necessary to save lives" and the cutbacks would have to be "immediately rescinded."[16]

The layoff crisis of April–May 1939, when combined with the onset of normal seasonal unemployment, created what Edwards termed Michigan's "most serious relief crisis in recent years." The severity of the cutbacks induced Edwards to undertake an effort to revitalize the union's welfare and unemployed committees, which in some locals had been "allowed to slack off" or even expire. He instructed local presidents to reestablish or reinvigorate their unemployed organizations and mobilize for action on the political front. Without immediate action, Edwards foresaw a summer unemployment problem that would produce "evictions, hunger, loss of morale, and disillusionment in the union." As WPA welfare director, he was committed to aggressive unemployed organizing, confident that his work was "respected in the union nationally."[17]

Edwards' enthusiasm reflected a conviction that the department was crucial to the creation of the worker community that his Socialist conscience yearned for. This belief was evident in his 1939 report to the board, which observed simply but eloquently, that "solidarity of the industrial and unemployed workers built the WPA Department of the UAW-CIO." The department's value became clear during the General Motors tool-and-die-makers' strike in June, when the unemployed picketed regularly in support of their striking brothers. (See figure 18.) Moreover, it provided advice and aid for strikers in need of welfare assistance during the walkout and provided research support to the Michigan Unemployment Compensation Commission, which ultimately ruled that striking unionists were eligible for benefits. In short, Edwards and his organization served as advocates for the strikers, while they also succeeded in preventing the unemployed from being exploited as scab labor during the walkout. As noted by GM's William Knudsen, management efforts to recruit strikebreakers on the WPA projects encountered stiff resistance from the organized workers on WPA.[18]

While the UAW consolidated its position in Michigan and elsewhere, Communists struggled to survive. In June 1939 Benjamin reported to CP officials that the Alliance remained the unemployed

Figure 18 Roy Reuther Joins Picketers During General Motors Tool and Dye Strike, June, 1939 [Center foreground, without hat] *(Archives of Labor and Urban Affairs, Wayne State University)*

organization "best adapted to do the job," but that it was essential for it to cooperate with the CIO. Acknowledging the "tremendous contribution" made by the CIO in the battle for relief, Benjamin argued that it was nonetheless deficient as a mass organization because unlike the Alliance, the CIO did not adequately serve the unorganized, nonunion unemployed and relief recipients. In a tortured twist, he insisted that while the CIO's "political work" and "voice" were essential to the success of the unemployed movement, the Alliance was needed to promote the "actual mobilization of the masses for active struggle in this field."[19]

Benjamin's analysis was on target in at least one respect: during the first six months of 1939, the CIO had become the primary political force behind the fight to preserve WPA funding and protect the nation's unemployed. Enraged by lingering unemployment, Lewis never wavered in his insistence on massive federal expenditures to combat persistent softness in the national economy. In January 1939, CIO unemployment director Ralph Hetzel moved to mobilize locals in support of Roosevelt's proposed $875 million deficiency appropriation for WPA. While the Alliance mounted nationwide street demonstrations, the CIO worked in Congress and with its locals to turn up the political heat by urging congressmen to resist a proposed $150 million reduction of the appropriation. Despite these efforts, Roosevelt was forced to approve a $725 million Deficiency Act on 4 February 1939.[20]

No sooner had the furor over the deficiency appropriation subsided than Congressmen Clifton Woodrum and John Taber opened an Appropriations Committee investigation of WPA. It might better have been called an attack on the Workers Alliance, whose national leaders, Benjamin and Lasser, were grilled endlessly by committee members, with emphasis on their political views. While the committee skewered the Alliance for its Communist ties, the press sensationalized the charges of Communist control.[21]

In the midst of a circus atmosphere, then, Roosevelt asked Congress for a WPA appropriation of $1.477 billion for fiscal year 1940. Convinced that the administration bill would be slashed significantly, Lewis endorsed the more sweeping House legislation introduced in May 1939 by Massachusetts Democrat Joseph Casey. Casey's bill proposed a $2.2 billion appropriation designed to create three million jobs. Lewis demanded easy qualification provisions, the right to organize on WPA, projects that were socially useful, and wages that would maintain "an American standard of living." Hetzel submitted to the CIO Executive Board a strong statement of support for the Casey Bill, which the board embraced in June as "an alternative to the gutting of the WPA." He later endorsed the companion bill introduced in the Senate by James E. Murray of Montana, while attacking House Democrat Clifton Woodrum's more conservative proposal as a "Tory" measure that would "sabotage recovery" and "destroy WPA." At the same time, *CIO News* blistered Congress for its abject failure to confront the unemployment problem. The union organ quoted Lewis's denunciation of the "reactionaries" for their "open cynicism" in "tearing the vitals out of the meager provisions already existing to help the unemployed eke out a living."[22]

Throughout the crisis, the Michigan UAW steadfastly supported Lewis, Hetzel, and the CIO Unemployment Office. When the battle over the Murray-Casey Bill entered the critical stage in June 1939, Edwards reacted to Hetzel's call with a well-orchestrated campaign to generate popular pressure in support of the legislation. Working with UAW Regional Directors and local WPA Welfare Committees, he engineered a series of events and activities, including a telegram, letter, and postcard campaign, which culminated in mass demonstrations in communities where the WPA Auxiliary was organized. The largest mass meeting, held in Detroit's Clark Park, united WPA workers, LNPL, the CIO Industrial Council, and UAW members in a demand to "save WPA" by enacting the Murray-Casey Bill. Complementing the public demonstration, both Edwards and Addes took to the airwaves with addresses supporting the bill and urging Michigan citizens to make their voices heard in Washington.[23]

Addes focused on the central theme in UAW policy, emphasizing the need for solidarity between employed and jobless workers as the only hope for the preservation of WPA. To organized labor, there was only one way to reduce WPA rolls: reabsorption of project workers into private industry; and until private enterprise could sustain reemployment, there could be "no justification for the curtailment of WPA." The only answer was the Casey Bill, which would again bind worker with worker:

> The same union which fought for you in the shops is now fighting for you on WPA. That slogan has always been opportune. UAW-CIO members working in the shops, UAW-CIO members who are now laid off, and UAW-CIO members who are working on WPA—their fight is the same fight. Their cause is the same cause. Their foe is the same foe. . . . The job of saving WPA is one part of the larger program of the UAW affiliated with the CIO—a program based on the proposition that there can be no justice for anyone until there is justice for all who labor.[24]

Addes, Edwards, and the UAW-CIO bureaucracy had prepared the ground in Michigan for the showdown in Washington. Finally, Edwards coordinated a last-minute pressure campaign from Washington as he prepared to testify before the Senate Appropriations Committee. Orchestrating a gradually escalating offensive, he prompted last-minute wires and letters from home and arranged a series of interviews with Senators Prentiss Brown, Arthur Vandenberg, Sherman Minton of Indiana, Robert LaFollette of Wisconsin, and Robert Wagner of New York. The UAW bolstered his forces by sending a WPA Welfare Department delegation from Detroit, Flint, Toledo, Cleveland, Anderson, and Racine to assist him in "buttonholing Senators." Although the prospects were dismal, he held out the hope that a provision could be inserted permitting the full appropriation to be expended in less than a year.[25]

On 20 June Edwards appeared before the Senate Appropriations Committee to urge passage of the Murray Bill, which would create 3 million WPA jobs, eliminate proposed wage cuts, and remove a planned eighteen-month layoff provision that would affect long-term WPA employees. He denounced the House-passed WPA bill as legislation that undermined wage standards in both public employment and private industry and sentenced hundreds of thousands of workers to the "dole." Edwards insisted that the House bill would result in a return to the "tremendous social unrest which was occasioned by inadequate relief and soup lines in the 1932 depression days."[26]

Turning to the job crisis in Michigan, Edwards stressed the seasonal unemployment problem as a special reason for the UAW's deep concern over the threatened WPA cutbacks. He insisted that support for WPA was "unquestioned" by all political parties in Michigan and cited as evidence Detroit mayor Reading's assertion that it had been the "salvation of Detroit" from "social unrest and municipal bankruptcy." Similarly, he said, the city's welfare administrator had predicted that the House bill's job cutbacks would bring about the "complete collapse" of the Detroit relief system. Reviewing the dismal employment statistics for Michigan, Edwards reminded the Senate committee that the crisis would certainly worsen by midsummer, when the state's annual unemployment peak would be reached. He concluded with an assertion that similar figures could easily have been provided for the UAW cities of Cleveland, Toledo, Anderson, South Bend, Milwaukee, and Racine, all subject to similar fluctuations.[27]

Despite the efforts of UAW, CIO, and LNPL, the House bill became the basis for the Emergency Relief Act finally passed by both houses. Not only had the congressional conservative coalition stymied supporters of progressive relief legislation and successfully challenged the administration, but they produced a conference bill that contained several provisions that unemployed groups and the administration found objectionable. The bill's new security wage system meant that WPA wages in the Midwest and North would be cut; the eighteen-month layoff requirement mandated thirty-day layoffs for needy families regardless of circumstances; the Federal Theater Project was killed; and an important amendment excluded aliens and security risks from WPA employment, an especially harsh blow for an already struggling Workers Alliance.[28]

The enactment of the Relief Act had several important consequences. Most significant was the cutback in WPA jobs from 3 million to 2 million in fiscal year 1940. Coupled with this setback was the pay cut forced by the 130 hours per month standard, which destroyed the prevailing wage previously enjoyed by skilled craftsmen and the building trades. Indeed, cost-of-living variations from area to area resulted in wage reductions for all areas outside the South. Finally, the relief fight of 1939 hastened the decline of the Workers Alliance, which suffered not only from the withering attacks of the Dies Committee and the Senate Appropriations Committee, but also from escalating internal tensions between Communist and non-Communist elements.[29]

Immediately after the Woodrum Bill's enactment, spontaneous protest strikes broke out on WPA projects throughout the United States. The AFL, though it acknowledged that these demonstrations represented the "state of mind" of WPA workers, quickly announced that the actions had "never been ordered by the American Federation of Labor." An AFL emergency conference did urge Congress to redress project worker grievances, starting with the critical issue of a restored prevailing wage, which was never far from the organization's consciousness. Meanwhile, AFL allies in the UWPAUWA proposed a slowdown strike that would compensate for the move to a 130-hour monthly work period on WPA.[30]

While the AFL and its supporters in Michigan confined themselves to such pronouncements, the UAW WPA Welfare Department swung into action. On the bureaucratic front, Edwards fired off a bitter protest to Francis Harrington in Washington against an impending layoff of 3,000 WPA workers in Detroit. He pointed out that the proposed cutback would complicate an "already intolerable" welfare situation. On 7 July Edwards informed WPA officials that spontaneous demonstrations were under way as Michigan project workers left their jobs "in complete disgust." Ten days later he followed up with a plea to halt the next set of layoffs scheduled to go into effect on 20 July. Reminding Harrington that seasonal unemployment in Michigan was approaching its peak, Edwards warned of "deep social unrest" as workers began to lose faith in a government that was "shirking" an "inescapable responsibility."[31]

To emphasize its commitment to the unemployed, the UAW also coordinated a national one-day protest strike that focused on Michigan. On 11 July, WPA workers throughout the state failed to report for work. The Detroit demonstration idled 28,000 of the city's 35,000 project workers. Unlike some previous protest actions, this strike had the united support of UAW, UWPAUWA, WAA, and the AFL unions. In this instance, the Detroit Building Trades were reportedly the most militant organizations, as evidenced by their pledge to extend the one-day walkout for as long as it took to restore the prevailing wage for WPA workers. CIO added its endorsement. Confirming the existence of momentary consensus in the unemployed movement, Herbert Benjamin expressed the national Workers Alliance's satisfaction with a "good situation" based on "unity down below" as AFL, CIO, and WAA closed ranks in support of the strategy of "short protest strikes."[32]

Equally enthusiastic was George Edwards, who claimed 100 percent cooperation on the one-day strike from WPA local auxiliaries around the state of Michigan. Particularly significant was the solidarity evident in communities outside Detroit, such as Flint, Pontiac, Dearborn, Royal Oak, Belleville, and Mt. Clemens, where 100 percent walkouts had occurred. And beyond Michigan, effective demonstrations took place in Racine, Kenosha, Cleveland, Toledo, Anderson, and Evansville. Edwards asserted that the strike had gone "exceedingly well, with WPA officials admitting we closed all projects" in the Detroit area. Moreover, he noted that the protest had resulted in "a great deal of good publicity and good organizational work."[33]

The UAW maintained that the strike had won significant support from unorganized WPA workers, many of whom joined the union in response to its militance in fighting for the "preservation of WPA as a national institution." The Workers Alliance gained less from the strike, partly because it did not openly challenge the Roosevelt administration in the strike's formative stage. As late as 6 July, Lasser was attempting to persuade Roosevelt to discuss the WPA cutbacks informally. Finally, under pressure from militants within its ranks, the national Alliance mounted its own one one-day demonstration on 20 July, which produced a walkout by more than 300,000 WAA members and supporters. So late was the Alliance's action that some CP hard-liners bitterly attacked the organization for its deference to Roosevelt. Even Benjamin admitted that the WAA decision to confine itself to a one-day demonstration produced "much demoralization" by creating the "impression of calling off the strikes."[34]

In Michigan, the response to the belated Workers Alliance protest strike was mixed. The day's major event occurred in Jackson, where the Michigan Alliance's state secretary, Frank Ingram, led a "Citizen's Protest Rally" that united area religious leaders and labor leaders from AFL, CIO, and WAA. Meanwhile in the Michigan Alliance's other center of strength, the UP, protest activity was continuous from 11 July through the 20 July demonstration. The Alliance sponsored public meetings in Iron River, Wakefield, and Houghton-Hancock, all to criticize the impending cutbacks mandated by the hated Woodrum Bill. Among the hotbeds of resistance were Iron and Gogebic counties, where the Alliance had long been entrenched. In Iron River, speakers blamed Wall Street and "reactionary business interests" for the enactment of the recent WPA legislation.[35]

Despite the bold pronouncements, the cutbacks were implemented on schedule. In August the Michigan Alliance's Frank Ingram toured the state "completing plans" for "organized actions . . . against starvation." Blaming the work relief crisis on Michigan Republicans and the conservative coalition in Washington, he saw recent suicides as "ghastly evidence" of "this reactionary policy that cut workers off from relief and government employment while private industry could not absorb them into the work force." In Jackson the WAA coordinated a mass rally to protest the "betrayal of the people" by the Woodrum Bill. The result of this meeting was the creation of yet another Alliance-CIO-AFL committee to promote labor unity in the effort to save WPA and publicize the collusion between "GOP and Garnercrats" who had mortally wounded the WPA.[36]

Efforts to maintain a labor coalition were also evident in the UP, where in late August, CIO Regional Director Adolph Germer worked to organize a CIO constituency of lumberjacks and miners that also included the WPA workers. On 25 August he met with the Iron River Workers Alliance to explain the CIO policy on WPA affiliation. Speaking later in Ironwood for Labor's Non-Partisan League, Germer cited the UP as a "living indictment" of an economic situation created by "predatory wealth, aided and protected by the Republican Party." One month later, the Michigan Workers Alliance convened a UP "Right to Work Conference" that mapped out a program to deal with both the regime of Republican governor Luren Dickenson and the attack on WPA. A new UP Coordinating Committee was appointed to implement the conference decision to reemphasize aid for relief recipients and to work directly with recently laid off WPA workers. Behind the desperate maneuvers lay the reality of a decayed organization. According to Michigan State Police informants, the UP Alliance had gone underground and finally "ceased functioning by the end of 1939."[37]

A new realism soon surfaced in Benjamin's thinking on the future of the Workers Alliance, which increasingly stressed the creation of a mass movement not solely dependent on work with WPA employees. Rather, he proposed that the Alliance recognize mass unemployment as a "permanent phenomenon" and move towards a new organizational structure that developed "community or neighborhood locals" as a more "stable form." The underlying theme in the Alliance's new departure was the recognition that because of CIO initiative and WPA cutbacks, its organizational base was shrinking. Its problem in Michigan was compounded by the vigor of the UAW, which continued to organize the unemployed in southern Michigan. Symptomatic of the UAW's success in unemployed work was the wholesale defection of the Lansing Workers Alliance, which in November 1939 voted to affiliate with the UAW WPA Welfare Department.[38]

Under the watchful eye of the International Executive Board's designated WPA directors, Addes and Thomas, Edwards had succeeded in rebuilding and reorganizing the new WPA Welfare Department, which had been chartered in early 1939 by the UAW-CIO to establish unity between workers in the plants and on the projects. With the job now complete, the board adopted a new organizational structure for "WPA auxiliary locals" that implemented the old CIO policy of organizing both auto workers on WPA and other project workers from those CIO unions that waived jurisdiction. Unlike the Workers Alliance, UAW concentrated on organizing the CIO unemployed and initiating new unionists from the ranks of the jobless. It was a meaningful distinction, in that UAW moved away from the sweeping community organizing pattern increasingly espoused by the outflanked Alliance. It also served the long-run interest of a rapidly bureaucratizing union that looked to future expansion based on jobless workers returning to the work force.[39]

Having accomplished his primary task, Edwards now resigned his position as UAW national welfare director. His replacement, Joseph Pagano of the Hudson local, brought a tough but less sophisticated style of leadership to the union's unemployed organizing. During Pagano's apprenticeship, however, Edwards continued to serve as assistant director. Since the July protest strike, the WPA Welfare Department had worked to ameliorate the effects of the 130-hour month and the eighteen-month layoff provisions of the new Relief Bill. After conferring with Michigan WPA officials, Edwards went to Washington to discuss the problem with WPA assistant administrator Fred Rauch. Supported by UAW-generated letters and telegrams from Detroit and Grand Rapids and backed by both Congressmen Rudolph G. Tenerowicz and Frank Hook, he urged Rauch to authorize a liberalization of the Michigan quota of WPA jobs. A confidential memo from Larned, moreover, made it clear that Harrington was well aware of organized protests in Michigan that had been coordinated by the UAW. As a result of Edwards' lobbying, 5,000 workers regained their WPA jobs in October.[40]

While Edwards battled the federal bureaucracy, the Flint auxiliary organization explored a CIO tie beyond the state borders. In Genessee County, Genora Johnson and Claude Workman had reconstructed a strong WPA Welfare Department, which by August 1939 had enrolled five hundred members and placed stewards on all projects. Convinced of the need for a more stable organization, the Flint militants were drawn to a new scheme to create a national CIO Project Workers Union under the aegis of Philip Murray, David McDonald, and O. B. Allen of the Steel Workers Organizing Committee. In response to a call from SWOC's Project Worker's Organizing Committee, the Flint WPA organization sent Johnson and Workman to Pittsburgh as delegates to a fifteen-state conference to launch the new unemployed union with CIO sponsorship.[41] The idea of a national project workers' union was completely consistent with the sentiments expressed by UAW-CIO ever since its founding convention in March.

The Pittsburgh conference was widely reported as the first step in the organization of the unemployed into a huge CIO union, but Lewis prudently adopted a policy of watchful waiting. Although the United Project Workers Organizing Committee had the "blessings of the CIO," its incorporation into the national organization depended on its progress, as well as "union desirability," according to CIO regional director Anthony J. Federoff. Federoff made it clear that the CIO would do all possible to help the fledgling union "attain desirability." With John Grittie of the New Castle Industrial Union Council as permanent chairman and Fred Carreno of the Pittsburgh United Project Workers as secretary, the UPWOC was clearly dominated by SWOC and the steel workers of the Pennsylvania–West Virginia–Ohio region. It was, therefore, "not very representative" of the nation's unemployed and WPA workers.[42] Although the UAW was cautious about the new departure and Lewis held back on a full endorsement, the new national unemployed union was a natural extension of the pioneer work done by both the auto workers and the national CIO.

UPWOC expressed the CIO social vision in its strong commitment to the right to work. It placed its faith in a strong national government that would act on behalf of the underclass to guarantee every citizen a "socially useful job" at a wage "compatible with American standards of health and decency." Despite the similarity between the views of Lewis, the CIO, and UPWOC, the organization never developed into a national union, in large measure because its emergence coincided with the expansion of the early wartime economy in late 1939. It was the economic revival more than any other factor that gradually weakened the entire unemployed movement,[43] and it was the fate of UPWOC to be caught in the transition back to full employment.

George Edwards saw the handwriting on the wall. In October 1939 he told his father that the "war boom" had returned Detroit employment to levels near the 1937 mark. Confirming this report, Pagano noted that the turnover in WPA Auxiliary membership had increased dramatically and that he had been forced to train many new project stewards in October. Because project and welfare problems had "very suddenly become mitigated" and since WPA was "phasing down," Edwards returned to organizing for Local 174.[44]

With the departure of the urbane George Edwards for the west side local, the UAW lost an effective spokesman for the jobless. Yet not for long, for shortly thereafter, Detroit mayor Edward Jeffries appointed Edwards secretary of the city's housing commission. Named to this position in part because of his high profile in unemployed work,[45] he gained a new platform from which to serve workers' social needs and launched a new career in bureaucratic politics.

With Edwards gone, Pagano brought a new, gritty leadership to a department that had become a fixture in the expanding UAW bureaucracy. The major work stoppage at Chrysler in October and November 1939 presented Pagano with his first major test as leader of the WPA Welfare Department. For the department, the key issue raised by the Chrysler strike was immediate access to welfare benefits for striking workers. Pagano's office coordinated the activities of local union welfare committees and guided them through the complicated welfare bureaucracy, at all times fighting problem cases in cooperation with the locals. The union complemented these efforts with a pressure campaign to maintain adequate welfare funds, which was most successful in Oakland County. Following UAW advice, county officials extended welfare benefits until the appropriation ran out, after which the union local pressed county agencies for aid. The WPA Welfare Department claimed that relatively few Chrysler workers went without help.[46]

A constant concern for the union was the threat of various back-to-work campaigns instigated through the welfare offices, where authorities sometimes conditioned eligibility for relief on worker promises of a willingness to return to work. According to a Red Squad informant, one Communist striker reported that Chrysler workers "fear[ed] that workers [would] be cut from the WPA and relief roll and told to go to Chrysler's," where "jobs would be waiting." In several instances, "anonymous sources" tried to induce WPA workers to provide scab labor, but without success. Pagano proudly reported in December that the WPA Welfare Department had taught the "would-be scab herders" the meaning of solidarity when many WPA workers spent their free time on the picket lines. Moreover, WPA authorities cooperated by accepting Pagano's advice to refuse reassignment of Chrysler workers to WPA. As a result the welfare offices were unable to force active pickets off the line. Finally, black WPA workers generally resisted Homer Martin's efforts to use them against the Chrysler strikers as scab labor.[47] When Chrysler capitulated, at least a portion of the credit was due to the active work of a WPA Welfare Department that had made significant progress towards uniting the employed and unemployed in class solidarity.

Assessing its progress over a two-year gestation period, the WPA Welfare Department claimed victory in its battle to "keep alive the spirit of unionism among the unemployed." Having built a strong union on WPA, UAW insisted that it had achieved something heretofore unknown in American labor history by turning economic adversity and potential strikebreakers into "union-building weapons." And there was one important bonus. Pagano was confident that when WPA workers went back to the private sector they would "continue their union-building in the shops." The thousands of Ford workers who were returning to work by 1940 after employment on the projects had "heard the message of unionism."[48] The battle lines had been drawn. CIO resisted defense spending as the solution to lingering unemployment and redoubled its efforts to promote social spending and an extension of the New Deal as solutions to economic stagnation. In Michigan, Joseph Pagano and the UAW stood ready to fight for WPA and organize project workers in self-interest and self-defense. But so long as the unemployed movement centered on the union jobless and organizable government employees, its shrinking base would continue to contract. An expanding war economy was threatening to permanently undermine the WPA Welfare Department that the union had worked so hard to create.

The UAW Welfare Department at Maturity

Despite the modest recovery under way in early 1940, neither the UAW nor the CIO could afford to relax their efforts on behalf of the unemployed. Lewis argued that the union movement was forced to continue its fight to prevent the destruction of WPA. He insisted that significant hard-core unemployment remained a problem, and that war-driven economic growth was illusory, in that it was unlikely to outlive the wartime crisis. Symptomatic of the lingering economic problem were the 775,000 workers dropped from the WPA rolls as a result of the eighteen-month layoff provisions of the WPA Bill of 1939. According to WPA Commissioner F. C. Harrington, 87 percent of dismissed project workers had not found employment in the private sector as of December 1939. In Detroit 46 percent were receiving direct relief and 20 percent were unemployed and not on relief. While 1,500 of the 9,000 dismissed workers had found jobs and another 1,500 had been reassigned to WPA, 6,000 were unable to support themselves.[49]

Confronted by a nagging unemployment and welfare problem in 1940, Pagano and the union leadership determined that UAW could be most effective as a coordinator for all worker groups affected by local, state, and federal cutbacks. As early as 9 March, the UAW brought together all CIO welfare directors, Workers Alliance leaders, unemployed activists, and some AFL representatives at a conference to plan a united effort to resolve the problems facing the Detroit-area unemployed. In an attempt to support the UAW initiative, the Workers Alliance imported David Lasser for an address emphasizing the importance of unity among progressive forces in opposition to the budget trimmers. The end result was a coordinated protest when the Common Council met to consider cuts in the welfare budget. While a variety of left groups provided the shock troops, it is nonetheless clear that the UAW WPA Welfare Department mapped and directed the strategy that succeeded. Not only were the budget cuts reversed, but UAW secured new rights in representing workers, including approval for direct contacts at district welfare offices.[50]

While the welfare crisis hit close to home for Michigan's unemployed, a parallel controversy threatened the long-term interests of the jobless even more directly: the unrelenting struggle to maintain federal funding for the WPA program in the face of yet another congressional economy drive. By early April, no new project assignments were being made in Michigan and additional layoffs seemed imminent. To counter the congressional economy bloc, the UAW Welfare Department endorsed H.R. 960, which funded three million new WPA jobs and rescinded the hated eighteen-month layoff provision. Scoring the "Congressional Blind Mice Club," the union's WPA Worker exhorted sympathetic readers to escalate the pressure by warning their representatives that reelection was dependent on a correct vote. In support of Pagano's effort, the UAW Executive Board expressed alarm at the impending layoffs and called for a deficiency appropriation to stave off disaster until the beginning of the new fiscal year in July.[51]

Before the deficiency appropriation was enacted, another related issue emerged in Michigan to test the mettle of WPA authorities. Because of the funding shortfall, many Wayne County locals, the Detroit IUC, and the UAW Welfare Department launched an effort to secure a revised quota of WPA jobs for the summer and fall quarters. The heart of their argument lay in the impact of seasonal unemployment in Michigan, which had historically resulted in widespread joblessness between July and October. Tracy Doll and John Gibson, representing the Detroit and Michigan IUC's, pressured WPA for a solution to the state's unique problem. Doll indicted the Michigan WPA administration, angrily asserting that "were it the intention of the WPA to reach an unemployment peak during the summer of 1940, they could have done no better job of figuring in reverse." Meanwhile Pagano and a delegation of hundreds demanded that Abner Larned pressure the Washington WPA authorities for redress. Eventually, Howard Hunter did agree to authorize a six-month quota as soon as a new appropriation had passed,[52] thus providing stability and immediate hiring authority that could be increased during the height of the seasonal layoff.

In fact, the gains had been modest at best. To be sure, Michigan secured an exceptional quota arrangement, but by July, when the figures were released, Pagano and the union were disappointed that the Michigan allocation was not higher. Pagano told Senator Brown that more jobs were required in July, August, and September when Michigan employment figures would "reach their valley." He insisted that the situation in the state was "extremely acute" and that spontaneous protests were becoming "very difficult to control." At the same time, the WPA Welfare Department pledged that the union was "determined that the needs of the state be met."[53]

The outcome of the fight for the WPA Bill was not satisfying. The result was a parsimonious $975 million for fiscal year 1940–1941, though Roosevelt was permitted to expend the entire appropriation in an eight-month period, if necessary. The union could not conceal its disappointment in the bill. Warning of "witch-hunts," the UAW Welfare Department especially deplored the provision for compulsory affidavits (the non-Communist affidavit) relating to WPA workers' political affiliations.[54]

While the union pressed for an acceleration of WPA quotas, the emerging war economy was undermining the argument for greater government expenditures on work relief programs. Moreover, there was increased emphasis in Washington on the defense buildup, which distracted the Roosevelt administration's attention from a program that had gained powerful political enemies in the congressional economy bloc. And the WPA cutbacks meant that Pagano's position was fatally weakened by the reality that the UAW Welfare Department's function and constituency were gradually eroding.

The result was a predictable decision to return to the primary problem confronting the WPA Welfare Department, namely the drive to boost the WPA job allocation for Michigan. An increase would provide not only badly needed assistance to the remaining jobless, but also a new supply of organizable workers for the union. While the WPA Welfare Department thus gave the problems of the unemployed on direct relief a lower priority, it could credibly argue that any expansion of job opportunity served the interest of all the jobless. In this instance, a humane program coincided with the bureaucratic interests of a union department which, if truly successful, would face ultimate extinction.

At its St. Louis convention in August, UAW crafted a dual-track strategy for organizing the unemployed in a time when public attention was becoming distracted from the plight of the jobless. When Detroit Local 154 advanced a resolution calling for a stronger UAW commitment to the unemployed, including a constitutional amendment to institutionalize the WPA Welfare Auxiliary and the immediate appointment of a national WPA Welfare Director (Pagano's official title was Assistant Director), the Constitution Committee adroitly maneuvered the resolution and the issue into the hands of the executive board. The board also received authority to explore a second line of attack by pursuing the possible creation of a nationwide CIO International for all unemployed workers, should CIO be willing to adopt this course. This resolution, proposed by the more conservative Lansing Local 14, reflected growing concerns about the long-term prospects for maintaining a permanent UAW initiative at the forefront of the state's unemployed movement. Deference to the new executive board also revealed the growing strength of the Reuthers and their allies, who emerged from St. Louis with a strengthened presence in the UAW inner circle.[55]

By late 1940, then, Pagano and the WPA Welfare Department were beset by a myriad of problems that foreshadowed a dramatic shift in the UAW commitment to the unemployed. Not only was the union moving to place the financial and organizational burden on the CIO, but the department also experienced increased frustration on the political front. Despite Pagano's ongoing campaign for an upward revision of the Michigan WPA quota, the Washington WPA authorities were unwilling to make any adjustment. Worse yet, Pagano admitted an even more serious problem: the hard fact that rising private employment and federal defense spending had created "an illusion of prosperity." Despite 750,000 on the WPA waiting list, "wishful thinking on the part of industry and its politicians" had "spread the idea that all those who are willing to work can now find jobs."[56]

The security of the WPA Welfare Department within the UAW bureaucracy was in jeopardy, and Pagano saw, only too clearly, the threat to his position. In response to changed circumstances, he moved to protect his office and the union's commitment to the jobless. In December 1940 he launched a project to develop a detailed profile of Michigan's WPA work force for use in a new campaign to preserve the federal jobs program. Preliminary findings revealed that the overwhelming majority were men over forty, men with physical disabilities, or women with little occupational experience. Moreover, many were blacks who had been barred from employment in most shops because of racial discrimination. Nearly all WPA workers were "ineligible," for one reason or another, for employment in private industry. In view of both state and national trends, the WPA Welfare Department concluded that WPA should become a permanent program, which could be a valuable asset in the burgeoning national defense effort, but which also should serve other important social and cultural purposes. In an internal memorandum, Pagano urged that the International Union press these demands on the Roosevelt administration and secure the full cooperation of Philip Murray and the CIO.[57]

By January 1941 Pagano had sold the plan within UAW and was prepared to go public with a visionary program for the unemployed, based upon the Michigan experience but defended as a response to unemployment as a national problem. The WPA Welfare Department asserted that nationwide, ten million jobless workers had not yet been absorbed by private industry. In a boldly progressive proposal, the department then advanced a program for the "unemployable employables"—women, minorities, the elderly, and the inexperienced young. The union's statistical breakdown of the Michigan WPA rolls revealed that 60 percent were over 40, 13 percent under 25, 14 percent female, and 17 percent black. The employment of these hard-core unemployed was deemed essential to national security, which required adequate public facilities and an educated public. The department maintained that WPA could be a "program with a definite direction," the employment of "the millions for whom private industry has no place and will have no place for years to come." With the adoption of the UAW program, there would never again be a time "when our nation weeps over a 'forgotten man.' "[58] (See figure 19.)

An independent report from Michigan WPA administrator Abner Larned confirmed important aspects of Pagano's analysis, especially his emphasis on the persistence of transitional unemployment due to reconversion to defense industry and his description of the

The Menace of the Machine—A Problem for GM Workers

Figure 19   The UAW Warns Against Technological Unemployment, April, 1940 *(Archives of Labor and Urban Affairs, Wayne State University)*

structure of Michigan unemployment. Much to UAW's displeasure, WPA officials in Washington were helpless in view of legislative limitations on the program. While the Michigan WPA authorities acknowledged the value of Pagano's examination of project workers "frequently overlooked," they could only promise to do what they could subject to the "financial limitations . . . imposed by the Congress." The exchange was entirely cordial but nonetheless unproductive. Pagano's proposal for a broadened WPA program "went nowhere."[59]

Pagano's shift to higher moral ground emphasizing the "unemployables" mirrored the WPA Welfare Department's growing concern that the volatile economy endangered its own future in the UAW's burgeoning bureaucracy. On 24 January 1941, *The WPA Worker* nervously asserted that the Department had been needed when grievances on the projects had gone unredressed and whenever the WPA appropriation had been threatened. Defending the UAW record, the Department organ argued that:

Now, if ever, you need your union. The WPA appropriation is threatened. The National Defense program has brought with it a prosperity-hysteria. The newspapers have fallen right in line. Employment has picked up—but there are still many more than three million men and women who need jobs on WPA. You have only one way of fighting for your right to work—through your union. That goes for your project, your welfare station, your city—and that goes for Washington.[60]

An important point stressed in the WPA Welfare Department's plea was the value of the CIO connection. Workers were reminded that CIO was "doing everything possible" to save WPA and convince Congress that WPA was "as vital to national defense as is the aircraft program." In fact, CIO was engaged in a broad effort to support unemployed workers on several fronts. In January 1941 John Brophy urged CIO state and local councils to lobby for uniform federal standards for state unemployment compensation systems that would result in equalizing benefits from state to state. One month later, James Carey of the CIO Unemployment Committee charged that the Roosevelt administration's $375 million deficiency appropriation request for WPA was "wholly inadequate." Demanding at least $500 million, the *CIO News* asked, "Is America so poor that it must starve the poor and defenseless in the name of national defense?" In support of Carey's appeal, R. J. Thomas, George Addes, and Joseph Pagano informed the Congressional Appropriations Committees that $500 million was essential to prevent "untold suffering." The UAW insisted that "national defense is based on security— not suffering."[61]

On 11 March 1941, Pagano complained bitterly to WPA administrator Howard Hunter that proposed quota reductions for Michigan would be "unfortunate" if they were "based on the delusions of prosperity now current in the minds of newspaper and editorial writers and other well-fed persons." Pagano insisted that most Michigan WPA workers were unlikely to be hired by private industry for the foreseeable future. Reminding Hunter of Michigan's peculiar seasonal employment problem, he noted that the situation would inevitably deteriorate by the end of the fiscal year and that defense contracts could not offset "this general cycle." Despite Pagano's demand for higher quotas for Michigan's industrial areas, Washington made no changes.[62]

One reason for the persistence of chronic unemployment lay in the auto industry's resistance to full-scale conversion to defense production. Because they were enjoying their first substantial profits in several years, auto managers were reluctant to curtail production of automobiles for the domestic market. Manufacturers therefore insisted on the simultaneous production of domestic goods and military supplies. Throughout 1940 and 1941, the industry resisted any governmental interference with normal business, and as late as summer 1941 remained preoccupied with domestic auto production and the profit margins it guaranteed.[63] Although the human resources to support expanded war production existed, industry was unprepared to mobilize those resources if a shift to defense materials entailed the risk of losses or other uncertainty.

In at least one sense, then, Pagano's argument was on target. Although the Michigan economy was gradually improving, the impact of defense spending was insufficient to reverse the chronic unemployment that plagued the state's auto workers. And in some instances, defense priorities exacerbated an already severe unemployment problem. Production of automobiles in July 1941 reached 461,000 units, almost twice the figure for July 1940. But full-scale automobile production had exhausted supplies of scarce materials such as chrome, copper, lead, steel, and zinc. As a result, some companies without defense contracts were forced to curtail production, which led to increased "priorities unemployment." On the heels of this setback, Office of Production Management Director William Knudsen, himself former president of General Motors, announced a 20 percent cut in scheduled automobile production for the period August 1941–July 1942, which threatened further employment cutbacks.[64] While the shift would not occur until 1 August 1941, Pagano correctly saw that existing conditions threatened to deepen the traditional summer doldrums.

As spring slipped into summer 1941, then, the WPA Welfare Department was mired in an unsuccessful effort to prevent WPA reductions and to reshape the agency as a bureaucratic advocate for the "unemployables" on the bottom rung of the industrial ladder. In large measure, the union's plea fell on deaf ears, partly because the nation was engaged in the early stages of a defense buildup that dwarfed the concerns of automakers and UAW workers who feared the strains of transitional unemployment. As the conversion process went forward, moreover, the concerns of a union bureaucracy in decline were overshadowed by an economy on the verge of a massive expansion. It was Pagano's misfortune to be caught in the transition.

Year of Decision at Ford: The Barriers Fall

While Pagano and the WPA Welfare Department struggled to combat the shrinkage of federal employment programs, a movement of much greater long-term significance for UAW was cresting at the last bastion of the open shop, the Ford empire. The triumph of interracial unionism at Ford has been described by many students of labor history and automobile unionism. Less well known, but also important, was the role played by the unemployed, especially WPA organizers, in forging the link between the black and white workers who laid the foundations of the militant Dearborn Local 600. It is clear, in retrospect, that the UAW's WPA Auxiliary constituted a critical bridge between the exclusionary practices of the past and the solidarity that marked the development of the UAW at Ford.

A key factor in the early mobilization of black workers was the role of the Communist Party, which may be traced back to the militance of the Unemployed Councils of the early 1930s. Indeed, with a few exceptions, the Communists were virtually the only white unionists to fight militantly for black equality in the union from the outset. Moreover, the Party's position within the UAW was strengthened substantially by the CP decision to colonize basic industries in 1937 and 1938. The result of this drive was a significant increase in the number of black Communist auto workers. As a consequence of CP activism, the only Ford workers to hold union cards in early 1938 were those organized by Party activist Bill McKie and a smaller group belonging to Local 174.[65]

While the focal point of CP activity among the Detroit jobless remained the Workers Alliance, there is ample evidence of cooperation within UAW at Ford, where unemployed activity and union organizing went hand in hand. In February 1938, for example, McKie reported to Walter Reuther on a massive literature distribution program for unionists in Local 174. He also described a series of unemployed welfare meetings held in January and February, which were attended by 3,500 workers. Undertaken in connection with preparations for the Cadillac Square demonstration of February 1938, the welfare meetings placed emphasis on an inherent right to work and the consequent demand for a larger commitment in Washington to WPA. Even the CP militant Frank Sykes recalled that Reuther appointed Communists from the unemployed movement to union positions, although Sykes maintained that the union's objective was to secure the names of Party workers who were active in the shops. Among these activists were William Nowell and Walter Hardin in Detroit and Pontiac, both of whom became active in organizing blacks during the abortive Ford drive of 1938. This significant step in mobilizing black workers was neutralized in February when an already suspicious Homer Martin laid off several Ford organizers, including the entire black staff. Although Nowell and Hardin were eventually rehired, the Ford drive was already collapsing.[66]

Meanwhile, on the WPA projects, UAW was engaged in the process of organizing unemployed workers, both union and non-union. Black organizer Shelton Tappes later recalled that while union activity in the shops had receded because of recession layoffs, "on the WPA there was quite a lift." While there were few concrete gains made, it was the modest achievements of the UAW WPA Auxiliary that were significant. Tappes noted that improvements in working conditions on the projects showed workers from unorganized shops, "especially the Ford people . . . how unions worked, the effectiveness of having representation." He maintained that through the WPA organization, UAW was "able to establish a very good contact with the Ford workers." In effect, the WPA Auxiliary became a halfway house for blacks on the road to unionism. WPA Welfare Department staffer Ethel Polk recalled that black participation in union unemployed organizing helped dispel the fear that had resulted from management intimidation at Ford. This assessment was shared by Pagano, who later indicated that many of the future leaders of Ford Local 600 "received their primary training and their trade union experience as officers and members of the WPA local of UAW." And, according to Tappes, "whenever it became necessary for UAW to hold a big demonstration . . . for propaganda purposes or support . . . they could usually depend on the numbers of the UAW WPA Section."[67]

As the Ford drive accelerated, the WPA Auxiliary assumed greater prominence as an instrument for union organizing. In March 1938 Ford organizers were compiling lists of WPA jobs in progress for "immediate action." At least one organizer reported "progress in the enrollment of Ford workers into the union from the WPA Ford workers." These efforts climaxed with a major Ford rally on 5 June 1938 in Baby Creek Park, at which Homer Martin, William Taylor, George Edwards, Victor Reuther, and Fred Pieper combined to appeal for unemployed services, an expanded WPA, and the immediate organization of Ford. Most speakers asserted that the WPA Auxiliary was the channel through which the union's goals were being achieved. Most emphatic was Edwards, who insisted that "when Ford reopens to full production he will not be able to find men who are not members of the UAW."[68]

Despite the impressive progress made through the WPA Auxiliary in Dearborn, the Ford drive of 1938 was actually in serious trouble due to the divisive influence of the emerging Martin split. As Martin's anti-Communist machinations became more persistent, a great strain was placed upon unemployed organizers who had labored to promote UAW-Workers Alliance cooperation in working with the jobless. The tension surfaced in May 1938, when the Dearborn branch of the Alliance tried to sign up members for UAW at a mass meeting for Ford workers held at Dearborn High School. After promising union cooperation to provide a film and other support for the meeting, Martinites on the UAW staff reneged on the agreement at the last minute, leaving union loyalists in the Alliance with no backing for the rally. In an angry protest to the Executive Board, Henry Kraus argued that recruitment into UAW had been carried out at three previous Workers Alliance meetings and that the Alliance had been "of real assistance in keeping up the union drive at Ford."[69]

Kraus reported that Martin ally Morris Fields had denied the Alliance union assistance because it was viewed as a "dual organization," which both UAW and CIO had disowned. Alliance members correctly charged that Fields had misinterpreted the CIO "attitude." Moreover, Kraus noted that the Dearborn Alliance had "always regarded the UAW as the basic organization for the auto workers," as evidenced by its consistent efforts to bring unemployed auto workers into the union. To the Alliance the overall strategy and its justification were clear:

> The Executive Board should know that there is a great reluc-
> tance for Ford workers to function openly as members of UAW
> or its auxiliaries even when laid off, and consequently the
> Workers Alliance has supplied a stopgap means both of win-
> ning concessions for the unemployed Ford workers and of
> educating and directing them toward the union.[70]

The Alliance's argument had validity, and it is clear that it was
committed to collaboration with UAW in the campaign to organize
Ford.

Other UAW accounts confirmed the Workers Alliance's analysis of the problem confronted by unionists in Dearborn. Pagano
later noted that unemployed Ford workers had long faced the
speedup, restrictions on personal liberty, and the "brutality of
the Ford service system" and, as a result, tended to "regard with
great skepticism newspaper stories about the right to organize."
Once the WPA Welfare Department had succeeded in forcing the
removal of Ford service men from supervisory positions on WPA
projects, there was a "definite increase" in applications for union
membership from unemployed Ford workers. Pagano asserted
that the Dearborn local of the WPA Welfare Department, one of
the first organized, was a hotbed of militant unionism. Pagano
maintained that, from the beginning, the Dearborn WPA organization had been "of great service to the International" in that it
had sent "many good, experienced, union members back into the
shop—most of whom had been afraid to even think of the union
previously."[71]

As had often been true in the past, the spirit of unionism at the
Ford Rouge complex was kept alive by the tireless Communist
activist Bill McKie. McKie clearly understood the value of unemployed organizing as a tool in the UAW onslaught against Ford. In
October 1938, he revealed his strategy at a meeting of Local 600.
A Red Squad informant described McKie's approach as dependent
upon support from the jobless:

> In District #6 of the WPA there are more former Ford workers
> working on the projects and the scheme of this Red is to
> organize them on their projects as they have just about de-
> spaired of organizing the Ford plant from the inside and plan
> to do it from the outside.[72]

By early 1939 the Ford drive lay dormant, having fallen victim to the larger factional split that had driven Homer Martin from the councils of UAW leadership. But the setback was only temporary. In mid-1939 union activists at Ford began to regroup their forces for the next battle. Black organizers, many of them with Communist Party ties, strongly supported the new drive. In August 1939 Paul Kirk and Joseph Billups urged the UAW Executive Board to renew its drive to organize black workers. Their appeal resulted in the board's decision to hire Billups and Walter Hardin as paid organizers to work with the new Voluntary Organizing Committee, which included many blacks who had gained experience with the Unemployed Councils, Workers Alliance, and the WPA Auxiliary. Especially prominent were blacks with Communist ties, such as Billups, Kirk, Leon Bates, James Anderson, and Veal Clough. The revitalized Local 600 was by most accounts the product of dedicated organizational activity on the left, including the work of many activists who had been schooled in the unemployed movement during the days of the AWU and the Councils.[73]

One insight transferred from the unemployed movement to the broader union movement involved the indivisibility of racial justice and union solidarity. At the initiative of the WPA Auxiliary, for example, the Michigan Industrial Union Council demanded that WPA administrators force city and county officials to abolish discrimination in restaurants, taverns, and other public places. More significant, perhaps, were the members of Detroit WPA Locals 1 and 2, who in April 1939 asked the UAW Executive Board to make black activist James Anderson a paid organizer for the WPA Welfare Department. The unemployed locals argued that Anderson, recently fired for union activities, was a "militant, sincere, honest, and aggressive union-conscious WPA worker." Declaring their trust and admiration for him, Chairman George Leets told the board that the workers "love this negro worker and brother," who had been "popularly asked to become a WPA organizer."[74] Anderson soon went on payroll as an organizer.

When in August 1940 the Ford drive resumed in earnest, appeals to black workers drew new emphasis. As early as March 1940, a joint negro organizing committee, including seven salaried black organizers, operated under the direction of a veteran of the unemployed movement, Paul Kirk. And when the Ford organizing committee began using radio broadcasts to reach workers, the WPA

Welfare Department aided in making a direct appeal to the Ford work force. In August 1940 Joseph Pagano stressed the union's services to unemployed members, whose situation at Ford was precarious in the absence of a union contract. He argued that at union plants, seniority meant guaranteed rehiring, while Ford workers never knew whether they would be reemployed after layoff season. Pagano concluded that Ford employees, suffering from "a perpetual sense of insecurity," were now "groping for something to tie up to."[75] In short, the uncertainties of unemployment and the UAW's commitment to the jobless provided one strong argument for unionization.

By March 1941, the turning point in the Ford campaign had been reached, as the union petitioned for a representation election. After Ford's dismissal of eight union committeemen, a spontaneous sit-down occurred in several Ford departments, and the final confrontation began. In this last battle, the WPA organization assumed an important role. One Polish immigrant recalled his experience at Ford in 1941 as a slow and difficult process that began on the projects:

> I went to WPA and started creating leadership on the WPA, young fellows. It was interesting. While I was on WPA with the young people. There were over 50 in a group it was very bad. [sic] One day they dug a hole and one wanted to bury me. I was the chief steward. He wanted to bury me because I wanted to organize them into a union. I took 3 of them, the worst ones. I took them to the side and talked to them nice and they began to understand me. And later the rest fell into line. I sign them up in the union. I carry on the fight for them and teach them that they shouldn't do crazy things. There's nobody at home to do any work. They should look ahead because some day they'll go back to Ford's and I want them to be leaders of the unions, not me but I want them to be leaders. And I had pretty good results. They became active later. Its too bad I can't name very many of them. Most of them were Americans. Some Polish. Italians.[76]

Throughout the strike, the WPA Welfare Department assumed a high profile, especially in the protection of workers' rights to welfare services and to speedy reinstatement following the stoppage. The union established an emergency welfare operation in Dearborn, staffed by Ethel Polk and her assistants, who worked night and day during the strike to loan strikers money and aid worker families in securing public assistance, when necessary. Yet the Michigan Industrial Union Council asserted that the "most spectacular" of the WPA Welfare Department's activities during the strike was its key role in supplying a "tremendous number" of the most active strikers, many of them graduates of the WPA organization. The strike "clearly illustrated the prestige of the WPA Welfare Department."[77]

The UAW's success in the NLRB election of May 1941 was profoundly significant for the union's development. Greater stability in labor-management relations flowed from the organization of the last major holdout against the rising tide of industrial unionism in the automobile industry. Moreover, it is evident in retrospect that the UAW alliance with the leadership of the black community and the visible participation of black workers in strike activities marked a watershed in the development of interracial unionism—what August Meier and Elliot Rudwick regard as an important part of the Ford strike's legacy. There is also some validity in Harry Bennett's overdrawn conclusion that the outcome was a "great victory for the Communist Party."[78] While Bennett's remark was meant to be sensational, there can be no doubt about the key role of Communists as part of the coalition that won a landmark union victory. Finally, a review of the strike's background, stretching backward to the recession of 1937–1938, clearly reveals that unemployed workers, the Workers Alliance, and the UAW WPA Welfare Department all played important roles in the promotion of unionism in the last bastion of the open shop in Detroit. Whether raising worker consciousness, educating the unemployed in the union tradition, promoting interracial cooperation, or engaging the jobless in militant organizational work in the shop and on the line, organized unemployed activity provided a critical bridge to unionism at Ford.

The Decline of the Loyal Opposition:
The Workers Alliance in an Expanding Economy

The Ford strike had revealed the value of cooperation between the dominant WPA Welfare Department and the struggling-but-still-active Workers Alliance. While the Alliance's efforts served the union's interest in a narrow sense, its long-term prospects diminished significantly from 1939 on as a result of the UAW-CIO's tremendous prestige among Michigan workers, the decline of the national Alliance in the wake of an anti-Communist onslaught, and the gradual improvement of the state's unemployment situation as the war economy expanded. Eventually, the Michigan Workers Alliance was to fade from the scene after the dismissal from WPA of its state secretary, Rudolph Schware, as a result of his Communist Party ties.[79]

From 1938 on, the Workers Alliance's national organization suffered a series of body blows at the hands of WPA's congressional critics, including both Clifton Woodrum and Martin Dies, who attacked Lasser, Benjamin, Ingram, and the Alliance for their alleged Communist activities. Recognizing the leftist image as a handicap to the Alliance, Lasser first forced Benjamin to resign in February 1940, a move which brought Michigan's Frank Ingram to Washington as the new secretary-treasurer. Unfortunately for the Alliance, Ingram's Communist ties, though less direct, differed little from those of his predecessor. Eventually, Lasser concluded that Ingram was withholding information on certain Alliance board meetings from him and was working to achieve dominance over organizational policy for "a political group." The national Alliance struggled on until late 1941, when it disbanded because war preparations gradually absorbed the unemployed and Communist purposes were no longer served by an active commitment to the organization.[80]

Lasser's resignation in June 1940 marked an important turning point in the Alliance's history. By mid-1940, the New Deal had long since succeeded in coopting the Alliance into the bureaucratic structure of an evolving liberal capitalist state. Thus, by the time the CP came to dominate its activities, the Alliance had already declined as a militant peoples' movement. As Frances Piven and Richard Cloward have argued, the New Deal had "subverted the use of disruptive tactics" and undermined the ability of the unemployed movement to "exacerbate disorder" so that from a radical perspective, WAA "no longer mattered one way or the other." By 1938, the Alliance no longer represented the grass-roots militance of the early 1930s. Rather, it had been integrated into the political economy of the liberal welfare state as a legitimate but nonthreatening pressure group. And by 1940, checkmated by the CIO, the Alliance had only a "skeleton of an organization left."[81]

While the national Alliance disintegrated, its Michigan affiliate also fell on hard times. By 1940, it had become the near-exclusive domain of the state Communist Party and was led by CP activist

Rudolf Schware. In June, a Michigan State Police informant reported that the Michigan Alliance had moved its state headquarters to a secret location in Detroit because its leaders were "afraid of the office being knocked off and all of their records being confiscated." The state organization devoted much of its attention in early 1940 to an attack on Republican Governor Luren Dickenson's restrictions on property owned by welfare recipients, which the Alliance attacked as "persecution of the unemployed." The Alliance *Bulletin* exhorted the membership to mobilize the unemployed in their communities "without giving up a single right as an American citizen." Increasingly removed from a direct link with the union movement, the Alliance was long on rhetoric and short on action.[82]

Nowhere was the rhetoric more sweeping than at the Michigan Alliance's second annual convention in June 1940. The decision to hold the meeting in Yemans Hall in Hamtramck reflected the narrowing support base of the embattled organization, which now found support among the hardest hit elements of the Polish and black community. Hamtramck was one large community in which the Communist Party retained a large following, and Yemans Hall was owned by the Party. State president Wayne Adams of Flint acknowledged that only as a last resort would the unemployed go to the Alliance for help. Schware added that membership was declining in nearly all Michigan counties and that during the previous eighteen months, the number of locals had dropped from sixty-nine to twenty-three.[83] From all appearances the Michigan Alliance was in the final stages of decay.

Not only was the convention hall owned by the Communist Party, but many of the spokesmen present were long-time CP activists in the unemployed movement, including Nat Wald, Frank Ingram, and Rudolf Schware. Flint activist Garfield Maunder, who later provided evidence for WPA investigators, observed that "instead of being a convention of the Workers Alliance it had turned out to be a Communist convention." Further evidence of Communist control was to be found in Frank Ingram's role in directing convention deliberations, which included instructions to several speakers. Finally, much of the speakers' rhetoric was aimed as much at Roosevelt's foreign policy as at the problems of the unemployed, thus hewing the CP party line.[84]

Not long after the convention, the Michigan Workers Alliance suffered a final devastating blow when its secretary-treasurer, Rudolph Schware, was suspended from WPA, charged with false swearing of the non-Communist affidavit required of all project workers. Although admitting one-time Party membership, Schware denied that he had belonged at the time he took the oath. In an interview with a WPA investigator, he lamely argued that while a Party member, he had never "performed organization work" for the CP and that as of December 1940 he had "no connection with or interest in the Party." Persecuted for his political beliefs and without work, he was unsuccessful in reversing the WPA decision. The notoriety surrounding his case was the culminating event in the demise of the Michigan Workers Alliance.[85]

Beyond Detroit, the Alliance maintained a strong presence in the Flint area, home of the organization's state president, Wayne Adams. By most accounts, the Flint Workers Alliance was essentially a front organization for the CP. All local officers, with the exception of President Harvey Finch, were Party members. Schware, who was a prominent local Party figure, conducted weekly educational classes in Communist principles. In early 1940, Garfield Maunder, secretary of the Flint Alliance local, was especially active in seeking more generous welfare benefits for relief recipients.[86]

Maunder's activities were part of a more comprehensive effort by several CIO affiliates to reverse 137 WPA layoffs and avert a local relief crisis. In fact, this drive was led by Flint's UAW WPA and Unemployed Union, which in February 1940 urged that Genessee County provide sufficient local sponsor's funds to provide for 2,000 new WPA positions. The WPA union also cooperated with the Workers Alliance to force the restoration of the terminated WPA positions and followed up with a major organizing drive on the Flint projects. This campaign was greeted with enthusiasm by union men in the plants, who were reportedly impressed by the "spirit and militancy of the WPA workers." While the UAW WPA union did not object to collaboration with the Alliance on specific issues, it complained to the nascent United Project Workers Union in Pittsburgh that the national CIO "should give all support to a CIO union in the WPA field and not to the WA, a dual union, in this territory at least, outside the CIO."[87]

The project workers union had a point. All evidence indicates that by March 1940 the Flint Workers Alliance no longer existed, except as a paper organization that represented a few "perpetual reliefers." By this time all the Alliance's active rank-and-file members had joined the WPA union because of its link with UAW and the hope of CIO assistance. In Flint, it was the project workers union that best exemplified the spirit of militance and local initiative that had once characterized the early unemployed movement, and jobless workers supported its activist response to the shrinkage of relief and WPA programs. UAW unemployed organizers knew that they were in a strong position to capitalize on their relationship with a militant union that had demonstrated its power to achieve concrete results for workers. Genora Dollinger later recalled the essentially local initiative and dedication to community organizing that was expressed through the Flint WPA local. These efforts bore fruit when the majority of Flint's Alliance members switched their allegiances in 1940. As late as the summer and fall of 1941, the Flint unemployed union maintained its protests against further WPA cutbacks,[88] but by then, the day of massive job programs had passed and the administration had targeted remaining work projects primarily as a tool for defense preparations.

Despite the declining momentum of the Alliance's activity in lower Michigan, the problem of unemployment sustained its activities in the economically depressed Upper Peninsula. In January 1940 a WAA committee, including Ingram and Schware, managed to persuade State WPA administrator Abner Larned to recommend a $4.00 per month increase in wage scale for 4,000 project workers in Baraga, Iron, Alger, Luce, Mackinac, and Keweenaw Counties. As a followup, in March 1940 the Alliance sent a new organizer from Chicago, Harold Hoffman, into the UP to revitalize the organization, which had been relatively cautious since the great timber strike of 1937. And by June Hoffman was engaged in an effort to bring tighter organization to the UP counties. Consistent with past precedent, the centers of activity were Gogebic, Iron, and Alger counties, especially the cities of Ironwood, Wakefield, Iron River, Escanaba, Negaunee, and Ishpeming.[89]

Close examination of the Workers Alliance's claims of success reveals that the organization was actually working cooperatively with CIO unions, and that these advances were probably attributable more to CIO influence than Alliance pressure. This collaboration was not surprising, since prior to his arrival in the UP, Hoffman had been a CIO organizer in Chicago. However, the cooperative tactic was significant to the UP unemployed movement. At the forefront of this effort was the International Woodworkers of America and its fiery leader Matt Savola. In January the IWA publication, *Jacks New Deal*, denounced WPA reductions and relief cuts and demanded that Governor Dickenson call a special legislative session to deal with the relief crisis with a new $10 million relief appropriation. In doing so, it was endorsing the demands of the MIUC, which dovetailed neatly with the plans of the Michigan Workers Alliance. The close relationship between IWA and WAA was evident at a March meeting of IWA Local 15 in Ironwood, which endorsed Harold Hoffman's plea for "unity of action" between the Workers Alliance and the "progressive labor movement."[90]

One month later, the heart of the Escanaba unemployed movement was cut out when longtime CP activist Carl Anderson fell victim to the new WPA regulations barring the employment of Communists. By June 1940 Anderson had risen to become the Party's UP secretary and section leader, and his work was well known in the district. More defiant than Schware, he refused to deny his political beliefs and therefore would not sign the required affidavit. As a result, Anderson was removed from WPA and ceased his activities as a Workers Alliance leader. Despite the government's effort to restrict Anderson's activity, other UP Communists maintained the pressure for aid to the unemployed. Leading the pack was the IWA. In April 1940 Local 15 denounced the WPA cutbacks contained in the Relief Bill of 1939. *Jacks New Deal* noted that the war boom had not diminished unemployment in the UP, which stood at 32 percent in 1940. The lesson drawn by the woodworkers was simple: "organized demands for jobs, relief, and security" were the key to the problem of unemployment.[91]

While Savola and the IWA closed ranks with the jobless, a similar plea for solidarity came from the Copper Country, where in 1939 the fledgling United Copper Workers Union had broken management's tight grip on the copper workers with a stunning victory at the Copper Range Consolidated Mining Company. A key figure in the struggle was Gene Saari, a native of Sugar Island near Sault Saint Marie who had gained a political education at the Finnish Work Peoples College at Duluth. A dedicated CP activist, Saari was a veteran of the Timber Workers strike and a member of the IWA, whose organizing experience had included contacts with the unemployed and the Workers Alliance. It was Saari, more than any other labor organizer, who was responsible for the organization of the UP's copper workers by the UCWU, an affiliate of the CIO's Mine, Mill, and Smelter Workers Union.

Once the CIO had gained a foothold in Houghton and Keweenaw counties, the formerly isolated Workers Alliance saw the hope of a worker coalition on behalf of the unemployed, who still constituted the largest working-class interest group in the Copper Country. When the Calumet Workers Alliance appealed to the Painesdale CIO for support in the then-raging battle over the WPA appropriation for fiscal 1941, it stressed the potential threat posed by WPA cutbacks to the "labor movement in general." Alliance secretary Leonard Somero told Saari and the CIO that the "newly organized miners union" had a clear interest in full solidarity with the UP unemployed:

> Reactionary forces are working at top speed to cripple and restrict the progressive record the CIO has made. With the WPA and relief under their control it will be easy to recruit scabs and strikebreakers by forcing these hungry men to work. They are now throwing hundreds of thousands in the streets to look for work and the more off the WPA, the better . . . [when] . . . the worker cannot look to the WPA as a sort of last hope, he's got to take what he can get. This makes it much harder to unionize and as in the Copper Country here it is apt to cripple or maybe to destroy it [the union] entirely.[92]

The message was not lost on the CIO, which had recently demonstrated a rising interest in the UP. When CIO regional director August Scholle decided to make a speaking tour through the UP, Savola counseled him on the subjects to emphasize with area workers. Especially applicable to conditions in the UP were three problems: unemployment, organizing the unemployed, and the burgeoning relief crisis in Michigan. Few were surprised, therefore, when in February 1940 Scholle came out swinging in Ironwood with an attack on unemployment, which was "the greatest problem with which we must contend" and the "greatest menace" to the achievements of organized labor. Scholle's words revealed the CIO's rock-solid commitment to the jobless:

> If these 15,000 [unemployed] remain unorganized, they will remain an external menace to your own possibilities of retaining your own job because these men want work. I have heard some Republicans make statements that these people would not accept a job if you offered it to them. The CIO knows better than that. . . . The CIO advocates a program for unemployment. The Federal Government should sponsor a meeting

of the Representatives who should sit down and bring forth some specific program as a solution to this problem.[93]

The outcome of Scholle's missionary work was the formation in March 1940 of the Upper Peninsula CIO Coordinating Committee. Meeting in Ironwood on 10 March, eight unions joined "to establish closer cooperation" between CIO locals and to organize the unorganized. In the UP, this pledge meant a commitment to unemployed as well as employed workers. Consequently, the Coordinating Committee agreed to invite the Workers Alliance to send fraternal delegates to the committee. The delegates went on to endorse the CIO unemployment program. And in a show of unity they listened to an address by Workers Alliance UP chairman Harold Hoffman, who urged the CIO to organize the 50 percent of the UP's citizens dependent on relief.[94] Hoffman was subsequently elected state president of the Workers Alliance, but by summer 1940 he was riding a dead horse.

Although the Copper Workers, Timber Workers, and the Coordinating Committee were unable to provide financial support, Saari and Savola worked within the committee to keep the problem of unemployment at the forefront of CIO concerns in the UP. When the Coordinating Committee laid plans for a major legislative conference in June 1940, Savola recommended that a separate caucus on unemployment be established. Saari supported Savola's position with a plea that the committee approach the conference seriously by establishing a continuation committee that would carry on the work proposed by the delegates.[95] While the rhetoric flowed more smoothly than the cash, the deliberations of the Coordinating Committee revealed close cooperation between its most prominent CP members in a determined effort to strengthen the Workers Alliance and aid the unemployed by encouraging Hoffman's organizational activities.

Although the Workers Alliance could be found in the UP as late as July 1941, it is clear that by that time the CIO had come to dominate the unemployed movement in Michigan's Upper Peninsula. The principal distinction between unemployed activity in the UP and that of the southeast was that intergroup cooperation between mainstream unionism and the independent unemployed movement persisted much longer in the far north. This tendency towards unity of action was rooted in the strength of the Communist element in the IWA and the UCWU, as well as the union leadership provided by Matt Savola, Gene Saari, and other leftists.

Moreover, the significance of Finnish political culture must not be underestimated. Although Finnish-American Communism had reached its greatest influence in the early 1930s and had never fully recovered from the losses sustained as a result of the Karelian migration, it was by no means a spent force in the years prior to the Nazi-Soviet Pact.[96] Finns gave leadership to the Timber Workers Strike, the IWA, and the United Copper Workers Union. From their union base, they also provided aid and comfort to a militant unemployed movement. It was only in 1940 that outside organizers came to dominate the UP Workers Alliance in a period during which the state and national Alliances took on a more sectarian hue as the CP fixed its hold on an organization in decline.

Despite the persistence of Communist influence, the Alliance was anxious to explore linkage with an expanding CIO, which itself took the initiative in 1940 to embrace the still-vigorous unemployed organizations of the UP. Recognizing danger in lingering unemployment, the CIO, under the leadership of Gus Scholle, endorsed the cause of the unemployed as a useful tactic in its own drive to bring industrial unionism to the unfriendly terrain of the UP in the late 1930s. In the final analysis, the CIO came to dominate the organization of the UP unemployed through a route different from that taken in the industrial southeast. The result was the ascendancy of a powerful industrial union movement in the effort to aid the jobless. Just as the foothold was established, however, American entry into World War II provided an economic stimulus that made the notion of unemployed organizing an anachronism, even in the depressed back-country of Michigan's last frontier.

10

Into the War
Prosperity and the "Unemployables"

The acceleration of government defense spending after 1939 clearly fueled the engines of recovery throughout the United States, and nowhere was its impact more dramatic or unsettling than in urban industrial Michigan. Between September 1939 and May 1940 the federal government poured more than $20 million in defense expenditures into the state. Despite this stimulus, Michigan businessmen were slow to respond to the new demands made on them for fear of disrupting domestic production and the more stable long-term recovery it promised. In the crucial automobile industry, management resistance meant substantial delays in conversion to defense production and opposition to new government controls.[1] The result was widespread residual unemployment in a period of controlled expansion, joblessness which Pagano and the WPA Welfare Department frequently used to discount exaggerated tales of full employment. And as the structure of unemployment changed, the union persisted in a fruitless effort to meet the needs of workers untouched by the new prosperity.

By February 1941 WPA cutbacks and increased employment had undercut the WPA Welfare Department's position in the union bureaucracy. Genora Dollinger later recalled that by this time, the Flint WPA union was collapsing because production had increased and its officers had found work. Meanwhile, in Detroit the WPA Welfare Department rallied in desperation to the cause of the needy "unemployables" and fought to counter the "false propaganda" that welfare and WPA programs were unnecessary due to "so-called prosperity."[2] By March 1941 the department's days were numbered.

The position taken by the UAW had some basis in fact. As early as February 1941 Michigan WPA officials had identified the beginning of priorities unemployment, which resulted from competition for increasingly scarce resources. In summer 1941, when cuts in domestic automobile production occurred, the number of jobless escalated further. Most dramatic was the 50 percent cutback announced in July by Leon Henderson of the Office of Price Administration and Civilian Supply. Henderson acknowledged that the result of his action would be increased unemployment, but maintained that materials shortages mandated the change. One day after Henderson's bombshell, Pagano wrote to the WPA's Howard Hunter to demand an increased quota for Michigan due to both the proposed cut in production and anticipated August-September seasonal layoffs. He argued that an increased WPA commitment was essential to prevent "greater chaos than exists even at present."[3]

Concern over worker dislocation escalated as the months passed and priorities unemployment increased throughout the state of Michigan. In August 1941 UAW president R. J. Thomas forecast joblessness that would make Flint, Pontiac, and Saginaw ghost towns. To combat these disastrous results, Thomas advocated an accelerated government-coordinated retooling program, planned allocation of scarce resources, federal retraining programs, seniority-based transfer of area workers to critical occupations, and a delay in reduced auto production until defense work was readily available. As a complement to this plan, UAW also urged that American unions be assured both the right to strike and a "labor voice in government defense policy." Within two weeks, Addes reported that the National Defense Advisory Commission and a union committee had worked out a tentative plan for the transfer of laid-off auto workers to defense occupations. The key provision of the program was the immediate identification of those auto workers who possessed adequate skills to work on defense projects. In addition, reemployment committees were to ease local transition problems while experienced workers received preference in defense hiring. At all points, union representatives were guaranteed participation in the reassignment process. The bottom line in the Six-Point Transfer Agreement accepted by UAW in September 1941 was the protection of seniority rights in all transfers, layoffs, and recalls.[4]

Meanwhile, the WPA Welfare Department, its lobbying function increasingly carried out by the Reuthers, Thomas, and other UAW leaders, refocused its attention on the day-to-day problems of project workers. In early September 1941, the department began to raise questions about the inadequacy of WPA wage rates in a period of sharp inflation. The first inquiry produced a bureaucratic expression of sympathy from Washington but no change in policy. Unwilling to accept this result, the department escalated the pressure on Washington WPA officials for a wage increase, which finally came in October 1941. *The WPA Worker* used a front-page editorial to attack the 15-cent hourly raise as inadequate to offset the burgeoning cost of living. A modest gain was made when most WPA workers were declared eligible for the federal food stamp program, but the UAW WPA Welfare Department remained unimpressed. To Pagano and his office, the 10 percent wage increase was "not even a drop in the bucket." The department therefore pledged to carry on the fight for a WPA pay hike beyond the modest increase allowed, a matter the union considered "a matter of gravest concern."[5]

By the end of the year, the WPA Welfare Department had returned to its broader social concerns of early 1941, when the issue of the "unemployables" had first been raised. The department continued along the same path in November 1941 by questioning the disproportionate number of women among the unemployed awaiting WPA assignment. Over 70 percent of those on the Wayne County assignment list were women, while only 36 percent of project workers were female. To union unemployed organizer Alex "Scotty" McKay, the statistics made it clear that "the women are not having the same opportunity for employment on the program" as men.[6]

Behind the numbers lay a lack of deep concern for women's employment in the prewar UAW. Women auto workers were frequently denied access to defense jobs as a result of both management preference and union policies that sanctioned separate seniority lists for men and women, which meant that under the UAW-OPM Six-Point Transfer Agreement, employers were free to give hiring preference to male auto workers. Moreover, when Defense Employment Committees were established in Detroit, Flint, Lansing, Saginaw, and Pontiac to ensure management compliance with the pact, women members were conspicuous by their absence. When challenged on the all-male committee policy, UAW defense employment coordinator George Addes flatly told female unionists "not to make an issue at this time of women's rights."[7] One predictable consequence of the union's emphasis on employment opportunity for men was the presence of unemployed women on the WPA waiting lists.

Although women were denied equal access to defense jobs with union support, the increasingly impotent WPA Welfare Department demonstrated some concern for female workers as an element in the "unemployable" category. McKay again wrote Pagano, who was headed for Washington, that the placement of women on WPA was a major problem in Wayne County. McKay was fresh from a meeting with Michigan WPA administrator Abner Larned, during which the union delegation and Larned had agreed to pursue several options to increase women's employment on the projects. McKay argued that the women's plight could be used to support the case for higher Michigan WPA quotas, but that there was real danger that the new quotas would be used to aid those workers soon to be "disemployed as a result of the national defense changeover."[8]

Although McKay pointedly noted that he and his WPA Welfare Department negotiating committee could accept any arrangement that prevented hardship for victims of priorities unemployment, they urged that the desperate situation faced by the "unemployables" not "get lost in the shuffle." McKay argued that an "overwhelming majority" of WPA employees were from the "group who face permanent need of WPA." He insisted that in the effort to aid those unemployed as a result of conversion, "the other group must not be affected by a new kind of 'priority' unemployment."[9] While the self-preservation instinct of a beleaguered bureaucracy cannot be discounted as a factor in McKay's argument, there is evidence that the "unemployables" were not without a voice within the UAW in 1941.

On 15 January 1942, Thomas and Addes urged Roosevelt to refocus WPA on the needs of those workers who were "unemployed as a result of ten years of depression," many of whom were awaiting assignment to the projects. The union appeal emphasized the plight of women, blacks, mature workers, and the handicapped, all of them anxious to make their contribution to the war effort. Insist-

ing that workers in these categories needed to gain useful employment "if the morale of the nation is to remain at a high level," UAW
urged that Roosevelt not permit them to be "lost in the shuffle."[10]

In the final analysis, the administration was not the problem.
Roosevelt's proposal for $300 million in supplementary relief ben-
efits went down to defeat in February as a result of conservative
opposition in Congress. Undaunted, the Michigan CIO Council
renewed its effort to aid the "unemployables." In May 1942 MIUC
went on record against the attempt to eliminate WPA for fiscal
year 1943. On the contrary, the council demanded an $875 million
appropriation that would include a substantial wage increase for
project workers. The MIUC protest, like the January plea to
Roosevelt, emphasized the needs of marginal workers, most of them
unskilled workers over the age of fifty, who had a "right to be
gainfully employed."[11]

Meanwhile, the union attacked both the Office of Production
Management and auto management for their apparent "business
as usual" policies. UAW published prominent advertisements criti-
cizing OPM, and insisted that the monthly conversion rate for new
jobs could be dramatically increased. The union protest reached a
crescendo on 24 March when an estimated ten to twenty thousand
workers rallied in Cadillac Square to dramatize the delays in conversion. Both UAW and other Detroit CIO leaders questioned the
government-management commitment to a timely changeover. Addes
chided the corporations for their reluctance to convert production
as rapidly as they did in peacetime when model changes were
required. The rank-and-file concurred in their leaders' indictment
of management delays, though they tended to fix greater blame on
a fumbling government.[12]

While union leaders chastised management and government, the
WPA Welfare Department addressed other concerns. It was, in fact,
engaged in a desperate struggle for survival against those UAW
officers who anticipated that the department would be irrelevant in
a full-blown wartime economy. The first internal crisis of the wartime era came in January 1942, when George Addes told the International Executive Board that "considerable money and time" was
being expended on the WPA auxiliaries for a modest return. Addes
noted that the WPA organization made little financial contribution
to the union, although he did acknowledge that it had provided
crucial welfare assistance to unemployed UAW members. In view
of this unfavorable cost-benefit ratio, Addes suggested that the board

consider abolishing the union's "WPA structure." Upon motion by Walter Reuther, the board disbanded the WPA Welfare Department and decided to retain a union welfare division for an indefinite period of time. As an afterthought, the board also chose to advise remaining local WPA auxiliaries to affiliate directly with the CIO.[13]

But the board's action proved so unpopular with the rank-and-file jobless that local unemployed units failed to comply with the order. After substantial discussion between President Thomas and Secretary Addes, the board reconsidered its draconian measure at the March meeting and decided to resurrect the WPA organization even though it was not a "financial asset" to the union. Several factors influenced the reversal. First, the union had failed in an effort to promote the congressional enactment of an $100 million defense training program. Moreover, it was clear that unemployed workers on WPA considered it an "honor" to belong to UAW. Finally, Addes noted that the WPA Welfare Department's work in "supporting the morale" of unemployed members had "caused favorable sentiment for the UAW." Aware of substantial worker sentiment for the unemployed organization, the board endorsed former welfare director Richard Leonard's motion to reinstate the "WPA setup."[14] The WPA Welfare Department had dodged a bullet, but the episode revealed the unemployed organization's vulnerability within the councils of UAW.

Union pressure on behalf of WPA workers resurfaced sporadically throughout the remainder of the year, but as early as April 1942 the handwriting was on the wall. When Victor Reuther attempted to halt the rumored elimination of WPA, he learned that the entire program was in jeopardy due to accumulated "prejudice against the WPA and confusion and overlapping of the various government departments in Washington." And not long thereafter, an interoffice memo from the depths of the WPA bureaucracy, attached to McKay's April plea, revealed the agency's perspective on the UAW entreaties on behalf of the "underprivileged" who clung to the program for support: "does anyone in the division keep this stuff?" With a war economy expanding rapidly, the question was pertinent. By June 1942, Abner Larned could refer to a downward trend in unemployment compensation, relief, and relief work, with direct relief cases below levels to which "authorities on social welfare problems predicted they would never fall in Michigan." Although unemployment was still "critical" in Flint and "depressed" in middle-western Michigan, most state areas were stable or improving, including Detroit and the UP. By autumn 1942, automotive conversion had been completed and the Michigan economy was booming.[15]

Although the WPA and its unemployed constituency was shrinking, the UAW stubbornly resisted legislative efforts to kill the program. As late as August 1942, George Addes called for the continuation of the union's WPA Department with a reduced staff. He insisted that the department was needed as a coordinating body to oppose efforts to terminate WPA. To underscore the UAW commitment to the WPA program, President R. J. Thomas appointed Richard Frankensteen director of the UAW WPA Department.[16]

But union pressure could not save a program with so many enemies, especially in view of wartime prosperity. In December, when Roosevelt dissolved the WPA, the UAW board prudently accepted the inevitable. Overriding Frankensteen's objections, it opted for a strategy calling for a new federal works agency to carry on the WPA mission. Keenly aware of Michigan's peculiar seasonal unemployment problem, Victor Reuther had proposed a sweeping public works program to carry on the WPA ideal by constructing needed public buildings, including day care facilities, recreation centers, and community centers. He argued that such facilities would be essential because women would be reluctant to return home in the postwar period. Finally, Reuther emphasized that to survive, the new agency must be distinct from WPA in the public mind. It was important that it command the respect of workers and the general public, who had often associated WPA with welfare and the dole. A successful new agency would have to broaden the "base of social security" and shed the "relief stigma."[17] The plan never came to fruition, and with the disappearance of WPA, the union's WPA Welfare Department slipped into memory in 1943.

Since its remaining constituency consisted primarily of the dispossessed and forgotten men and women who existed on the outer fringes of the labor market, the WPA Welfare Department's demise was not surprising. Equally predictable was the UAW's necessary focus on the concerns of the millions of employed auto workers it represented. By the end of 1943 the Michigan unemployment rate had plummeted to .6 percent of the total workforce, which compared favorably with a national figure of 1.2 percent. Since the war had put middle America to work, few noticed that in June 1943

WPA closed its doors for good.[18] In one sense, it was an agency that had stood as a reminder of hard times that many wanted to forget. In the flush of wartime prosperity, it was also possible to argue that the WPA Welfare Department's self-defined mission to serve the outcasts of industrial society was irrelevant to the successful prosecution of a "good war."

But all good wars must come to an end. And the future would bring new generations of what Pagano had once labeled the "unemployable employables": women, minorities, and elderly workers for whom the marketplace seemed to have no place. For these workers, the progressive vision of the UAW Welfare Department, fully articulated in 1941 when its original function had decreased in significance, held meaning for the postwar era. The Great Depression cast a long shadow on the future, and the lessons of the 1930s influenced the UAW as it responded to the new uncertainties confronting workers in a state economy dominated by a burgeoning automotive industry. But the intensity of purpose that had driven the unemployed movement could not be replicated once the moment of opportunity had passed.

Epilogue

Although its social mission as defined in 1941 was never fulfilled, the UAW Welfare Department expressed a vision that survived, albeit in an altered form, in the postwar years. For a brief moment, the department had expressed both the idealism and potential for mobilization characteristic of a great social movement. Yet after the Depression, the possibility of industrial unionism as the vehicle for fundamental social change slipped away. In the short run, the Department's achievements were modest. Many unemployed Michigan workers were never touched by the union's efforts, and a significant number turned left for economic solutions, especially in the desperate days of the early 1930s.

The Unemployed Councils and the Workers Alliance played important roles in the mobilization of both the underclass and those who fell from middle-class grace. The Councils were dramatically effective in the great struggles of the period 1930–1933, most notably in Wayne County. In the early 1930s, the Communist Party was clearly the leading organizational force among the jobless. The predominance of the CP in the darkest days of the Depression marked the failure of Michigan's conservatives and liberals to confront the problems of the dispossessed and dislocated. Until late 1933 it was the radicals who met the economic outcasts on their own ground to offer direct assistance and a glimmer of hope.

To be sure, the membership of the Unemployed Councils and Workers Alliance never matched that of the labor unions which later developed. But to evaluate these grass-roots organizations solely in terms of incomplete and sterile statistics is to miss the social significance of an embryonic mass movement that rejected "politics as usual" in favor of a challenge to the established order— if only momentarily. Not only are the membership figures notoriously unreliable, but they fail to encompass the aspirations of the jobless legions for whom the modest price of membership was too great. Moreover, mass support for street actions often revealed wider latent sympathy for those who questioned political authority. Finally, the record clearly shows that unemployed organizations cooperated across political and jurisdictional lines to express dissent against mainstream political solutions and to make demands on community leaders. This capacity to generate occasional or selective mass mobilization was sometimes sufficient to produce political or economic concessions from civil authorities. The disruptive potential of the organized unemployed simmered beneath the surface of a broken economy, at least in the pre–New Deal years.

As the Roosevelt programs began to take effect, the unemployed movement displayed a new diversity. The Socialist initiative that gave rise to the early Workers Alliance signaled a new competitiveness in the battle for the sympathies and loyalties of the jobless. For five years, WAA and its Michigan affiliates functioned as legitimate labor unions for the unemployed, simultaneously operating as grass-roots community action organizations that responded to the immediate needs of the jobless. After the unity meeting of 1936 the development of a class-conscious social movement again seemed within reach. The strength of the Michigan Alliance lay primarily in Wayne County, Genessee County, Jackson County, and the sharply depressed UP. Crucial to its development between 1936 and 1938 was the rapid growth of WPA, which expanded the membership base for all unemployed organizations.

As WAA matured, however, its influence in Michigan was undercut by two parallel developments. First, growing Communist influence within the Alliance in both Washington and Michigan limited the organization's usefulness. Herbert Benjamin, David Lasser, and Frank Ingram all made valuable contributions to the Alliance, but after 1938, CIO organizing successes and the negative image created by the organization's Communist ties combined to undermine WAA as a mass organization and as a labor union for the unemployed. The Michigan Alliance's collapse was hastened by the Red-baiting tactics of such union leaders as the cautious Frank Martel and the erratic Homer Martin.

Second, and more significant than any other influence, was the rise of industrial unionism in Michigan under the leadership of the militant United Automobile Workers of America. Once UAW entered the picture, its decisions on unemployed organization exerted a determinative influence on the future of the entire effort to serve the jobless, at least in the industrial southeast. From the moment that the UAW embraced the unemployed, other competing groups were at a decided disadvantage. The Workers Alliance never recovered, though its work with the unemployables and its pursuit of a CIO affiliation raised the possibility of meaningful mass mobilization.

Paradoxically, the expansion of CIO also spelled disaster for the Workers Alliance as a mass organization. Herbert Benjamin later recalled that the Alliance carried on the "thankless unrewarding work among the unemployed" while Socialists and other unemployed leaders "grabbed the well-paying jobs being offered by the CIO." By 1940 he recognized that whereas the jobless of the early 1930s were without organized protection, the industrial unions had come to "consider unemployment the number one domestic problem of the nation." He readily admitted that CIO initiative had reduced the Workers Alliance's constituency to the "permanently unemployed" and those outside the orbit of unionism.[19]

An expression of the union alternative, the UAW WPA Welfare Department emerged in 1937 as the predominant institutional mechanism for the organization of Michigan's unemployed. Under the pressure created by increased joblessness during the recession of 1937–1938, Richard Leonard, William Taylor, and George Edwards Jr. molded the department into a vigorous advocacy organization that spoke for jobless unionists, as well as the wider community of the dispossessed. The interests of the nonunion unemployed assumed greater significance when UAW moved to extend its hegemony over all WPA workers in 1938. As the process of union bureaucratization accelerated, the needs of project workers became more and more important to the department's survival in the context of a reviving economy.

Despite this increased emphasis on WPA and its preservation, critics on the left argued with some justification that the UAW's institutional approach to the unemployment problem neglected the concerns of the nonunion occupants of the bottom rail. It is equally clear that the CIO was unable to reach significant jobless populations in the more remote areas of Michigan beyond the reach of the UAW. These caveats notwithstanding, the dominating presence of UAW-CIO made it the controlling force in the state's unemployed movement. It is also true that the unemployed and their organizers had played a key role in the organizational struggles that led to the birth of the modern UAW in 1937. Mirroring a nationwide pattern, many of the activists who had gained their first union experience in the Unemployed Councils and the early Workers Alliance surfaced as union organizers in the CIO army assembled by John L. Lewis in 1936 and 1937. In no case were the unemployed and the UAW's WPA organization more valuable as union advocates than in the successful Ford drive of 1941. At Ford and elsewhere, hundreds of "union-conscious members" were "trained in union procedures" while they were still attached to the WPA Auxiliary. In this way union discipline was maintained and the unemployed became an "additional force" rather than a "threat against organized labor" in strike situations.[20] Between 1937 and 1941, unemployed organizing became a vehicle for union-building and the reinforcement of class solidarity. In the end, the great reserve army became a dedicated union-conscious force, though its radical potential was smothered by the resultant bureaucratization.

Given Michigan's distinctive labor history, the ascendancy of the UAW WPA Welfare Department and the decline of the Workers Alliance are not surprising. These trends reflected the intense popularity of the CIO among the state's workers as well as the rise of Walter Reuther and the eventual success of his effort to outflank Communist elements in the UAW. With Reuther's presence came a concept of the union which transcended the limits of business unionism to articulate a vision rooted in the Socialist view of organized labor as a sweeping social movement. Convinced that the union must become the worker's extended family, Reuther and his backers accepted the organization's responsibility to support individual members in their hour of greatest need. This conclusion does not, however, alter the reality that the Reuther faction was quick to grasp the usefulness of a controlled unemployed movement in its relentless and sometimes brutal attack on the Communist opposition. After cooperating with the CP forces in the UAW and the Workers Alliance when pragmatic to do so, the Reuther-Edwards element in the UAW WPA Welfare Department vanquished both the Martinites and the radical left as it moved to consolidate its position in 1939.

The ideological struggle within the union mirrored another reality that characterized unemployed organizing throughout the Depression years—tension between independent mass action and coordinated protest at the instigation of interest groups. While spontaneous acts of defiance by the unemployed occurred, especially during the first phase of organizational activity from 1930 to 1933, rallies and demonstrations took on a more organized form as unemployed groups became more diverse and the New Deal developed institutional channels for the expression of complaints. At all stages of the unemployed movement, political and economic groups worked to aid the unemployed while they also served their own interests. Communists, Socialists, liberals, and other unionists embraced the jobless as both needy victims and useful instruments. As a result, unemployed activism reflected a sometimes confusing amalgam of grass-roots militance and interest-group stimulus. It is clear that in most instances, external coordination was an important factor in mass protest, and that after 1934 this tendency became more pronounced.

Once the UAW came to dominate unemployed organizing in 1938, the expression of discontent was increasingly channeled through the developing union bureaucracy to a burgeoning WPA bureaucracy in both Michigan and Washington. Both the more structured UAW and the Workers Alliance, which was less institutionalized, were integrated into the evolving New Deal labor relations system. Indeed, there is evidence to indicate that the WPA regarded both organizations as allies in the struggle to preserve the agency as an important component of the welfare state. This rapproachment suggests that the New Deal's management of unemployed activism was one dimension of the larger social process by which organized labor made its peace with American industrial capitalism. As Nelson Lichtenstein has shown, World War II marked an important phase in the domestication of American labor, during which management and government reached an accommodation with a rapidly bureaucratizing union movement. The UAW's incorporation of the jobless into the union family and structuring of unemployed protest in politically acceptable forms reveals that the roots of bureaucratized industrial unionism may be found in the 1930s. And with the triumph of bureaucracy the development of a radical and independent labor movement, once promised by the militance of the Unemployed Councils, was contained within the channels of progressive business unionism.

Whether its genesis is found in the Socialist vision of the union as family or the Communist concept of mass organization as vanguard, the UAW's preoccupation with unemployment and its remedies outlived the systemic crisis of the 1930s. Although the WPA Welfare Department ceased operations in 1943, its function remained an important dimension of UAW activity. The Michigan CIO War Relief organization gave rise to a new union commitment to social service. After Detroit social worker Charles Livermore of CIO War Relief projected a vision of a postwar union community service program, UAW responded by creating a Community Services Division to manage UAW relations with social agencies, the United Fund, and union families in need of welfare services. Through the division, UAW recommitted itself to the concept of the union as extended family.[21]

There is also a strong line of continuity between the union's Depression-era concern over seasonal unemployment and the UAW's long-term search for worker security. One important product of Depression insecurity was the institutionalization of the seniority system as the basis for the management of layoffs. And the union's focus on worksharing and the guaranteed annual wage (GAW), which surfaced in the late 1930s, is directly related to Reuther's postwar preoccupation with full production and the necessity of a supplemental unemployment benefits program. These social and economic assumptions had evolved out of the uncertainties of the Depression-era economy of scarcity. Had it been adopted, Philip Murray's well-known industrial councils scheme would have established labor's power and legitimacy as a full participant in national economic planning.[22] It also offered hope that the ongoing ravages of seasonal unemployment and market-driven insecurity might be mitigated through a planned economy in the future.

Since 1980, the UAW commitment to the rank-and-file has been sorely tested in an era of cutbacks, shutdowns, and chronic unemployment. New armies of modern workers confront structural and technological unemployment that disrupts the work lives they once prepared for. Life in a service economy threatens to create a two-class system in the United States. In view of increased class polarization, the uncertain future of the American welfare state raises new questions about the potential for mass mobilization among the economic outsiders. If the current effort to shred the fabric of the social safety net accelerates, some modern workers will face the ravages of unemployment without the protections provided by the social contract established in the 1930s. Early retirement schemes, private pensions, two-income family economies, and a work-based welfare system will enable a shrinking middle class to avoid disaster, but no such cushion against hardship will shield marginalized men and women.

If American unionism is to be revitalized, it cannot afford to ignore workers on the fringes of the modern economy. As labor turns to new leaders for a new century, the union consciousness of the 1930s gains new relevance. The Depression vision of unionism as a social movement, now clouded by changing values and the uncertainties of the modern competitive environment, may be revived as a solution to the problem of deepening social divisions. An effective union reaction to the impending crisis will require all the idealism and creativity of the UAW's formative years. Labor's response is likely to shape the future of industrial democracy in America.

NOTES

Chapter 1

1. Alexander Keyssar, *Out of Work: The First Century of Unemployment in Massachusetts* (Cambridge: Cambridge University Press, 1986), 304–307; Albert Prago, "The Organization of the Unemployed and the Rise of the Radicals, 1929–1935" (unpublished Ph.D. dissertation, Union Graduate School, 1976), 22.

2. Leo Genzeloff, "The Effect of Technological Changes Upon Employment Opportunities in the Automobile Industry" (unpublished MA thesis, University of Wisconsin, 1939), 168–69; Steve Babson, *Working Detroit* (Detroit: Wayne State University Press, 1986), 50; Joyce Shaw Peterson, *American Automobile Workers, 1900–1933* (Albany: State University of New York Press, 1987), 52–54.

3. Martin Edward Sullivan, " 'On the Dole': The Relief Issue in Detroit, 1929–1939" (Unpublished Doctoral Dissertation, University of Notre Dame, 1974), 30–37; Thomas Klug, "Employers' Strategies in the Detroit Labor Market, 1900–1929," in Nelson Lichtenstein and Stephen Meyer, *On the Line: Essays in the History of Auto Work* (Urbana: University of Illinois Press, 1989), 63, 65; Peterson, 52.

4. Larry Lankton, *Cradle to Grave: Life, Work, and Death at the Lake Superior Copper Mines* (New York: Oxford University Press, 1991), 247, 250–52; William B. Gates, *Michigan Copper and Boston Dollars: An Economic History of the Michigan Copper Mining Industry* (Cambridge: Harvard

University Press, 1951), 155–56; Arthur W. Thurner, *Strangers and So-journers: A History of Michigan's Keeweenaw Peninsula* (Detroit: Wayne State University Press, 1994), 237–38.

5. William Haber, "Financing Unemployment Relief in Michigan," *Michigan Municipal Review* 6 (February 1933), 21–22; State Emergency Welfare Relief Commission, *Unemployment, Relief, and Economic Security* (Lansing: State of Michigan, 1936), 17; State Emergency Welfare Relief Commission, *Emergency Relief in Michigan, 1933–1939,* (Lansing: State of Michigan, 1939), 1–2; State Emergency Welfare Relief Commission, *Unemployment and Relief in Michigan* (Lansing: State of Michigan, 1935), 2; Richard T. Ortquist, "Unemployment and Relief: Michigan's Response to the Depression During the Hoover Years," *Michigan History* 57 (Fall 1973), 210–11; Ortquist, *Depression Politics in Michigan* (New York: Garland Press, 1982), 126.

6. Quoted in Jean Rusing, "The Works Progress Administration in Detroit" (unpublished MA thesis, Wayne State University, 1974), 1; Babson, 53. The severity of the economic crisis in Detroit is fully discussed in Sullivan, chapters 2 and 3. See also Peterson, 130–34; Jess Gilbert and Craig Harris, "Unemployment, Primary Production, and Population in the Upper Peninsula of Michigan," in *A Half Century Ago: Michigan in the Great Depression* (East Lansing: Michigan State University, 1980), 25.

7. *Unemployment and Relief in Michigan*, 2, 9–10, 30–32; Haber to Mr. Stanchfield, 6 June, 1935, in William Haber Papers, Ann Arbor, Michigan Historical Collections, box 5; Gates, 164–67; Lankton, 255; Thurner, 238; U.S. Bureau of the Census, *Fifteenth Census of the United States: 1930; Unemployment*, 500; Russell M. Magnaghi, *The Way It Happened: Settling Michigan's Upper Peninsula* (Iron Mountain: Mid-Peninsula Library Cooperative, 1982), 91; Gilbert and Harris, 25–26.

8. State Emergency Welfare Relief Commission, *Social, Economic, Occupational Classification of Workers in Selected Industries* (Lansing: State of Michigan, March, 1937), 1–2, 5; *Industrial Classification of Unemployed and Gainfully Employed Workers* (Lansing: State of Michigan, December 1936), 1–2.

9. *Unemployment, Relief, and Economic Security*, 77–81; Peterson, 85–86, 89–90.

10. *Unemployment, Relief, and Economic Security*, 80–81; Magnaghi, *An Outline History of Michigan's Upper Peninsula* (Marquette: Belle Fontaine Press, 1979), 39. The best study of the socioeconomic composition of the auto industry's work force is Peterson, *American Automobile Workers, 1900–1933*. For discussion of the ethnocultural and racial character of the labor force, see especially chapter 2, 14–29. See also 85–87, 89–90, 105–106. An

excellent account of the Ford work force will be found in Stephen Meyer, III, *The Five Dollar Day: Labor Management and Social Control in the Ford Motor Company, 1905–1921* (Albany: State University of New York Press, 1981).

11. *Unemployment, Relief, and Economic Security,* 154–56.

12. Alice E. Stenholm, "Report on Michigan Field Trip," 2 October 1931; Roland Haynes, "Report of Visit of Roland Haynes to Michigan," 10 November 1931, West Branch, Herbert Hoover Presidential Library, PECE/POUR State Files, box 1110; Ortquist, "Unemployment and Relief," 211.

13. Rusing, 2–4; Peterson, 135–36; Sullivan, 42–43, 46; Helen Hall, "When Detroit's Out of Gear," *Survey* 64 (1 April 1930), 9–14, 51–54.

14. Ortquist, *Depression Politics in Michigan,* 127; Sullivan, 45–48; Peterson, 135–36; Roy Rosenzweig, "Organizing the Unemployed: The Early Years of the Great Depression, 1929–1933," *Radical America,* 10 (July–August 1976), 38. The view that the unemployed tended to accept their fate and reject radical solutions to their problems is expressed in John A. Garraty, *The Great Depression: An Inquiry into the Causes, Course and Consequences of the Worldwide Depression of the Nineteen-Thirties as Seen by Contemporaries and in the Light of History* (New York: Harcourt, Brace, Jovanovich, 1986), 165, 172, 175, 179–80; Bernard Sternsher, *Hitting Home: The Great Depression in Town and Country* (Chicago: Quadrangle, 1970), 22–23, 25, 27–28, 33, 35. More recently, Sternsher has expressed doubts about the depth of self-blame and loss of morale (see *Hitting Home,* rev. ed. [Chicago: Elephant Paperbacks, 1989]); the militance and anger of the unemployed are discussed by James T. Patterson, who argues that scholars should avoid generalization about loss of morale. See James T. Patterson, *America's Struggle Against Poverty, 1900–1980* (Cambridge: Harvard University Press, 1981), 51–55. For a colorful account of the rebellious side of the unemployed and their activities, see Franklin Folsom, *Impatient Armies of the Poor: The Story of Collective Action of the Unemployed, 1808–1942* (Niwot: University Press of Colorado, 1991), chapters 18–36.

15. It is the first period of the unemployed movement which has drawn the greatest scholarly attention. Stressing the role of the Communist Party, the Trade Union Unity League, and the Unemployed Councils, historians have examined the period prior to 1936 in substantial detail. See, for example, Rosenzweig, "Organizing the Unemployed"; "Radicals and the Jobless: The Musteites and the Unemployed League, 1932–1936," *Labor History* 16 (Winter 1975), 52–76; and "Socialism In Our Times: the Socialist party and the Unemployed, 1929–1936," *Labor History* 20 (Fall 1979), 485–509. Taken together, the Rosenzweig articles provide a comprehensive introduction to the efforts of Communists, Socialists, Musteites, and

Trotskyites in the organized unemployed movement of the early Depression years. Prago, in "The Organization of the Unemployed and the Role of the Radicals, 1929–1935," examines the same period from a standpoint sympathetic to the goals and successes of the Communist Party's Unemployed Councils. Daniel J. Leab ("United We Eat: The Creation of and the Organization of the Unemployed Councils in 1930," *Labor History* 8 [Fall 1967], 300–315), explores the earliest reaction to the economic downturn in 1930, with emphasis on the first hunger march of March 1930. A Socialist perspective is developed in Virgil J. Vogel, "Communist Activity Among the Unemployed, 1929–1935" (unpublished manuscript in hands of the author, Northbrook, Illinois).

16. The most important study of the Workers Alliance of America is James E. Sargent, "Roosevelt, Lasser, and the Workers' Alliance: Organizing WPA Workers and the Unemployed, 1935–1940," paper presented at the Annual Meeting of the Organization of American Historians, Philadelphia, April 1982; see also Sargent, "Woodrum's Economy Bloc: the Attack on Roosevelt's WPA," *Virginia Magazine* 93 (April 1985), 175–207; Wilma B. Leibman, "The Worker's Alliance of America" (senior thesis, Barnard College, 1972). The Alliance is also discussed in Harvey Klehr, *Heyday of American Communism* (New York: Basic Books, 1984); Barbara Blumberg, *The New Deal and the Unemployed* (Lewisburg: Bucknell University Press, 1979); Donald S. Howard, *The WPA and Federal Relief Policy* (New York: Russell Sage Foundation, 1943); Frances Fox Piven and Richard Cloward, *Poor People's Movements: Why They Succeed, How They Fail* (New York: Vintage, 1977); and Rosenzweig, "Radicals and the Jobless," 66. For evidence of Alliance growth in Michigan, see Sullivan, 181; *Workers Alliance*, December 1935, 2; Alan Strachan, *From Picket Line to Protocol: Recollections of a United Auto Worker* (unpublished manuscript), 70–72.

17. Piven and Cloward have developed a clear and comprehensive definition of social protest movements which incorporates the activism of the unemployed in the 1930s into the category of "movement." Even their critics have conferred "movement" status on the activities in which the jobless were engaged. See Piven and Cloward, 3–5; see also Steve Valocci, "The Unemployed Workers Movement of the 1930s: A Reexamination of the Piven and Cloward Thesis," *Social Problems* 37 (May 1990), 191–92, 202–203.

18. The significance of linkage between unemployed activism and the wider labor insurgency of the 1930s is discussed in Valocci, 201–203.

19. For a thoughtful analysis of the UAW's considerable insight into this relationship, see David Riddle, "The Detroit Federation of Labor, the United Automobile Workers, and the Works Progress Administration in Detroit, 1937–1939," seminar paper, 23 June 1991, Wayne State University (in possession of the author).

Chapter 2

1. Roger Keeran, *The Communist Party and the Auto Workers Union* (New York: International Publishers, 1980), 61–62; Babson, 53; Peterson, 130–32; Prago, 30–31; *Unemployment and Relief in Michigan*, 2.

2. Eleanor Nora Kahn, "Organizations of Unemployed Workers as a Factor in the American Labor Movement" (unpublished MA thesis, University of Wisconsin, 1934), 65; Helen Seymour, "The Organized Unemployed" (unpublished MA thesis, University of Chicago, 1937), 31, 46; John Brophy, *A Miner's Life* (Madison: University of Wisconsin Press, 1964), 250–51; Philip Taft, Notes, "Unemployment," 11 October 1930; AFL Executive Board Minutes, 1930, in Philip Taft Papers, Margaret Catherwood Library, Cornell University School of Industrial Labor Relations, Ithaca, box 13; Interview, Louis Weinstock, New Yorkers at Work Oral History Collection of the Robert F. Wagner Archives, New York University, New York, 16; Piven and Cloward, 72; Daniel Nelson, *Unemployment Insurance: The American Experience, 1915–1932* (Madison: University of Wisconsin Press, 1969), 153–55.

3. Interview, Alan Strachan, Washington, D.C., 2 February 1989; *Michigan Federationist* (January 1930), 1–2; Michigan Federation of Labor, *Official Bulletin* (November 1930), 2; ibid. (August 1931), 2; see also *Proceedings*, 41st Annual Convention of the Michigan Federation of Labor, 11–14 February 1930, Grand Rapids, 50; Sullivan, 44–45; *American Federationist* (March 1931), 273–74. Corporate paternalism and the open shop environment are discussed in Peterson, chapter 4; David Gartman, *Auto Slavery: The Labor Process in the American Automobile Industry, 1897–1950* (New Brunswick: Rutgers University Press, 1986), chapter 1; Meyer, chapters 6, 7, 8.

4. Interview, Dave Moore, Detroit, 5 May 1989; Strachan interview; Interview, Victor Reuther, Washington, D.C., 23 June 1989; Membership Report By State, 1928–1933, Socialist Party of America Papers, Durham, Duke University (microfilm edition), reel 28 (hereafter SPA Papers); John Barnard, *Walter Reuther and the Rise of the Auto Workers* (Boston: Little, Brown, 1983), 7–8; Irving Bernstein, *The Lean Years* (Boston: Houghton, Mifflin, 1960), 426. For a comment on the Old Guard emphasis on educational activities, see Frank A. Warren, *An Alternative Vision: The Socialist Party in the 1930s* (Bloomington: Indiana University Press, 1974), 27; Folsom, 224.

5. Ortquist, "Unemployment and Relief," 218–19; Reuther interview; Alex Londal to Clarence Senior, 17 February 1931; Helen M. Bell to Senior, 3 July 1931; SPA Papers, reels 15, 17; Arthur E. Kent to Frank Martel, 25 February 1932, Metro Detroit AFL-CIO Papers, Detroit, Archives of Labor

History and Urban Affairs, Wayne State University (hereafter ALH), boxes 17, 19. Platform, Socialist Party of Michigan, 1930, Vertical File, ALH; John Panzner Papers, ALH, box 2. For evidence of the national Socialist Party endorsement of unemployment insurance, see "Good Unemployment Insurance," ca. January 1930, SPA Papers, reel 15; *The Unemployed* (February 1931), 18–19.

6. Fraser M. Ottanelli, *The Communist Party of the United States: From the Depression to World War II* (New Brunswick: Rutgers University Press, 1991), 28; Klehr, 50; Folsom, 264–65; Piven and Cloward, 68–69.

7. Leab, 304; Piven and Cloward, 68–69; Wyndham Mortimer, *Organize: My Life as a Union Man* (Boston: Beacon, 1971), 52–53; Steve Nelson et al., *Steve Nelson: American Radical* (Pittsburgh: University of Pittsburgh Press, 1981), 75, 78, 86; Interview, Henry Kraus, Labor History Project, University of Michigan–Flint, 10–11; Philip Bonosky, *Brother Bill Mckie: Building the Union at Ford* (New York: International Publishers, 1953), 59–62; Garman Karsh, "The Political Left," in Milton Derbur and Edwin Young, eds., *Labor and the New Deal* (New York: Da Capo Press, 1972), 87; Irving Bernstein, *A Caring Society* (Boston: Houghton, Mifflin, 1985), 282–83; Bert Cochran, *Labor and Communism: The Conflict that Shaped American Unions* (Princeton: Princeton University Press, 1977), 77, 79; Interview, Herbert Benjamin, 30 October 1970; Benjamin to Theodore Draper, 22 November 1970; Draper to Benjamin, 23 November 1971, Theodore Draper Papers, Atlanta, Special Collections, Robert W. Woodruff Library, Emory University, box 17; Prago, 50; Carl Winter, "Unemployed Struggles of the Thirties," *Political Affairs* (September–October 1969), 54–56; William Allan, "The Jobless Fought Back," Folsom-Elting Papers, Boulder, Special Collections Department, University of Colorado at Boulder, box 3, file 3.

8. Nelson, 50.

9. Christopher H. Johnson, *Maurice Sugar: Law, Labor, and the Left in Detroit, 1912–1950* (Detroit: Wayne State University Press, 1988), 106–8; Keeran, 42–45, 59; Nelson, 51: Klehr, 162, 164.

10. Herbert Benjamin, interview No. 5, 18 November 1976, Folsom-Elting Papers, box 1, file 9. See also "Unemployment Organizing in the 1930s: An Interview with Herbert Benjamin," *Yesterday's Lessons*, 19, University of Michigan, Labadie Collection; Keeran, 66–67; Leab, 302–3; Interview, Nat Ganley, Oral History Collection: Unionization of the Auto Industry, ALH, 5, 34; "Radical Underground Strategy," n.d., John E. Pokorny Papers, Labadie Collection, box 1; Klehr, 50; Ottanelli, 28–29.

11. Keeran, 32–37; Peterson, 124–29; Ottanelli, 23; Harvey A. Levenstein, *Communism, Anticommunism, and the CIO* (Westport: Greenwood, 1981), 20.

12. *Auto Workers News*, December–January 1930; Keeran, 64–65; Phil Raymond, "Report on Automobile Industry," ca. November 1929, Henry Kraus Papers, ALH, box 1; *Labor Unity*, 11 January 1930; Peterson, 125.

13. *Auto Workers News*, December 1929–January 1930.

14. "To All Shop Committees, Trade Unions, and Other Labor Organizations: To All Workers in Detroit," 14 December 1929, American Federation of Labor Papers (hereafter AFL Papers), Madison, State Historical Society of Wisconsin (hereafter SHSW), series 11, box 7; *Auto Workers News*, December 1929–January 1930; Klehr, 50; for background on Goetz, see Nelson, 42; Keeran, 47; Leo J. Kirchner, "Gabby Goetz, Muscovite," *Detroit Saturday Night*, 29 May 1937; see also NA, RG 69, WPA, Records of the Division of Information, 1934–1943, Michigan, Young Workers League File.

15. Keeran, 66; Ottanelli, 28–29; Prago, 101–2; Allan, "The Jobless Fought Back." Klehr emphasizes external CP influences in the establishment of the Councils; see Klehr, 49–50.

16. Prago, 59–63; Hall, 51; Keeran, 66; Ottanelli, 29.

17. *Industrial Intelligence Bulletin*, 3 March 1930, U.S. Department of Justice, Federal Bureau of Investigation, file no. 61-6699-13 (obtained through FOIA Request).

18. "Final Tasks . . ."; *Detroit Labor News*, 26 February 1930, both in U.S. Congress, House, *Investigation of Communist Propaganda: Hearings Before A Special Committee to Investigate Communist Activities in the United States*, 71st Cong., 2nd Sess. (Washington, D.C., 1930), 113; "Unemployed Workers! Organize," 6 March 1930, Joe Brown Papers, ALH, box 9; *Labor Unity*, 1 March 1930; Seymour, 12; Sullivan, 45; William Z. Foster, *Pages from a Worker's Life* (New York: International Publishers, 1939), 184.

19. Peterson, 138; Prago, 82–83; Leab, 304; Folsom, 258; Winter, 54–55.

20. Leab, 307; Prago, 83; Rosenzweig, "Organizing the Unemployed," 41; Sullivan, 46; Piven and Cloward, 50–51, Keeran, 67–68; Bonosky, 58.

21. Quoted in Keeran, 68–69; *Investigation of Communist Propaganda*, 111; Report on Civil Liberties Situation, January–March 1930, ACLU Papers (Microfilm Edition), reel 3; Ottanelli, 31; Folsom, 258.

22. Keeran, 65; Ottanelli, 32, 34; Rosenzweig, "Organizing the Unemployed," 41; Johnson, 117; Frank Marquardt, *An Autoworkers Journal: The UAW from Crusade to One-Party Union*, (University Park: Pennsylvania State University Press, 1975), 52; Folsom, 259–60.

23. "Minutes of the Auto Workers Conference," 8 March 1930, Kraus Papers, box 1; *Auto Workers News*, 15 March 1930; Keeran, 69. In Detroit,

follow-up protests were held to gain maximum publicity value from the police brutality evident on 6 March. "Answer Bowles-Emmons Brutality," March 1913, Ross Papers, box 8.

24. Interview, Frank Sykes, Detroit, 8 May 1989; Babson, 57; Keeran, 69; Ottanelli, 32; *Investigation of Communist Propaganda*, 113, 189, 233, 292.

25. Keeran, 69; Leab, 313; *Investigation of Communist Propaganda*, 22.

26. Interview, Shelton Tappes, Maurice Sugar Papers, ALH, box 54; Interview, Josephine Gomon, Oral History Collection: Unionization of the Auto Industry, ALH, 8; Federated Press Central Weekly Letter, sheet 2, no. 0620, 20 June 1930, in AFL Papers, series 11, file B, box 7; Sullivan, 47.

27. Interview, Dave Moore, Detroit, 5 May 1989; Babson, 57–58; Interview, Chris Alston, Detroit, 22 July 1987; Sykes interview.

28. Johnson, 117; Moore interview.

29. Sykes, Moore, Alston, Tappes interviews; Interview, Joseph Billups, Oral History Collection: Blacks in the Labor Movement, ALH, 8–9; Mary Gosman Scarborough, *Whirlwinds of Danger: the Memoirs of Mary Gosman Scarborough* (New York: David Walker, 1990), xiv; Allan, "The Jobless Fought Back"; Bonosky, 645; Sullivan, 47; Johnson, 158; Babson, 57; for evidence of black reliance on relief in Detroit, see Prago, 110; CP claims of "strong growth" among blacks in the nation's urban centers, including Detroit, are detailed in "Report," Communist Party Plenum, 1930, Earl Browder Papers, Syracuse, George Arents Research Library, Syracuse University microfilm edition), reel 6. By 1930, the Party had determined to focus on the organization of black Americans; see Ottanelli, 36–37. An excellent analysis of the black role in the unemployed movement is found in Scott Ian Craig, "Automobiles and Labor: the Transformation of Detroit's Black Working Class, 1917–1941" (unpublished MA thesis, Wayne State University, 1986).

30. Keeran, 70–71; Rosenzweig, 44; Interview, Mr. and Mrs. Joseph Billups, Oral History Collection: Blacks in the Labor Movement, ALH, 4–5; Joseph Billups interview, 6, 8–9; Moore, Sykes, Tappes, Alston interviews; Babson, 58; Johnson, 117; Broadsides, January, February, October, November, and December, 1931, Detroit Mayor's Papers (hereafter MP), 1931, Burton Historical Collection, Detroit Public Library, box 2; Piven and Cloward, 55.

31. Interview, Carl Winter, Detroit, 9 May 1989; Interview, Stanley and Margaret Novak, Detroit, 4 May 1989; Moore, Alston, Tappes interviews; Joseph Billups interview, 12; Mortimer, 50; Rosenzweig, 44; Prago, 103, 226; Leab, 309; Winter, "Unemployment Struggles of the 1930s," 54–56; Bonosky, 61; Folsom, 276.

32. Mortimer, 253; Tappes, Alston, Sykes interviews.

33. Sullivan, 61; Leab, 313; Rosenzweig, 42–43; Klehr, 50–51.

34. Clarence Hathaway, "An Examination of Our Failure to Organize the Unemployed," *The Communist* 9 (September 1930), 792–94.

35. Sullivan, 62–63; "Trade Union Unity League," 1930, Detroit, Midwest Institute for Labor Studies; *Labor Unity*, 10 September 1930; *Daily Worker*, 14 August 1930; "Fellow Workers: Fight for the Workers Unemployment Insurance Bill," 1 Sept. 1930, Metro Detroit AFL-CIO Papers, box 1; *Detroit Times*, 30 October 1930; Leab, 313.

36. Sidney Fine, *Frank Murphy: The Detroit Years* (Ann Arbor: University of Michigan Press, 1975), 399–403; *Detroit News*, 26 February 1931, MP, Unemployment Clippings File; *Labor Unity*, 8 October 1930 and 1, 22, and 29 November 1930; Murphy to Harry Slavin, 3 December 1931; "Proposals for Emergency Unemployment Relief"; Handbills, November 1931; MP, 1931, box 2; Sullivan, 61–62; Bernstein, 428.

37. Sullivan, 66; Frank Murphy, "About the Unemployed," *The Unemployed*, Spring 1931, 19, 29–30, Labadie Collection; Gomon interview, 9; Josephine Chaplin Brown, *Public Relief, 1929–1939* (New York: Henry Holt, 1939), 106–7; Rusing, 14; Babson, 55–56; Piven and Cloward, 62.

38. Sullivan, 80–86; "Platform of the Communist Party," 1931, Brown Papers, box 6; William Reynolds to Murphy, 9 July 1931; Alfred Goetz to Murphy, 14 April 1931, MP, 1931, box 2; Piven and Cloward, 59.

39. *Labor Unity*, 2 May, 6, 20 June 1931; Folsom, 284–85.

40. "Official Announcement of the First National Hunger March," October 1931, Benjamin Papers, 1932 file; Benjamin interview no. 10, n.d., Folsom-Elting Papers, box 1, file 9; Folsom, 286; Klehr, 56; "To All Unions and Workers Organizations," 26 October 1931, Metro Detroit AFL-CIO Papers, box 1; "Resolution on Why Unemployment Demonstration December 6th Failed," December 1931, Silver Spring, George Meany Memorial Archives (hereafter Meany Archives), William Green Papers, collection 2, reference files, box 16.

41. W. Reynolds, "Unemployment Work," *Party Organizer* 4 (January 1932), 8–9; "Official Announcement of National Hunger March"; planning for local arrangements are discussed in Foster, 189–90; see also Klehr, 57–58.

42. "Confidential Memorandum," n.d. (ca. 1931); Green to Charles W. Anderson, 17 February 1931, Green Papers, collection 2, box 5; ibid., collection 3, box 6; AFL Executive Committee Minutes, 1931, 79–80; see also Taft, Notes, AFL Executive Committee Minutes, 22 January 1931, Taft Papers, box 13; Nelson, 156–57.

43. "Why Unemployment Insurance," 1932, Meany Archives, Miscellaneous Pamphlets File; "Unemployment Insurance and the AFL," 1932, New York Reference Center for Marxist Studies, Pamphlet Collection; Weinstock interview, 16–17. For discussion of the rising dissension within the AFL, including the fatal defection of the Metal Trades and United Mineworkers, see Nelson, 158.

44. Michigan Federation of Labor, *Proceedings of the 43rd Annual Convention*, Kalamazoo, 9–12 February 1932, 12; Interview, Louis Weinstock (telephone), 15 August 1990; Weinstock to Brothers, n.d. (ca. 1932), ILGWU Papers, box 34; Weinstock interview, Oral History of American Left Collection, 17, 128–29; Klehr, 58.

45. *Party Organizer* 5 (January 1932), 4–7; *Young Worker*, 7 December 1931; Prago, 128–29; Klehr, 58; Folsom, 286–87.

46. For discussion of Henry Ford's impact on technology, the work process, and workers, see Meyer, especially chapters 2, 3, 5, 6; Gartman, 77–82; 84–95; 199–211; Wayne Lewchuk, "Fordism and the Moving Assembly Line: The British and American Experience, 1895–1930," in Lichtenstein and Meyer, 17–41; Peterson, 43–45; 56–59; 73–74; Allen Nevins and Frank Ernest Hill, *Ford: Expansion and Challenge: 1915–1933* (New York: Charles Scribners Sons, 1963).

47. Sykes, Moore interviews; Mr. and Mrs. Joseph Billups Interview, 1; Susan Webb, "Auto Workers' Legacy," *Daily World*, 18 March 1982, in Folsom-Elting Collection, box 3, file 3; Carl Raushenbusch, *Fordism: Ford and the Workers, Ford and the Community* (New York: League for Industrial Democracy, 1937), Lansing, Michigan State University Libraries, Special Collections, Radicalism Collection; Sullivan, 96; Prago, 165. For the Communist analysis of Ford's place in the demonology of the Left, see Foster, 191–92.

48. Charles R. Walker, "Relief and Revolution," *Forum* (August 1932), 78; Benjamin, "Draft Autobiography," Chapter 14, 30, in Benjamin Papers, "Between Hunger Marches" file. Full details on the Ford Hunger March are available in Sullivan, 96; Prago, 165–66; Keeran, 71–73; Folsom, 304–6; Johnson, 120–23; Babson, 59; Benjamin, "Draft Autobiography," Chapter 14, 29–31; Webb. A complete scholarly account may be found in Alex Baskin, "The Ford Hunger March—1932," *Labor History* 13 (Summer 1972), 331–60. A strident analysis, sympathetic to the marchers, is the memoir of labor lawyer Maurice Sugar, who handled legal defense work in the wake of the 7 March incident. See Maurice Sugar, *The Ford Hunger March* (Berkeley: Meiklejohn Civil Liberties Fund, 1980). Numerous and often passionate first-hand observations are housed in the Walter P. Reuther Archives of Labor and Urban Affairs. See, for example, "Why they Marched,"

Kraus Papers, box 1; William Reynolds, "Ford Hunger March and Massacre" and "Statements by Workers," Sugar Papers, box 53; see also Scarborough, 25–28; for an alternative analysis that emphasizes Communist leadership and CP political goals, see Fine, 403–5; Klehr, 59.

This study relies at various points on documents generated by the Detroit Police Department Red Squad. These materials have become available as a result of a lawsuit filed in 1974 and settled in 1990. One provision of the settlement mandated that upon request, facsimiles of files be made available to individuals and organizations illegally surveilled by the Detroit Red Squad between 1930 and 1974, when it was abolished. The Michigan District of the Communist Party U.S.A. has generously permitted the author to review copies of the files now in its possession, which will be referred to as Detroit Red Squad/Communist Party Collection (hereafter DRS/CPC). Reference to folder numbers will be to the Communist Party Collection numbering system rather than the folder numbers in the Red Squad Files. For evidence of Communist Party efforts to mobilize the unemployed through the Unemployed Councils in 1931, including its role in the encouragement of industry-based hunger marches in December 1931, see "Communist Unemployment Meeting, 11 January 1931; CPUSA District Seven, "Weekly Letter #43," 11 December 1931, DRS/CPC, files 28, 29.

49. "After the Dearborn Massacre," *New Republic*, 30 March 1932, Folsom-Elting Collection, box 3, file 6; Murphy to Young Communist League, *Daily Worker*, 11 March 1932; Statement by Maurice Sugar for the International Labor Defense, Sugar Papers, box 53; "Ford Riot—Protests File," MP, 1932, box 4; *Detroit Labor News*, 11 March 1932; "Report of the American Civil Liberties Union," 12 March 1932, Kraus Papers, box 1; Socialist Party of Michigan, Protest March, 1932, SPA Papers, reel 98; *Nation*, 30 March 1932, Brown Papers, box 25; Keeran, 73–74; Folsom, 307; Babson, 60. Although Roger Baldwin and the ACLU exonerated the Murphy Administration with regard to the killings, it was critical of the Detroit Police Department's role in a series of raids on radical group headquarters in the aftermath of the clash. Baskin, 346–47; Fine, 408–9; Minutes, Executive Board, ACLU, 14 March 1932, ACLU Papers, reel 3.

50. Memorandum, Roland Haynes to Mr. Croxton, 14 March 1932, NA, RG 73, Office of Assistant Director, State Files, box 245; Hoover Library, PECE/POUR State Files, box 1110. Foster asserted that his role was confined to a speech at the preliminary meeting which "went off peaceably." Foster, 192. Charles Sorenson to Sir Percival Perry, 11 March 1932, Dearborn, Ford Motor Company Archives (hereafter FMCA), accession no. 572, box 31; E. G. Liebold, "Reminiscence," FMCA, Reminiscences, vol. 12, p. 1053. The Employers' Association and Detroit police eventually concluded that a show of leniency would be the best policy to defuse the

appeal of radicalism. As a result charges against Foster were dropped. Folsom, 308.

51. Memorandum, Haynes to Croxton, 14 March 1932, NA, RG 73, Office of Assistant Director, State Files, box 245; Hoover Library, PECE/ POUR Files, box 1110.

52. "Statement of a Ford Worker," n.d.; R. Rondot to Comrade Editor, 17 March 1932; "Bloody Monday in Dearborn," 14 March 1932; *New Force*, Ford Massacre Number (March–April 1932), Sugar Papers, boxes 53, 117; Moore interview; Babson, 60; *Party Organizer* 5 (March–April 1932), 18; Keeran, 75–77. For the impact of the Ford March on Sugar's political views, and his growing confidence in the CP, see Johnson, 124.

53. Webb, "Auto Workers Legacy."

54. Benjamin, "Draft Autobiography," chapter 14, 31; Mary Gosman, "Bloody Monday in Dearborn," Sugar Papers, box 53; Keeran, 74; Johnson, 122.

55. Ford Riot Protests File, MP, 1932; Webb, "Auto Workers Legacy."

56. Scarborough, 28; "Beginning of an Article on the Subject by Some Individual," n.d., Kraus Papers, box 1; Sullivan, 98; Baskin, 360; Benjamin, "Draft Autobiography," chapter 14, 31; Folsom, 308.

57. A. Allen, "Unemployed Work: Our Weak Point," *The Communist* 11 (August 1932), 685–86; "An Open Letter to Mayor Murphy," 3 August 1932; Unemployed Councils to Mayor Murphy, 7 October 1932; P. Smith to Mayor Murphy, 26 October 1932; "Communist File," MP, 1932, boxes 2, 7a; Reports, 6 and 8 August 1932, United States Army Military Intelligence Reports (microfilm edition), Taminent Institute, reel 24; *Daily Worker*, 6 and 8 June, 29 August 1932; *Detroit News*, 6 and 7 June 1932; *Detroit Times*, 7 June 1932, Sugar Papers, box 117; Bernstein, 422–23.

58. Donald J, Lisio, *The President and Protest: Hoover, Conspiracy, and the Bonus Riot* (Columbus: University of Missouri Press, 1974), 119–20, 305; A. E. Fredetto, Memorandum, "Meeting of the Unemployed Council . . .," 2 September 1932; Nugent Dodds to Attorney General, 9 September 1932; Attorney General to the President, 9 September 1932; J. C. Patton, "Report of a Committee of 15 Men of the Rank and File Organization of the Workers Ex-Service Men's League," 19 July 1932, Hoover Papers, President's Official File (hereafter POF), boxes 375, 376; Klehr, 61–62; Bernstein, 466. After 1935, Pace left the Communist Party and testified three times before the House Committee on Un-American Activities. His testimony indicated that from the earliest discussions in April 1932, the Detroit movement for a march on Washington was the result of CP initiative. See U.S. Congress, House, Committee on Un-American Activities,

Hearing Before the Committee on Un-American Activities, 82nd Cong., 1st Sess. 1951, 1930–32.

59. "Labor–Ideological Organizations–Communists—1932," 1 August 1932, FMCA, accession 940, box 16; *Daily Worker*, 1, 21 and 29 November, and 29 September 1932; Prago, 150–51; Karl Lochner to Murphy, 26 November 1932, MP, 1932, box 2; Benjamin to Draper, 26 November 1971, Draper Papers, box 17; "Mass Meeting," 17 November 1932, MP, 1932, box 2; Klehr, 68. The reasons for Pace's incarceration are discussed in Benjamin Gitlow, Communist Party Notes, Benjamin Gitlow Papers, Stanford, Hoover Institution for the Study of War, Peace, and Revolution, box 9.

60. Italics are mine. "Resolution on Why Unemployment Demonstration on December 6th Failed," ca. December 1931, Green Papers, collection 2, box 16. For a discussion of the unemployed movement's failures, see Ottanelli, 35.

61. Ottanelli, 35–36.

62. "Memorandum," n.d., Metro Detroit AFL-CIO Papers, box 1; Moore, Sykes, Alston, Tappes interviews; Joseph Billups interview, 8–9; Benjamin interview, 23; Prago, 116–17; see also Benjamin interview no. 10, Folsom-Elting Collection.

63. Alston interview; Interview, Carl Winter, Detroit, 22 and 29 July 1987; Keeran, 85, 89; "Briggs Minutes," 11 January 1932; "The Briggs Waterloo Strike," January 1933, Kraus Papers, box 1; Jack Stachel, "The Strikes in the Auto Industry," 1933, Nat Ganley Papers, ALH, box 30; "Special Report on Present Day Conditions in the Communist Movement in Detroit, Michigan," 13 February 1933, DRS/CPC, file 29; James R. Prickett, "Communists and the Automobile Industry in Detroit before 1933," *Michigan History* (Fall 1973), 204; Johnson, 136.

64. "Stand Solid Behind the Briggs Strike," January 1933; "Auto Workers Union Organizes for Strike," January 1933, Kraus Papers, box 1; Keeran, 89–90; "Memorandum to Labor Committee Members from Leo Krzycki, Chairman," Powers Hapgood Papers, Bloomington, Lilly Library, Indiana University, box 6; "Your History and Membership with Local 212–UAW," UAW Local 212 Papers, Miscellaneous Publications File; "Strikers and Workers" (Broadside), FMCA, accession 572, box 33; Michael Whitty, "Emil Mazey: Radical as Liberal," (unpublished doctoral dissertation, Syracuse University, 1969), 35–36; Reuther interview; "Smash the Wage Cutting Starvation Program of the Automobile Bosses," January 1933, Brown Papers, box 6; *Auto Workers News*, 27 January 1933.

65. *Detroit Hunger Fighter*, February 1933; *Daily Worker*, 9 February 1933; Sykes interview; Keeran, 90.

66. The foregoing summary is based on more extensive accounts of the Briggs Strike in Keeran, 75–95; Johnson, 135–38; and Fine, 412–24. The attempt by the Briggs Company to dismiss the strike as the product of Communist agitation is detailed in W.O. Briggs to Rev. H. Ralph Higgins, 6 February 1933, FMCA, accession 572, box 33.

67. John Schmies, "The Auto Union and the Unemployed," *Labor Unity*, May 1933; Jack Stachel, "The Strikes in the Auto Industry," *Labor Unity*, March 1933; *Daily Worker*, 27 June 1933; Gomon interview, 16–18; Prickett, 185, 206–7; Interview, Philip Raymond, Oral History of the American Left Collection, Wagner Archives; Cochran, 65; Johnson, 138; Keeran, 95; Babson, 63.

68. Informant's Report, 6 March 1933, encl., Henry Shearer to Charles E. Sorenson, 9 March 1933, FMCA, accession 572, Espionage File.

69. Informant's Report, 8 March 1933, encl., Shearer to Sorenson, 9 March 1933, FMCA, accession 572, Espionage File. The Detroit Red Squad files contain ample evidence that the Councils retained a dedicated, though shrinking, following in March and April 1933. Minutes of Regular Meeting, Unemployed Council, Auto Workers Union, 4 March 1933; Informant's Report, 25 March and 21 and 29 April 1933, DRS/CPC, file 29.

70. Max Salzman, "Building the United Front in Ford-Controlled Dearborn," *The Communist* 12 (August 1933), 796–97; *Daily Worker*, 22 May and 17 March 1933; "Dearborn Workers Continue Struggle Against Relief Cuts," n.d., Kraus Papers, box 1; Schmies, "The Auto Union and the Unemployed"; Keeran, 76; "Minutes of Regular Meeting, Unemployed Council, Auto Workers Union," 4 March 1933, DRS/CPC, file 29.

71. "On to the Ford Plant June 5th," n.d.; "Protest Police Killings," 23 May 1933; Informants' Reports, 11 and 12 May 1933, DRS/CPC, file 29.

72. Quoted in Baskin, 358–59; "All Out June 5, Ford Hunger March," Brown Papers, box 9; Communist Party Notes, 5 June 1933, Gitlow Papers, box 9; "How Katava Organized WPA Workers," interview, Ganley Papers, box 33.

73. Keeran, 76; Moore, Alston, Winter interviews. Benjamin later maintained that although the unemployed movement allowed the Communist Party to "involve the masses more immediately than we would involve them in any other way, the *primary* focus was always on the workers *in industry* because they occupy a more strategic position." Benjamin interview, 23 (italics are mine).

Chapter 3

1. Piven and Cloward, 70, 75; Folsom, 347–48; Rosenzweig, "Radicals and the Jobless," 66; Joann Ooiman Robinson, *Abraham Went Out: A Biography of A. J. Muste* (Philadelphia: Temple University Press, 1981), 49–50.

2. National Unemployed League, *Second Annual Convention of NUL*, 30 July–1 August 1934, Columbus, OH; A. J. Muste to Elmer Cope, 7 October 1932; Federation of Unemployed Workers Leagues of America to All Organizations Affiliated with the Organization, March 1933; "Declaration of Workers and Farmers of America," 4 July 1933; Elmer Cope and Arnold Johnson, "Report on Unemployed Activities," 11 November 1933, Elmer Cope Papers, Ithaca, Margaret Catherwood Library, Labor-Management Documentation Center, Cornell University (microfilm edition), reels 6, 7.

3. Wayne County Public Welfare Commission, *Proceedings*, 28 March 1933, 25 April 1933, 30 January 1934; Unemployed Citizens' League of Michigan vs. Ralph Dooley, Ray Sheldon, Jack Cannon, George Schaefer, 1933, Metro Detroit AFL-CIO Papers, box 19; "The Unemployed Citizens' League," 18 August 1932; "Unemployed Citizens' League of Michigan," 1933, Brown Papers, boxes 9, 25; Whitty, 37–38. For discussion of the self-help alternative, see Folsom, 277–83. Somewhat more successful was the independent Lansing cooperative, which engaged in food and clothing manufacture and operated a farm. Supported by a modest FERA investment, this self-help venture was to become self-sustaining by 1934, when federal official Lorena Hickok reported its progress to Harry Hopkins as "damned interesting." See Hickok to Hopkins, 31 May 1934, in Richard Lowitt and Mourine Beasley, eds., *One Third of a Nation: Lorena Hickok Reports on the Great Depression* (Urbana: University of Illinois Press, 1981), 263–68.

4. Mauritz Hallgren, *Seeds of Revolt*, (New York: Alfred Knopf, 1933), 105–6; "Memorandum to Labor Committee Members from Leo Krzycki, Chairman," 1933, Hapgood Papers, box 6; Prago, 190–92, 207–8; Keeran, 90.

5. *Detroit Hunger Fighter*, 1 March 1933, quoted in Seymour, 13.

6. Bob Repas, "History of the Christian Labor Association," *Labor History* 5 (Spring 1964), 168–69.

7. *Grand Rapids Press*, 7 March 1930.

8. John I. Croshaw, "Communist Report," 3 September 1932, Thomas Walsh Papers, Grand Rapids, Michigan Room, Grand Rapids Public Library, box 12; *Daily Worker*, 14 May 1932; *Labor Unity*, 23 May 1931; "Report of the Committee on Subversive Activities, Presented to the Union

League of Michigan," 21 February 1931, NA, RG 73, POUR 620.1, box 84; Victor Woodward to George Welsh, 9 May 1931; Resolution no. 56434, 14 May 1931; Arnold Zeigler to the City Commission, 24 November 1930; Resolution no. 55326; Recommendation, 1 December 1930, Resolution no. 55372; James Field to the City Commission, 23 November 1931, Resolution no. 57502; all in Grand Rapids City Archives (hereafter GRCA), City Commission Records, 1930–1931, 1931–1932.

9. *Grand Rapids Labor News*, 24 October 1930.

10. *Proceedings of the 43rd Annual Convention of the MFL*, Kalamazoo, 9–11 February 1932, 53; *Grand Rapids Labor News*, 17 January 1930; Joanna C. Colcord, *Emergency Relief Work* (New York: Russell Sage Foundation, 1932), 86–90; *Survey* 68 (November 1932), 595–96. The best account of the scrip program may be found in Richard H. Harms, "Work Relief and the New Deal: The Grand Rapids Scrip Labor Program," paper presented at Great Lakes History Conference, Grand Rapids, 1990.

11. Walter J. Morris to Clarence Senior, 26 October 1931, SPA Papers, reel 18; *Grand Rapids Press*, 18 February 1930.

12. Harms, 20.

13. J. Field, L. A. Fabiano, and B. Korf to the City Commission of Grand Rapids, 16 November 1931, GRCA, City Commission Records, 1931–1932, no. 57468.

14. Harms, 19; "Report of the Committee of 100," 28 July 1932, Michigan Room, Grand Rapids Public Library; *Survey* (15 November 1932), 595–97; Z. Z. Lydens, ed., *The Story of Grand Rapids* (Grand Rapids: Kregel, 1966), 562. Ann Arbor was also in the process of abandoning a commissary relief system in late 1932. See *Survey* 68 (December 1932), National Social Workers Assembly Papers, Supplement, Minneapolis, Social Welfare History Archives, University of Minnesota, box 42.

15. *Our Gang*, February 1933, Labadie Collection; Official Proceedings of the Grand Rapids Welfare Advisory Council, 4 January 1933; ibid., 7 October 1932; United Front Conference Committee to the Honorable City Commission, 5 June 1933, all in GRCA, City Commission Records, no. 61141.

16. *Monthly Bulletin of the Christian Labor Association*, December 1932, encl., Official Proceedings of the Grand Rapids Welfare Advisory Council, GRCA, City Commission Records, no. 61141; Repas, 169–70.

17. Welfare Advisory Council to Honorable City Commission, 29 December 1932; ibid., 13 March 1933; Christian Labor Association to Honorable City Commission, 20 December 1932, Official Proceedings of Grand Rapids Welfare Advisory Council, GRCA, City Commission Records, no. 61141.

Notes • 311

18. Dean Selby et al. to the Mayor and City Commission, October 1931, SPA Papers, reel 18; *Michigan Worker*, 6 November 1932; *Daily Worker*, 5 September and 11 November 1932.

19. Selby to Senior, n.d., May 1931, and 11 December 1931; Senior to Hallen M. Bell, 10 December 1931; National Executive Committee Memo 8, 7–8 October 1931, SPA Papers, reels 17, 18.

20. Gilbert and Harris, 22–27, 43; Magnaghi, *The Way It Happened*, 91; see also Lankton, chapters 1, 14; Gates, chapter 6; Thurner, chapter 8, especially 242–48.

21. Michael G. Karni, "Struggle on the Cooperative Front: The Separation of Central Cooperative Wholesale from Communism, 1929–1930," in Michael G. Karni, Mattie E. Kaups, and Douglas J. Ollila Jr., *The Finnish Experience in the Western Great Lakes Region: New Perspectives* (Turku: Institute for Migration Studies, 1975), 200; David John Ahola, *Finnish-Americans and International Communism: A Study of Finnish-American Communism from Bolshevization to the Demise of the Third International* (Washington, D.C.: University Press of America, 1981), 259–60. For coverage of the Finnish-American experience from a labor perspective, see Carl Ross, *The Finn Factor in American Labor, Culture, and Society* (New York Mills, MN: Parta Printers, 1982), esp. chapter 11. Broader treatment is given the Finnish-American radical tradition as background for the developments of the 1930s in Michael G. Karni and Douglas J. Ollila, eds., *For the Common Good: Finnish Immigrants and the Radical Response to Industrial America* (Superior: Tyomies Society, 1977); Auvo Kostiainen, *The Forging of Finnish-American Communism, 1917–1924* (Turku: Institute for Migration Studies, 1978); John I. Kolehmainen, "The Inimitable Marxists: The Finnish Immigrant Socialists," *Michigan History* 36 (December 1952), 395–405. For emphasis on the radical tradition in Michigan's Upper Peninsula, see Michael G. Karni, "Yhteishyva . . . or For the Common Good: Finnish-American Radicalism in the Western Great Lakes Region, 1900–1940," (unpublished doctoral dissertation, Department of History, University of Minnesota, 1975); and Al Gedicks, "Ethnicity, Class Solidarity, and Labor Radicalism Among Finnish Immigrants in Michigan Copper Country," *Politics and Society* 7 (1977), 127–156. A complete ethnic breakdown for Gogebic County in 1930 may be found in Marianne Triponi, "The Ironwood Theatre as Symbol," (unpublished MA thesis, Department of Art, Michigan State University, 1989), 141–42. For a discussion of the ethnic character of Houghton and Keweenaw Counties, see Lankton, 211–14; and Thurner, chapter 5.

22. "Resolution," 12 April 1933, Walter Harju Papers, Minneapolis, Immigration History Research Center (hereafter IHRC), University of Minnesota, folder 11; Karni, "Yhteishyva," 363, 367; *Progressive* (August

1982), Ernest Koski Papers, IHRC, box 1. For evidence of the Finnish Workers Federations' rapid growth in the UP, see Minutes, Finnish Workers Federation of the United States, 18 March, 23 May, and 15 August 1932, Finnish Workers Federation of the United States Papers, IHRC, box 1; Lowell K. Dyson, *Red Harvest: The Communist Party and American Farmers* (Lincoln: University of Nebraska Press, 1982), chapter 3.

23. *Progressive* (August 1982).

24. Interview, Rachel Kangas, Iron River, 14 July 1989; Interview, Carl and Melvin Anderson, Escanaba, 13 July 1989; Interview, Frank Walli, Superior, 9 June 1989; Interview, Edwin Spiegal, Hancock, 11 July 1989; Interview, Ernest Koski, Superior, 9 June 1989; Interview, Helvi Savola, Minneapolis, 22 May 1989; Interview, Charles Symon, Escanaba, 13 July 1989; Interview, Wilbert Salmi, Hancock, 12 July 1989; Interview, Carl Ross, St. Paul, 24 May 1989; John Wiita, "Some Experiences of My Work at Upper Michigan as Communist Party District Secretary," John Wiita Papers, IHRC, box 1, folder 11; *Daily Worker*, 27 February 1932; ibid., (n.d.) April 1932; *Labor Unity*, 20 August 1930, September 1932, and January 1933; Debra Bernhardt, "We Knew Better: The Michigan Timber Workers' Strike of 1937" (unpublished MA thesis, Department of History, Wayne State University, 1977), 4–6; Magnaghi, *The Way It Happened*, 92.

25. Lankton, 200–213; 219–43; Gates, 113–15, 134–36; Dear Mrs. . . ., n.d., Copper Range Company Papers, accession 232, Houghton, Michigan Technological University Archives and Copper Country Collection (hereafter MTUA), box 2; Thurner, chapter 7.

26. *Labor Unity*, April and September 1932, November 1930, October 1931, January 1933; *Daily Worker*, 30 December 1932; *Producers News*, 25 November 1931; Spiegal, Walli interviews.

27. Walli interview.

28. Walli, Spiegal, Ross interviews; *Labor Unity*, October 1931, September 1932, January 1933. The accelerated union activity among unemployed miners was consistent with national CP-TUUL policy. In 1931–1932, NMU was deeply engaged in the organization of mass marches by unemployed miners and their families, designed to challenge local public officials and law enforcement agencies. See Melvin Dubofsky and Warren Van Tyne, *John L. Lewis: A Biography* (New York: Quadrangle/New York Times Book Co., 1977), 171–72.

29. William Heikkila to Mike, 23 February 1959, Koski Papers, box 1; Summary of Transcript, Decision of Special Inquiry Officer, Heikkila Exclusion Proceedings, William Heikkila Papers, IHRC, box 2.

30. *Crystal Falls Diamond Drill*, 10 February 1933 and 10 July 1931; Heikkila to Mike, 23 February 1959, Koski Papers, box 1.

31. Ward Paine to W. H. Schacht, 5 January 1933; Schacht to Paine, 24 December 1932; Copper Range Company Papers, accession 232, box 1; Lankton, 254–55; Lankton and Charles Hyde, *Old Reliable: An Illustrated History of the Quincy Mining Company* (Hancock: Quincy Mine Hoist Association, 1980), 141–43; Jeffrey Singleton, "Unemployment Relief and the Welfare State, 1930–1935," (unpublished doctoral dissertation, Boston University, 1987), 186; 202–4.

32. John Kova, "Watch the Iron Range," *Labor Unity*, January 1933; see also *Labor Unity*, 15 November 1930 and 10 October 1931; C. Harry Benedict, *Red Metal: The Calumet and Hecla Story* (Ann Arbor: University of Michigan Press, 1952), 233; Walli interview; Summary of Transcript, Heikkila Papers, box 2; Paul F. Abrahams et al., "A Study of Labor Relations at Calumet Division of Calumet and Hecla" (unpublished MA thesis, Michigan Technological University, 1969), 37–38.

33. Kangas Interview; "An Iron Miner to the Editor," *Labor Unity*, September 1932. Workers interviewed were unanimous in confirming the pervasiveness of fear and repression in the mining communities of the UP (Walli, Spiegal, Salmi, Savola, Kangas interviews). For discussion of elite group pressures and vigilante activity in the UP, with particular reference to the timber workers strike of 1937, see Bernhardt, 41–45. While the issues in 1937 differed from those present in 1932, the social atmosphere in the two situations was comparable.

34. Ross, Spiegal, Anderson, Kangas interviews.

35. Kangas interview.

36. *Marquette Mining Journal*, 11 and 12 February 1931.

37. *Labor Unity*, 16 May 1931; Spiegal, Kangas interviews.

38. Koski interview (author); Interview, Ernest Koski, Finnish American Family History Project, IHRC, box 3.

39. Dyson, 52–56; see also Klehr, 138; Koski interview (author).

40. Gates, 164; Lankton, 255; Carter Goodrich, "What Would Horace Greeley Say Now?", *Survey Graphic* 25 (June 1936), 359, 361; Gilbert and Harris, 38–40; Magnaghi, *The Way It Happened,* 91–92.

41. Dyson, 103–4; *Producers News*, 27 November 1931; Summary of Transcript, Heikkila Papers, box 2.

42. Dyson, 70, 101; *Producers News*, 27 November 27 and 11 December 1931.

43. *Producers News*, 11 December 1931.

44. *Producers News*, 4 December 1931.

45. *Producers News*, 25 December 1931.

46. *Producers News*, 1 January 1932 and 25 December 1931.

47. *Daily Worker*, 9 July 1932; *Producers News*, 6 May, and 25 November 1932; Jacob Anderson Interview, MTUA; Thurner, 243.

48. *Daily Worker*, 7 March and 7 April 1933; *Producers News*, 3 February 3, 17 and 24 March, and 21 April 1933; Magnaghi, *The Way It Happened*, 91–92; Gilbert and Harris, 38–40; Kangas interview.

49. *Producers News*, 3 and 17 February and 10 March 1933.

50. *Producers News*, 31 March, 21 April, 26 May, and 2 June 1933; *Farmers Unite Their Fight: Report, Discussion, and Resolutions of the Farmers Second National Conference, Held in Chicago, 15–18 November 1933* (Philadelphia: Farmers National Committee for Action, January, 1934), 12; Dyson, 108–9; 113.

51. Kangas interview; Reino Kero, "Emigration of Finns from North America to Soviet Karelia in the Early 1930s," in Karni et al., *The Finnish Experience in the Western Great Lakes Region*, 212; Magnaghi, *The Way It Happened*, 93; Kaarlo Tuomi, "The Karelian Fever of the Early 1930s," *Finnish Americana* 3 (1980), 61–63; Reino Akkala, "Material from Reino Akkala, Chatham, MI," courtesy Charles Symon, Gladstone, MI; "Exodus," *Grand Forks Herald*, 25 November 1988.

52. Kero, 215–17; "Exodus," *Grand Forks Herald*, 25 November 1988; Koski interview (author); Tuomi, 62–63.

53. Tuomi, 63–64; "Material from Reino Akkala, Chatham, MI"; *Marquette Mining Journal*, 24 October 1931; "Exodus," *Grand Forks Herald*, 25 November 1988; Kero, 216, 219.

54. "Exodus," *Grand Forks Herald*, 25 November 1988; Kero, 221.

Chapter 4

1. Sullivan, 117–19; "Make the Democrats Keep Their Promises," 1933, Reference Center for Marxist Studies, Pamphlet Collection; *Unemployment and Relief in Michigan*, 1935, 2, tables 5 and 7; *Emergency Relief in Michigan, 1933–1939*, 87.

2. Brown, 148, 216; Singleton, 203–4.

3. Nelson, 158–60; Weinstock interview, OHAL, 20–22; Folsom, 394–95.

4. *American Federationist* 40 (March 1933). For full discussion of the historical origins of AFL's conservative approach to the unemployed, see Nelson, 64–78; 152–61.

5. Frank Morrison to Martel, 21 November 1933, Metro Detroit AFL-CIO Papers, box 24. A review of the Wayne County AFL files makes it clear that the primary Federation concern when dealing with the unemployed was the maintenance of union wage standards.

6. Ottanelli, 52–53; Klehr, 129; Keeran, 104–7; Matthew Smith, "The Mechanics Educational Society," December 1934, Brown Papers, box 15; Cochran, 70; Johnson, 140–41; *Daily Worker*, 7 November 1933.

7. "On to Bessemer," April 1933; "Protest Resolution," April 1933; "Are You Satisfied with the Present Relief Program," April 1933, Frank Walli Papers, in possession of Frank Walli, Superior, WI; *Producers News*, 21 April 1933; *Daily Worker*, 10 February and 20 March 1933.

8. *Daily Worker*, 31 May 31 and 6, 12, and 19 June 1933; R.F.C. Notice; William McNamara to Walli, 27 April 1933, Walli Papers.

9. *Producers News*, 29 September 1933; Klehr, 141–43.

10. *Producers News*, 29 September and 3 November 1933; Dyson, 144.

11. Dyson, 118–20; "Farmers Unite Their Fight," 12, 82; Klehr, 144.

12. *Ironwood Daily Globe*, 15 December 1933; *Marquette Mining Journal*, 15 December 1933; *Daily Worker*, 19 December 1933; *Crystal Falls Diamond Drill*, 15 December 1933; *Iron Mountain News*, 23 December 1933. For evidence of YCL organizational activity among Iron County young people seeking CWA employment, see *Young Worker*, 2 January 1934. On the national scene, CWA strikes occurred occasionally, but the agency was so short-lived that sustained worker opposition failed to develop. When disputes did break out, however, Communist influence was often involved. Forrest A. Walker, *The Civil Works Administration: An Experiment in Federal Work Relief, 1933–1934* (New York: Garland, 1979), 78–81.

13. *Detroit Labor News*, 22 December 1933; *Mt. Clemens Daily Leader*, 20 December 1933; *Ann Arbor News*, 29 December 1933, *Muskegon Chronicle*, 16 December 1933, Mortimer Cooley Papers, Bentley Historical Library, Michigan Historical Collections, Ann Arbor, box 60, Scrapbook.

14. Complaints similar to Martel's and Thal's were common, and William Green was on record to the effect that CWA officials did not treat skilled labor fairly. See Walker, 76. For discussion of CWA classification procedures, wages, and hours, see Walker, 65–71. John Carmody to Ed Thal, 17 March 1934; Martel to Harry Hopkins, 9 March 1934; Carmody to

Fred R. Johnson, 27 January 1934; Martel and Thal to National Board of Labor Review, 24 January 1934, National Archives, Record Group 69, Records of the Works Progress Administration (hereafter NA, RG 69), Central Files, Federal Emergency Relief Administration (hereafter FERA), Administrative Correspondence, State File, Michigan, box 22.

15. Thal to Hopkins, 18 May 1935, NA, RG 69, Central Files, FERA Administrative Correspondence, State File, Michigan, box 22; see also Thal to Carmody, 1 December 1933; Thal to Hopkins, 5 December 1933, box 22.

16. Gil Green, "Towards a Mass Y.C.L.," Report to the 7th National Convention, Young Communist League, 22–27 June 1934, MSU Radicalism Collection; *Auto Workers News*, 14 June 1934; *Daily Worker*, 31 March and 9, 14, and 23 June 1934; "Relief Workers Protective Association," n.d., DRS/CPC, file 28.

17. *Auto Workers News*, 13 January and 4 August 1934; "Relief Workers Protective Association," n.d., DRS/CPC, file 28; *Daily Worker*, 3 and 17 January and 12 July 1934; "Resolution Supporting Program of Action of the League of Struggle of Negro Rights," 3–5 February 1934, Labadie Collection.

18. *Auto Workers News*, 21 July 1934; *Daily Worker*, 2 and 6 July 1934.

19. Croshaw, "Monthly Intelligence Report Covering Communistic Subversive Activity for Month of February, 1934," 1 March 1934, Walsh Papers, box 12; A. Briggs to the City Commission of Grand Rapids, 8 February 1934; Grand Rapids Federation of Labor to City Commission, 24 July 1933; "Resolution," 3 August 1933, GRCA, City Commission Proceedings, 1933–1934, nos. 61069, 61151, 62366; John Monsma to Roosevelt, 18 December 1933, NA, RG 69, Central Files, FERA Administrative Correspondence, State File, Michigan, box 22; *Grand Rapids Press*, 10 and 19 July 1933.

20. *Daily Worker*, 4, 6, 15, 16 and 18 October 1934; *Unemployed News Service*, 17 October 1934, 3; T. H. Maynard to H. L. Kerwin, 2 August 1934, NA, RG 69, FERA State Files, Michigan, box 139; Ludington Labor Unions, FERA Workers and Workers League to Mason County Welfare Relief Administrator, 23 April 1935, AFL Papers, series 9, box 3; *Auto Workers News*, 21 April 1934.

21. Louisa Wilson to Hopkins, 30 November 1934, Harry Hopkins Papers, Hyde Park, Franklin D. Roosevelt Presidential Library, box 67; Interviews, Tom Klasey, 46, and William Weinstone, 36, University of Michigan–Flint Labor History Project; Interview, Genora Dollinger, ALH, 6, 27. For full discussion of the Flint relief program, see William H. Chafe, "Flint and the Great Depression," *Michigan History* 53 (Fall 1969), especially 227–35.

22. Wilson to Hopkins, 30 November 1934, Hopkins Papers, box 67.

23. Ibid.

24. Charles Killinger et al. to the Officers and Members of AFL Local Unions in the city of Flint," ca. November 1934, Kraus Papers, box 8; University of Michigan–Flint Labor History Project.

25. *Daily Worker*, 1 January 1935; Wilson to Hopkins, 24 November 1934, Hopkins Papers, box 65; *Auto Workers News*, 24 April 1934; Thaddeus Radzilowski, "Introduction," Margaret Collingwood Nowak, *Two Who Were There: A Biography of Stanley Nowak* (Detroit: Wayne State University Press), 16–17; Arthur Evans Wood, *Hamtramck: A Sociological Study of an American Community* (New Haven: College and University Press, 1955), 56.

26. "Special Report Covering Activities of the Communist Party," 26 August 1935, DRS/CPC files 44, 73; Interview, Stanley and Margaret Nowak, 3 May 1989; *Daily Worker*, 29 and 30 June, 5, 6, 9, 17 and 20 August 1935; *Detroit Free Press*, 20 July 1935; Radzilowski, 17–18; Johnson, 154; Wood, 59–60, 62–63. For a CP perspective on the Communist role in the meat boycott, see *Party Organizer*, September 1935, 15–18; December 1935, 1148.

27. Michigan State Police, Complaint no. 18446, FBI, "Request for Information Concerning the Officers, Activity, and Background of the Workers Alliance in the Vicinity of Houghton and Hancock, Michigan," 26 December 1942, Benjamin Papers, Michigan State Police File; Spiegal interview; *Houghton Daily Mining Gazette*, 4 July 1934; *Daily Worker*, 16 July and 13 September 1934. For the management view of these events, see Angus Murdoch, *Boom Copper: The Story of the First U.S. Mining Boom* (Calumet: Roy W. Drier and Louis G. Koepel, 1964), 238. Murdoch's interpretation is based on information provided through the offices of Calumet and Hecla Mining Company. Spiegal to James J. Lorence, 17 August 1989.

28. Michigan State Police, Complaint; Spiegal interview; *Daily Worker*, 13 September 1934; *Houghton Daily Mining Gazette*, 4 July 1934.

29. *Crystal Falls Diamond Drill*, 5 October 1934; *Producers News*, 27 April 1934.

30. Prago, chapter 5, especially 180, 213–14; Seymour, 94; Communist Party, U.S.A., "8th National Convention," 1934, Browder Papers, reel 3; "Memorandum, 1 September 1934, Clarence Senior Papers, SHSW, box 2; Socialist Party, "Report of the NEC to the National Convention," 1, 2, and 3 June 1934, SPA Papers, reel 29. For a Socialist view of the Communist movement toward a united front among unemployed organizations, see Vogel, especially 11–15.

31. "Convention Demands Real Program for the Unemployed"; "Program of the Workers Alliance of America," 2, 3, and 4 March 1935; "Constitution and Declaration of Principles, Workers Alliance of America," Workers Alliance of America Papers, SHSW, packet (the full program is discussed in Sargent, "Roosevelt, Lasser, and the Workers' Alliance," 4–5); Liebman, 25–26. Despite the sharp rhetoric, the Socialists argued that it was an error to organize the unemployed as a revolutionary vanguard because such an approach would clash with the short term goal of immediate aid to the unemployed. See Liebman, 20. For discussion of the Socialist position in the unemployed movement at this time, see Rosenzweig, "Socialism in Our Time," especially 502–9.

32. *Detroit Labor News*, 2 December 1932; Green to Martel, 13 October 1932, Metro Detroit AFL-CIO Papers, box 1; Craig Phelan, *William Green: Biography of a Labor Leader* (Albany: State University of New York Press, 1989), 57–59; Nelson, *Unemployment Insurance*, 159–61.

33. Nelson, 198–204; "Resolutions Adopted by the First National Conference of the United Automobile Workers Federal Labor Unions," 24 June 1934, Francis Dillon Papers, ALH, box 2.

34. *Auto Workers News*, February and April 1934; *Daily Worker*, 14, 15, 21, 22, 23 and 24 November 1933; Klehr, 120; for discussion of the national activities of the Rank and File Committee, see *Rank and File Federationist*, January 1934, Labadie Collection; "Behind the Scenes at the 53rd Annual Convention of the AFL-CIO," (AFL Trade Union Committee for Unemployment: January 1934).

35. Martel to A. E. Kent, 20 March 1934; International Workers Order and Unemployment Councils, "To All Mass Organizations," ca. April 1934, Metro Detroit AFL-CIO Papers, boxes 17, 1; *Auto Workers News*, 10 March 1934; *Daily Worker*, 3 and 27 March and 16 and 23 April 1934; Seymour, 75; Prago, 232–42. An excellent discussion of grass-roots pressure for unemployment insurance may be found in Prago, chapter 5; see also Folsom, 390–93; Klehr, 284–89; Weinstock interview, New Yorkers at Work Oral History Collection, 28–30.

36. *Rank and File Federationist*, September–October 1934, Labadie Collection; F. J. Dillon to Harry Green, 30 October 1934, Metro Detroit AFL-CIO Papers, box 5; *Daily Worker*, 16 August 1934; Weinstock interview, 15 August 1990; "How Katava Organized the WPA Workers."

37. "Minutes of Unemployment Relief Conference, 11 November 1934; "Detroit Conference for Unemployment Relief and Insurance," 26 November 1934; "A Call to Action," ca. November 1934, Metro Detroit AFL-CIO Papers, boxes 1, 2, 5; *Daily Worker*, 12 November 1934.

38. *Daily Worker*, 11 and 15 December and 27 November 1934.

39. W. A. Harju, "Workers and Farmers Co-Operative Unity Alliance N.E.B. Holds Meeting," ca. 1935; Harju Papers, folder 18; Karni, "Yhteishyva," 367; *Daily Worker*, 11 and 15 December 1934.

40. Benjamin Interview, 21; *Proceedings, 46th Annual Convention, Michigan Federation of Labor*, Lansing, 12–14 February 1935, 24, 47; *Unemployment Insurance Review*, 1935, MSU Radicalism Collection; Prago, 242–53. For a summary of the AFL position, see "Unemployment Insurance and Other Economic Problems To be Considered at White House Conferences," 7 November 1934, Green Papers, collection 3, box 2.

41. Nelson, 205–11; Folsom, 397–98.

42. Wilson to Hopkins, 17 November 1934, Hopkins Papers, box 67; "Special Report Covering Communist Party Activities," 16 September 1935, DRS/CPC, files 44, 73. Piven and Cloward note that as the unemployed movement matured, it was integrated into the developing welfare system, with a resultant loss of militancy. They argue that when the unemployed organizations abandoned disruptive tactics, their ability to influence relief administration declined. See Piven and Cloward, 79–82.

43. Alston, Winter interviews; Sullivan, 167.

44. "Revolution on the Unemployed Question," October 1935, Socialist Workers Party Papers (microfilm edition), SHSW, reel 32; Prago, 254–55; Piven and Cloward, 75–76; Derbur and Young, 92. For discussion of WPA as a stimulus to union interest in the unemployed, see Seymour, 32–33.

45. Alan Strachan to Paul Porter, 7 June 1935; John Panzner to Porter, 1 February 1935, SPA Papers, reels 30, 29; Senior to Norman Thomas, 3 August 1934, Norman Thomas Papers, New York, New York Public Library Rare Books and Manuscripts Division (microfilm edition), reel 3; Socialist Party, "Membership Report by States," Browder Papers, reel 6; "Comparative Membership Report," 30 September 1933; "Memorandum #5," 22 March 1935, Senior Papers, box 2; Interviews, Alan Strachan, Washington, D.C., 2 February 1989; George Edwards Jr., Cincinnati (telephone), 28 June 1988; "Why Are We Idle?" Labadie Collection, Unemployed League of Detroit File; Rosenzweig, "Radicals and the Jobless," 66; Piven and Cloward, pp 74–75.

46. Strachan interview; Strachan, *From Picket Line to Protocol*, 70–72; "Your History and Membership with Local 212–UAW," (Detroit: UAW Local 212), 3; Minutes, Meeting of the State Executive Committee, Socialist Party of Michigan, 10 February 1935, SPA Papers, reel 98. For evidence of the spurt of Socialist activity among the unemployed in 1934, see Arthur

G. Mcdowell, Testimony, 21 December 1953, U.S. Congress, Senate, Sub-committee of the Judiciary Committee, *Hearings Before the subcommittee to Investigate the Administration of the Internal Security Act and other Internal Security Laws*, 83rd Cong., 1st and 2nd Sessions, 1954, 11; Social-ist Party, "Convention Memo #3," 1936, Browder Papers, reel 6.

47. D. B. Hovey to Porter, 30 March 1935; National Headquarters to F. A. Halstead, 22 March 1935; "What the Ford Federal Local is Doing and Planning to Organize the Unorganized," ca. March 1935, SPA Papers, reel 30; "Newsletter to All Unions and Automobile Workers Affiliated with the AFL," 3 October 1934, Dillon Papers, box 1; Hovey to Lundeen, 2 April 1934, Ernest Lundeen Papers, Stanford, Hoover Institution for the Study of War, Revolution, and Peace, box 322; *Trade Union Advocate*, April 1935, Kraus Papers, box 16; Interview, Paul A. Rasmussen, Miami, FL (tele-phone), 3 May 1988.

48. *Socialist Call*, 13 April 1935; Green to Lasser, 4 March 1936, SPA Papers, reel 30; *Proceedings of the 47th Annual Convention of the Michi-gan Federation of Labor*, Escanaba, 7–9 July 1936, 68; John R. Stockham, "An Analysis of the Organizational Structure, Aims and Tactics of the Workers Alliance of America in Franklin County and Cuyahoga County, Ohio and In Hennepin County, Minnesota, and of the Federal Workers' Section of the General Drivers Union, Local 544, in Hennepin County, Minnesota" (unpublished MA thesis, Ohio State University, 1938), 163–64.

49. George McJimsey, *Harry Hopkins: Ally of the Poor and Defender of Democracy* (Cambridge: Harvard University Press, 1987), 81–83; John Reid to Martel, 5 September 1935, Metro Detroit AFL-CIO Papers, box 8; Inter-view, Tom Klasey, University of Michigan–Flint Labor History Project, 40; Unemployed Workers Union to City Commission, 25 July 1935, GRCA, City Commission Proceedings, 1935–1936, no. 65942; UAWA Federal Union 18536 to Roosevelt, 16 September 1935; Workers Protective Union to Roosevelt, 16 September 1935; ibid., 20 September 1935; Workers Alliance of America, Bay City Local, to Hopkins, 18 August 1935, NA, RG 69, WPA Central Files, State Series, Michigan, boxes 1569, 1568; *Proceedings of the 46th Annual Convention of the Michigan Federation of Labor*, Lansing, 12–14 February 1935, 12; *Proceedings of the First Constitutional Convention of the International Union, United Automobile Workers of America*, 26–31 August, 1935, 61–62, 81, 95; Harold Ickes, Diary, Harold Ickes Papers, Washington, D.C., Manuscripts Division, Library of Congress, 763; Irving Bernstein, *A Caring Society: The New Deal, the Worker, and the Great Depression* (Boston: Houghton, Mifflin, 1985), 77.

50. American Federation of Labor, *Report of Proceedings*, 7–19 October 1935, 678; Derber and Young, 95; Croshaw, "Monthly Intelligence Report," 1 October 1935, Walsh Papers, box 12; *Michigan Organizer*, June 1935, MSU Radicalism Collection; Carl B. Waters to Senior, 5 July 1935, SPA

Papers, reel 31; Departmental Communication, RE: Flint, FMCA, accession 572, box 30; "Remember the Ford Martyrs," ca. March 1935, Labadie Collection, handbills, box 1. By this time, the Communist position in Michigan had deteriorated, if the party's own published estimates are to be believed. With membership and dues receipts in decline, the faithful were urged to redouble efforts to rebuild the party. See *Michigan Organizer*, September 1935.

51. The spurt of unemployed organizing in 1935 is discussed in Nels Anderson, "Are the Unemployed a Caste?" *Survey Graphic* (July 1935), 346–47; *Detroit Labor News*, 8 and 22 November 1935; Frank Morrison to Martel, 21 November 1935, Metro Detroit AFL-CIO Papers, box 24; *Proceedings, 47th Annual Convention, Michigan Federation of Labor*, 70–71; *Workers Alliance*, 2 October 1935. For discussion of the wage issue, including its implications for unionization of WPA workers, see Beulah Amidon, "WPA—Wages and Workers," *Survey Graphic* (October 1935), 493–97, 504–505.

52. Rasmussen to John Brophy, 22 November 1935, Congress of Industrial Organizations Papers, Washington, D.C., Department of Archives and Manuscripts, Catholic University of America (hereafter CIO Papers, CUA), Labor's Non-Partisan League Series, Workers Alliance of America File; Rasmussen to Martel, 22 October 1935; "Facts about the Workers Alliance of America," ca. October 1935, Metro Detroit AFL-CIO Papers, box 23; *Workers Alliance*, 1 and 15 September and 2 October 1935. While Brophy remained cordial, financial support was not forthcoming and full cooperation did not materialize in 1935 and 1936. Brophy to Lasser, 29 November 1935, CIO Papers, CUA, Labor's Non-Partisan League Series, Workers Alliance of America File.

53. Rasmussen interview.

54. "Memorandum," n.d., Metro Detroit AFL-CIO Papers, box 1; *Michigan Organizer*, 15 October 1935, MSU Radicalism Collection; *Daily Worker*, 25 October 1935. For comment on the organization committee and its objectives, see "Special Report Covering the Activities of the Communist Party," 16 and 23 September and 16 and 25 October 1935, DRS/CPC, files 44, 73; Riddle, 15.

55. *Daily Worker*, 3 and 11 November and 11 December 1935; *Detroit News*, 18 and 23 December 1935, Stanley and Margaret Nowak Papers, ALH, box 9; *Detroit Times*, 19 December 1935, Pierson Papers, box 1; M. Schultz to Martel, 1 November 1935; Metro Detroit AFL-CIO Papers, box 23; Rusing, 85–86; Riddle, 15–16. For comment on the WPA policy of transferring militants, see *Michigan Organizer*, 15 November 1935, MSU Radicalism Collection.

56. *Daily Worker*, 31 December 1935; see also Rusing, 85–86.

57. A. W. D. Hall to Fred Fulton, 17 December 1935; Workers' Protective Association of Washtenaw County to Hopkins, 21 October 1935; Workers Alliance of America, Hazel Park, MI, to Ickes, 3 November 1935; James G. Bryant to Nels Anderson, 26 November 1935; Jacob Baker to Howard O. Hunter, 9 November 1935, NA, RG 69, WPA Central Files, State Series, Michigan, boxes 1566, 1567, 1568, 1569; *Daily Worker*, 11 November 1935. For the WPA official authorization of collective bargaining rights for project workers, see *WPA Bulletin #36—Labor Relations*, 13 November 1935, NA RG 69, WPA Central Files, State Series, Michigan, box 1570.

58. "Special Report Covering District Plenum of District 7 (State of Michigan and Toledo, Ohio) of the Communist Party, Held in Detroit, Saturday and Sunday, December 14 and 15, 1935," DRS/CPC, file 44.

59. Sullivan, 168.

60. *WPA News*, 15 January 1936, DRS/CPC, file 30.

61. "Report on the PWA [*sic.*] Union Complaint"; "Report on Investigation of PWA [*sic.*] Union Complaint" *WPA News*, 15 January 1936, DRS/CPC, files 32, 72, 30.

62. *Daily Worker*, 27, 30 January and 13 May 1936; "Some Successful WPA Strikes and Stoppages," in Herbert Benjamin, *Handbook for Project Workers*, January 1936, MSU Radicalism Collection; Detroit Public Schools to Police Department (with enclosure), 11 and 13 February 1936, DRS/CPC, file 72.

63. *Daily Worker*, 11 January 1936; Martel and Reid to Clyde Austin, 8 January 1936; John D. Dingell to Roosevelt, 28 February 1936; Metro Detroit AFL-CIO Papers, box 24; Martel to Edwin McGrady, 7 January 1936, NA, RG 69, WPA Central Files, State Series, Michigan, box 1568. The DFL rapprochement with Local 830 took place side by side with a reassertion of the Federation's traditional desire to maintain union standards through a role in the administration of government policy. In January 1936, Martel urged the appointment of DFL representatives to positions that would enable the Federation to influence welfare administration. He was especially concerned about Public Works Administration and WPA wage schedules and the selection of project workers. On the latter point, Martel was determined that when PWA contractors requested union members, "no man is a union man unless he is in possession of a current working card showing his dues are paid to date" (quoted in Riddle, 22).

64. Minutes, "Special Meeting Called by the Arbitration Board," 26 February 1936; Alfred K. Hebner to Edwin Kuhnlein, 27 February 1936; Martel to Ray Taylor, 27 March 1936, Metro Detroit AFL-CIO Papers, boxes 23, 24; *Daily Worker*, 2 March 1936; *Detroit Labor News*, 3 January 1936, in

Pierson Papers, box 1. The collaborative relationship between the DFL and WPA administrators is discussed in Riddle, 25–27. For comment on the increasing conservatism in the Hod Carriers Union and its gradual withdrawal from unemployed organizing, see Robin D. G. Kelly, *Hammer and Hoe: Alabama Communists During the Great Depression* (Chapel Hill: University of North Carolina Press, 1990), 153–54.

65. *Daily Worker*, 25 January 1936; Interview, Mrs. Howard Foster, 35; Interview, Tom Klasey, 40; Interview, Charles Killinger (tape), University of Michigan–Flint Labor History Project; *Flint Journal*, 28 and 30 January 1936, Flint Public Library, Clippings, Automotive History Collection.

66. *Workers Alliance*, November, December 1935; Rasmussen to Lorence, 12 March 1988; Sullivan, 181.

67. C. Sweisberger to Federal Relief Administration, 24 October 1935, NA, RG 69, WPA Central Files, State Series, Michigan, box 1569; *Workers Alliance*, December 1935.

68. Frederic S. Schouman, "Seventh Confidential Report of the Michigan Works Progress Administration, Covering the Period From February 3 to March 1, 1936," 4–6, Pierson Papers, box 1; Bryant to Nels Anderson, 22 January 1936; E. L. Kalling et al. to Hopkins, 26 January 1936; Charles K. Vanduren to Hopkins, 6 March 1936; Guy VanderVeer to Albert J. Engel, 24 February 1936; VanderVeer to Engel, 13 January 1936; Bryant to Dean R. Brimhall, 11 February 1936; August Fischer to Hopkins, 11 February 1936; Anderson to Margaret Fish, 17 January 1936, NA, RG 69, WPA Central Files, State Series, Michigan, boxes 1568, 1569; *Daily Worker*, 6 February 1936; *Grand Rapids Herald*, 3 and 8 March 1936; *Lansing State Journal*, 18 March 1936, NA, RG 69, WPA Division of Information, Clippings File, 1936–1944, Michigan-Minnesota, box 259.

69. Schouman, "Eighth Confidential Report of the Michigan Works Progress Administration, Covering the Period from March 1st to March 31st, 1936," 2–3, Pierson Papers, box 1.

70. Schouman, "Seventh Confidential Report," 4; *Workers Alliance*, January 1936; *Daily Worker*, 28 February 1936.

71. *Proceedings, 2nd National Convention, Workers Alliance of America,* 1936, 56–7; *Workers Alliance*, January 1936.

72. *Workers Alliance*, December 1935; Ralph J. Kennelly to Hopkins, 15 November 1935, NA, RG 69, WPA Central Files, State Series, Michigan, box 1568; Anderson interview; Michigan State Police File, Carl Raymond Anderson.

73. *Marquette Mining Journal*, 26 November 1935; see also 22, 27, 29 and 30 November and 5 December 1935; *Workers Alliance*, December 1935; Paul E. Balzell to Dean R. Brimhall, 2 December 1935, NA, RG 69, WPA Central Files, State Series, Michigan, box 1568; Communist Party, Escanaba Section, "To All Workers and Farmers," n.d., Lawrence Farrell Papers, Ann Arbor, Michigan Historical Collections, Bentley Library, box 2; Anderson interview.

74. *Workers Alliance*, December, 1935; *Ironwood Daily Globe*, 8 and 19 January 1936; Anderson interview.

75. Wiita, "Some Experiences of My Work at Upper Michigan," 2–4; Walli, Savola, Bednar interviews.

76. Spiegal, Salmi, Anderson, Kangas interviews; Spiegal to Lorence, 17 August 1989; Michigan State Police File, Request for Information, Workers Alliance, Benjamin Papers.

77. *Daily Worker*, 6 March 1936; *Workers Alliance*, January 1936; *Ironwood Daily Globe*, 8 and 10 January 1936; Anderson interview.

78. Bryant to Nels Anderson, 13 January 1936; "Resolution," January 1936, NA, RG 69, WPA Central Files, State Series, Michigan, boxes 1568, 1569; *Ironwood Daily Globe*, 11 and 13 January 1936; *Daily Worker*, 17 January 1936; Walli interview.

79. *Daily Worker*, 17 January 1936; *Workers Alliance*, Second January Issue, February 1936; *Marquette Mining Journal*, 15 January 1936.

80. *Workers Alliance*, February 1936; *Daily Worker*, 17 January 1936; Rasmussen interview; Rasmussen taped interview, tape 4; *Marquette Mining Journal*, 15 January 1936.

81. L. G. Brasser to Roosevelt, 13 February 1936, NA, RG 69, WPA Central Files, State Series, Michigan, box 1568; *Marquette Mining Journal*, 10 January, 24 February, and 2 March 1936; Kangas interview. For comment on Matt Savola's role in the Iron River resistance to evictions, see Bernhardt, 21–22.

82. Folsom, 416–17; Brown, 265; Interview, Ernest Rice McKinney, CUOHC, 19.

83. Benjamin, "Memorandum," ca. January 1936, Browder Papers, reel 5. For discussion of CP activity in the Unemployed League and Workers Alliance *prior to merger*, see Klehr, 296; Folsom, 416.

84. Rasmussen taped interview, tape #3; "Report of the National Labor Secretary to the National Convention of the Socialist Party, Cleveland, Ohio," 23 May 1936, SPA Papers, reel 33; Klehr, 296; Sargent, "Roosevelt, Lasser,

and the Workers Alliance," 6–7; Liebman, 34–35; Prago, 256; Vogel, 14–15; Brendan Sexton, "Socialists in the Workers Alliance, *American Socialist Monthly* 5 (February 1937), 53–56; Rosenzweig, "Socialism in Our Time," 506–7; Folsom, 417. Despite a Socialist majority on the national executive board, the presence of Benjamin in the critical position of secretary ensured that the Communist line would be effectively expressed in the Alliance's internal councils. Rasmussen clashed with the CP operative from the beginning, while Lasser proved more accomodating. Moreover, Benjamin later claimed that with the support of "sleepers" and wavering Socialists on the board it was often possible for Communists to exert controlling influence on WAA policy. It is impossible to prove or disprove this assertion, but it is clear that although Lasser remained as president until 1940, the Alliance expressed a Communist viewpoint on many issues from 1937 on. For the new Workers Alliance Constitution, see Folsom, appendix O.

85. Rasmussen, Alston interviews; Rasmussen to Lorence, 12 March 1988; *Proceedings of the 2nd National Convention, Workers Alliance of America*, 1936, 8–9, 36, 56–57; Ganley interview, 5, 34; *Daily Worker*, 6 April 1936. For discussion of the unity meeting, see Klehr, 295–97; Piven and Cloward, 75–76; Leibman, 34–38; Sargent, "Roosevelt, Lasser, and the Workers' Alliance," 6–7; Folsom, 417. At the time of merger, Michigan's Unemployment Councils were small, though Benjamin persisted in the dubious claim that on a national scale they were dominant. This assessment exaggerated Council strength. In numerical terms, the Unemployment Councils were weak. This weakness was evident in Michigan, where membership languished. The CP's own estimates revealed that as of November 1935, statewide Council membership stood at 296, which placed Michigan twenty-third out of thirty-four states in which Unemployment Councils existed. See National Unemployment Council, "Report on Supplies," 1 January–1 November 1935; "Summary and Conclusions," ca. March 1936; Benjamin Papers, Financial File.

Chapter 5

1. Ottanelli, 140–41, 145, 148–49; Keeran, 140–46; Barnard, 37–38.

2. Ford Thompson to Brophy, 18 March 1936, CIO Central Files, Labor's Non-Partisan League Series, Workers Alliance of America File; "Ninth Confidential Report of the Michigan Works Progress Administration, Covering the Period from April 1st to April 30th, 1936," and "Tenth Confidential Report of the Michigan Works Progress Administration, Covering the Period from May 1st to May 31st, 1936," Pierson Papers, box 1; *Proceedings of the 2nd National Convention, Workers Alliance of America*, 1936, 2–3; Seymour, 48.

3. *Detroit News*, 2 June 1936; *Workers Alliance*, July 1936; *Daily Worker*, 15 June 1936; "A Survey of Communist Activity in the City of Detroit and Vicinity (Confidential)," 1 July 1936, 8, Metro Detroit AFL-CIO Papers, box 1.

4. *Detroit News*, 7, 8, 12, 13, and 15 August 1936; *Detroit Times*, 29 July and 3 August 1936; *WPA Progress*, June 1936, 2 (all in Pierson Papers, box 1); McMahon to Editor, *Detroit News*, 16 August 1936, NA, RG 69, WPA Division of Information, Clippings File, 1936–1944, Michigan-Minnesota, box 259; *Daily Worker*, 3 and 27 July and 14 and 17 August 1936; McMahon to Hopkins, 7 August 1936; Allen Forsberg to McMahon, 11 August 1936, NA, RG 69, WPA Central Files, State Series, Michigan, boxes 1568, 1572.

5. Sullivan, 167; David Ziskind, *One Thousand Strikes of Government Employees* (New York: Columbia University Press, 1940), 139–41, 151, 155, 160, 166, 172; *Detroit News*, 15 and 17 August 1936, Pierson Papers, box 1; *Daily Worker*, 29 August 1936.

6. Benjamin, "Report to the Ninth Convention, C.P.," Benjamin Papers, 1936 file; *Workers Alliance*, First July Issue, 1936; Leibman, 44; Sargent, "Roosevelt, Lasser, and the Workers Alliance," 8.

7. Benjamin, "Unemployed Work," 2 October 1936; David Lasser, "Report to the National Executive Board, Workers Alliance of America," 12 September 1936, Benjamin Papers, 1936 file; "A Survey of Communist Activity in the City of Detroit and Vicinity," 8; Thompson to Anderson, 20 May 1936; Bryant to Thompson, 28 May 1936; Anderson to Ray Cooke, 4 August 1936; Floyd McDonald to Hopkins, 13 September 1936; Glenn McCoy to Hopkins, 16 March 1936, NA, RG 69, WPA Central Files, State Series, Michigan, box 1568; *Daily Worker*, 21 March 1936; *Workers Alliance*, Second July Issue, 1936; Benjamin, "Memorandum," ca. Fall 1936, Draper Papers, series 2.3, reel 9.

8. L. M. Nims to James Myers, 9 September 1936; Anderson to Myers, 9 September 1936; Myers to Hopkins, 2 September 1936 and 18 September 1936; Myers, et al., "Petition," n.d.; Houghton County Board of Supervisors, "Resolution," 20 October 1936; Forsberg to Otto Alatalo, 6 November 1936; Meyers to Frances Perkins, 18 September 1936, NA, RG 69, WPA Central File, State Series, Michigan, box 1568; NA, RG 174, Records of the Secretary of Labor, General Subject File, 1933–1941, box 108; *Mining Gazette*, 20 September 1936; *Proceedings of the 47th Annual Convention of the Michigan Federation of Labor*, 5–7 July 1936, Escanaba, 12, 46.

9. Leo J. Smith to Hopkins, 12 September and 29 September 1936; Anderson to Smith, 3 October 1936; Anderson to Nims, 3 October 1936, NA, RG 69, WPA Central Files, State Series, Michigan, box 1568. The

Alliance's standing in Iron River was strengthened not only by traditional CP influence in the area, but also the AFL's refusal to consider an affiliation with a local unemployed group seeking a Federation tie. See Secretary-Treasurer to Eddie Klimik, 14 September 1936, AFL Papers, series 9, box 3.

10. Lewis to Lasser, 2 September 1936; Green to Lasser, ca. September 1936; Lasser to Lewis, 24 September and 21 December 1936, CIO Files of John L. Lewis, part 1, reel 6; Lewis to Lasser, 9 October 1936, in "How to Win Work with the Workers Alliance of America," 1936, Reference Center for Marxist Studies, Pamphlet Collection.

11. Houghton *Daily Mining Gazette*, 14 October 1936; Marquette *Mining Journal*, 14 September 1936; *Detroit News*, 12 September 1936, Pierson Papers, box 1; Anderson, Spiegal interviews. Ironically, Michigan Democrats attacked WPA for *insufficient* attention to partisan interests. A frequent complaint was that the state WPA administration was honeycombed with "black-hearted Republicans" unsympathetic to the New Deal. John D. Dingell to James A. Farley, 10 August 1936, Roosevelt Papers, POF no. 39; Farley to Dingell, 19 August 1936, Hyde Park, Roosevelt Library, Democratic National Committee Papers, box 1096.

12. Rasmussen interview; "Unemployed Work," 2 October 1936, Benjamin Papers, 1936 file; *Workers Alliance*, 7 November and 19 December 1936, 2 January 1937.

13. Lasser, "Report to the National Executive Board," 12 September 1936; "Unemployed Work," 2 October 1936; Stockham, 66–67.

14. "Report on the Workers Alliance Mass Meeting," 9 January 1936, DRS/CPC, file 46.

15. *Detroit News*, 6, 7, and 9 March 1937, NA, RG 69, WPA Central Files, Division of Information, Clippings File, 1936–1944, Michigan-Minnesota, box 259; *Detroit Labor News*, 4 December 1936, 15 March 1937; *Peoples Press*, 13 March 1937; Workers Alliance of Wayne County, "Resolution," 13 March 1937, McMahon to FDR, 10 December 1936, NA, RG 69, WPA Central Files, State Series, Michigan, boxes 1572, 1608. The reinstatement order is quoted in "Agreement," 7 March 1937, Haber Papers, box 5.

16. Harry Mikuliak and Leo Maciosek, "Memorandum," 20 March 1937; 11 June 1937; 14 October 1937, U.S. Military Intelligence Reports, reel 30; *Daily Worker*, 5 May and 22 April 1936.

17. Reuther, Edwards interviews; Interview, Frank Marquardt, Unionization of the Auto Industry Collection, ALH, 9–10; Interview, Ben Fischer, July 1991, Pittsburgh.

18. Fischer interview; Reuther interview.

19. Reuther interview; *Detroit News*, 11 April 1936; Matthew Smith to Hopkins, 20 February 1936, NA, RG 69, WPA Central Files, State Series, Michigan, box 1568; Minutes, Joint Relief Committee, 13 February 1936, Homer Martin Papers, ALH, box 1; Adolph Germer to Brophy, 7 January 1936, CIO Files of John L. Lewis, part 1, reel 2; Sullivan, 193; Harold Hartley, "Report of the Welfare and Unemployment Committee, Local 174, UAW, for Period May, 1937 to June, 1938," 1; Joe Brown Papers, box 33. Communist-Socialist cooperation at Kelsey-Hayes is discussed in Keeran, 157.

20. Keeran, 114–16; Folsom, 352–53; Irving Bernstein, *Turbulent Years: A History of the American Worker, 1933–1941* (Boston: Houghton, Mifflin, 1979), 218–28; Piven and Cloward, 121–22.

21. Interview, Charles Killinger (telephone), 25 July 1989; Killinger taped interview; Foster interview, 35; Charles M. Stewart to J. C. Wyszelski, 6 April 1937, NA, RG 69, WPA, Division of Investigation Records, reel B 1295; Killinger to Martin, 25 July 1936, Martin Papers, box 1; George Starkweather to Green, 5 March 1937, AFL Papers, series 11, file C, box 39; Keeran, 151, 173; Edsforth, 169.

22. Sidney B. Fine, *Sitdown: the General Motors Strike of 1936–1937* (Ann Arbor: University of Michigan Press, 1969), 220–21; Edsforth, 168–69; Interview, Roy Reuther, *Detroit Free Press*, 2 February 1966, 1–2, Roy Reuther Papers, ALH, box 3; Victor Reuther interview; "Highlights of a Letter Sent to Miss Hilda Smith by Frances Comfort," 13 February 1937, *United Automobile Worker*, 9 July 1938; "Michigan WPA Workers' Education Program," ca. 1937, Dorothy Hubbard Bishop Papers, ALH, box 1; Rusing, 109; Victor Reuther, *The Brothers Reuther and the Story of the UAW* (Boston: Houghton, Mifflin, 1979), 199. Because of its firm commitment to the principles of unionism, the Workers Education Program came under attack as Communist-oriented and biased towards CIO. Marquardt interview, 4–5; Rusing, 88–90; "Notes Regarding the Article in *Business Digest* for September, 1937, Entitled WPA Cash Backs CIO," Metro Detroit AFL-CIO Papers, box 24; Hartley Barkley, "WPA Cash Backs CIO," Bishop Papers, box 1. For discussion of the workers education program and its significance for the developing labor movement, see Joyce Kornbluh, *A New Deal for Workers Education: the Workers Service Program, 1933–1942* (Urbana: University of Illinois Press, 1987); see also Brown, 270–72.

23. Interview, Hy Fish, University of Michigan–Flint Labor History Project, 17; "To the Delegates," 26–29 March 1937, Special Convention of the Socialist Party, SPA Papers, reel 35; Dollinger interview, ALH, 32; Dollinger interview (Lorence); Keeran, 164–65; Klehr, 232–33; see also Edsforth, 168–70.

24. Edsforth, 153; "But the Evil Remains," *United Automobile Worker*, December 1936, Brown Papers, box 25; Haber to Kraus, 1 December 1936; Victor S. Woodward to Mrs. Walter Reed, 28 October 1936, Kraus Papers, box 8; Charles Killinger, Walter Moore, and Burdine Simon, "The Relief Situation," 6–7 November 1936, NA, RG 46, Records of United States Senate, in University of Michigan–Flint Labor History Project files.

25. *Survey* 73 (March 1937), 69–70; Interview, Roy Reuther, University of Michigan–Flint Labor History Project, 39; Roy Reuther interview, Roy Reuther Papers, box 3; "Dear Brother," December 1936, CIO Files of John L. Lewis, part 1, reel 1; Dollinger interview (Lorence). For discussion of the Flint relief system in the 1930s, see Chafe, "Flint and the Great Depression," especially 231–37. The background for the development of the city's relief program is examined in Edsforth, 142–44. Murphy's decision is covered in Sullivan, 193–94; Fine, 202–3.

26. Ella Lee Cowgill, "Field Representative's Report," 27 January 1937; Cowgill to Killinger, January 22, 1937; Robert C. Travis to Haber, 22 January 1937, Haber Papers, box 5; *Flint Journal*, 28 January 1937, Flint Public Library, Automotive History Collection, Clippings Book; Sullivan, 194; Fine, 203–4; G-2 Report, 22 January 1937, Michigan National Guard Papers, Department of Military Affairs Records, Michigan Archives, Lansing, box 2.

27. Hartley, "Report of the Welfare and Unemployment Committee, Local 174," 1; Sullivan, 194.

28. Edwards, Victor Reuther interviews.

29. Hartley, "Report of the Welfare and Unemployment Committee, Local 174," 5; Edwards, Strachan, Fischer interviews; Interview, Ethel Polk, Chicago, 20 August 1991; Brown, "Welfare Committees Set Up in UAW Because of Strike Needs," 25 February 1937, Brown Papers, box 33; Sullivan, 194.

30. Hartley, "Report of the Welfare and Unemployment Committee, Local 174," 5; Victor Reuther interview.

31. Hartley to Daniel Hoan, 6 April 1935, Daniel W. Hoan Papers, Milwaukee, Milwaukee County Historical Society, boxes 8, 33; *Daily Worker*, 13 June 1935. Stuart Strachan later recalled that Hartley was often accused of being a CP member. Strachan to Lorence, 7 April 1989. Homer Martin also alleged that in 1937, Hartley served on the State Committee of the Communist Party of Michigan. Martin, Speech, n.d., "Speeches on Communism" file, Martin Papers, box 4.

32. *Peoples Press*, 15 December 1936; *General Motors Conveyor*, Local 174, UAWA, ca. February 1937, Brown Papers, box 21; Sullivan, 194, 217.

33. Sullivan, 194–95; Minutes, Wayne County Welfare Relief Commission, 1 April 1937; Workers Alliance of Wayne County to G.R. Harris, 4 February 1937; Harris to Hartley, 9 February 1937, *Proceedings, Wayne County Welfare Relief Commission*, 1937, 19–21, 25; Margaret Riopelle to Roosevelt, 11 January 1937, NA, RG 69, WPA Central Files, State Series, Michigan, box 1608; Riddle, 28.

34. "Harris and Lipson Must Go! Strike for Increased Relief!", March 1937, Kraus Papers, box 16; U.S. Congress, House of Representatives, *Investigation and Study of the Works Progress Administration, Hearings Before the Subcommittee of the Committee on Appropriations* (Washington, D.C., 1939), vol. 1, 114–15; Sullivan, 182.

35. *Proceedings and Resolutions of the 3rd National Convention, Workers Alliance of America*, 1937, 1–2, 4, 8, 37, Labadie Collection; "Unemployed Work," 1936, 3, Benjamin Papers, 1936 file. The policy of cooperation without affiliation with existing unions dated from the Workers Alliance founding convention of 1935. "Our Relations with Organized Labor," SHSW, Workers Alliance of America Papers, packet 1.

36. Hartley, "Report of the Welfare and Unemployment Committee, Local 174," 1–2; *United Automobile Worker*, 11 December 1937 and 15 January 1938; George Edwards Jr., "History of WPA-Welfare Department, UAWA-CIO," in George Edwards Jr. Papers, ALH, part 3, box 2.

37. Hartley, "Report of the Welfare and Unemployment Committee, Local 174," 4–5; *United Automobile Worker*, 15 January 1938; Edwards, "History."

38. *Detroit Free Press*, 28 May 1937, NA, RG 69, WPA Central Files, Division of Information, Clippings File, 1936–1944, Michigan-Minnesota, box 281; Alston interview; *United Automobile Worker*, 12 June 1937; Minutes of Executive Board of the West Side Local 174, 4 June 1937, Stuart Strachan Papers, ALH, box 1.

39. Barnard, 53; Babson, 80–81; Fischer, Polk, Novak, Victor Reuther interviews; Dubofsky and Van Tine, chapter 12; Zieger, 90–96.

40. *Detroit News*, 28 February and 7 March 1937, Brown Papers, box 11; Sullivan, 192; Sidney B. Fine, *The Automobile Under the Blue Eagle: Labor, Management, and the Automobile Manufacturing Code* (Ann Arbor: University of Michigan Press, 1963), 412.

41. Riddle, 31.

42. Interview, Mort Furay, ALH; *Detroit News*, 4, 17, 22 and 25 June 1937; *New York Times*, 4 June 1937; all in SHSW, Russell Sage Foundation Papers, Clippings Files, box 1; *Daily Worker*, 3 and 11 June 1937; *Party*

Organizer 10, (July 1937), 4; Sullivan, 206–7. In early July the Detroit Common Council established several subcommittees to examine the condition and cost of housing in the city. *Detroit News*, 30 June and 3 July 1937; Riddle, 32.

43. *Detroit Saturday Night*, 17 July 1937; Report on Meetings, 11 and 26 June 1937; "Information on Communist Activities," 18 September 1937, DRS/CPC, files 46, 51; Minutes of Executive Board, 10 September 1937, Strachan Papers, box 1; *Daily Worker*, 6 July and 11 November 1937; *Detroit Labor News*, 30 July 30 and 6 August 1937; Furay interview; Riddle, 31–32. For discussion of the rapid politicization of the Polish community, see Johnson, 209–11, Radzilowski, 8–11; Wood, chapter 4.

44. Hartley, "Report of the Welfare and Unemployment Committee, Local 174," 4; Mortimer to Hopkins, 10 January 1937, NA, RG 69, WPA Central Files, State Series, Michigan, box 1570; Craig, 104–5. The origins of the Ford drive are discussed in Johnson, 223–25; Keeran, 218–20; Babson, 103–8.

45. Tappes interview, 12; Tappes interview, in Sugar Papers, box 54; Sykes interview; Craig, 106–7. The key role of Communists in the organization of Ford is confirmed by Keeran, 218–19.

46. Interview, Joseph Pagano, ALH, Unionization of the Auto Industry Collection, 24, 37; Sykes interview; Tappes interview, Sugar Papers, box 54; Hartley, "Report of the Welfare and Unemployment Committee, Local 174," 5; Billups interview, no. 2, p. 5. The best discussion of the black role at Ford may be found in August Maier and Elliot Rudwick, *Black Detroit and the Rise of the UAW* (New York: Oxford University Press, 1979), 34–106, Richard W. Thomas, *Life for Us Is What we Make It: Building Black Community in Detroit, 1915–1945* (Bloomington: Indiana University Press, 1992, 277–304, and Craig, 105–31; see also Babson, 103–8.

47. Maier and Rudwick, 40, 48–49; Thomas, 287; Interview, LeBron Simmons, p. 9, in Ganley Papers, box 33; Sykes interview; Paul Kirk to John B. Davis, 16 July 1937, National Negro Congress Papers, Schomburg Collection, New York Public Library (microfilm edition), roll 5.

48. Interview, John W. Anderson, ALH, Unionization of the Auto Industry Collection, 70; Sullivan, 206.

49. *Marquette Mining Journal*, 6 June 1937; *Peoples Press*, 8 and 29 May 1937; Rintala to Roosevelt, 7 June 1937; Niles to Rintala, 10 June 1937, NA, RG 69, WPA Central Files, State Series, Michigan, box 1570.

50. *Marquette Mining Journal*, 10, 14, 15 and 26 June 1937; *Peoples Press*, 19 June 1937; *Crystal Falls Diamond Drill*, 18 June 1937; *Milwaukee Sentinel*, 12 June 1937.

51. *Proceedings and Resolutions, Third Annual Convention, Workers Alliance of America*, 1937, 3, 13; *Peoples Press*, 3 July 1937; *Ironwood Globe*, 18, 22, 23 and 25 June 1937; *Marquette Mining Journal*, 24 July 1937; Rintala to Hopkins, 30 June 1937; Niles to Rintala, 2 July 1937, NA, RG 69, WPA Central Files, State Series, Michigan, box 1571; Rintala to Murphy, 1 July 1937, Murphy Papers, box 18.

52. The best analysis of the Timber Workers' strike is Bernhardt, "We Knew Different: the Michigan Timber Workers Strike of 1937." For further comment on the strike, see Jerry Lembcke and William M. Tattam, *One Union in Wood: A Political History of the International Woodworkers of America* (New York: International Publishers, 1984), 47–52. See also William Beck, "Radicals in the Woods: The 1937 Timber Workers Strike in the Lake Superior Region" (paper presented at Missouri Valley History Conference: Omaha, 14–16 March 1991), especially 10–12. Veteran CP activist Carl Ross confirms the close relationship between the unemployed movement and the timber workers strike (Ross interview; Symon interview).

53. *Marquette Mining Journal*, 12 June 1937; Bernhardt, 18–19.

54. Bernhardt, 19; Wiita, 5.

55. Bernhardt, 30; *Midwest Labor*, 6 June 1937; *Ironwood Daily Globe*, 27 May 1937; Wiita, 5–6; Symon interview; John W. Maki to Hopkins, 24 June 1937, NA, RG 69, WPA Central Files, State Series, Michigan, box 1571.

56. Bernhardt, 30, 38; Interview, Helvi Savola, 22 May 1989, Minneapolis; Walli interview.

57. *Midwest Labor*, 6 and 27 August and 24 December 1937; Savola to F. Granger, 31 December 1937, NA, RG 69, WPA Central Files, State Series, Michigan, box 1571; Bernhardt, 39.

58. Margaret Riopelle to UAW Local 212, 1 July 1937; McMahon to All Secretaries of Local Unions, 3 July 1937, UAW Local 212 Papers, ALH, box 4.

59. *Daily Worker*, 16 and 19 July 1937, Strachan Papers, box 1; *Detroit Labor News*, 16 and 23 July 1937.

60. UAW Local 174 *Conveyor*, 31 August 1937; *Daily Worker*, 4 September 1937; *Detroit Labor News*, 3 September 1937; *Midwest Labor*, 13 August 1937; "Minutes of the Meeting of the Management Committee of the Peoples Cooperative Society, Superior," 17 August 1937, Central Cooperative Wholesale Papers, box 13; Labor's Non-Partisan League, *National Bulletin*, 15 August 1937, CIO Central Files, CUA, Labor's Non-Partisan League Series; *Detroit News*, 21 August 1937; Minutes, Executive Board, Local 174, 30 July 1937, Strachan Papers, box 1; Hartley, "Report of the

Welfare and Unemployment Committee, Local 174," 4; Memorandum, Attached Letter, 11 August 1937, DRS/CPC, file 6; Folsom, 421; Klehr, 298.

61. "Resolutions Adopted at the Special Joint Council Meeting, West Side Local 174, UAWA," 1 August 1937, Strachan Papers, box 1; UAW Local 174 *Conveyor*, 20 and 27 July 1937; Handbill, "Relief Hearing, Pontiac High School," 15 July 1937, Walter Reuther Papers, box 6; *New York Herald Tribune*, 3 August 1937; *New York Sun*, 3 August 1937; *Washington Morning Herald*, 3 August 1937; *Grand Rapids Herald*, 3 August 1937, NA, RG 69, WPA Central File, Division of Information, Clippings File, Michigan-Minnesota, 1936–1944, box 259.

62. "Resolutions Adopted at the Special Joint Council Meeting, West Side Local 174, UAWA," 1 August 1937; *Second Annual Convention of the IUUAW of A.*, 23–24 August 1937, Milwaukee, appendix 3, 57, 60–61.

63. "Policy—WPA Workers," 17 August 1937; Walter Smethurst to Lowell Hollenbeck, 27 September 1937, CIO National Secretary-Treasurer's Papers, ALH, box 49; Smethurst to Lasser, 6 August 1937, CIO Central Files, CUA, Labor's Non-Partisan League Series, Workers Alliance of America File; Lasser to Thomas, 22 September 1937, Thomas Papers, reel 7.

64. "Outline for Local Welfare Committees," Hartley to Brother, ca. October 1937, Ross Papers, box 2; *West Side Conveyor*, 5 October 1937.

Chapter 6

1. For discussion of the CIO initiative in historical perspective, see David Montgomery and Ronald Schatz, "Facing Layoffs," in David Montgomery, ed., *Workers' Control in America: Studies in the History of Work, Technology and Labor Struggles* (Cambridge: Cambridge University Press, 1979), 139–49.

2. Benjamin to Lewis, 4 November 1937; CIO, "Legislative Program," October 1937, The CIO Files of John L. Lewis, part 1, reel 6; Robert H. Zieger, *John L. Lewis: Labor Leader* (Boston: Twayne, 1988), 101–2; Dubofsky and Van Tine, 329–30.

3. Montgomery and Schatz, 145; Zieger, 106, 129; see also Zieger, *The CIO, 1935–1955* (Chapel Hill: University of North Carolina Press, 1995), 81.

4. Hartley, "Report of the Welfare and Unemployment Committee, Local 174," 1–2; Katherine Pollak, "Suggestions on Letter to Local Industrial Unions On Unemployment," 22 November 1937, Katherine Pollak Ellickson

Papers, ALH, box 19; Jim Gillan, "CIO Activity in Unemployment Situation," 17 January 1938, Mary Heaton Vorse Papers, ALH, box 95; Ralph Hetzel Jr., Report on CIO Unemployment Activities, 12 April 1938, John Brophy Papers, CUA, 1937–1938 file; Montgomery, 144–45.

5. Benjamin to Lewis, 4 November 1937; Benjamin to Sir or Brother, 18 November 1937, CIO Files of John L. Lewis, part 1, reel 6; CIO Central Files, CUA, Labor's Non-Partisan League Series, Workers Alliance File.

6. John L. Lewis to All National and Industrial Unions et al., 7 December 1937, CIO Press Release, 7 December 1937, CIO Central Files, CUA, Workers Alliance File; "Report of John L. Lewis to the First Constitutional Convention of CIO, 14 November 1938, CIO Secretary-Treasurer's Papers, ALH, box 89; *Peoples Press*, 18 December 1937; Dubofsky and Van Tine, 330.

7. Brophy to all Regional Directors and Field Representatives, 30 December 1937, CIO Files of John L. Lewis, part 2, reel 2; Brophy to Local Industrial Unions and Industrial Union Councils, 18 December 1937, Ellickson Papers, box 19.

8. *Peoples Press*, 18 December 1937; Benjamin and Lasser to Ralph Hetzel, Jr., 9 December 1937, Ellickson Papers, box 19.

9. *Emergency Relief in Michigan, 1933–1939*, 12; Walter Galenson, *The CIO Challenge to the AFL: A History of the American Labor Movement, 1935–1941* (Cambridge: Harvard University Press, 1960), 157; Sullivan, 204; Keeran, 194; Rusing, 43–44; "Martin's Report to the Executive Board," *United Automobile Worker*, 14 May 1938, Ganley Papers, box 10.

10. WPA Welfare Department, UAWA, "You Asked for It," 1940, George Clifton Edwards Papers, ALH, series 2, box 11; *Peoples Press*, 6 November 1937; "Re: History of WPA-Welfare Department, UAWA-CIO," 1940, George Edwards Jr. Papers, part 3, box 3; *West Side Conveyor*, 30 November 1937; *Daily Worker*, 18 and 25 November 1937; Sullivan, 205; Polk interview; Interview, Lester Washburn, 1 August 1990, Tomahawk, WI; Frankensteen, "UAW Aids Jobless," *Technical America*, n.d., Frankensteen Papers, box 5.

11. Fred H. Cole to Richard W. Reading, 25 January 1938, MP, 1938, box 3; Hartley, "Report of Welfare and Unemployment Committee, Local 174," 1 ; Sullivan, 194, 217.

12. Martin to All Local Unions of UAW, 9 December 1937, Kraus Papers, box 11; Victor Reuther, Edwards interviews. See also Local 174 Joint Council Minutes, 4 December 1937, Daniel M. Gallagher Papers, AHL, box 3.

13. *United Automobile Worker*, 18 December 1937, Joe Brown Papers, box 31; ibid., 11 December 1937, ALH, UAW Biography File; "Re: History WPA-Welfare Department, UAWA-CIO"; "You Asked for It"; *Detroit News*,

12 December 1937; Riddle, 28–29; Henry Kraus, *Heroes of Unwritten Story: The UAW, 1934–1939* (Urbana: University of Illinois Press, 1995), 366.

14. Report, 11 January 1938, DRS/CPC, file 50.

15. Polk interview.

16. Hartley, "Report of the Welfare and Unemployment Committee, Local 174," 2, 6; *United Automobile Worker*, 11 December 1937 and 15 January 1938, ALH, UAW Biography File; "Re: History of WPA Welfare Department, UAWA-CIO"; Polk interview.

17. *CIO News*, 29 December 1937; *Detroit News*, 20 December 1937, Brown Papers, box 31; *Midwest Labor*, 10 and 24 December 1937; *Peoples Press*, 16 December 1937; Adolph Germer diary, 14, 19, and 21 December, 1937, Germer Papers, box 24.

18. Johnson, 226–27; Barnard, 54–56; Irving Howe and B. J. Widick, *The UAW and Walter Reuther* (New York: Random House, 1949), 71; Klehr, 7–13; Robert J. Alexander, *The Right Opposition: The Lovestoneites and the International Communist Opposition of the 1930s* (Westport: Greenwood, 1981), 56–60; David Dubinsky and A. H. Raskin, *David Dubinsky: A Life With Labor* (New York: Simon and Schuster, 1977), 241–43; Strachan, Polk, Fischer interviews.

19. Jay Lovestone to Frankensteen, 20 December 1937, W. Jett Lauck Papers, Archives and Manuscripts Division, University of Virginia, Charlottesville, boxes 40, 96; ALH, box 1; Jay Lovestone Papers, Stanford, Hoover Institution on War, Revolution, and Peace, box 629; *Workers Age*, 18 December 1937; Lovestone, *New Frontiers for Labor* (New York: Workers Age Press, 1938), 14, in Michigan State University Radicalism Collection. See also "Report of Lester Washburn, President of Local 182-UAW at Joint Council Meeting of 18 December 1937," Lovestone Papers, box 567 and Kraus, *Heroes of Unwritten Story*, 366–367.

20. Edwards interview; Mortimer, "Only a Determined Policy Will Halt Mass Layoffs and Depression," December 1937; "Layoffs," ca. 10 December 1937, Kraus Papers, box 11; Lovestone to Lauck, 4 January 1938, Lauck Papers, ALH, box 1; Clayton W. Fountain, *Union Guy* (New York: Viking, 1949), 80.

21. Memorandum, 15 December 1937, UAW Public Relations Department Papers, Ford Series, box 2; "Draft Resolution, Unity Caucus," 9 December 1937, Kraus Papers, box 12.

22. Executive Board Minutes, 18 January 1938, Sugar Papers, box 79; "Resolution," 18 January 1938, in Department Reports, Board Meeting, 4 December 1939, George Addes Papers, ALH, box 1; Martin to All Local Unions, 20 January 1938, Kraus Papers, box 12; *Daily Worker*, 8 and 24

January 1938; R. J. Thomas to Hopkins, 6 January 1938, NA, RG 69, WPA Central Files, State Series, Michigan, box 1571; Press Release, 26 January 1938, Brown Papers, box 31; *Socialist Call*, 29 January 1938; Galenson 157.

23. Carl Haessler, "First Act of Detroit Mayor is to Sabotage Relief," Federated Press, 12 January 1938, Brown Papers, box 25; Riddle, 10–11.

24. "Consultation Visit, Confidential," 23 February 1938, Family Service Association of America Papers, Social Welfare History Archives, Minneapolis, University of Minnesota, box 57; "You Asked for It"; Harris to Reading, 7 January 1938, MP, 1938, box 9; *Detroit News*, 8, 9, and 11 January 1938, Brown Papers, box 31; Germer diary, 12 and 13 January 1938, Germer Papers, box 25; Sullivan, 207.

25. Germer diary, 18 January 1938, Germer Papers, box 25; "Frankensteen Radio Talk," 8 March 1938, Frankensteen Papers, box 4; *United Automobile Worker*, 15 January 1937, ALH, UAW Biographical File, Richard Leonard; Leonard to Reading, 8 January 1937, MP, 1938, box 8.

26. Sullivan, 209–211; Press Releases, 21, 26 and 29, January 1938, Brown Papers, box 31; Germer diary, 25 January 1938, Germer Papers, box 25; Leonard and Germer to Reading (telegram), 19 January 1938, MP, 1938, box 9; "Re: History of WPA-Welfare Department, UAWA-CIO."

27. Nat Wald and A. J. Tarini to Prentiss Brown, 7 January 1938; Niles to Brown, 14 January 1938; UAW WPA Welfare Department to Abner Larned, 9 January 1938; NA, RG 69, WPA Central Files, State Series, Michigan, box 1572; Minutes, State Emergency Welfare Commission of Michigan, 9 March 1938, Frankensteen Papers, box 4; *United Automobile Worker*, 15 January 1938, UAW Biographical File, Leonard File.

28. "Re: History of WPA-Welfare Department UAWA-CIO"; Sullivan, 216; *Milwaukee Sentinel*, 11 January 1938; *United Automobile Worker*, 15 January 1938; Germer diary, 12, 13 and 14 January 1938; Germer Papers, box 25; Gillan, "CIO Activity in Unemployment Situation"; Lorin Cary, "Adolph Germer, Farm Labor Agitator to Labor Professional," (doctoral dissertation, University of Wisconsin, 1968), 119; Riddle, 12; for Martin's detailed brief on Michigan's WPA needs, see Martin, "Memorandum," February 1938, NA, RG 69, WPA Central Files, State Series, Michigan, box 1571; *United Automobile Worker*, 5 February 1938, Brown Papers, box 31.

29. Leonard and Germer to All Unions Affiliated with the CIO, 26 and 27 January 1938; ibid., 21 February 1938; Emil Mazey To Highland Park Chief Stewards, 28 January 1938; Edwards to Brothers, 28 January 1938, UAW Local 212 Papers, boxes 4, 5; Press Releases, 27 January and 1 February 1938, Brown Papers, box 31; Edwards to "Darlings," 3 December 1937;

Edwards to Family, 9 January 1938, George Clifton Edwards Sr. Papers, series 2, box 11. Lovestoneite endorsement of UAW's activism on behalf of the unemployed is clearly stated in "Memorandum on the Relief and Unemployment Situation," 2 February 1938, Lovestone Papers, box 566.

30. *West Side Conveyor*, 1 February 1938; Joint Council Minutes, 22 January 1938, Gallagher Papers, box 3; Mortimer, 149; "You Asked for It."

31. Lewis to Martin, 3 February 1938; Leonard to Lewis, 1 February 1938, CIO Files of John L. Lewis, part 1, reel 2; Germer diary, 3 February 1938, Germer Papers, box 25; Edwards interview; Interview, Henry Kraus, ALH, 98–99; Mortimer, 149.

32. Federated Press, Press Release, 7 February 1938, Brown Papers, box 31; *Detroit Free Press*, 5 February 1938, Brown Clippings, vol. 12; Martin, "Notes for Mass Meeting in Cadillac Square," February 1938, Martin Papers, box 3; *Daily Worker*, 5 February 1938; Mortimer, 149; Sullivan, 216; Piven and Cloward, 88–89; Kraus, *Heroes of Unwritten Story*, 366.

33. "You Asked for It"; *Socialist Call*, 12 February 1938; *Daily Worker*, 5 February 1938; Mortimer, 149; Germer to Lewis, 4 February 1938, the CIO Files of John L. Lewis, part 1, reel 2; Germer diary, 4 February 1938, Germer Papers, box 25.

34. Brophy, "The CIO and Unemployment," 13 February 1938, Brophy Papers, Speeches File, 1938.

35. Frankensteen, "Press Release," 10 February 1938; Federated Press, Press Release, 7 February 1938, Brown Papers, box 31; Mortimer, 150; Edwards interview; Leonard to Lewis (telegram), 6 February 1938; Germer to Lewis, 4 February 1938, the CIO Files of John L. Lewis, series 1, reel 2; "Re: History of WPA-Welfare Department, UAWA-CIO."

36. *Workers Age*, 12 February 1938; Sullivan, 217; Martin to Lauck, 18 February 1938, Lauck Papers, box 45; Press Releases, 10 and 15 February 1938, Brown Papers, box 31; Frankensteen to Reading, 15 February 1938, Frankensteen Papers, box 1; Rusing, 48; Alan Brinkley, "The New Deal and the Idea of the State," in Fraser and Gerstle, 96.

37. "All Unemployed and WPA Workers" (handbill), 28 March 1938; "The UAW is Organizing Its Members on WPA Jobs . . . ," (handbill), 11 March 1938, Brown Papers, box 33; Hartley to Reading, 20 April 1938, MP, 1938, box 9; "Everybody Out! Picket Line" (handbill), March 1938, Reuther Papers, box 1; "Confidential Information on Communist and UAW Activities," 16 February 1938, DRS/CPC, file 50; *West Side Conveyor*, 29 March 1938. For discussion of union efforts to modify some of WPA's more arbitrary labor practices, see Rusing, 91–92.

38. Martin to All Local Unions, 10 February 1938, Reuther Papers, box 1; "Re: History of WPA-Welfare Department, UAWA-CIO"; Rusing, 91.

39. Reuther to Joseph Schlossberg, 14 March 1938, International Ladies Garment Workers Union (hereafter ILGWU) Papers, Ithaca, Labor-Management Documentation Center, Margaret Catherwood Library, Cornell University, Joseph Schlossberg File, box 143; "You Asked for It"; Riddle, 16–17; Polk interview.

40. Germer diary, 24, 25, and 26 March 1938, Germer Papers, box 25; Brophy to Mortimer, 24 March 1938; Mortimer to Brophy, 22 March 1938, Brophy Papers, 1937–1938 File; Kraus Papers, box 12.

41. "You Asked for It"; "Re: History of WPA-Welfare Department, UAWA-CIO"; *Detroit News*, 24 March 1938; "Immediate Release," 17 March 1938, Brown Papers, box 31; Germer diary, 31 March and 1 April 1938, Germer Papers, box 25; *Detroit News*, 13 March 1938.

42. *Detroit News*, 21 March 1938, Brown Papers, box 31; "Statements and Accusations Reported to Have Been Made by Bob Travis in Lansing on March 30 and Replies Thereto by Homer Martin," 30 March 1938, Martin Papers, box 3; "Re: History WPA-Welfare Department, UAWA-CIO"; "You Asked for It."

43. Len De Caux, *Labor Radical: From the Wobblies to CIO* (Boston: Beacon, 1970), 306–7; Victor Reuther interview; *Detroit News*, 19 and 27 March 1936, NA, RG 69, Division of Information, Clippings File, 1936–1944, box 281.

44. Author unidentified, draft manuscript, Mary Heaton Vorse Papers, ALH, box 95; Hartley, "Report of the Welfare and Unemployment Committee, Local 174"; Interview, John W. Anderson, UAW Oral History Collection, 70–71; Polk interview; Homer Martin to All Local Unions, 10 February 1938 and 9 April 1938, Reuther Papers, box 1; Sullivan, 206; Frankensteen, "Tactics, Strategy, Conditions of Ford Organizing Drive," ca. January 1938, Lovestone Papers, box 566. Montgomery and Schatz have demonstrated that the UE used its WPA auxiliary in a similar way. The result was a new "link between the industrial workers of the community as a whole and the new industrial unions." See Montgomery and Schatz, 146.

45. Leonard to All Local Unions, 21 March 1938, Martin to All Locals, 9 April 1938, Reuther Papers, box 1; "Immediate Release," 18 March 1938, George Edwards Jr. Papers, part 3, box 3; "Leonard Appointed Director of Drive to Organize Project Workers," *United Automobile Worker*, 19 March 1938, in UAW Vertical File, ALH; Minutes, International Executive Board, UAW, 9–20 May 1938, 13, Sugar Papers, box 54; Joseph Alsop and Robert Kintner, "The Capitol Parade," n.d. (1938), Vorse Papers, box 95; Memorandum, 3 June 1938, 11–12, Frankensteen Papers, box 4; "Report of Homer

Martin," Special Convention, United Automobile Workers of America, Detroit, 4 March 1939, Offices of Allied Industrial Workers, Milwaukee; Rusing, 93–94.

46. Anderson interview, 70–71; *West Side Conveyor*, 4 June 1938; *United Automobile Worker*, 28 May 1938, Brown Papers, box 31; "You Asked for It"; Polk interview; Rusing, 93–97; Sullivan, 217.

47. Kintner and Alsop; "Digest of Proceedings of Conference of Representatives of the Affiliated Organizations of the CIO," 12–13 April 1938, CIO Files of John L. Lewis, part 2 reel 3; "Afternoon Session of First Day," 12 April 1938; Hetzel, "Report on CIO Unemployment Activities," 12 April 1938; "Report of Director John Brophy to Meeting of the CIO," 12 April 1938, Brophy Papers, 1937–1938 File; Hetzel, "CIO Statement," ca. 1938, Kraus Papers, box 12; "Report of Chairman John L. Lewis, to the First Constitutional Convention of the CIO," 14 November 1938, CIO Secretary-Treasurer's Files, ALH, box 89; De Caux, 306–7; Martin, "The Successes of the UAWA—What They Mean to American Labor," 26 April 1938; "Speech Delivered by President Homer Martin in Lansing," 1 April 1938, Martin Papers, box 3.

48. Hetzel to Regional Directors et al., 1 July 1938; New Relief and Recovery Bill, 25 June 1938 (reprint), Frankensteen Papers, boxes 1, 4; Irving Bernstein, *A Caring Society: The New Deal, the Worker, and the Great Depression* (Boston: Houghton, Mifflin, 1985), 112–13; James T. Patterson, *Congressional Conservatism and the New Deal: the Growth of the Conservative Coalition in Congress, 1933–1939* (Lexington: University of Kentucky Press, 1967), 238; "Three and a Half Million Federal Relief Jobs for the Unemployed," May 1938, Gallagher Papers, ALH, box 2; "Labor's Program for Jobs" (leaflet), 1938, CIO Central Files, CUA, Labor's Non-Partisan League Series; "Statement of John L. Lewis," 2 May 1938, Brophy Papers, 1937–1938 File.

49. Hetzel, "Memorandum for Mr. Lewis," 7 July 1938; "Organization of WPA Project Workers," 30 June 1938, CIO Files of John L. Lewis, part 2, reel 3; "Memorandum," 3 June 1938, Frankensteen Papers, box 4; "Report of Chairman John L. Lewis to the First Constitutional Convention of the CIO."

50. Martin and Addes to the Officers and Members of Local Unions, ca April 1938, UAW Local 212 Papers, ALH, box 6; Anderson interview, 71; Martin to All Local Unions, n.d., Kraus Papers, box 12; Reuther Papers, box 1; Minutes, UAWA Executive Board, 9–20 May 1938, 13, 48, Sugar Papers, box 54, 79; *Socialist Call*, 28 May 1938.

51. "You Asked for It"; *United Automobile Worker*, 28 May 1938; Sullivan, 206; Rusing, 96–97; Riddle, 35–36.

52. *West Side Conveyor*, 21 May 1938; "You Asked for It"; *United Automobile Worker*, 28 May 1938; "Joint Council Minutes," West Side Local 174, 14 May 1938, Gallagher Papers, box 3; N. Dragon to Frankensteen, 1 March 1938, Frankensteen Papers, box 1; Sullivan, 206; Rusing, 96–97.

53. "Report on UAWA Meeting at Baby Creek Park," 5 June 1938, DRS/CPC, file 50.

54. Immediate Release, 8 and 20 May 1938, Brown Papers, boxes 13, 31; "Re: History of WPA-Welfare Department, UAWA-CIO"; "Report of Homer Martin," 4 March 1939; *CIO News*, 30 April 1938; GEB, "Resolution," ca. May 1938, Reuther Papers, box 17; Martin and Addes to Officers and Members of Local Unions Affiliated with IUUAWA, Metropolitan Area of Detroit, 18 June 1938, George Clifton Edwards Papers, series 2, box 11; Barnard, 60.

55. Keeran, 196–97; Johnson, 231; Barnard, 60; Frankensteen to All Officers and International Executive Board Members, 21 April 1938, Frankensteen Papers, box 1; "Dear Fellow Worker," 24 March 1938, Kraus Papers, box 13; William B. Mason to All Local Unions in the UAW, 6 May 1938, UAW Local 212 Papers, box 5; Martin to All Officers and Members, International Union, UAWA (enclosure), 16 May 1938, Lauck Papers, box 45; "Report of R. J. Thomas, President, IUUAWA-CIO," May 1939, 1, Ethel Polk Papers, ALH, box 1. For discussion of the growing Lovestoneite influence on Martin and within UAW, see Alexander, 56–59.

56. Memorandum, 3 June 1938, 12, Frankensteen Papers, box 3; "Report of Homer Martin," 4 March 1939; see also Keeran, 197.

57. Taylor to All Local Unions, 6 May 1938; Taylor to All Units of Dodge Local 3, May 1938; "Unemployed Youth: Meeting of Special Committee," 18 May 1938, John Zaremba Papers, ALH, box 4; Leonard to All Local Unions, 23 April 1938; Taylor to All CIO Locals, 11 May 1938, UAW Local 212 Papers, box 5; P.E. Worley to Frankensteen, 19 May 1938, Frankensteen Papers, box 1; Niles to Taylor, 17 May 1938; Zaremba to Hopkins, 21 May 1938; Gill to George D. O'Brien, 7 May 1938, NA, RG 69, WPA Central Files, WPA State Series, Michigan, box 1572; *West Side Conveyor*, 29 April 1938; "Immediate Release," 20 April 1938, Brown Papers, box 31; Hartley to Rose Lipson, 12 April 1938, MP, 1938, Welfare, box 9.

58. "Information," 1 June 1938; "Report of Investigation," 3 June 1938; "Supplementing Report of June 3rd, 1938," 17 June 1938, DRS/CPC, Files 44, 50; Riddle, 33–34.

59. To Fellow Member, Local 203, 3 June 1938; "Dear Comrade," 4 June 1938, DRS/CPC, file 50.

60. Delegation to Governor Murphy, Minutes, 14 June 1938, Ganley Papers, box 8; "Dear Comrade," 4 June 1938, DRS/CPC, file 50; Riddle, 34.

61. *UAW-WPA Department Bulletin*, August 1938, Polk Papers, box 1; "Information on Communist Activity," 14 June 1938, DRS/CPC, file 50.

62. *Work*, 30 July 1938; "Bulletin: Unemployed," June 1938; Handbill, 14 June 1938, Reuther Papers, box 1; "Report of the Welfare and Unemployment Committee, Local 174," 7.

63. *UAW-WPA Department Bulletin*, August 1938, Polk Papers, box 1.

64. Taylor to Suzanne, n.d. (1938), Reuther Papers, box 1; Germer to Lewis, 5 August 1938, CIO Files of John L. Lewis, part 1, reel 2; Memoranda of Conversations (William Munger and Martin, Munger and Lovestone), 3–5 August 1938, Daniel Bell Papers, New York, Taminent Institute, Robert Wagner Archives, box 3; "Who Are the Labor Splitters?"; "Report of Homer Martin, 4 March 1939." For reaction to Martin's actions, see "Press Release," "Ed Hall on WJR," 4 August 1938; "Frankensteen Press Conference," n.d. (1938), Frankensteen Papers, box 3.

65. *UAW-WPA Department Bulletin*, August 1938, Polk Papers, box 1; Polk interview.

66. *UAW-WPA Department Bulletin*, August 1938, Polk Papers, box 1.

Chapter 7

1. Fischer interview; Polk interview; Lovestone to Lauck, 4 January 1938; Lovestone to Frankensteen, 20 December 1937, Lovestone Papers, box 629; Lauck Papers, boxes 40, 45; Edward Barth and Rudolph Schware to Reuther, 19 April 1938; Wayne County Workers Alliance of America to Nat Wald, 15 April 1938, Reuther Papers, box 1; Hartley, "Report of the Welfare and Unemployment Committee, Local 174," 1, 8.

2. *Work*, 9 April 1938; Workers Alliance of America, *Proceedings, Fourth Annual Convention*, Cleveland, 1938, 25–26; Lasser to Lewis, 12 April 1938, CIO Files of John L. Lewis, part 2, reel 3; "Morning Session of Second Day," CIO Conference, 13 April 1938, Brophy Papers, 1937–1938 File.

3. H. B., "Unemployment: An Old Struggle Under New Conditions," *The Communist* 17 (May 1938), 428; *Daily Worker*, 18 April 1938; *Proceedings, Fourth Annual Convention*, 26; Lovestone to Dubinsky, 4 April 1938, ILGWU Papers, box 115; see also *Work*, 21 May 1938; Stockham, 81–2.

4. *Proceedings, Fourth Annual Convention*, 27; "Resolution on CIO, Adopted by National Executive Board, Workers Alliance of America," 5 June 1938; Lasser, et al., to James Carey and Ralph Hetzel, 6 June 1938, CIO Files of John L. Lewis, Part 1, reel 6.

5. "Memorandum-Workers Alliance," 13 July 1938, Benjamin Papers, 1938 File; see also Draper Papers, Benjamin File, series 2.3, reel 9; *Proceedings, Fourth Annual Convention*, 27; "Agenda, Committee on Unemployment," 6 June 1938; "Memorandum on CIO Unemployment and Relief Division," 31 May 1938, Frankensteen Papers, box 4.

6. "Memorandum-Workers Alliance," 13 July 1938; "Conclusions of the Joint Meeting of Committee on Unemployment and Regional Directors," 15 June 1938; CIO Files of John L. Lewis, part 2, reel 3; "Abstract of Minutes, Joint Meeting of Committee on Unemployment and Regional Directors," 15 June 1938, Brophy Papers, 1937–1938 File; Stockham, 87–88.

7. "Report of Chairman John L. Lewis to the First Constitutional Convention of the CIO"; Reuther interview; "Memorandum—Workers Alliance," 13 July 1938; *Proceedings, Fourth Annual Convention*, 27.

8. *Proceedings, Fourth Annual Convention*, 27; "Memorandum on Proposals of CIO for WPA and Relief Division," ca. August 1938; Lasser to A.D. Lewis, 8 August 1938, CIO Files of John L. Lewis, part 1, reel 6.

9. Lasser to Dubinsky (with enclosure), 10 October 1938, ILGWU Papers, box 159; Lasser, "Work and Security," 23 September 1938, MSU Radicalism Collection; *Proceedings, Fourth Annual Convention*, 27–28, 52, 98–99; *Daily Worker*, 27 September 1938.

10. "Report of the Committee on the Officers' Report," 13 November 1938, CIO Secretary-Treasurers Papers, box 89.

11. "Memorandum—Workers Alliance," 13 July 1938; *Daily Worker*, 26 September 1938; Nels Anderson, *The Right to Work* (New York: Modern Age, 1939), 120; Stockham, 19, 166.

12. Rusing, 85; *Work*, 24 September 1938; *Proceedings, Fourth Annual Convention*; Alston interview.

13. Abner Larned, "Final Report of the WPA," (Detroit: WPA, 1943), 48; Sullivan, 168; "Smash Wall Street's Sabotage of Business Recovery" (Detroit: Communist Party of Michigan, 1937); see also Anderson, *The Right to Work*, 115–16.

14. Fountain, 76–79; Hartley, "Report of the Welfare and Unemployment Committee, Local 174," 2, 3, 5; Rudolph Schware to FDR, 15 March 1938; Niles to Schware, 29 March 1938, NA, RG 69, WPA Central Files, State Series, Michigan, box 1570; "Single Men's Unemployment League, *News*," 2 February 1938; "Attention, Unemployed," January 1938, Brown Papers, box 9; *Peoples Press*, 30 November 1937; *Daily Worker*, 17 January 1938; *Work*, 9 April 1938.

15. "Call for Eastside Federation of Unemployed," 21 April 1938; "Mass Meeting for All Unemployed" (broadside), UAW Local 212 Papers, box 5; "Information on Communist Activities, Meetings, Etc.," 5 March 1938; "Confidential Information on Communist and UAW Activities," 16 February 1938, DRS/CPC, file 50. The Alliance's activities received warm support from the developing National Negro Congress, which in April 1938 endorsed both it and the Renters and Consumers League. Resolution, "Program," 23 April 1938, National Negro Congress Third City Wide Conference, Detroit, National Negro Congress Papers, roll 8.

16. *Ford-Dearborn Worker*, March 1938; 1 May 1938, Kraus Papers, box 16.

17. Mazey to Detroit Welfare Commission, 25 March 1938; M. J. Furay to Local 212, UAW Local 212 Papers, box 5; *Detroit News*, 12 March 1938, Brown Papers, box 25; John Netschke to Reading, 11 February 1938; Tom Parry and George Mitchell to Reading, 12 February 1938 (telegram); Wald to Reading, 11 February 1938 (telegram); Hartley to Reading, 12 February 1938 (telegram); William Hulle to Reading, 11 February 1938 (telegram), MP, 1938, Welfare, box 9; *Daily Worker*, 18 January 1938; Sullivan, 206–7, 213, 217. Between 1 January and 17 April 1938, twenty unemployed demonstrations occurred in Detroit, most of them sponsored by either the Workers Alliance or the UAW. "Reply to Attached Letter," 19 April 1938, DRS/CPC, file 30.

18. Schware and Edward L. Barth to Reuther, 19 April 1938, Reuther Papers, box 1; *Work*, 9 April 1938; Levenstein, 55.

19. Hartley, "Report of the Welfare and Unemployment Committee, Local 174," 8; *New York Times*, 18 April 1939; Germer diary, 4 May 1938, Germer Papers, box 25; Nat Wald to Reuther, 15 April 1938, Reuther Papers, box 1.

20. Fred J. Dalton to John L. Lewis, 4 August 1938; Alexander W. Burnas to Lewis, 7 August 1938; Robert L. Poe to Lewis, 27 July 1938; Jacob Lorenz to Lewis, 1 August 1938; Otha Lowry to Lewis, 2 August 1938, CIO Files of John L. Lewis, part 1, reel 2; Benjamin to Aubrey Williams, 28 January 1938; Niles to Benjamin, 5 February 1938; Nims to Howard O. Hunter, 10 December 1937; Workers Alliance, Pontiac to Niles, 26 August 1938; Niles to Nims, 26 August 1938, NA, RG 69, WPA Central Files, State Series, Michigan, box 1573.

21. Brophy Speech, 22 April 1938, Brophy Papers, Speeches File, 1937–1938; Niles to Benjamin, 25 February 1938; Nims to Niles, 19 February 1938; Arthur Knapp to Hopkins, 1 August 1938; Niles to Knapp, 9 August 1938; Niles to Mildred Wright, 15 March 1938; Wright to Hopkins, 10 March 1938; Niles to Howard Wilson, 24 March 1938; Tom Mattimore and

Stanley Moore to Hopkins, 4 January 1938; Hopkins to Mattimore, 13 January 1938, NA, RG 69, WPA Central Files, State Series, Michigan, boxes 1569, 1570, 1571.

22. *Grand Rapids Herald*, 15 February 1938, NA, RG 69, WPA Division of Information, Clippings File, 1936–1944, box 281; P. B. Jensen to WPA, 16 February 1938, NA RG 69, WPA Central Files, State Series, Michigan, box 1570; George W. Welsh to Prentiss Brown, 12 April 1938, Prentiss Brown Papers, Ann Arbor, Michigan Historical Collections, Bentley Library, University of Michigan, box 2; Interview, Leonard Woodcock (telephone), 2 October 1990. For discussion of Welsh's background, including his role in the controversy over the scrip system and the delivery of welfare services in Grand Rapids, see Harms, 3–8, 13, 17.

23. Albert De Byle to FDR, 1 June 1938; Neal O. Eastman to Harrington, ca. June 1938, NA, RG 69, WPA Central Files, State Series, Michigan, boxes 1570, 1573; *Grand Rapids Press*, 13 April 1938.

24. *Detroit News*, 18, 19, 20, and 25 August 1938; *Lansing State Journal*, 30 June, and 20 August 1938, NA, RG 69, WPA Central Files, Division of Information, Clippings File, 1936–1944, box 259; Lasser to Niles, 3 August 1938; Niles to Lasser, 13 September 1938, NA, RG 69, WPA Central Files, General File, 1935–1944, box 58; "Immediate Release," March 2, 1938, Brown Papers, box 31.

25. Lawrence R. Klein to Lorence, 12 December 1990; Leon K. Zimmerman to Edwards, 6 April 1938, George Edwards Jr. Papers, part 2, box 5; *Lansing State Journal*, 27 March 1938, NA, RG 69, WPA Central Files, Division of Information, Clippings File, 1936–1944, box 281; Workers Alliance Local G-1006 to Hopkins, 23 April 1938, NA, RG 69, WPA Central Files, State Series, Michigan, box 1571.

26. Edsforth, 146, 184; Chafe, 234–36; Dollinger interview (Lorence).

27. Dollinger interview (Lorence); Klasey Interview, 40–43; Edsforth, 184; *United Automobile Worker* (Flint Edition), 8 January 1938.

28. *Flint Daily Journal*, 28 March 1938; *United Automobile Worker* (Flint Edition), 8, 19, and 26 March 1938; Edsforth, 184.

29. International Representatives, Local 156 to Lewis, 12 February 1938, CIO Files of John L. Lewis, part 1, reel 2; Klasey Interview, 41–42; Edsforth, 184.

30. Frank Johnson to Green, 10 April 1938; John Reid to Green, 19 April 1938; Green to Reid, 15 April 1938, AFL Papers, series 11, file C, box 39; "Demonstrate," 9 April 1938, Kraus Papers, box 16; *Socialist Call*, 9 April 1938; *United Automobile Worker*, 9 April 1938.

31. *United Automobile Worker* (Flint Edition), 9 April 1938; *Detroit News*, 10 April 1938, Brown Papers, Clippings Book, vol. 12, p. 62; *Socialist Call*, 9 and 16 April 1938.

32. *United Automobile Worker*, 7 May 1938, Brown Papers, box 31; Gilbert R. Clark to Hopkins, 29 April 1938; Niles to Clark, 2 May 1938; Genessee County Workers Alliance to FDR, 22 April 1938, NA, RG 69, WPA Central Files, State Series, Michigan, boxes 1570, 1571; *Flint Daily Journal*, 28 March 1938; Klasey interview, 41.

33. Mortimer to Ed Geiger, 9 June 1938; Kraus Papers, box 13.

34. *United Automobile Worker* (Flint Edition), 23 July 1938; *Detroit Free Press*, 20 July 1938, NA, RG 69, WPA Central Files, Division of Information, Clippings File, 1936–1944, box 259; *Work*, 24 September 1938; Edsforth, 184; Chafe, 236.

35. *Manistique Times*, 9 June 1938; Bernhardt, 57.

36. *Timber Worker*, 27 November 1937.

37. Matt Savola to F. Granger, 31 December 1937, NA, RG 69, WPA Central Files, State Series, Michigan, box 1571; Savola interview; *Midwest Labor*, 7 and 14 January 1938; *Timber Worker*, 22 January and 5 February 1938.

38. By June 1938, 1800 UP lumberjacks were employed by WPA. *Midwest Labor*, 13 May and 11 March 1938; "Minutes of the Executive Board Meeting of Local 15," 13 February 1938; Herbert Norris to B. J. McCarty, 12 March 1938, International Woodworkers of America Papers, Eugene, University of Oregon Library, Local 12-15 File; Savola interview; *Timber Worker*, 5 February and 4 June 1938; Minutes, State Emergency Welfare Relief Commission, 9 March 1938, Frankensteen Papers, box 4; W. D. Connor to G. R. Berkeland, 20 June 1938, Connor Land and Lumber Company Papers, SHSW, Stevens Point, Area Research Center, University of Wisconsin-Stevens Point, box 10.

39. *Midwest Labor*, 8 July 1938.

40. Germer Diary, 25 and 27 August 1938, Germer Papers, box 25.

41. Interview, Edwin Spiegal, Hancock, 10 July 1989; Spiegal to Lorence, 17 August 1989; Michigan State Police File, 26 December 1942, Complaint 80-1446 (Calumet); "Request for Information Concerning the Officers, Activities, and Background of the Workers Alliance in the Vicinity of Houghton and Hancock, Michigan," Benjamin Papers, Michigan State Police File. The persistence of depressed economic conditions in Houghton and Keewenaw Counties is discussed in Gates, 166–69; see also Lankton, 256–58.

42. Spiegal interview.

43. Henry Kurre and Eric Mikkola to FDR, 16 August 1938; Petition to Hopkins, August 1938; "Resolution," August 1938; Niles to Carl E. Skogan, 19 August 1938, NA, RG 69, WPA Central Files, State Series, Michigan, box 1569; Spiegal to Lorence, 17 August 1989.

44. Interview, Carl Raymond and Melvin Anderson, Escanaba, 13 July 1989; "Resolution," n.d., NA, RG 69, WPA Central Files, State Series, Michigan, box 1570; Michigan State Police File, Raymond Anderson, 1949–1950, in possession of Carl Raymond Anderson, Escanaba.

45. Anderson interview; Michigan State Police File, Raymond Anderson.

46. *Crystal Falls Diamond Drill*, 11 July, 6 August, 3 September 1937 and 8 July 1938; Kangas, Spiegal, Walli interviews.

47. Martel to Ingram, 25 August 1938; Ingram to Martel, 24 August 1938, Metro Detroit AFL-CIO Papers, box 23; Taylor to All Local Unions, IUUAWA, 23 August 1938, UAW Local 212 Papers, box 5; *Work*, 13 August 1938.

48. *Marquette Mining Journal*, 30 August 1938; *Work*, 25 August and 30 September 1938; *Detroit News*, 30 August 1938, NA, RG 69, WPA Central Files, Division of Information, Clippings File, 1936–1944, box 368; Walli interview; Murphy, "To the Members of the Legislature," 29 August 1930, Murphy Papers, box 78.

49. *Work*, 25 August and 10 September 1938; *Marquette Mining Journal*, 30 and 31 August 1938; *Detroit News*, 30 August 1938, NA, RG 69, WPA Central Files, Division of Information, Clippings File, 1936–1944, box 369.

50. WPA Department, IUUAWA to FDR, 22 September 1938; Paul Silver to WPA, 24 September 1938; Silver to FDR, 23 September 1938; NA, RG 69, WPA Central Files, State Series, Michigan, box 1572; "Immediate Release," 22 September 1938, Brown Papers, box 31.

51. "Immediate Release," 27 October 1938, Brown Papers, box 31; Taylor to All UAW Locals and Locals Affiliated with the CIO, 10 September 1938, Reuther Papers, box 1; Alan Strachan to Hopkins, 22 September 1938 (telegram); Russell Burghorn to FDR, 15 September 1938 (telegram); Niles to Burghorn, 20 September 1938; David Gilman to FDR, 19 September 1938; Niles to Zaremba, 20 September 1938, NA, RG 69, WPA Central Files, State Series, Michigan, boxes 1570, 1571, 1572.

52. Polk interview.

Chapter 8

1. *Socialist Call*, 16 July 1938; Arthur McDowell to Socialist Comrades in Auto, 28 July 1938; "Registered Socialist Members of Auto Workers Union," 1938, Bell Papers, box 30; Socialist Party Papers, reel 35.

2. Fischer interview.

3. Klehr, 247–48; William W. Weinstone and B. K. Gebert, "Factionalism—the Enemy of the Auto Workers," ca. June 1938, MSU Radicalism Collection; *Socialist Call*, 16 July 1938; Michigan Auto League, "Socialist Policy in Auto," 2–4 July 1938, Socialist Party Papers, reel 35. Socialist-Communist tensions in 1938 are summarized in Keeran, 197–98, 203; Johnson, 227, 231; Barnard, 59–60; Alexander, 58. The initial tendency of UAW Socialists to cooperate with the CP is discussed in Levenstein, 108.

4. "Auto League Report #1," 7 June 1938, Bell Papers, box 30; "Confidential Report of the Socialist Party on the Inner Situation in the Auto Union," 16 June 1938, Sugar Papers, box 41; see also Kraus Papers, box 16; Edwards to Family, 12 June 1938, George Clifton Edwards Papers, series 2, box 11.

5. "Auto League Report #1."

6. "Auto League Report #8," 29 October 1938, Socialist Party Papers, reel 35; Taylor to All Stewards, 15 July 1938; Taylor to All Regional Directors, Local Union Presidents, WPA Organizing Committees, and Welfare Committee Chairmen, 21 July 1938; "Notes from Foreman's Handbook, for the Information of UAW-WPA Stewards," ca. July 1938, UAW Local 212 Papers, boxes 5, 6; *Workers Age*, 9 July 1938.

7. Alan Strachan, "History of the 1938 Michigan Political Campaign," 18 September 1940, Strachan Papers, ALH, box 2; *Work*, 28 August and 10 September 1938; Germer diary, 1 November 1938, Germer Papers, box 25; Germer to Lewis, 30 September 1938, CIO Files of John L. Lewis, part 2, reel 11; "Communists Back Murphy In Fight to Win Michigan Over to Reds," Michigan Republican Party, Murphy Papers, box 57; Arthur D. Maguire to FDR, 26 October 1938, FDR Papers, POF 300; Fountain, 87–88. For Red Squad observations on the Communist analysis of Murphy's defeat, see "Information on Communist Activity," 26 November 1938, DRS/CPC, file 50.

8. Radio Address by Governor Frank Murphy, WJR, Detroit, 29 October 1938; Radio Address by Governor Frank Murphy, WXYZ–Detroit, 2 November 1938, Murphy Papers, box 78.

9. David Halkola, "The Citadel Crumbles: Political Change in the Upper Peninsula of Michigan in the Great Depression," in *A Half Century Ago: Michigan in the Great Depression, Symposium Proceedings* (East Lansing: Michigan State University, 1980), 75–77; Savola, "Radio Address," 14 October 1938, International Woodworkers of America Papers, Local 12-15 File; John B. Bennett, speeches, 4 November 1938, ca. October 1938 and 22 August 1938, John B. Bennett Papers, Ann Arbor, Michigan Historical Collections, University of Michigan, box 1; *Crystal Falls Diamond Drill*, 8 July 1938.

10. Strachan, "History of the 1938 Michigan Campaign"; Mort J. Furay, "The Results of the Michigan Elections," 1938, Labor's Non-Partisan League Papers, box 8; "Governor Murphy's Defeat," CIO National-International Union Files, Catholic University of America, UAW file.

11. Samuel McSeveny, "The Michigan Gubernatorial Campaign of 1938," *Michigan History*, 45 (June 1961), 104, 106–7; Babson, 96; Dudley W. Buffa, *Union Power and American Democracy: The UAW and the Democratic Party, 1935–1972* (Ann Arbor: University of Michigan Press, 1984), 6; Keeran, 203; Barnard, 56; Sullivan, 221.

12. "Auto League Report #8"; Minutes, International Executive Board, IUUAWA, 4–7 October 1938, Martin Papers, box 2; see also CIO Files of John L. Lewis, part 1, reel 2; *CIO News*, 15 October 1938; *Detroit News*, 7, 9, and 11 October 1938; *Detroit Times*, 8 October 1938, Brown Papers, Clippings Books, vol. 13, pp. 99, 102, 106; Mazey to International Executive Board, UAWA, 7 October 1938 (telegram), UAW Local 212 Papers, box 4; Polk interview. The 32-hour minimum appears to have been a line of demarcation acceptable in other industrial unions; see Montgomery, 148–49.

13. Leonard to Hopkins (with enclosure), 6 October 1938; Evelyn Strachan to FDR, 28 September 1938, Niles to E. Strachan, 7 October 1938; Anthony C. Tenerowicz and Cassie A. Domin to Hopkins, 12 October 1938, NA, RG 69, WPA Central Files, State Series, Michigan, boxes 1570, 1572; "Stewards Report—UAWA-WPA Department," 10 November 1938, George Clifton Edwards Papers, series 2, box 11.

14. Williams to Leonard, 29 November 1938; Niles to Leonard, 21 November 1938; Leonard to Hopkins, 15 November 1938; Leonard to FDR, 17 November 1938; Silver to Mr. Marbury, 1 December 1938 (telegram), NA, RG 69, WPA Central Files, State Series, Michigan, box 1572.

15. Leonard to Hopkins, 15 December 1938; Nims to Hopkins, 10 December 1938; Niles to Nims, 14 December 1938; Leonard and Edwards to Hopkins, 17 November 1938 (telegram); Hartley to Hopkins, 26 October 1938, NA, RG 69, WPA Central Files, State Series, Michigan, box 1572; "Report of R. J. Thomas," May 1939, Polk Papers, box 1; "Immediate Re-

lease," 17 November 1938; *United Automobile Worker*, 3 December 1938, Brown Papers, box 31; *Detroit Free Press*, 25 November 1938; *Detroit News*, 17 November and 11 December 1938, NA, RG 69, WPA Central Files, Division of Information, Clippings File, 1936–1944, box 321; Hetzel to Regional Directors et al., 27 October 1938, CIO Files of John L. Lewis, part 2, reel 3; *West Side Conveyor*, 10 December 1938; Sullivan, 221–22.

16. Haessler, "Union Pressure Brings WPA Reforms," 12 December 1938; "Immediate Release," 9 December 1938, Brown Papers, box 31; Germer diary, 10 December 1938, Germer Papers, box 25; Leonard to FDR, 9 December 1938, NA, RG 69, WPA Central Files, State Series, Michigan, box 1572; *Detroit Free Press*, 10 December 1938.

17. Minutes, Executive Board, UAWA, 2–20 November 1938, Sugar Papers, box 79-15; Socialist Auto League, "Auto Report #9," 21 December 1938, Bell Papers, box 30 (see also #8); Martin, "Report," March 1939; George Edwards Jr. to "Darlings," 10 November 1938, George Clifton Edwards Papers, series 2, box 11; GFM to Lovestone, 8 December 1938, ILGWU Papers, box 115; Barnard, 60–61; Galenson, 163; Keeran, 198.

18. "Who Are The Labor Splitters"; GFM to Lovestone, 8 December 1938, ILGWU Papers, box 115.

19. Victor Reuther interview; "Toward Bringing about Unity of the Employed and Unemployed Workers Under the Leadership of the Trade Unions," ca. 1939, Arthur Le Sueur Papers, St. Paul, Minnesota Historical Society, box 4; "The CIO and the Organized Unemployed," ca. 1939, Benjamin Papers, AFL Committee for Unemployment Insurance File; "Workers Alliance Convention," 5 October 1938; Jack Stachel to All State Secretaries, 27 December 1938, Draper Papers, series 2.3, reel 9; Martin, "Report," March 1939; "Auto Report #9."

20. "For Immediate Release," 9 January 1939; *Union News Service*, 6 January 1939; "Memo from Ralph Hetzel for Mr. L. Prior to Talk with Harry Hopkins," December 1938, CIO Files of John L. Lewis, part 3, reels 4, 3; Hetzel to Presidents of National and International Unions, 23 December 1938, Milwaukee, Area Research Center, University of Wisconsin–Milwaukee, Milwaukee County Industrial Union Council Papers, box 1.

21. George Edwards Jr. to George Clifton Edwards, 16 January 1939, George Clifton Edwards Papers, series 2, box 12; "Re: History, WPA Welfare Department,, UAWA-CIO"; *West Side Conveyor*, 7 January 1939; Alexander McKay et al. to Harrington, 6 January 1939 (telegram), NA, RG 69, WPA Central Files, State Series, Michigan, box 1572.

22. Martin, "Report of Homer Martin to the International Executive Board," 10 January 1939, Frankensteen Papers, box 5; Kraus Papers, box 14; Martin to Sir and Brother, 5 January 1939, Reuther Papers, box 10;

George Edwards Jr. to George Clifton Edwards, 16 January 1939, George Clifton Edwards Papers, series 2, box 12; Martin to All Officers and Members of Local Unions, UAWA, 23 January 1939, Socialist Party of America Papers, reel 35.

23. "You Asked For It"; "Re: History WPA Welfare Department, UAWA-CIO"; "Information," 17 January 1939, DRS/CPC, file 30; "Immediate Release," 11 January 1939, Brown Papers, box 31.

24. Mazey, "Radio Address," 25 January 1939, UAW Local 212 Papers, Miscellaneous Publications; "You Asked for It"; "Re: History WPA Welfare Department, UAWA-CIO"; Polk interview; R. J. Thomas, "Report on WPA Welfare Department," May 1939, Polk Papers, box 1; Keeran, 198; Riddle, 19.

25. *Work*, 28 January 1939; "Re: History WPA Welfare Department, UAWA-CIO"; *Socialist Call*, 29 January 1939.

26. *Detroit Free Press*, 21 January 1939; *Detroit News*, 21 January 1939, Brown Papers, Clippings Book, vol. 15, p. 26; box 33.

27. "National Conference of All Executive Officers of Local Unions Affiliated with IUUAWA Called by Homer Martin," 29 January 1939, Strachan Papers, box 2; Martin to Lewis, 23 January 1939, CIO Secretary-Treasurers Papers, box 89; "Re: History of WPA Welfare Department, UAWA-CIO"; UAW Executive Board Minutes, 23 January 1939, Addes Papers, box 4; "Auto Report," 23 January 1939, Socialist Part of America Papers, reel 35; Polk interview; Keeran, 198–99; Barnard, 61; Galenson, 165–66; Howe and Widick, 77. For the organizational structure of the WPA-Welfare Department, as reconstituted by the Executive Board, see "By-Laws of the WPA-Welfare Department, UAW-CIO," 19 January 1939, Polk Papers, box 1.

28. "For Release 5:45 p.m.," 21 March 1939, Martin Papers, box 4; *Proceedings, Special Convention*, 4 March 1939, Detroit 120–21; "Know the Truth," 1 March 1939, UAW Public Relations Department, Ford Series, box 2; *United Automobile Worker* (Martin Edition), 18 February and 11 March 1939, Brown Papers, box 31; "Re: History WPA Welfare Department UAWA-CIO"; Interview, Gilbert Jewell, 4 August 1990, Milwaukee (telephone). For summary of the Martin Group convention deliberations, see Galenson, 167–69.

29. Edwards to FDR, 20 March 1939 (telegram); Edwards to Louis Rabaut, 13 February 1939 (telegram); Fred R. Rauch to Edwards, 20 February 1939, NA, RG 69, WPA Central Files, State Series, Michigan, boxes 1572, 1573; "Re: History WPA Welfare Department, UAWA-CIO"; *United Automobile Worker*, 11 February 1939, UAW Local 212 Papers, box 33; "By-

Laws of the WPA-Welfare Department," 19 January 1939, Polk Papers, box 1; Rusing, 48.

30. Polk to Edwards, 20 March 1939; Edwards, "Report, WPA Welfare Department," August 1939, George Edwards Jr. Papers, part 3, box 3; Polk interview; Minutes, Joint Council, Local 174, 14 January and 18 March 1939, Gallagher Papers, box 3.

31. *United Automobile Worker* (Thomas Edition), 11 March 1939, Brown Papers, box 31; "Memorandum," ca. 1939, George Edwards Jr. Papers, part 3, box 3.

32. "Report, WPA Welfare Department," August 1939; "Open Letter to Local, State, and Federal Officials and Legislators from the United WPA and Unemployment Workers of America," April 1939; Taylor to Harrington, 20 April 1939, NA, RG 69, WPA Central Files, State Series, Michigan, box 1572; Jewell interview.

33. Dollinger interview (Lorence); Genessee County Board, *Proceedings*, 1939–1940, 61, 75, 107, 123; Lasser to Williams, 20 December 1938, NA, RG 69, WPA Central Files, General Series, 1935–1944, box 58.

34. Dollinger interview (Lorence); "Notes," 8 April 1989, Los Angeles, Genora Dollinger Papers; Edsforth, 186.

35. Dollinger interview; *United Automobile Worker* (Martin Edition), 18 and 25 March 1939.

36. Perry Coon and Emitt Irvine to Hopkins, 21 December 1938; D. B. Hovey to FDR, 8 December 1938; H. L. Campbell to Hopkins, 20 December 1938; Niles to Coon, 29 December 1938, NA, RG 69, WPA Central Files, State Series, Michigan, boxes 1569, 1570, 1571; Leonard to Grand Rapids City Council, 1 December 1938 (telegram), Resolution 72681, GRCA, City Commission Proceedings, 1938–1939.

37. Niles to Nims, 20 December 1938; Benjamin to Niles, 30 December 1938; Fred Graham to FDR, November 1938; C. M. Stewart to Hopkins, October 1938; Fay Hill to U.S. Administrator of WPA, 25 January 1939, NA, RG 69, WPA Central Files, State Series, Michigan, boxes 1570, 1571, 1572, 1573.

38. Sargent, "Roosevelt, Lasser, and the Unemployed," 24, 41–42; WPA, Michigan, Division of Employment, Grievance Reports, Ingham and Van Buren Counties, 20 January 1939, NA, RG 69, WPA Central Files, State Series, Michigan, box 1573.

39. Niles to Herbert Norris, 26 September 1938; W. H. Roberts to Nims, 1 October 1938; Norris to Niles, 19 September 1938; Matt Savola and

Norris, "Resolution," Timber Workers Union, Local 15, 27–28 August 1939; Earl F. Toomey to Hopkins, 3 September 1938; Niles to Toomey, 8 September 1938, NA, RG 69, WPA Central Files, State Series, Michigan, box 1571; Anderson, Walli interviews.

40. Matt Bari and John Spiegal to Hopkins, 19 December 1938, NA, RG 69, WPA Central Files, State Series, Michigan, box 1571.

Chapter 9

1. *Proceedings of the Special Convention of the IUUAWA, Affiliated with the Congress of Industrial Organizations*, 27 March–6 April 1939, Cleveland, 287–89; *Cleveland Plain Dealer*, 1 April 1939, Brown Papers, Clippings Book, vol. 16, 1; "Constitutional Provisions Regarding Organization of WPA Workers," April 1939, Polk Papers, box 1. For discussion of the Cleveland meeting's deliberations, see Barnard, 61–62; Keeran, 199–200; Galenson, 171–73.

2. "Minutes of Socialist Party Conference on Unemployment"; Fischer to Pearl Weiner, 18 May and 22–23 April 1939, Pittsburgh, Socialist Party of America Papers, reel 36; UAW Executive Board Minutes, 24–25 April 1939, Sugar Papers, box 82; *Proceedings of the Special Convention*, 287; *Cleveland Plain Dealer*, 3 April 1939, Brown Papers, Clippings Book, vol. 16, p.3; "Constitutional Provisions Regarding Organization of WPA Workers."

3. Memorandum, Mr. Mulcahy to Mr. Larned, 22 April 1939; Joseph A. Mulcahy to Howard Hunter, 24 April 1939; NA, RG 69, WPA Central Files, State Series, Michigan, box 1558; *Detroit News*, 23 April 1939; United Automobile Worker (Martin Edition), 8 April 1939, Sugar Papers, box 1; "Minutes of the Regional Council," Niles, Michigan, 16 April 1939, Strachan Papers, series 3, box 2.

4. "Brief of Recommendations to Welfare Commission, City of Detroit," 9 May 1939; "Report of WPA Welfare Department," August 1939, George Edwards Jr. Papers, part 3, box 3; "Information and Adjustment Service," 8 May 1939, Metro Detroit AFL-CIO Papers, box 24; "Labor Relations Policy," 11 May 1939, NA, RG 69, WPA Central Files, State Series, Michigan, box 1573; *United Automobile Worker*, 26 July 1939, Brown Papers, box 31; Rusing, 95.

5. "Report of R. J. Thomas, President, IUUAWA," May 1939; *WPA Welfare Department Bulletin*, 1 June 1939, Polk Papers, box 1.

6. "Report of July 8, 1939," in Lovestone to Dubinsky, 11 July 1939, ILGWU Papers, box 115; *Detroit Free Press*, 23 and 24 June 1939, NA, RG

69, WPA Division of Information, Clippings File, 1936–1944, box 259; *Detroit News*, 23 June and 7 July 1939; *United Automobile Worker*, 14 June 1939, Brown Papers, Clippings Book, vol. 16, pp. 71, 85, box 31; "Report of WPA Welfare Department, IUUAWA," August 1939, George Edwards Jr. Papers, part 3, box 3.

7. "Report of WPA Welfare Department, IUUAWA," August 1939, George Edwards Jr. Papers, part 3, box 3; Secretary-Treasurer's Report, July 1939, Addes Papers, box 2; see also Walter Reuther Papers, box 2.

8. U.S. Congress, House, Subcommittee of the Committee on Appropriations, *Investigation and Study of the Works Progress Administration*, 76th Congress, 1st Sess., 1939, 37.

9. Sargent, "Roosevelt, Lasser, and the Workers Alliance," 23.

10. *Work*, 20 May 1939; *Daily Worker*, 9, 11, and 22 May 1939; Novak interview; Margaret Collingwood Novak, *Two Who Were There: A Biography of Stanley Novak* (Detroit: Wayne State University Press, 1989), 154.

11. Novak interview; Germer diary, 25 April and 15 May 1939, Germer Papers, box 25; Michigan Industrial Union Council, *Proceedings, Annual Meeting*, June–July 1939; Larned to Luren D. Dickenson, 17 May 1939; "Report of WPA Welfare Department, IUUAWA," August 1939, George Edwards Jr. Papers, part 3, box 3.

12. "The CIO Will Fight All Lay-offs on WPA!" Dollinger Papers; Taylor to Harrington, 16 March 1939 (telegram); Irvan Cary to FDR, 15 March 1939; H. R. Loudon to Cary, 31 March 1939, NA, RG 69, WPA Central Files, State Series, Michigan, box 1573; *Chicago Tribune*, 26 April 1939; *United Automobile Worker*, Flint Edition, 22 April 1939.

13. Memorandum, 1 May 1939; Resolution, UAWA, CIO, WPA Division, Flint, Michigan, 1 May 1939, Dollinger Papers; Dollinger interview; "Report of WPA Department, IUUAWA," August 1939, George Edwards Jr. Papers, part 3, box 3.

14. Fred R. Rauch to Hook, 15 March 1939, NA, RG 69, WPA Central Files, State Series, Michigan, box 1573; Kangas interview; *Marquette Mining Journal*, 11 March 1939.

15. Rauch to Hook, 18 April 1939; Paul A. Henley to Harrington, 26 April 1939; NA, RG 69, WPA Central Files, State Series, Michigan, box 1572; "Notice," ca. April 1939, WPA Division of Investigation File, reel 1294.

16. "Resolution," n.d.; Michael J. Manning to FDR, 5 May 1939; Edwards to Harrington (telegram), 12 May 1939; Edwards to FDR (telegram), 4 May 1939; Thomas to FDR (telegram), 4 May 1939, NA, RG 69, WPA Central

Files, State Series, Michigan, box 1572; Joint Council Minutes, West Side Local 174, UAW-CIO, 29 April 1939, Gallagher Papers, box 3; Addes to FDR, 25 April 1939, Addes Papers, box 2; "Welfare Situation in the City of Detroit," 15 May 1939, George Edwards Jr. Papers, part 2, box 3.

17. George Edwards Jr. to George Clifton Edwards, 23 May 1939, George Clifton Edwards Papers, series 2, box 12; Edwards to All Local Union Presidents, 12 May 1939, UAW Local 212 Papers, box 5; "Welfare Situation in Detroit and State of Michigan," 15 May 1939, George Edwards Jr. Papers, part 2, box 3.

18. Barnard, 64; Jean Gould and Lorena Hickok, *Walter Reuther: Labor's Rugged Individualist* (Dodd, Mead 1972), 161; *CIO News*, 10 June 1939; "Report on WPA Welfare Department, IUUAWA," August 1939, George Edwards Jr. Papers, part 3, box 3; "You Asked for It."

19. Benjamin, "Memorandum—Right to Work Congress," 16 June 1939, Draper Papers, series 2.3, reel 9; Benjamin, "End of the Alliance with Roosevelt," 1940, Folsom-Elting Collection, box 1, file 9.

20. Hetzel to Presidents of National and International Unions et al., 17 January 1939; Press Releases, 18, 26 and 29 January 1939, CIO Files of John L. Lewis, part 2, reel 4; Sargent, "Roosevelt, Lasser, and the Workers Alliance," 25; Lichtenstein, 29; Dubofsky and Van Tine, 330.

21. Sargent, "Roosevelt, Lasser, and the New Deal," 28–32.

22. Press Release, 13 June 1939, CIO Files of John L. Lewis, part 2, reel 4; *CIO News*, 19 and 26 June 1939; "Report of Activities of CIO National Office on Unemployment (Since November, 1938)," Brophy Papers, 1938–1939 File; *Union News Service*, 23 June 1939; U.S. Congress, Senate, Committee on Appropriations, *Work Relief and Public Works Appropriation Act of 1939*, 76th Congress, 1st Sess., 21 June 1939, 287–93; Donald E. Spritzer, *Senator James E. Murray and the Limits of Post-New Deal Liberalism* (New York: Garland, 1985), 43.

23. Local 235 News, 10 June 1939; Edwards to Regional Directors et al., 7 June 1939, Walter Reuther Papers, boxes 10, 17; "Mass Meeting to Save WPA," ca. June, 1939, Brown Papers, box 33; "Report of WPA Welfare Department, IUUAWA," August 1939; *WPA-Welfare Department Bulletin*, 1 June 1939, Polk Papers, box 1.

24. George F. Addes, Radio Speech, 14 June 1939, WJR, Brown Papers, box 33.

25. George Edwards Jr. to Family, 20 June 1939, George Clifton Edwards Papers, series 2, box 12; Notes, ca. 20 June 1939; Edwards to Charles Walters, 20 June 1939 (telegram), George Edwards Jr. Papers, part 3, box 3; Edwards to William Cody, ca. June 1939 (telegram), Milwaukee Indus-

trial Union Council Papers, box 2; *Work*, 20 May 1939; Ingham County Workers Alliance to Whom It May Concern, 12 June 1939, UAW Local 650 Papers, ALH, box 24; Silver to Harrington, 2 June 1939 (telegram); NA, RG 69, WPA Central Files, State Series, Michigan, box 1572; *United Automobile Worker*, 28 June 1939; "Report of WPA Welfare Department, IUUAWA," August 1939; *Bulletin, WPA Welfare Department, UAW-CIO*, ca. June, 1939, Polk Papers, box 1.

26. *Work Relief and Public Works Appropriation Act of 1939*, 293–95; "Statement by George Edwards, Welfare Director of the IUUAWA," 20 June 1939, George Edwards Jr. Papers, part 3, box 2; *United Automobile Worker*, 28 June 1939, Brown Papers, box 31.

27. Ibid

28. Sargent, "Roosevelt, Lasser, and the Workers Alliance," 36–37; Porter, 88; George Edwards Jr. to George Clifton Edwards, 1 July 1939, George Clifton Edwards Papers, series 2, box 12.

29. Sargent, "Roosevelt, Lasser, and the Workers Alliance," 37–38; Liebman, 63–67; Sargent, "Woodrum's Economy Bloc," 200–201.

30. "Who Is Responsible for Your Layoff," ca. July 1939, Strachan Papers, series 3, box 2; *American Federationist*, August 1939; "Report of Special Committee to the Conference of Representatives of National and International Unions on the W.P.A. Situation," 12 July 1939, Roosevelt Papers, POF 142, box 1; see also Taft Papers, box 14; Sargent, "Roosevelt, Lasser, and the Workers Alliance," 38; Herman Erickson, "WPA: Strike and Trials of 1939," *Minnesota History* 42 (Summer 1971); 204–5; Sidney B. Fine, *Frank Murphy: the Washington Years* (Ann Arbor: University of Michigan Press, 1980), 92. For reportage of the nationwide scope of the WPA walkout, see *New York Times*, 16 July 1939; *CIO News*, 10 July 1939.

31. Edwards to Harrington, 7 and 17 July 1939 (telegrams), NA, RG 69, WPA Central Files, State Series, Michigan, box 1572.

32. "Memorandum: WPA Situation," 14 July 1939, Benjamin Papers, 1939 File; see also Draper Papers, series 2.3, reel 9; *Union News Service*, 14 July 1939; *Detroit News*, 11 and 12 July 1939; *Daily Worker*, 12 July 1939; "Chronology of Events," 1939, Irene Paull Papers, St. Paul, Minnesota Historical Society, box 1.

33. "Report, WPA Welfare Department," August 1939; George Edwards Jr. to "Darlings," 14 July 1939, George Clifton Edwards Papers, series 2, box 12; UAW Pamphlet, June 1940, Ganley Papers, box 33.

34. "Memorandum II: WPA Developments," 21 July 1939, Benjamin Papers, 1939 File; *Work*, 29 July 1939; "To the Members of the Communist Party Only," 1 August 1939, ILGWU Papers, box 115; Benjamin, "Meeting

Reaction's Assault on the Unemployed," *Communist*, August 1939, 698–99; Lasser to Roosevelt, 6 July 1939 (telegram), Roosevelt Papers, PPF 7649; Sargent, "Roosevelt, Lasser, and the Workers Alliance," 38; "Report of WPA Welfare Department," August 1939; George Edwards Jr. to "Darlings," 14 July 1939, George Clifton Edwards Papers, series 2, box 12.

35. Wakefield Workers Alliance, "Resolution," 12 and 17 July 1939; Workers Alliance of Iron River to Harrington, 17 August 1939, NA, RG 69, WPA Central Files, State Series, Michigan, box 1564.

36. *Work*, 12 August 1939.

37. Michigan State Police File no. 454, Benjamin Papers, Michigan State Police File; *Work*, 12 October 1939; "Resolution on the WPA Bill," 26–27 August 1939, Timber and Sawmill Workers Union, Local 15, Iron River, NA, RG 69, WPA Central Files, State Series, Michigan, box 1573; Germer, Radio Address, Ironwood, 29 August 1939, August Scholle Papers, ALH, box 4; Germer diary, 25 August 1939, Germer Papers, box 25.

38. "Report of the WPA Welfare Department, IUUAWA," 4 December 1939, Addes Papers, box 6; "Report of the General Secretary-Treasurer," WAA National Executive Board Meeting, 21–23 October 1939, Draper Papers, series 2.3, reel 9; Benjamin, "End of the Alliance with Roosevelt," 1940.

39. *CIO News*, 6 September and 30 October 1939; "Organizational Structure—WPA Auxiliary Locals, UAWA-CIO," in WPA Board Minutes, 8–12 August 1939; Addes, "Report of the Secretary-Treasurer, UAW-CIO," 8–12 August 1939, Addes Papers, box 3; see also "Report of WPA Welfare Department, IUUAWA," August 1939; *Bulletin, WPA Welfare Department*, 6 July 1939, Polk Papers, box 1.

40. George Edwards Jr. to Mater, Pater, and Nicky, 5 October 1939, George Clifton Edwards Papers, series 2, box 12; *CIO News* (Michigan Edition), 2 October 1939; *Bulletin, WPA Welfare Department*, ca. September 1939, Polk Papers, box 1; Larned to Harrington, 29 September 1939; Hook to Howard Hunter, 16 September 1939; Tenerowicz to FDR, 18 September 1939 (telegram); Max Ireland to FDR, ca. September 1939; Henrietta Wendell to FDR, 16 September 1939 (telegram); George Edwards Jr. to Rauch, 15 September 1939; C. Walters to Harrington, 9 September 1939; "Statement of Position," ca. September 1939, NA, RG 69, WPA Central Files, State Series, Michigan, boxes 1572, 1573, 1574; ibid., file# 190, box 281.

41. Dollinger interview; Philip Murray, David McDonald, and Anthony Federoff to Sir and Brother, 3 August 1939; O. B. Allen to All International Unions et al., 8 August 1939, CIO Files of John L. Lewis, part 1, reel 9; Milwaukee Industrial Union Council Papers, box 2; "Report of the WPA Welfare Department, IUUAWA," August 1939.

42. Dollinger to Lorence, 6 December 1991; *Post-Gazette*, 11 September 1939, Murray Papers, scrapbook, 1939; Fred Carreno to James Carey, 3 October 1939; "Outline of Program for Organizing Project Workers," CIO Files of John L. Lewis, part 1, reel 9; "Minutes: National Consultative Conference of United Project Workers Organizing Committee," 9–10 September 1939, Dollinger Papers.

43. Dollinger interview; "Report of Program Committee," 9–10 September 1939, Dollinger Papers.

44. Edwards interview; George Edwards Jr. to "Mater," "Pater," and Nicky, 5 October 1939, George Clifton Edwards Papers, series 2, box 12; "Report of the WPA Welfare Department, IUUAWA," 4 December 1939; *CIO News* (Michigan Edition), 16 October 1939. For comment on the recovery of 1939, see Alan Clive, *State of War: Michigan in World War II* (Ann Arbor: University of Michigan Press), 14–15; Sullivan, 225.

45. "You Asked for It."

46. "Report of the WPA Welfare Department, IUUAWA," 4 December 1939; "Meeting of Chrysler Executive Boards and Shop Committees," 7 November 1939, Zaremba Papers, box 4; *Non-Partisan News*, 16 November 1939, Labor's Non-Partisan League Papers, box 8. For comment on the origins and development of the Chrysler strike, see Babson, 99–101.

47. "Report of the WPA Welfare Department, IUUAWA," 4 December 1939; "You Asked for It." Babson notes the important role of Detroit's black leadership in sustaining the strike; see Babson, 101–2. For evidence of the WPA Welfare Department's efforts to prevent the reassignment of Chrysler strikers to WPA jobs, see *Non-Partisan News*, 16 November 1939, Labor's Non-Partisan League Papers, box 8. For Red Squad observations, see "Report," 21 November 1939, DRS/CPC, file 51; see also Riddle, 38.

48. UAW Pamphlet, June 1940, 66–70, Ganley Papers, box 33; "Report of WPA Welfare Department, IUUAWA," 4 December 1939; "You Asked for It"; the WPA Welfare Department had by this time chartered sixteen local auxiliary unions throughout the UAW states, including three in Detroit, and single units in Grand Rapids, Pontiac, Mt. Clemens, Muskegon, Dearborn, Flint, and Lansing. Three locals operated in Wisconsin, with one each in Indiana and Ohio. "Report of the WPA Welfare Department, IUUAWA," 4 December 1939.

49. Federal Works Agency, WPA, "Press Release," 26 January 26 and 14 February 1940, Meany Archives, Legislation Department Files, box 56; Brophy, Oral History, 817, Brophy Papers.

50. *United Automobile Worker*, 16 March and 3 April 1940; *The WPA Worker*, 28 March 1940, "You Asked for It."

51. *The WPA Worker*, 1 April and 1 May 1940; *United Automobile Worker*, 3 April 1940, Brown Papers, box 33; "Act Now: Don't Gamble with Your Future Security," April 1940, Brown Papers, box 9; UAW Executive Board, "Resolution," 30 April 1940; UAW Local 602, "Unemployed and WPA Workers," April 1940; UAW Local 3 to Harrington, 17 May 1940, NA, RG 69, WPA Central Files, State Series, Michigan, boxes 1572, 1573.

52. Larned to Harrington, 7 June 1940; Hunter to Larned (telegram), 11 June 1940; Larned to Edward Jeffries, 20 June 1940; John W. Gibson to FDR, Michigan Senators and Congressmen, Hunter, Harrington, Jeffries, Governor Dickenson, and Larned, 8 June 1940; Tracy Doll to Harrington, 6 June 1940, NA, RG 69, WPA Central Files, State Series, Michigan, boxes 1567, 1572, 1573.

53. *The WPA Worker*, 12 July 1940; Pagano to Brown, ca. July 1940, NA, RG 69, WPA Central Files, State Series, Michigan, boxes 1572, 1573.

54. "You Asked for It"; WPA Department Report, 16 December 1940, Addes Papers, box 18; *The WPA Worker*, 28 June 1940, Brown Papers, box 33.

55. *Proceedings of the Fifth Annual Convention of the IUUAWA*, 29 July–6 August 1940, St. Louis, 190–91, 422–23. The growing strength of the Reuther forces is discussed in Keeran, 210–11; Barnard, 71–73; Cochran, 153; Lichtenstein, 86.

56. *UAW Conveyor*, 15 December 1940; *Michigan CIO News*, 6 December 1940; WPA Department Report, 16–20 December 1940; Pagano to Addes, 26 November 1940, Addes Papers, box 18; Rauch to Pagano, 26 November 1940; Pagano to Hunter, 20 November 1940, NA, RG 69, WPA Central Files, State Series, Michigan, box 1573.

57. "Memoranda on Present Situation Regarding the Works Project Administration," 3 December 1940, Joseph Pagano Papers, Detroit, ALH, box 1; Polk interview.

58. "National Security: For All the Nation," January 1941, UAW Research Department Papers, ALH, box 32; see also NA, RG 69, WPA Central Files, General Correspondence Series, 1935–1944, box 62.

59. Polk interview; Ernest L. Marbury to Pagano, 15 January 1941, NA, RG 69, WPA Central Files, General Correspondence Series, 1935–1944, box 62; Larned to Rauch, 20 January 1941; "Economic Conditions in Michigan," n.d., NA, RG 69, WPA Central Files, State Series, Michigan, box 1567. A significant decline in unemployment did not occur until late Winter, 1941. Lichtenstein, 45.

60. *The WPA Worker*, 24 January 1941, NA, RG 69, WPA Central Files, General Correspondence Series, 1935–1944, box 62.

61. Thomas, Addes, and Pagano to House and Senate Appropriations Committee, 1 February 1941; Carey to Edward T. Taylor, 5 February 1941, Labor's Non-Partisan League Papers, box 5; *CIO News*, 6 January and 10 February 1941.

62. Malcolm J. Miller to Pagano, 21 March 1941; Pagano to Hunter, 11 March 1941, NA, RG 69, WPA Central Files, State Series, Michigan, box 1574.

63. Nancy F. Gabin, *Feminism in the Labor Movement: Women and the United Auto Workers, 1935–1975* (Ithaca: Cornell University Press, 1990), 48–49; Barton J. Bernstein, "The Automobile Industry and the Coming of the Second World War," *Southwestern Social Science Quarterly*, 47 (June 1966), 23–29; Lichtenstein, 40.

64. Clive, 23; Bernstein, 24–25; *Labor Market Report for Michigan*, 1 July–15 August 1941, UAW War Policy Division Papers, ALH, box 6.

65. Craig, 107; Lloyd H. Bailer, "The Negro in the Automobile Industry" (unpublished doctoral dissertation, Dept. of History, University of Michigan, 1943), 323; Keeran, 218; Meier and Rudwick, 40–48.

66. Craig, 126; Sykes interview; "Calling All Workers: Ford Workers Specially Invited," January 1938; William McKie to Walter Reuther; "West Side Local 174 Mimeographed Handbills for Unemployed and Welfare Meetings," Walter Reuther Papers, box 1; *Party Organizer* 10 (September 1937), 24; "Tactics, Strategy, Conditions of Ford Organizing Drive," ca. January 1938, Lovestone Papers, box 566.

67. Tappes interview, 11–12, 24; Pagano interview, 34; Polk interview.

68. "Report on UAWA Meeting at Baby Creek park, 5 June 1938," 6 June 1938, DRS/CPC, file 50; *Detroit News*, 6 June 1938, NA, RG 69, WPA Central Files, Division of Information, Clippings Files, 1936–1944, box 281; "UAW Ford Rally," Leaflet, June 1938, Kraus Papers, box 16; Memorandum, "Ford," ca. 1938; M. Dragon to Frankensteen, 1 March 1938, Frankensteen Papers, boxes 1, 5.

69. Members of the UAW Ford Local and Workers Alliance of Dearborn to International Executive Board, 24 May 1938, Kraus Papers, box 16; Craig, 126–27.

70. Ibid.

71. Report of the WPA Welfare Department, IUUAWA," 4 December 1939, Addes Papers, box 6; Polk interview; "You Asked for It"; *Michigan CIO News*, 4 September 1939; *CIO News*, 30 October 1939.

72. "Information on Communist Activities," 6 October 1938, DRS/CPC, file 50; Riddle, 38–39.

73. Craig, 131, 134; Keeran, 219; Babson, 107–8; Meier and Rudwick, 44–45.

74. George Leets to Brother Addes, 18 April 1939, Addes Papers, box 2; *Proceedings, Michigan Industrial Union Council*, June–July 1939; Craig, 134; Meier and Rudwick, 74–76.

75. Pagano, "Radio Broadcast," WJBK, 19 August 1940, Pagano Papers, box 1; Meier and Rudwick, 82.

76. Katana interview, Ganley Papers, box 33.

77. *Fourth Annual Convention Proceedings, Michigan CIO Council*, Jackson, 22–24 May 1941, in CIO Files of John L. Lewis, part 2, reel 11; "Official Daily Memorandum for Members of Ford Organizing Committees Staff, 26 April 1941, Harry Ross Papers, ALH, box 4; Polk interview.

78. Quoted in Maurice Isserman, *Which Side Are You On? The American Communist Party During the Second World War* (Middletown: Wesleyan University Press, 1982), 88; Meier and Rudwick, 107; Keeran, 220. For a militant assertion of the argument for substantial Communist influence on the result, see Interview, Billy Allan, Ganley Papers, box 33.

79. Rusing, 85–86.

80. Leibman, 68–69; Sargent, 38–40; *The Communist*, February, 1941, 147; *New York Times*, 20 June 1940. Benjamin later asserted that his resignation was influenced by Earl Browder, who urged him to make "this last sacrifice for the united front." See Benjamin to James E. Sargent, 31 August 1981, in Folsom-Elting Papers, box 1, file 9.

81. Benjamin, "End of the Alliance with Roosevelt," 1940; Piven and Cloward, 91.

82. *Michigan Workers Alliance State Bulletin*, 20 January 1940, Brown Papers, box 8; "Report," June 1940, Benjamin Papers, Michigan State Police File.

83. Ray M. Mix to Richard Thompson, 3 February 1941; "Second State Convention of the Michigan Workers Alliance," 14–16 June 1940; Garfield Maunder, Deposition, 23 January 1941, NA, RG 69, WPA Central Files, Records of Division of Investigation, Michigan, Ingham County, file 4-MC-322. See also memorandum, "Second State Convention of Michigan Workers Alliance," 14–16 June 1940, Benjamin Papers, Michigan State Police File.

84. "Second State Convention of the Michigan Workers Alliance," 14–16 June 1940; Maunder, "Deposition."

85. Abner E. Larned, "Final Report," Michigan WPA (March 1943), 48; Rusing, 85–86; Schware to Larned, 22 November 1940; "Supplemental

Report; Mix to Thompson, 1 November 1940; 3 February 1941, NA, RG 69, WPA Central Files, Records of Division of Investigation, Michigan, Ingham County, file 4-MC-322.

86. "Second State Convention of the Michigan Workers Alliance"; Maunder Deposition; "Supplemental Report," 8 February 1941, NA, RG 69, WPA Central Files, Records of Division of Investigation, Michigan, Ingham County, file 4-MC-322.

87. Joseph Duprey to Fred Carreno, 1 February 1940; "Open Letter to the Taxpayers of Flint," 5 February 1940; "WPA-CIO Scores Victory For Unemployed," n.d., Dollinger Papers; Dollinger interview.

88. Carl A. Swanson to Hunter, 17 July 1941; Jacob Waldo to Hunter, 30 October 1941; Duprey to Carreno, 1 February 1940, Dollinger Papers; Dollinger interview; "Second State Convention of the Michigan Workers Alliance," 14–16 June 1940; Dollinger to Lorence, 6 December 1991.

89. "Second State Convention of the Michigan Workers Alliance," 14–16 June 1940; Corrington Gill to Paul A. Henley, n.d., NA, RG 69, WPA Central Files, State Series, Michigan, box 1558; *Work*, 4 January 1940.

90. *Midwest Labor*, 1 March and 10 May 1940; *Jacks New Deal*, 12 January 1940, in International Woodworkers of America Papers, Local 12-15 File.

91. *Jacks New Deal*, 4 April 1940, International Woodworkers of America Papers, Local 12-15 File; Gilbert and Harris, 26; Anderson interview; Michigan State Police File, Raymond Anderson, Complaint 9-2475, in Anderson Papers.

92. Leonard Somero to CIO of Painesdale, 22 January 1940, Gene Saari Papers, ALH, box 13; Lankton, 258.

93. Minutes, Upper Peninsula CIO Conference, 11 February 1940; Savola to Scholle, 29 January 1940, Scholle Papers, box 4; Savola to Irving Uitti, 23 January 1940; Savola to Leonard Jukkala, 24 January 1940, Saari Papers, box 13; *Midwest Labor*, 16 February 1940.

94. Minutes, Upper Peninsula CIO Organizing Committee, 10 March 1940, Scholle Papers, box 4; see also Saari Papers, box 13; *Midwest Labor*, 15 March 1940; *Michigan CIO News*, 25 March 1940.

95. Minutes, Upper Peninsula CIO Coordinating Committee, 9 June 1940, Saari Papers, box 13.

96. David John Ahola, *Finnish-Americans and International Communism: A Study of Finnish-American Communism from Bolshevization to the Demise of the Third International* (Washington: University Press of America, 1981), 216–32; Henley to Vandenberg, 9 July 1941, NA, RG 69,

WPA Central Files, State Series, Michigan, box 1573; see also Ross, 172–74.

Chapter 10

1. Clive, 18–19; Bernstein, "The Automobile Industry," 24; Lichtenstein, 39.

2. Addes, "Quarterly Report," 1 November 1940–28 February 1941, Addes Papers, box 15; Dollinger interview.

3. Pagano to Hunter, 21 July 1941, NA, RG 69, WPA Central Files, State Series, Michigan, box 1567; Bernstein, "The Automobile Industry," 28; Clive, 23.

4. *Detroit News*, 22, 23, and 27 August 1941; *New York Times*, 4 August 1941, Brown Papers, Clippings Book, vol. 21, pp. 46, 60–61; Gabin, 53. See also "The Editor's Point of View," *UAW Conveyor*, 1 August 1941; Victor G. Reuther, "Memorandum Regarding Estimated Displacement of Automobile Workers, Assuming Passenger Car Production at 25% of Normal Program," n.d., UAW War Policies Division Papers, box 3.

5. *The WPA Worker*, 12 and 31 October 1941; Polk to Research Division, WPA, 3 September 1941; Malcolm J. Miller to Polk, 13 September 1941, NA, RG 69, WPA Central Files, State Series, Michigan, box 1574.

6. Alex McKay to Pagano, 5 November 1941, NA, RG 69, WPA Central Files, State Series, Michigan, box 1574.

7. Gabin, 54. Gabin convincingly demonstrates that the UAW's primary concern throughout the conversion process was the preservation of jobs and wage levels for male workers.

8. McKay to Pagano, 8 November 1941, NA, RG 69, WPA Central Files, State Series, Michigan, box 1574.

9. Ibid.

10. Thomas and Addes to Roosevelt, 15 January 1942, NA, RG 69, WPA Central Files, State Series, Michigan, box 1574.

11. Ben Probe to All Michigan Congressmen and Senators, 20 May 1942; "Resolution," ca. May 1942; Probe to All CIO State Councils, 1 June 1942, NA, RG 69, WPA Central Files, State Series, Michigan, box 1573; Labor's Non-Partisan League of Wayne County, "Proceedings, Election Results, Constitution," 26–27 June 1942, Labor's Non-Partisan League Papers, ALH, box 1; *United Automobile Worker*, 1 March 1942; *The WPA Worker*, 13 March 1942.

12. Clive, 27; Larned to Hunter, 21 January 1942, NA, RG 69, WPA Central Files, State Series, Michigan, box 1567; Howe and Widick, 14.

13. Minutes, International Executive Board, 22–23 January 1942, Sugar Papers, box 84.

14. Minutes, International Executive Board, 15–22 March 1942, Sugar Papers, box 84.

15. Clive, 28–29; Larned to F. H. Dryden, 20 June 1942; "Memorandum," 13 May 1942, attached to McKay to FDR, 23 April 1942; Pagano to Philip Fleming, 14 July and 24 September 1942; Addes to Roosevelt, 14 September 1942; NA, RG 69, WPA Central Files, General Correspondence, 1936–1944, box 62; State Series, Michigan, box 1567, 1574; Mark Starr to Victor Reuther, 22 April 1942; Reuther to Starr, 17 April 1942, UAW War Policies Division Papers, box 16.

16. Minutes, International Executive Board, IUUAAAIWA, 24–31 August 1942, UAW Executive Board Minutes, box 1.

17. R. J. Jacobson to Victor Reuther, 9 December 1942; "Notes on Conference with Vic Reuther," n.d., UAW War Policies Division Papers, box 16; Minutes, International Executive Board, 15 December 1942, UAW Executive Board Minutes, box 1.

18. Clive, 50.

19. Benjamin, "End of the Alliance with Roosevelt," 1940; Benjamin to Sargent, 31 August 1981, Folsom-Elting Collection, box 1, file 9.

20. UAW Pamphlet, June 1940, Ganley Papers, box 33; *Michigan CIO News*, 30 October 1939. For discussion of efforts by other CIO unions to control layoffs and manage relief to union members, see Montgomery and Schatz, 139–49.

21. Polk Interview.

22. For discussion of the producerist mentality in UAW, see Stephen Amberg, "The Old Politics of Inequality: The Autoworkers Union and the Liberal Keynesian State," paper presented at the Annual Meeting of the American Historical Association, 27–30 December 1988, Cincinnati.

SELECT BIBLIOGRAPHY

Primary Sources

Manuscript and Oral History Collections

Ann Arbor, MI. Bentley Historical Library. Michigan Historical Collection.

John B. Bennett Papers.

Prentiss M. Brown Papers.

Mortimer Cooley Papers.

Lawrence Farrell Papers.

Josephine Gomon Papers.

William Haber Papers.

Michigan State Emergency Welfare Commission Papers.

Frank Murphy Papers.

Harry Lynn Pierson Papers.

Ann Arbor, MI. Joseph E. Labadie Collection. Special Collections Library. University of Michigan. Joseph Pokorny Papers.

Miscellaneous Collections

Subject Vertical File

Atlanta, GA. Woodruff Library. Emory University. Theodore Draper Research Files.

365

Bloomington, IN. Lilly Library. University of Indiana. Powers Hapgood Papers.

Boulder, CO. University of Colorado at Boulder Libraries. Special Collections. Folsom-Elting Collection.

Charlottesville, VA. Manuscripts Division. Special Collections Department. University of Virginia Library. W. Jett Lauck Papers.

Detroit, MI. Ford Motor Company Archives (Dearborn).

Detroit, MI. Wayne State University. Walter P. Reuther Library. Archives of Labor and Urban Affairs.

George Addes Papers.

Dorothy Hubbard Bishop Papers.

Merlin Bishop Papers.

Blacks in the Labor Movement Oral History Collection

Joe Brown Papers.

CIO Secretary-Treasurers Office Papers.

Francis Dillon Papers.

George Edwards Jr. Papers.

George Clifton Edwards Papers.

Kathryn Pollock Ellickson Papers.

Richard Frankensteen Papers.

Daniel M. Gallagher Papers.

Nat Ganley Papers.

Henry Kraus Papers.

Homer Martin Papers.

Metro Detroit AFL-CIO Papers.

Michigan AFL-CIO, Lansing Office Papers.

Stanley Nowak Papers.

Joseph Pagano Papers.

John Panzner Papers.

Ethel Polk Papers.

Roy Reuther Papers.

Walter P. Reuther Papers.

Harry Ross Papers.

Gene Saari Papers.

August Scholle Papers.

Stuart Strachan Papers.

Maurice Sugar Papers.

R. J. Thomas Papers.

Unionization of the Auto Industry Oral History Collection.

UAW Chrysler Department Papers.

UAW General Motors Department Papers.

UAW Local 155 Papers.

UAW Local 174 Papers.

UAW Local 212 Papers.

UAW Local 602 Papers.

UAW Local 650 Papers.

UAW Public Relations Department, Ford Motor Company Series Papers.

UAW Research Department Papers.

Mary Van Vleeck Papers.

Mary Heaton Vorse Papers.

John Zaremba Papers.

Eugene, OR. Special Collections. University of Oregon. International Wood-workers of America Papers.

Flint, MI. University of Michigan–Flint. Labor History Project Archives.

Grand Rapids, MI. Public Library. Michigan Room. Thomas Walsh Papers.

Houghton, MI. Michigan Technological University. Copper Range Company Papers.

Hyde Park, NY. Franklin D. Roosevelt Library.

Harry Hopkins Papers.

Eleanor Roosevelt Papers.

Franklin Delano Roosevelt Papers.

Aubrey Williams Papers.

Ithaca, NY. Martin P. Catherwood Library. Labor-Management Documentation Center. Cornell University.

Elmer Cope Papers.

David Dubinsky Papers.

International Ladies Garment Workers Union Papers.

Philip Taft Papers.

Los Angeles, CA. Genora Dollinger Papers (in possession of Genora Dollinger).

Madison, WI. State Historical Society of Wisconsin. Archives and Manuscripts Division.

American Federation of Labor Papers.

Adolph Germer Papers.

Labor's Non-Partisan League Papers.

John L. Lewis Papers.

Russell Sage Foundation Papers.

Clarence Senior Papers.

Socialist Workers Party of America Papers (microfilm).

Workers Alliance of America Papers.

Milwaukee, WI. Milwaukee County Historical Society. Daniel W. Hoan Papers.

Milwaukee, WI. State Historical Society of Wisconsin Area Research Center. University of Wisconsin-Milwaukee. Milwaukee County Industrial Union Council Papers.

Minneapolis, MN. Social Welfare History Archives. University of Minnesota Library.

Family Service Association of America Papers.

Helen Hall Papers.

Paul Kellogg Papers.

New York, NY. Columbia University Oral History Collection, Part II (microfiche edition).

New York, NY. Tamiment Institute Library. New York University.

Daniel Bell Papers.

Oral History of the American Left Collection.

New York, NY. Schomburg Center for Research in Black Culture. National Negro Congress Papers (microfilm edition).

New York, NY. Rare Books and Manuscripts Division. New York Public Library. Norman Thomas Papers.

Saint Paul, MN. Minnesota Historical Society.

Audio-Visual Archives Oral History Collection.

Irene Paull Papers.

Project on Twentieth Century Radicalism Papers.

Saint Paul, MN. University of Minnesota. Immigration History Research Center.

Central Cooperative Wholesale Papers.

Finnish Workers Federation of the United States Papers.

Walter Harju Papers.

William Heikkila Papers.

Ernest Koski Papers.

John Wiita Papers.

Silver Spring, MD. George Meany Memorial Archives.

Department of Legislation Files.

William Green Papers.

Silver Spring, MD. Herbert Benjamin Papers (in possession of Ernst Benjamin).

Stanford, CA. Hoover Institution on War, Revolution, and Peace Archives.

Benjamin Gitlow Papers.

Jay Lovestone Papers

Ernest Lundeen Papers.

Superior, WI. Frank Walli Papers (in possession of Frank Walli).

Syracuse, NY. Syracuse University. George Arents Research Library. Department of Special Collections. Earl Browder Papers (microfilm edition).

Washington, D.C. Catholic University of America.

John Brophy Papers.

CIO Central Office Files.

CIO Collection. Labor's Non-Partisan League Series.

Phillip Murray Papers.

Washington, D.C. United Mineworkers of America Collection. CIO Files of John L. Lewis (microfilm edition).

West Branch, IA. Herbert Hoover Library.

Frederick Croxton Papers.

Herbert Hoover Papers.

President's Organization on Unemployment Relief Papers, 1927–1933.

Unpublished Government Documents

Detroit Public Library. Burton Historical Collection.

Mayor's Papers, 1931–1941.

Proceedings of the Wayne County Public Welfare Commission, 1930–1941.

Grand Rapids City Archives.

City Commission Files, 1930–1941.

Welfare Relief Advisory Commission Files, 1930–1933.

Michigan Archives. Lansing.

Department of Military Affairs, Office of the Adjutant General, Flint Sitdown Strike.

National Archives.

Record Group 69. WPA Central Files.

Record Group 73. Records of President's Organization on Unemployment Relief.

Published Government Documents

Abner E. Larned. *Final Report: A Critical Evaluation of the Experience of the WPA in Michigan with Recommendations for the Operation of a Future Federal Work Program.* Michigan WPA. March 1943.

Michigan State Emergency Welfare Relief Commission. *Emergency Relief in Michigan, 1933–1939.* Lansing: May 1939.

———. *Michigan Census of Population and Unemployment.* Lansing: October 1936; December 1936; March 1937.

———. *Unemployment and Relief in Michigan.* Lansing: January 1935.

———. *Unemployment, Relief, and Economic Security: A Survey of Michigan's Relief and Unemployment Problem.* Lansing: March 1936.

U.S. Congress, House, Special Committee to Investigate Communist Activities in the United States. *Investigation of Communist Propaganda: Hearings Before a Special Committee to Investigate Communist Activities in the United States.* 71st Congress, Second Sess., July 25–26, 1930.

U.S. Congress, House, Committee on Appropriations. *Investigation and Study of the Works Progress Administration: Hearings Before the Subcommittee of the Committee on Appropriations.* 76th Congress, First Sess., Part 1, 1939.

U.S. Congress, Senate, Committee on Appropriations. *Work Relief and Public Works Appropriation Act of 1939: Hearings Before the Committee on Appropriations, United States Senate.* 76th Congress, 1st Sess., 1939.

U.S. Congress, House, Committee on UnAmerican Activities. *Investigation of Communist Activities in the State of Michigan: Hearings Before the House Committee on UnAmerican Activities*. 83rd Congress, 2nd Sess., Part 8, 1954.

U.S. *Military Intelligence Reports: Surveillance of Radicals in the United States, 1917–1941*. University Publications of America, 1984 (microfilm).

Proceedings, Minutes, and Transactions of Private Organizations

American Federation of Labor. *Report of Proceedings, Annual Convention*, 1932–1936.

CIO, Minutes of Executive Board (microfilm). Archives of Labor History and Urban Affairs. Detroit.

Farmers National Committee for Action. *Farmers Unite Their Fight: Report, Discussion, and Resolutions of the Farmers Second National Conference*. Chicago, November 15–18, 1933.

Michigan Federation of Labor. *Proceedings*, 1930–1942.

Michigan Industrial Union Council. *Proceedings, Annual Convention*, 1939–1941.

National Unemployed League. *Second Annual Convention of the National Unemployed League*. Columbus, July 30–August 1, 1934.

UAW-AFL. *Report of Homer Martin: UAWA Special Convention*. Detroit, March 4, 1939.

UAW-CIO. *Proceedings*, 1935–1941.

Workers Alliance of America. *Proceedings of the 2nd National Convention, Workers Alliance of America*. Washington, D.C., April 7–10, 1936.

———. *Proceedings and Resolutions, 3rd Annual Convention, Workers Alliance of America*. Milwaukee, June 22–27, 1937.

———. *Reports and Proceedings, 4th Annual Convention, Workers Alliance of America*. Cleveland, September 23–26, 1938.

Memoirs, Pamphlets, and other Contemporary Works

Amidon, Beulah. "WPA—Wages and Workers." *Survey Graphic* 24 (October 1935): 493–497.

"Behind the Scenes at the Fifty-Third Annual Convention of the AFL-CIO." New York: AFL Trade Union Committee for Unemployment, January 1934.

Benjamin, Herbert. "Extending the Unity of the Unemployment Movement." *Political Affairs* 16 (August 1937): 760–770.

———. "Unemployment: An Old Struggle Under New Conditions." *Political Affairs* 17, (May 1938): 425–427.

Borders, Karl. "When Unemployed Organize." *The Unemployed* (June 1934): 22–23, 34.

Brophy, John. *A Miner's Life*. Madison: University of Wisconsin Press, 1964.

Brown, Josephine Chapin. *Public Relief, 1929–1939*. New York: Henry Holt, 1939.

Colcord, Joanna, William C. Koplovitz, and Russell H. Kurtz. *Emergency Work Relief, as Carried Out in Twenty-Six American Communities, 1930–1931, with Suggestions for Setting Up a Program*. New York: Russell Sage Foundation, 1932.

De Caux, Len. *Labor Radical: From the Wobblies to the CIO: A Personal History*. Boston: Beacon, 1970.

Dubinsky, David, and A. H. Raskin. *A Life With Labor*. New York: Simon and Schuster, 1977.

"Fight, Don't Starve: Demands for Unemployment Insurance." New York: Trade Union Unity League, 1931.

Foster, William Z. *Pages from a Workers Life*. New York: International Publishers, 1939.

Fountain, Clayton W. *Union Guy*. New York: Viking, 1949.

Hall, Helen. "When Detroit's Out of Gear." *The Survey* 64 (April 1, 1930): 9–14, 51–54.

Hallgren, Mauritz A. *Seeds of Revolt: A Study of American Life and the Temper of the American People During the Depression*. New York: Alfred A. Knopf, 1933.

Kraus, Henry. *The Many and the Few*. Urbana: University of Illinois Press, 1985.

———. *Heroes of Unwritten Story: The UAW, 1934–1939*. Urbana: University of Illinois Press, 1995.

Lowitt, Richard, and Maurine Beasley, eds. *One Third of A Nation: Lorena Hickok Reports on the Great Depression*. Urbana: University of Illinois Press, 1981.

Marquardt, Frank. *An Auto Worker's Journal: The UAW from Crusade to One Party Union*. University Park: Pennsylvania State University Press, 1975.

Mortimer, Wyndham. *Organize: My Life As A Union Man*. Boston: Beacon, 1971.

Nelson, Steve, James R. Barrett, and Rob Ruck. *Steve Nelson: An American Radical*. Pittsburgh: The University of Pittsburgh Press, 1981.

Nowak, Margaret Collingwood. *Two Who Were There: A Biography of Stanley Nowak*. Detroit: Wayne State University Press, 1989.

Reuther, Victor G. *The Brothers Reuther and the Story of the UAW*. Boston: Houghton, Mifflin, 1979.

Scarborough, Mary Gosman. *Whirlwinds of Danger: The Memoirs of Mary Gosman Scarborough*. New York: David Walker Press, 1990.

Sugar, Maurice. *The Ford Hunger March*. Berkeley: Meiklejohn Civil Liberties Institute, 1980.

"The TUUL: Its Program, Structure, Methods and History." New York: Trade Union Unity League, 1930.

Vorse, Mary Heaton. *Labor's New Millions*. New York: Modern Age, 1938.

Weinstone, William. "The Great Flint Sitdown Strike." New York: Workers Library Publishers, March 1937.

Winter, Carl. "Unemployment Struggles of the Thirties." *Political Affairs*. (September–October 1969): 53–63.

Ziskind, David. *One Thousand Strikes of Government Employees*. New York: Columbia University Press, 1940.

Newspapers and Journals

American Federationist, 1930–1941.
Auto Worker News, 1929–1934.
Christian Labor Herald, Grand Rapids, 1939–1941.
Communist, 1929–1941.
Crystal Falls Diamond Drill, 1930–1939.
Daily Mining Journal, Marquette, 1930–1940.
Daily Worker, 1929–1941.

Detroit Labor News, 1930–1941.
Grand Rapids Labor News, 1928–1930.
Ironwood Daily Globe, 1930–1941.
Labor Unity, 1930–1935.
Midwest Labor, Duluth, 1937–1941.
Mining Gazette, Houghton, 1933–1941.
New York Times, 1936–1941.
Party Organizer, 1929–1938.
Producer's News, 1931–1937.
Rank and File Federationist, 1934–1935.
Socialist Call, 1935–1941.
Survey Graphic, 1933–1941.
The Timber Worker, 1936–1941.
The Unemployed, 1930–1932.
Unemployed News Service, 1934–1935.
Union News Service, 1936–1941.
United Automobile Worker, 1936–1941.
United Automobile Worker (Flint Edition), 1936–1941.
United Automobile Worker: West Side Conveyor, 1937–1941.
Work, 1938–1940.
Worker's Age, 1932–1941.
Workers Alliance, 1935–1936.

Special Collections

Automotive History Collection. Flint Public Library. Flint.

Detroit Police Department Red Squad Files. Michigan District, Communist Party U.S.A. Collection.

Pamphlet Collection. Reference Center for Marxist Studies. New York.

Radicalism Collection. Special Collections. Michigan State University Libraries. Lansing.

Secondary Sources

Books

Ahola, David John. *Finnish-Americans and International Communism: A Study of Finnish-American Communism from Bolshevization to the Demise of the Third International*. Washington, D.C.: University Press of America, 1981.

Alexander, Robert J. *The Right Opposition: The Lovestoneites and the International Communist Opposition of the 1930s.* Westport, CT: Greenwood, 1981.

Babson, Steve. *Working Detroit: The Making of a Union Town.* Detroit: Wayne State University Press, 1988.

Barnard, John. *Walter Reuther and the Rise of the Auto Workers.* Boston: Little, Brown, 1983.

Bernstein, Irving. *A Caring Society: The New Deal, the Worker, and the Great Depression.* Boston: Houghton Mifflin, 1985.

————. *The Lean Years: A History of the American Worker, 1920–1933.* Boston: Houghton Mifflin, 1960.

Blumberg, Barbara. *The New Deal and the Unemployed: The View from New York City.* Lewisburg: Bucknell University Press, 1979.

Bonasky, Phillip. *Brother Bill McKie: Building the Union at Ford.* New York: International Publishers, 1953.

Brody, David, ed. *Workers in Industrial America: Essays on the 20th Century Struggle.* New York: Oxford University Press, 1980.

Buffa, Dudley. *Union Power and American Democracy: The UAW and the Democratic Party, 1935–1972.* Ann Arbor: University of Michigan Press, 1984.

Clive, Alan. *State of War: Michigan in World War II.* Ann Arbor: University of Michigan Press, 1979.

Cochran, Bert. *Labor and Communism: The Conflict that Shaped American Unions.* Princeton: Princeton University Press, 1977.

Derber, Milton, and Edwin Young, eds. *Labor and the New Deal.* Madison: University of Wisconsin Press, 1957.

Dubofsky, Melvyn, and Warren Van Tine. *John L. Lewis: A Biography,* abridged ed. Urbana: University of Illinois Press, 1986.

Dyson, Lowell K. *Red Harvest: The Communist Party and American Farmers.* Lincoln: University of Nebraska Press, 1982.

Edsforth, Ronald. *Class Conflict and Cultural Consensus: The Making of a Mass Consumer Society in Flint, Michigan.* New Brunswick: Rutgers University Press, 1987.

Fine, Sidney. *The Automobile Under the Blue Eagle: Labor, Management, and the Automobile Manufacturing Code.* Ann Arbor: University of Michigan Press, 1963.

———. *Frank Murphy: The Detroit Years.* Ann Arbor: University of Michigan Press, 1975.

———. *Frank Murphy: The New Deal Years.* Chicago: University of Chicago Press, 1979.

———. *Frank Murphy: The Washington Years.* Ann Arbor: University of Michigan Press, 1984.

———. *Sit-down: The General Motors Strike of 1936–1937.* Ann Arbor: University of Michigan Press, 1969.

Folsom, Franklin. *Impatient Armies of the Poor: The Story of Collective Action of the Unemployed, 1808–1942.* Niwot: University Press of Colorado, 1991.

Fraser, Steve and Gary Gerstle, eds. *The Rise and Fall of the New Deal Order, 1930–1980.* Princeton: Princeton University Press, 1989.

Friedlander, Peter. *The Emergence of a UAW Local, 1936–1939: A Study in Class and Culture.* Pittsburgh: University of Pittsburgh Press, 1975.

Gabin, Nancy F. *Feminism in the Labor Movement: Women and the United Auto Workers Union, 1935–1975.* Ithaca: Cornell University Press, 1990.

Galenson, Walter. *The CIO Challenge to the AFL.* Cambridge: Harvard University Press, 1960.

Gartman, David. *Auto Slavery: The Labor Process in the American Automobile Industry, 1897–1950.* New Brunswick: Rutgers University Press, 1987.

Gates, William B., Jr. *Michigan Copper and Boston Dollars: An Economic History of the Michigan Copper Mining Industry.* Cambridge: Harvard University Press, 1951.

Gould, Jean, and Lorena Hickok. *Walter Reuther: Labor's Rugged Individualist.* New York: Dodd, Mead, 1972.

Howe, Irving, and B. J. Widick. *The UAW and Walter Reuther.* New York: Random House, 1949.

Isserman, Maurice. *Which Side Were You On? The American Communist Party during the Second World War.* Middletown: Wesleyan University Press, 1982.

Johnson, Christopher. *Maurice Sugar: Law, Labor, and the Left in Detroit, 1912–1950.* Detroit: Wayne State University Press, 1988.

Karni, Michael G., Matti E. Kaups, and Douglas J. Ollila Jr., eds. *The Finnish Experience in the Western Great Lakes Region: New Perspectives.* Turku, Finland: Institute for Migration, 1975.

Karni, Michael G., and Douglas J. Ollila Jr., eds. *For the Common Good: Finnish Immigrants and Radical Response to Industrial America.* Superior, WI: Tyomies Society, 1977.

Keeran, Roger R. *The Communist Party and the Auto Workers Union.* Bloomington: Indiana University Press, 1980.

Keyssar, Alexander. *Out of Work: The First Century of Unemployment in Massachusetts.* Cambridge: Cambridge University Press, 1987.

Klehr, Harvey. *The Heyday of American Communism: The Depression Decade.* New York: Basic, 1984.

Kornbluh, Joyce L. *A New Deal for Workers Education: The Workers Service Program, 1933–1942.* Urbana: University of Illinois Press, 1987.

Kostiainen, Auvo. *The Forging of Finnish-American Communism, 1917–1924: A Study of Ethnic Radicalism.* Turku, Finland: Institute for Migration, 1978.

Lankton, Larry D. *Cradle to Grave: Life, Work, and Death at the Lake Superior Copper Mines.* New York: Cambridge University Press, 1991.

Lembcke, Jerry, and William M. Tattam. *One Union in Wood.* New York: International Publishers, 1984.

Levenstein, Harvey A. *Communism, Anticommunism, and the CIO.* Westport, CT: Greenwood, 1981.

Lichtenstein, Nelson. *Labor's War at Home: The CIO in World War II.* Cambridge: Cambridge University Press, 1982.

Lichtenstein, Nelson, and Stephen Meyer, eds. *On the Line: Essays in the History of Auto Work.* Urbana: University of Illinois Press, 1989.

Lisio, Donald. *The President and Protest: Hoover, Conspiracy, and the Bonus Riot.* Columbia: University of Missouri Press, 1974.

Magnaghi, Russell H. *An Outline History of Michigan's Upper Peninsula.* Marquette: Belle Fontaine, 1979.

———. *The Way It Happened: Settling Michigan's Upper Peninsula.* Iron Mountain: Mid-Peninsula Library Cooperative, 1982.

Meier, August, and Elliot Rudwick. *Black Detroit and the Rise of the UAW*. New York: Oxford University Press, 1979.

Meyer, Stephen. *The Five-Dollar Day: Labor Management and Social Control in the Ford Motor Company, 1908–1921*. Albany: State University of New York Press, 1981.

Montgomery, David. *Workers Control in America: Studies in the History of Work, Technology, and Labor Struggles*. Cambridge: Cambridge University Press, 1979.

Naison, Mark. *Communists in Harlem during the Great Depression*. Urbana: University of Illinois Press, 1983.

Nelson, Daniel. *Unemployment Insurance: The American Experience*. Madison: University of Wisconsin Press, 1969.

Nevins, Allan, and Frank Ernest Hill. *Ford: Expansion and Challenge, 1915–1933*. New York: Charles Scribner's Sons, 1957.

Ortquist, Richard T. *Depression Politics in Michigan, 1929–1939*. New York: Garland, 1982.

Ottanelli, Fraser. *The Communist Party of the United States: From the Depression to World War II*. New Brunswick: Rutgers University Press, 1991.

Peterson, Joyce Shaw. *American Automobile Workers, 1900–1933*. Albany: State University of New York Press, 1987.

Piven, Frances Fox, and Richard Cloward. *Poor Peoples' Movements: Why They Succeed, How They Fail*. New York: Pantheon, 1977.

Romasco, Albert U. *The Poverty of Abundance: Hoover, the Nation, the Depression*. New York: Oxford University Press, 1965.

Ross, Carl E. *The Finn Factor in American Labor, Culture, and Society*. New York Mills, MN: Parta Printers, 1982.

Sternsher, Bernard. *Hitting Home: The Great Depression in Town and Country*. Rev. ed. Chicago: Elephant Paperbacks, 1989.

Struthers, James. *No Fault of their Own: Unemployment and the Canadian Welfare State, 1914–1941*. Toronto: University of Toronto Press, 1983.

Thomas, Richard W. *Life for Us Is What We Make It*. Bloomington: Indiana University Press, 1992.

Thurner, Arthur W. *Strangers and Sojourners: A History of Michigan's Keeweenaw Peninsula*. Detroit: Wayne State University Press, 1994.

Trolander, Judith. *Settlement Houses and the Great Depression.* Detroit: Wayne State University Press, 1975.

Walker, Forrest A. *The Civil Works Administration: An Experiment in Federal Work Relief, 1933–1934.* New York: Garland, 1979.

Warren, Frank. *An Alternative Vision: The Socialist Party of the 1930s.* Bloomington: Indiana University Press, 1974.

————. *Liberals and Communism: The 'Red Decade' Revisited.* Bloomington: Indiana University Press, 1966.

Wood, Arthur Evans. *Hamtramck: A Sociological Study of a Polish-American Community.* New Haven: College and University Press, 1955.

Zieger, Robert H. *American Workers, American Unions, 1920–1985.* Baltimore: John Hopkins University Press, 1986.

————. *The CIO, 1935–1955.* Chapel Hill: University of North Carolina Press, 1995.

————. *John L. Lewis: Labor Leader.* Boston: Twayne, 1988.

Articles

Baskin, Alex. "The Ford Hunger March—1932." *Labor History* 13 (Summer 1972): 331–60.

Bernstein, Barton. "The Automobile Industry and the Coming of the Second World War." *Southwestern Social Science Quarterly* 47 (June 1966): 24–33.

Chafe, William. "Flint and the Great Depression." *Michigan History* 53 (Fall 1969): 225–39.

Erickson, Herman. "WPA Strike and Trials of 1939." *Minnesota History* 42 (Summer 1971): 202–14.

Garraty, John A. "Unemployment During the Great Depression." *Labor History* 17 (Spring 1976): 139–59.

Klehr, Harvey. "American Communism and the United Auto Workers: New Evidence on an Old Controversy." *Labor History* 24 (Summer 1983): 404–13.

Leab, Daniel J. "United We Eat: The Creation and Organization of the Unemployed Councils in 1930." *Labor History* 8 (Fall 1967): 300–315.

McSeveney, Samuel T. "The Michigan Gubernatorial Campaign of 1938." *Michigan History* 45 (June 1961): 97–127.

Ortquist, Richard T. "Unemployment and Relief: Michigan's Response to the Depression During the Hoover Years." *Michigan History* 5 (Fall 1973): 209–36.

Prickett, James R. "Communists and the Automobile Industry Before 1935." *Michigan History* 57 (Fall 1973): 185–208.

Repas, Bob. "History of the Christian Labor Association." *Labor History* 5 (Spring 1964): 168–82.

Rosenzweig, Roy. "Organizing the Unemployed: The Early Years of the Great Depression, 1929–1933." *Radical America* 10 (July–August, 1976): 37–61.

———. "Radicals and the Jobless: The Musteites and the Unemployed Leagues, 1932–1936." *Labor History* 16 (Winter 1975): 52–77.

———. "Socialism in Our Time: The Socialist party and the Unemployed, 1929–1936." *Labor History* 20 (Fall 1979): 485–509.

Sargent, James E. "Woodrum's Economy Bloc." *The Virginia Magazine* 93 (April 1985): 175–226.

Skeels, Jack. "The Background of UAW Factionalism." *Labor History* 2 (Spring 1961): 158–74.

Tuomi, Kaarlo. "The Karelian Fever of the Early 1930s." *Finnish Americana* 3 (1980): 61–75.

Valocci, Steven. "The Unemployed Workers Movement of the 1930s: A Re-examination of the Piven and Cloward Thesis." *Social Problems* 37 (May, 1990), 191–205.

Wargelin, John. "The Finns in Michigan." *Michigan History* 24 (Spring 1940): 179–203.

Zieger, Robert H. "Nobody Here but the Trade Unionists: Communism and the CIO." *Reviews in American History* 10 (June 1982): 245–49.

Unpublished Studies

Bailer, Lloyd H. "Negro Labor in the Automobile Industry." Ph.D. dissertation, University of Michigan, 1943.

Bernhardt, Debra E. "We Knew Different . . . The Michigan Timber Workers' Strike of 1937." MA thesis, Wayne State University, 1977.

Cary, Lorin Lee. "Adolph Germer: From Labor Agitator to Labor Professional." Ph.D. dissertation, University of Wisconsin, 1968.

Craig, Scott Ian. "Automobiles and Labor: The Transformation of Detroit's Black Working Class, 1917–1941." MA thesis, Wayne State University, 1986.

Genzeloff, Leo. "The Effect of Technological Changes upon Employment Opportunities in the Automobile Industry." MA thesis, University of Wisconsin, 1939.

Harms, Richard H. "Work Relief before the New Deal: The Grand Rapids Scrip Labor Program." Paper presented at Great Lakes History Conference, April 1990, Grand Rapids, Michigan.

Kahn, Eleanor. "Organizations of Unemployed Workers as a Factor in the American Labor Movement." MA thesis, University of Wisconsin, 1934.

Liebman, Wilma. "The Workers' Alliance of America: The Organization of Relief Recipients." Senior thesis, Barnard College, 1971.

Prago, Albert. "The Organization of the Unemployed and the Role of the Radicals, 1929–1935." Ph.D. dissertation, Union Graduate School, 1976.

Repas, Robert F. "The Christian Labor Association." MA thesis, Michigan State University, 1963.

Riddle, David. "The Detroit Federation of Labor, the United Automobile Workers, and the Works Progress Administration in Detroit, 1937–1939." Seminar paper, Wayne State University, June 23, 1991.

Rusing, Jean. "The Works Progress Administration in Detroit, 1935–1939." MA thesis, Wayne State University, 1974.

Sargent, James E. "Roosevelt, Lasser, and the Workers' Alliance: Organizing WPA Workers and the Unemployed, 1935–1940." Paper presented at Organization of American Historians Annual Meeting, April 1982, Philadelphia.

Seymour, Helen. "The Organized Unemployed." MA thesis, University of Chicago, 1937.

Singleton, Jeffrey. "Unemployment Relief and the Welfare State, 1930–1935." Ph.D. dissertation, Boston University, 1987.

Stockham, John R. "An Analysis of the Organizational Structure, Aims, and Tactics of the Workers Alliance of America in Franklin County and Cuyahoga County, Ohio and in Hennepin County, Minnesota; and of the Federal Workers Section of the General Drivers Union,

Local 544, in Hennepin County, Minnesota." MA thesis, Ohio State University, 1938.

Sullivan, Martin Edward. " 'On the Dole': The Relief Issue in Detroit, 1929–1939." Ph.D. dissertation, University of Notre Dame, 1974.

Vogel, Virgil J. "Communist Activity among the Unemployed, 1929–1935." In possession of Virgil J. Vogel, Northbrook, Illinois.

Whitty, Michael D. "Emil Mazey: Radical as Liberal. The Evolution of Labor Radicalism in the UAW." Ph.D. dissertation, Syracuse University, 1969.

INDEX

Addes, George: on need for WPA and unity of employed and unemployed workers, 248; and UAW factionalism, 184, 227, 229; and UAW Welfare Department, 240, 253, 285–286, 287; and women, 284

AFL (American Federation of Labor), 15, 34, 35; and unemployed and WPA workers, 105–108, 116, 117, 134, 140, 162, 187; and unemployed organizing, 16, 82, 85, 103, 105–108; and unemployment compensation, 16, 35–36, 84–85, 97; and unionization of automobile industry, 126; voluntarism in, 16, 84–85, 97, 131; and Workers Alliance, 103–117, 127, 133, 199–200, 214; and WPA, 116, 250. *See also* Prevailing wage

AFL-CIO split: influence on unemployed movement, 131–132, 161–162

Alger County, MI, 66; United Farmers League in, 74

Alsop, Joseph, and Robert Kintner: on CIO unemployed organizing to build unions, 180

Alston, Christopher, 28; and direct action, 29, 30; on ineffectiveness of Detroit Workers Alliance, 124; on UAW welfare activities, 144

American Brass Company, 178; and collusion with Detroit Welfare Department, 186; 1938 strike at, 186

American Federationist: on AFL as advocate for unemployed, 85

Anderson, James, 113; as dismissed Black WPA organizer, 269

Ann Arbor, MI: relief project strike in, including skilled workers, 91; Trades and Labor Council in, and Civil Works Administration wage scale, 89

Arvola, Frank: and farmer-labor cooperation, 75, 87–88

Auto Worker's Union (AWU), 91, 98, 269; and Brigges-Waterloo

383

Lasser, David con't.
race, 220; on 1938 relief crisis, 215; realizes impact of union competition in serving unemployed, 163; red-baited in Congress, 242, 247; resigns as head of Workers Alliance, 272; warns CIO about concentrating on union unemployed, 163; on weakness of Workers Alliance in Michigan, 129–130
Leonard, Richard: appointed head of UAW Welfare Department, 165; elected head of Michigan Industrial Union Council, 182–183; named welfare director by Martin, 225–226; supports UAW WPA organizing, 177; on UAW cooperation with Detroit Welfare Department, 170, 171; and UAW Welfare Department, 203–204, 286, 290; on WPA cutbacks, 225, 232; on WPA wages, hours, and working conditions, 179, 224
Lewis, John L., 107; as advocate for unemployed, 192, 196; effort to end UAW factionalism, 225; on hard-core unemployed and WPA, 257; hears complaints about Martin, 201; policies and pronouncements on employed and unemployed during Roosevelt Recession, 160–163; on unemployed organizing, 131; and Workers Alliance, 131, 133, 193, 195, 291; works to extend PWA and WPA, 180, 227, 246, 247
Local 830 (Workers Alliance): fights WPA wage levels, 127–129
Lodge, Mayor John: receives unemployed demands, 22
Lodging houses, 33, 198; as housing for UAW pickets and demonstrators, 185–186

Lovestone, Jay: influence on Martin, 166–169; opposes CIO-Workers Alliance affiliation, 193; on unions taking over all unemployed activities, 167–168, 191–192
Lovestoneites, 10, 187, 218, 219, 220; influence in Lansing, 203–204; influence on Martin, 166–169, 184, 185, 188, 191–192; on unemployed organizing as key in anti-Stalinist struggle, 167
Ludington, MI, 203; work stoppages on relief projects, 92, 115–116
Lundeen Bill, 122; authorship of, 98–99; pressure from helps pass Social Security Act, 102

Marquette Mining Journal: on demands of unemployed marchers, 71–72; on WPA labor relations, 118; on WPA strikes, 150, 151
Martel, Frank, 14, 107, 108, 290; and 1938 relief crisis, 214; red-baits WPA organizing, 109, 113; and UAW in 1936 Motor Products strike, 136; and unemployed organizing, 84–85; on unemployment compensation, 18, 36, 99–102; on union scale for Civil Works Administration, Public Works Administration, and WPA projects, 89–90, 322n. 63; on WPA unions, 112
Martin, Homer: attack on UAW Left, 184–185, 188, 226; character of, 167, 188, 225; on CIO adoption of UAW unemployed organizing program, 179; complaints about reach Lewis, 201; criticizes Mayor Reading, 170–171; effort to take UAW into AFL, 225, 227, 240; effort to use black scabs

145, 292; impact on radicalism, 45, 90, 292; impact on unemployed movement, 11, 13, 81–82, 102–103, 130–131, 272; and relief programs, 1938, 180, 187
New Republic: on Ford Massacre, 40
Niles, David K.: as WPA administrator, 207, 224, 230, 233
Niles, MI: as early center of Workers Alliance activity, 115–117; WPA in, 129

Ontonagon County, MI, 3, 67, 71, 73, 74, 210; demonstration in, against May Day march ban, 72; United Farmers League-led action in, against foreclosures, 75
Owosso, MI, 56; relief strikes in, 92

Pagano, Joseph, 255, 281; activities in 1939 Chrysler strike, 255–256; appointed welfare director, 253; efforts for Detroit unemployed, 257–258; efforts to increase WPA funding, 263; position weakened by changes in UAW attitudes toward unemployed and unemployed organizing, 260–261, 264–265; position weakened by decline of WPA, 259, 261; on "unemployables," 288; urges permanent WPA, 261–262; as welfare director, 255–257, 259; on WPA and union movement, 266; on WPA wage rates, 283; on WPA workers and Welfare Department in organizing Ford, 268, 270
Pieper, Fred, 218, 267; effort to kill UAW Welfare Department, 188

Pierson, Harry Lynn: as WPA administrator, 111, 118, 129
Piven, Frances Fox, and Richard Cloward: on New Deal and decline of unemployed movement, 272
Poles, 6, 20, 51, 65, 231; and Workers Alliance, 273
Police: use of, in strikes and demonstrations, 25, 33, 37, 39-44, 49, 52, 59, 92, 112, 137, 152, 186, 238
Polk, Ethel, 171, 216, 230, 271; on blacks in unemployed organizing, 266; on dealing with welfare agencies, 166; on organizing unemployed UAW workers, 164; on UAW and WPA, 176
Pollock, James R.: opposes WPA in Flint, 243
Pontiac, MI, 4, 23, 34, 91, 92, 218, 219, 220, 284; factionalism in UAW local in, 201; Red Thursday in, 25; Unemployed Council in, 20, 22, 27; WPA in, 201, 220
Popular Front: as strategy and tactic and cause, 34–35, 73, 86, 91, 110, 117, 119–121, 123–126, 147–149, 153, 155, 156, 165, 191, 197, 199, 207, 213, 214, 217–218, 228, 250, 251, 252, 257
Prevailing wage: as an issue, 89–90, 92, 93, 105, 106, 109, 112, 127–131, 136, 141, 150, 151, 160, 175, 187, 224, 250, 251, 283
President's Organization for Unemployment Relief (POUR): on Ford Massacre, 41; on post-Crash economic distress, 6–8
Producers News: on arrests at White Cloud foreclosure protest, 77; on farm foreclosure actions in Upper Peninsula, 73; on United Farmers League

organizing drives, 267–269;
and Ford Hunger March, 44;
and Ford organizing drives,
265–271; growth of, 145;
International Executive Board
of, 225–227; Local 159, 201;
Local 174, 184, 187; Local 174
welfare committee, 140, 141,
143–144, 147–148, 161; Local
203, 186; Milwaukee
convention of, 1937, 155, 156;
and organizing WPA workers,
175–192; Progressive Caucus
in, 167, 184, 219; and relief
cutbacks, 242–243; St. Louis
convention of, 1940, 260; and
shifting attitudes toward
unemployed and unemployed
organizing, 260–263; and
Socialist Party idealism, 135;
and unemployed and
unemployed organizing, 9, 13–
14, 126, 134–160, 169–189,
174, 188; and uniting
unemployed and employed
union workers, 135–137, 141,
150, 165, 240, 245; and
unionism as a social
institution, 135, 140, 165–189,
293, 294; Unity Caucus in,
147, 156, 167, 168–169, 184,
199, 203, 217–218; and use of
relief benefits in strikes, 138–
139, 255–256, 270–271; and
local welfare committees, 9,
140; Welfare Department of,
disbanded, 286–288; welfare
operations of, and prevention
of scabbing, 141, 178, 255–256;
welfare operations of, copied
by CIO, 160; and women, 148–
149, 283–284; and Workers
Alliance, 140, 141–143, 147–
150, 153–156, 169, 187, 191–
192, 196–200, 203–204,
257–258, 267–268, 271–272,
290; and WPA, 134, 247–249,
258–259. *See also* United

Automobile Workers of
America, Welfare Department;
WPA Auxiliary
United Automobile Workers of
America, Welfare Department:
achievements of, 181, 188–189,
239–240, 245, 253; activities
and impact of, 143–144, 175–
192, 245, 247–251; and blacks,
182, 269; as bridge for
interracial organizing at Ford,
265, 266; bureaucratization
and, 159, 262–263; as
certifying agency for welfare
recipients and WPA workers,
141–142, 164, 169–171, 258;
Cochran ousted as director of,
225–226; compared to
Unemployed Councils and
Workers Alliance, 140; created,
165; creation of WPA Auxiliary,
144; death of, 285–288; decline
of WPA and, 259, 282; and
Detroit unemployed, 257–258;
and defense of Department,
262–263, 264; Edwards
appointed director of, 229;
Edwards resigns as director of,
253; educates workers on right
to work, 166; and effort to
become advocate for
"unemployables," 264; and
effort to move Department's
functions to CIO, 260;
emergence of, 139–140; and
Emergency Relief Act, 254,
258; and factionalism in UAW,
160, 182–185, 188, 201, 216,
217–231, 238–240; failures of,
189; and Ford organizing, 266–
271, 291; Frankensteen
appointed director of 287;
functions of, 140–141, 143–144,
165; growth of, 171, 240;
impact of war-related economic
revival on, 255, 257, 263, 282,
285–288; Leonard named
director of, by Martin, 225–

4, 15; unemployment in 1930s
in, 4–9, 64, 66; Workers
Alliance in, 9, 117–122, 150–
153, 210–214, 234, 244, 252–
253, 275–279; WPA as election
issue in, 221–222; WPA in,
117–122, 130, 150–151, 211–
214, 234–235, 244, 275–277,
WPA strikes in, 150–151

Wagner Act, 10, 11, 13, 63, 82,
125, 131, 145
Wagner-Lewis Bill: on
unemployment compensation,
97–98; weakened in Social
Security Act, 102
Wald, Nat, 113, 171, 199, 273
Walker, Charles R.: on Ford
Massacre, 40
Walli, Frank, 67, 87, 120, 121,
150, 151, 152, 234; on Popular
Front in Gogebic County, 119;
and transfer from mine
organizing to unemployed
organizing, 68
Washington Conference on
Unemployment, 100–101; on
organizing relief project
workers, 91; on racial
solidarity, 91
Wayne County, MI 58; WPA in,
244–245
Wayne County Social Workers
Association: presses for
prevailing wage on WPA
projects, 224
Weinstock, Louis: appointed head
of Rank and File Committee, 35
Welfare capitalism, 20, 37, 69
Welfare state, 13, 82, 97, 101–
103, 294; and craft unions, 85
Welsh, George, 58, 60, 61;
opposition to direct relief, 202
West Side Conveyor: on 1938
Cadillac Square demonstration,
172–173; on use of unemployed
to organize Ford, 182
Western Federation of Miners
(WFM), 66–67; in upper

Peninsula copper strike, 1913–
14, 67
White Cloud, MI: foreclosure
protest in, 77, 88
White, Reverend Horace, 146,
149
Wiita, John, 66, 87, 151, 152; on
Americanization of Communist
Party in Upper Peninsula, 119;
organizes in Gogebic County,
118–119
Williams, Aubrey: as WPA
administrator, 129, 215, 224
Wilson, Edmund: on Detroit
Unemployed Council and
evictions, 30
Wilson, Louisa: on unemployed
in Flint and Hamtramck, 93,
94; on decline of Detroit
Unemployed Council, 102
Winter, Carl: on Communist
Party training of organizers,
30
Women: and defense conversion,
283–285; and Ford Massacre
and gender solidarity, 42; in
labor force, 287; and UAW,
283–285
Woodson, Mattie: and race and
class solidarity in Ford
Massacre, 42
Woodrum Bill, 250, 252
Woodrum, Congressman Clifton;
investigates WPA, 247
Work, Merrill, 187; and Detroit
housing problems, 147
Work sharing, 160, 205, 235,
293; endorsed by Michigan
Federation of Labor; 16–17; at
mining companies, 69; UAW-
Chrysler agreement on, 223
Workers Alliance of America
(WAA), and Michigan, 11, 12,
165, 265; absorbs existing
unemployed organizations,
122–123; activities and impact
of, 103–125; 127–133, 192–216;
and AFL, 199–200; attacked by
Martin, 226; and blacks, 198,